COUNTRYMEN

COUNTRYMEN

BO LIDEGAARD

TRANSLATED FROM THE DANISH BY
ROBERT MAASS

ALFRED A. KNOPF · NEW YORK
2013

THIS IS A BORZOI BOOK
PUBLISHED BY ALFRED A. KNOPF

Library of Congress Cataloging-in-Publication Data
Lidegaard, Bo, [date]
    Countrymen / by Bo Lidegaard. — First English
language edition.
        pages ; cm
    Includes bibliographical references and index.
    ISBN 978-0-385-35015-0 (hardcover) —
ISBN 978-0-385-35016-7 (ebook) 1. Jews—Denmark—
History—20th century.   2. Jews—Persecutions—
Denmark. 3. Holocaust, Jewish (1939–1945)—Denmark.
4. World War, 1939–1945—Jews—Rescue—Denmark.
5. Denmark—History—German occupation, 1940–1945.
6. Denmark—Politics and government—1912–1947.
7. Denmark—Ethnic relations. I. Title.
    DS135.D4.L49 2013
    940.53'1809489—dc23   2013006349

Front-of-jacket image courtesy of Palle Marcus
Jacket design by Carol Devine Carson

Printed in the United States of America
First United States Edition

Friends, Romans, countrymen, lend me your ears;
I come to bury Caesar, not to praise him.
The evil that men do lives after them;
The good is oft interred with their bones.

—WILLIAM SHAKESPEARE, *Julius Caesar*

CONTENTS

This cartoon in the Göteborg Trade and Maritime Journal *gave birth to a widespread and long-lived myth that King Christian rode through the streets of Copenhagen wearing the yellow star in defiance of Nazi demands that the Jews do so.*

The drawing shows the Danish prime minister, Thorvald Stauning, in an overcoat, in thoughtful conversation with King Christian, easily recognizable by his riding boots and uniform. In the caption Stauning asks: "What shall we do, Your Majesty, if Scavenius says that our Jews also have to wear yellow stars?" The king replies: "Then we'll probably all wear yellow stars"—an almost literal transcription of an interview King Christian had had with Acting Prime Minister Vilhelm Buhl four months earlier. The fact that the tenacious myth is rooted in a real conversation has only been revealed recently, as the handwritten diary notes made by the king were made accessible to historians. Even if King Christian was prepared to do so, he did not ride through the streets of Copenhagen wearing the yellow star; in fact no one in Denmark was required to wear it.

Cartoon by Norwegian Ragnald Blix, January 10, 1942

THE BIRTH OF A MYTH

Toward the end of the conversation the acting prime minister raised the question of the Jews. He had come to confer with the aging king Christian X on the state of affairs in occupied Denmark. It was early September 1941, and the German advance into the Soviet Union seemed successful and unstoppable, the news going from bad to worse. The European continent was under totalitarian control, and the United States remained firmly neutral. Denmark insisted on its neutrality, too, but the country had been under German occupation since April 1940, and even if the firm Danish rejection of any Nazi representation in government was still holding up, the Germans were becoming more and more arrogant in their demands. Now Finance Minister Vilhelm Buhl, acting as head of government, sounded out the king on the delicate issue of the Danish Jews. Later the same day the king wrote down the main lines of the conversation in his private diary. According to the king, the finance minister expressed deep concern: "Considering the inhuman treatment of the Jews not only in Germany but also in other countries under German occupation, one could not help but worry that one day this request would also be presented to us. If so, we would have to reject it outright following their protection under the Constitution."

The king agreed "that [he] would also reject such demands in regard to Danish citizens. If the request was made, the right attitude would be for all of us to wear 'the star of david.' The Finance Minister interjected that that would indeed be a way out."[1]

Buhl did not keep the king's suggestion to himself, and four months later the conversation appeared as the text of a cartoon in a newspaper in neighboring Sweden, also neutral but not occupied by the Germans. The cartoon gave birth to the compelling image of King Christian riding the streets of occupied Copenhagen wearing the yellow star. The myth has never died, and new generations have taken it as a token of hope amid the dismal history of the Holocaust.

The history from the Swedish cartoon traveled widely and it proved both compelling and useful. It served those in the United States and the United Kingdom who were working to improve the public image of an occupied Denmark criticized for its cowardly appeasement of Hitler's Germany. In the United States the myth was spread by Danish-American and Jewish organizations, in the United Kingdom by the Political Warfare Executive as part of a targeted effort to drive a wedge between Denmark's allegedly pro-German government and the resistance-willing people rallying behind their king.

The myth, of course, is false. But the history behind it is even more fascinating: Not only did the king not wear the yellow star, but no one in Denmark did. The very attitude of the king and his prime minister, as reflected in their brief conversation—and indeed that of the entire people—prevented any provision in regard to Jews being passed in Denmark. This is what makes Denmark a unique example, an exception to the general picture of the Holocaust. The exception was more fundamental than the myth reveals. It went beyond the rejection of measures directed against the Jews by denying the very existence of a Jewish question. It simply stated the obvious: That before being of Jewish descent, these individuals were Danish citizens or at least protected by Danish law, which did not distinguish between citizens of different creeds. There was simply no issue—and thus there could be no measures to address it.

Family Tree

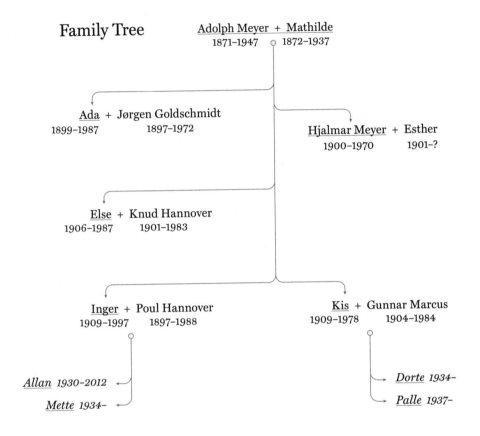

Adolph Meyer + Mathilde
1871–1947   1872–1937

Ada + Jørgen Goldschmidt
1899–1987   1897–1972

Hjalmar Meyer + Esther
1900–1970   1901–?

Else + Knud Hannover
1906–1987   1901–1983

Inger + Poul Hannover
1909–1997   1897–1988

Kis + Gunnar Marcus
1909–1978   1904–1984

Allan 1930-2012
Mette 1934–

Dorte 1934–
Palle 1937–

COUNTRYMEN

She went through the packing lists one more time. Somehow doing so comforted her. The children's clothes, Gunnar's, her own. They needed to be warm and practical and not take up too much space. Still, they also needed to look right. The whole thing seemed at once urgent and unreal. And she had no idea what to do. So she sat down to make packing lists. To establish a measure of normality in what suddenly seemed not to be normal at all. A few days later she noted: "We were optimistic, and couldn't and wouldn't believe that as Danes we could come to experience the horrors that Jews in the other German-occupied countries had gone through. From the middle of September the rumors began to circulate that persecution of the Jews would come, and we were nervous when Jewish books and records were stolen from offices of the Jewish congregation where they were kept. We lulled ourselves into a certain kind of calm thinking that maybe they would limit themselves to new laws and the like. And even though we heard about many of our own race who didn't sleep at home for fear of being picked up by the Gestapo at night, we stayed at home until Sunday, September 26."[1]

That was the last night for a long time that Kis Marcus slept in her own bed. The next morning she began a journey into the realm of uncertainty. Over the following days it would take her and her immediate family to parts of the country they had not previously known, and into situations they would not have conceived of as possible just a few days before. At the same time they would embark on a mental journey from being law-abiding and well-respected citizens to being cast as criminals wanted by German patrols for deportation to an unknown fate. During her escape, Kis Marcus took notes for her diary. She struggled to keep track of events, sequences, and emotions. Maybe she also struggled to stay aloof from the situation and to keep her emotions at bay. She wrote about the fear, the doubts, the confusion, and the hardships as well as about her fellow travelers and the children. She wrote about the uncertainty and—eventually—about the relief.

Kis and her family traveled with her twin sister, Inger, her husband, Poul Hannover, and their two children. Poul Hannover also kept a diary, as did his son Allan, who noted events from the perspective of an alert thirteen-year-old.

While the two small families headed south, the twin sisters' father, Dr. Adolph Meyer, headed north together with thousands of other refugees. The prominent pediatrician had declared that he would stay in Denmark until he was certain that his entire, numerous family was safe in Sweden. This hesitation proved to be almost fatal, as the doctor faced hardship and danger while he searched desperately for a safe route to Sweden. Adolph Meyer also kept a diary, and his meticulous records provide, together with his exchange of letters the following weeks with those who helped him escape, a rare firsthand account of the reflections and actions of those directly affected by the attempt to round up the Danish Jews. Eventually the doctor survived, and like his daughter, son-in-law, and grandson, he soon took the time to look over his notes and write an account of the dramatic getaway

When the family returned to Denmark after the war, the four diaries were kept as a private testimonial to the ordeal, shared only among members of the family and trusted friends. Now, as the last of the young children participating in the escape are themselves aging, the family has decided to share these accounts with a wider public—realizing that they constitute singular contemporary and personal witness to the making of a miracle. Here the experience of a wife and mother, another by a well-connected businessman, a third by a sharp-eyed young teenager, and the last by an aging patriarch of stature and influence—all describe the dramatic impact of sudden discrimination and persecution. Together with the few other known contemporary accounts, these diaries open the door into the mind-sets of both the refugees and their persecutors—and into that of the Danish helpers. Though each story is unique, their experiences were similar. It's a story thousands recognize, both then and today. A story of doubt, of despair—and of the determination to survive.

The history of the escape of the Danish Jews is but a small part of the much larger history of the Holocaust. But it does teach a lesson of self-preservation, of defiance, and of support from countrymen turning against the deportation in indignation and anger. In this way it is also the history of a society upholding its own view of what was right and what was wrong—even as it bowed before the superior force of German occupation.

Poul Hannover finishes his diary at Stadshotellet in Västerås, west of Stockholm, on October 10, 1943. He writes of his objective: "After I managed to get hold of a typewriter on Wednesday, I started to write down my memories of the trip—the most terrible trip I've ever experienced or ever hope to experience. This is not a novel—no fancy trimmings—it is for ourselves and our closest friends and family— I do not think others should read it." Like many other refugees, he felt no inclination to share his experience, and for the rest of his life, he kept his notes close. Some gladly told their stories after the war. But most did not, and Poul Hannover comments on this ambiguity: "As I begin to write down what happened in the last days, I ought to clarify why I'm doing it—and for whom. I know neither. I just feel the need to get this down on paper, incomplete though it surely is. I also don't know what others experienced—if it's more or less—but for us it seems, because we have experienced the unbelievable, that if I don't get this down, there will be barely anyone who will believe it."[2]

Gunnar
1 sæt vintertøj
2 slips
3 skjorter
1 sæt undertøj
1 par sko
1 impregneret frakke
1 hat
1 pyjamas
4 flipper
2 par handsker
1 slipsover
4 par sokker
4 lommetørklæder
1 par tøfler

What do you do if escape is the only way out? What do you take along, and what do you leave behind?

Kis Marcus was thirty-four years old and the mother of two small children when these urgent questions arose. Until then she had always been safe, and she had no experience of persecution or of being on the run. While her thoughts developed and she tried to decide what to do, she began to prepare, writing down what each of the family's four members should pack if necessary. Committing it to paper helped focus her mind, and in the following days Kis Marcus set the unfolding events down in black softcover notebooks.

But the notebook's first pages are perhaps the most telling: no narrative and no comments, only a list of the essentials, odd bits and pieces representing the daily life of her family and constituting the total of what she hoped to bring along from her previous life. Everything else had to be left behind, and it is as if her drawing up the packing lists was the beginning of her separation from the house, the furniture, and countless other items, big and small. The nonessentials.

Kis Marcus was already a refugee.   Private family collection

Kis	Kåår	Dorte	
1 frakke	1 par kunstsilke strømper	2 par sportsstrømper	1 par nyjere
1 kjole	1 " sko og slør	1 pyjamas	
2 tørklæder		1 frakke	
2 par handsker		1 nederdel	
1 strikket trøje		1 bluse	
1 pyjamas		1 strikket trøje	
4 par helsilkestrømper		1 par vanter	
1 " kunst -		1 " luffer	
1 par uldne -		1 hue	
2 sæt undertøj (1 daarligt)		1 par sko	
2 hofteholdere (")		1 " tøfler	
1 par uldne buhser		1 tørklæde	
1 underkjole		1 sæt uldent undertøj	
2 brystholdere		2 bomulds undertøjer	
1 par sko		2 — - buhser	
10 lommetørklæder		1 par silke buhser	
1 bælte		1 " uldne buhser	
1 par tøfler		2 lommetørklæder	
		1 livstykke	

Palle		
1 frakke	1 par nyjere	
1 hue	1 overall	
1 par luffer	1 par buhser (af k's nederdel)	
1 " sko	1 " sportsstrømper	
2 " sportsstrømper		
1 sæt tøj		
2 skjorter		
1 bomuldsundertrøje		
2 par underbuhser		
2 uldne undertrøjer		
1 halstørklæde		
4 lommetørklæder		
2 par seler		
1½ pyjamas		
1 par tøfler		
1 slipover		

Efter tyskernes overgreb paa Danmark d 29 aug 1943, regeringens afsættelse og kongens internering, begyndte der atter at komme rygter i omløb om særlige forholdsregler mod jøderne i vort land. - Vi blev beroliget af mange mennesker og levede saaledes mellem haab og frygt. Vi var dog mest optimistiske, kunde ikke og vilde ikke tro, at vi i Danmark kunde komme til at opleve de rædsler, som jøderne i andre af tyskerne besatte lande havde gennemgaaet. Fra midten af september begyndte rygterne at gaa om, at nu kom jødeforfølgelserne, og vi blev nervøse, da de jødiske bøger og protokoller blev stjaalet fra de kontorer, hvor de laa. Vi lullede os selv til ro med, at der maaske kun kom love o.l., og selvom vi hørte om mange af vore race fæller, der ikke var hjemme af frygt for at blive hentet af gestapo om natten, blev vi hjemme indtil søndag d. 26 sept. Vi fik da besøg om eftermiddagen først af Ruth Schottländer og derpaa af Poul og Inger, der raadede os til at tage væk om natten. Vi tog saa med til Ruth og Bolsa, som vi ingen

CHAPTER 1

SUNDAY, SEPTEMBER 26

THE LAST DAY OF THE PAST

Sunday Morning at Sorgenfri Castle

There was a hard rain on Sunday morning, and that wasn't a good omen. The trolleys plying the streets bore small flags to mark the king's birthday. But the aging king did not ride through the streets of occupied Copenhagen, as he since the beginning of the German occupation had made it a habit of doing every morning as a token of normality and defiance. After an equestrian accident the previous year, and his more-or-less voluntary confinement at Sorgenfri Castle, the royal family's summer residence a few kilometers north of Copenhagen, King Christian had stopped attending the usual festivities. The king was seen by many as a personification of hope. The hope for freedom and the hope for winning back the dignity betrayed when Denmark decided not to put up a real fight as the Germans attacked on April 9, 1940. Somehow the king managed to stay aloof from petty politics even if he had loyally supported every step the elected politicians had taken in administering the country under the German occupation and in warning the people against armed resistance and sabotage. Now Christian stood as the epitome of the popular attitude: Yes, we had bowed to the occupation. But we had not subjected ourselves. And behind the formal politeness between the occupying power and the occupied nation, both the king and the people showed their contempt through quiet rejection—dubbed "the cold shoulder"—making sure that the intruders were not treated as guests.

The king could look back on ten hard years. And looking ahead, the prospect was even bleaker. There was only one bright spot: The country

remained united. It had been the opposite in his younger days, when
World War I raged in Europe and Denmark fought to hold on to its
neutrality and stay clear of the destruction of war. The political parties had been deeply divided, but Denmark had managed to maintain a
delicate neutrality, trading with both sides. In the aftermath of the war,
the king had seen monarchies fall all over Europe; the Russian czar, the
German kaiser—both friends and relatives. And what replaced them?
Revolutions and social unrest. Denmark was also on the brink of revolution around Easter 1920, but the leader of the Social Democratic Party,
Thorvald Stauning, had intervened and stabilized the situation. Stauning later became prime minister, governing with a firm hand from
1929, and he steered the country in the critical years as the Depression
swept the world economy and the Nazi storm gathered south of the border. In the aftermath of the occupation Stauning had managed to keep
the political parties so tightly together that the occupation forces had not
been able to divide and rule. But in May 1942, the sixty-eight-year-old
prime minister had died, worn out and depressed. Still, the politicians
had remained united, and they stayed united even after August 29, 1943,
when the government resigned. That was the bright spot: unity.

Denmark and Nazism

Right from the outset the Danish government had been deeply troubled
by the Nazi tide rising in neighboring Germany. The uneasy feeling was
only reinforced when Hitler took power in 1933, and open anti-Semitism
declared itself everywhere. The center-left coalition government had settled early on a cautious course seeking to avoid any action that, rightly
or wrongly, could provoke Hitler's increasingly threatening Third Reich.
The government kept silent as far as possible and encouraged Danish
citizens to do the same. Better not to provoke, to avoid giving the Nazi
regime even the slightest pretext to take action against neutral Denmark. At the same time the coalition between the little Liberal Center Party and the huge Social Democratic Party was determined to do
everything possible to stem what they dreaded even more than they
did Germany: that totalitarianism would take root within Danish society. The government understood from the outset how closely related
Nazism was to Communism and fascism, and how utterly all three contradicted not only democracy but also the humanistic values underpinning democratic society. Therefore the government initiated a powerful

political and moral mobilization aimed at galvanizing the Danish people against totalitarian ideologies and uniting the country around democratic governance and humanitarian ideals as the very essence of the national community.

The analysis was that the Nazi takeover in Berlin was due not least to the fact that the Nazis had successfully made Nazism synonymous with Germany's recovery from World War I's human and social disasters, and with overcoming the humiliating terms the victorious powers had forced upon Germany at the Versailles conference. By mobilizing patriotism in its favor, the Nazi Party harnessed a great national force and legitimized its taking control of society's institutions. Danish politicians wanted at all costs to avoid something similar in Denmark. The strategy was to reverse the mechanism in order to mobilize patriotic forces in Denmark for the defense of democracy. It would also deprive the Danish Nazi Party of the ability to portray itself as a patriotic alternative to a "weak" and "indecisive" democratic government.

Following this logic, the Social Democratic Party from 1933 deliberately began, in their political rhetoric, to link "the Danish" with "the democratic"—using the two synonymously. Hence, to be a good, patriotic Dane was tantamount to resisting totalitarian ideas and defending representative government, democracy, and humanism. The Social Democrats argued that the patriotic political platform was too forceful to be left to the extreme Right, and their strategy gradually forced both the Conservatives and the Farmers' Party, the leading opposition parties, to confront anti-parliamentary forces within their own political movements.

The question of the Jews fitted precisely within such thinking. Despite the careful appeasement of Nazi Germany, it soon became clear to the Danish government that here was a line it would not and could not cross: If Denmark embarked on a differentiation between Jews and other Danish citizens, it would be betraying a fundamental pillar of its democracy—and thus of what was "Danish." As the government saw it, there was no "Jewish question" in Denmark. All talk of such a question originated with people who wanted to create a problem—and for a specific purpose. To be sure, prejudice against Jews appeared from time to time in Denmark, as did outright anti-Semitism. But the more discrimination and persecution of Jews became endemic in Germany, the more strongly the Danish government reacted to prevent racism from taking root in Denmark.

The government cooperated with the democratic opposition in rejecting all attempts to bring anti-Semitism into political life or to make it generally acceptable to refer to a "Jewish problem." Thus in March 1938, when the Conservative MP Victor Pürschel, who had overt Nazi sympathies, pointed out during a parliamentary debate that "Denmark is, after all, the Danish fatherland, and it is we who have the first right to be here," the remark provoked a strong response. Mercilessly stripping bare the emptiness of Pürschel's rhetoric, the speaker for the Social Democrats succeeded in enlarging the perspective to demonstrate that, contrary to defending good Danish values, Pürschel was "in the process of injecting anti-Semitism and the cloven hoof of Nazism into the political debate." Pürschel's motion was defeated and the common front against Nazism reinforced.

After Kristallnacht on November 9, 1938, when violence against the Jews was systematized in Germany, Justice Minister Karl Kristian Steincke introduced a specific statutory provision that addressed "Whoever by spreading false rumors or accusations pursues or incites hatred against a group of the Danish population because of its faith, descent, or nationality." When the opposition threw the necessity of this "Jewish law" into doubt, the minister of justice cited from the rostrum Hitler's *Mein Kampf* as well as Dr. Goebbels's explicit denunciation of democracy: "You cannot say that you have not been warned, or that you do not know what it is about," Steincke pointed out, arguing in favor of making racism illegal. His proposal was adopted, and hence the criminal code effectively banned anti-Semitic propaganda in Denmark, not only up to the German invasion but, remarkably, also during the occupation.[1]

Closing the Door on Refugees

Until 1937 Jewish refugees as well as other foreigners could freely enter Denmark and stay up to three months if they were able to support themselves or knew someone who could support them. Permits could be extended without particular difficulties as long as they were not filed as an application for permanent residence or a work permit—which generally were rejected, even for people who had stayed in the country for a long time. From 1937, when persecution of the Jews in Germany was intensified, Denmark, like most of Germany's other neighbors, tightened its procedures as Jewish refugees were stopped at the border. The few who still got in had only a short time to find another residence. Overall the main purpose of Danish refugee policy from 1933 to 1938 was to prevent Jews and other refugees from taking up permanent residence in the country—and from the summer of 1938 to prevent them from getting in at all. It succeeded to a great extent, and few of the persecuted found safe haven in Denmark. But there were loopholes, and despite the restrictions more than five thousand German refugees arrived. A little less than half of these were still in the country when Denmark was occupied, including some fifteen hundred Jewish refugees. Among them were 265 children aged fourteen to sixteen, known as the Aliyah-children, and 377 young Jews seeking agricultural education as part of a Zionist movement for later immigration to Palestine.

The government's restrictive immigration policy is sometimes interpreted as a response to fear of growing anti-Semitism and Nazi advances in Denmark. This did play a role, and was also behind the support for the policy from Jewish organizations in Denmark, which followed a pattern familiar from other countries bordering Nazi Germany. Discussions in the Foreign Policy Committee of the Danish parliament after Kristallnacht revealed "agreement that it would be unfortunate if the admission of refugees formed the basis for anti-Semitism." Probably more compelling was the simple fact that the politicians, in a socially turbulent time, did not want any influx of refugees who were socially exposed. It was fundamentally an issue of the social order, and the politicians utterly opposed the entry of anyone they didn't believe could be self-supporting and who they feared would further increase the country's already catastrophically high unemployment.

Over time a more convenient argument was developed to support the ever-more-restrictive immigration policies: The refugee problem had to find its solution somewhere else. Denmark was not unwilling to provide financial support for such an endeavor—for example in a "safe zone" if any country would make one available. It sounded nice, but it did not help the many refugees who were desperately seeking a way out of Nazi Germany, which was actively "encouraging" the emigration of its Jewish population.

Thus there was not much room in Denmark for either Jews or others fleeing the Nazis. The government had long since given up trying to counter the ominous developments south of the border and concentrated solely on the survival of the Danish nation. Steincke summarized the paradox in April 1937: "One does not want to be inhumane, and one dares not be humane because of the consequences." This policy was reflected in the Jewish community, which, under the strong pressure of the situation, backed up the restrictive refugee policy of the government and never openly committed itself to support the minority of activists who sought admission for numbers of German and Austrian Jews to Denmark. The community took a few discreet initiatives with charities that might mitigate the German and Austrian Jews' circumstances, just as they sought to provide work permits to the Jewish refugees who had already come to Denmark, so that in the long run they were not left to be supported by financial assistance from the community's better-established members.

In response to the growing Jewish refugee problem in Europe, thirty-two countries met at a conference held in Évian-les-Bains in July 1938, on the initiative of U.S. president Franklin D. Roosevelt. All agreed that something urgently had to be done—and that preferably this something should be done by anybody but themselves. (It reflects on the spirit of the conference that the Australian delegate declared that as Australia had no racial problems, obviously it did not want to import one.) Despite all the good words the Évian conference provided no solution and did not advance any common refugee and asylum procedures. As far as Denmark was concerned, its main effort at the conference—besides avoiding being noticed—was to steer clear of any "provocation" in the form of direct criticism of Germany and its manifest persecution of Jews and other minorities. Upon his return to Denmark, Steincke even felt obliged to reassure the public that he had not left room for one single Jewish refugee to cross the Danish border. But there was no need for such concerns. The main flow of refugees did not go north, and by 1940 fewer than six thousand Jews had sought refuge in the three Scandinavian countries.[2]

Still, the problem was conceived as one of numbers. There were more than a million Jews in Germany and Austria. How many of these unfortunates could and should Denmark receive? The apathy toward the disaster only grew with the numbers, and Denmark, like other countries, turned its back on the problem and reinforced immigration controls at the border.[3]

"Us" and "Them"

In his confinement at Sorgenfri Castle, King Christian had ample time to reflect on his own encounter with Herr Hitler. As the king was traveling through Germany in 1937, he had stopped over in Berlin, wanting to address the precarious question of the Danish-German border directly with the German chancellor. But the foreign minister, Peter Munch, who was also the leader of the Liberal Center Party, had warned the king not to interfere in this highly political issue. So, according to Christian's private notes, the conversation with Hitler had mainly turned on less controversial issues relating to "the achievements of Danes at the 1936 Olympic Games in Berlin and the sportive education of youth in general."

As Germany became increasingly threatening, the issue of Denmark's security bore down more and more. The threat came from both outside and within. The four democratic parties constituting the center of gravity in Danish politics had no confidence in the Danish Communists and Nazis. Neither was seen as a genuine democratic party but rather each was perceived as a fifth column with close ties to Moscow and Berlin, respectively. The government therefore pushed forward to curb the growth and appeal of these totalitarian movements, both through legislation and through a comprehensive ideological and political mobilization in favor of democracy. It is no coincidence that it was in the mid-1930s, facing the world crisis and growing support for Communism, fascism, and Nazism in most European countries, that Prime Minister Thorvald Stauning went to the polls on a platform labeled "Denmark for the People" or under the slogan "Stauning or Chaos." A robust national unity was meant to be forged around democracy, and the national flag, the Dannebrog, was flown by the labor movement alongside its traditional red flags.

Gradually a strong sense developed of a national "us," which included every citizen adhering to the principles of democracy and its underlying humanitarian values, opposed to a "them" of the political extremes not subscribing to those same ideas. The majority thus stigmatized Communists and Nazis not only as enemies of democracy but also as "un-Danish," thus as individuals on the margins of society, tolerated but not accepted as part of the community. This deliberate casting of "us" and "them" was to determine the fate of Denmark and that of many Danes during the turbulent times ahead. Indeed, it was meant to do exactly that.

The political mobilization, however, did not resolve the issue of military defense, or that of Denmark and Germany's shared border. After a century of battle and war over this issue, a national border was finally established by the Versailles conference and a referendum in 1920. This line meticulously followed the national majority in each and every village, and left as few as possible of the German-speaking minority north of the border and equally few Danish speakers south of it. But the boundary winding and twisting its way across the base of Jutland (Jylland) had never been recognized by Germany, which despite the popular vote in 1920 saw it as part of the unjust dictates of Versailles. Even worse: It was an unfortified line in lowlands, making it difficult—if not impossible—to defend against German armor. No wonder neither Britain nor Sweden would or could come to Denmark's aid, and that both countries carefully avoided any signal that could be interpreted by Denmark—or by Germany—as a military guarantee of the 1920 border.

Against this backdrop many within the governing parties considered a Danish military defense against a determined German attack impossible. But the prime minister realized that giving up on defending his country, even at very bad odds and against an overwhelming enemy, was no option. At a minimum, the government had to demonstrate that every possibility had been tried and that every effort had been made. Against his foreign minister's and coalition partners' advice, Prime Minister Stauning in 1931 appointed the most fervent advocate of national defense, General Erik With, as commander of the army. Unlike the admiral commanding the navy, the staunchly conservative and British-oriented general believed in the importance of a territorial defense, and indeed the possibility of territorial defense. He no longer did so five years later, having explored every possible military strategy in vain. Despite all his efforts and secret contacts with the Swedish high command, the general had not been able to present a credible plan for the defense of Denmark against the ever-growing German military might on flat terrain and with no prospect of reinforcement.

The four old democratic parties slowly adjusted themselves to the inevitable: If Germany demanded anything from Denmark, including access to Danish territory, there was nothing Denmark could do, other than bow so quickly that it would not be worth Hitler's while to destroy the country. This was the reason for the foreign minister's opposition to any informal consultation between Hitler and the king. The government realized that any hint of negotiations about the common border with Hitler's Germany was bound to lead to requests that Denmark would rather not face. The country was in no position to negotiate with the Reich—let alone to say no. This became even more manifest when Hitler in May 1939 imposed a bilateral nonagression pact in Denmark, the only one of the three Scandinavian countries not daring to refuse.

The Nazi-Soviet Nonaggression Pact in August 1939 confirmed Denmark's worst fears that the totalitarian powers had more in common than their ideological tirades seemed to suggest. The pact helped trigger the war, and Poland's fate during its first weeks made it abundantly clear that even a substantially larger and better-equipped army than Denmark's had little chance of stopping the German war machine—and that the price of making the attempt was cruelly and destructively high. That autumn the Soviet attack on Finland, a fellow neutral Nordic country, drove home the point. Despite stubborn and heroic Finnish resistance in the frozen polar regions, Britain and France failed to come to Finland's rescue, and struggling alone over the winter, Finland faced the inevitability of defeat. Denmark shivered, ducked, and reaffirmed its neutrality. Everybody realized that the worst was yet to come—and that Denmark could do little to avoid it.

Peaceful Occupation

The worst occurred on the morning of April 9, 1940, with the German onslaught on Denmark and Norway. In the early hours Germany initiated the first-ever combined land, sea, and air attack, landing troops simultaneously in fifteen different locations spread across the country, including the middle of Copenhagen. The scope and strength of the assault took Denmark by surprise. In the midst of it, the German minister to Denmark handed the stunned foreign minister, P. Munch, a unique ultimatum. It laid down a set of conditions, offers, and proposals constituting the outline of an arrangement under which Denmark could retain parts of its sovereignty provided the Danish government chose not to launch an all-out defense.

King Christian describes in his personal diary how he was summoned to an urgent session of the state council at 5:30 a.m., and how he reluctantly but also forcefully rejected the advice of the commanding general to fight on despite the immediate threat of destruction of the capital and massive civilian casualties. German heavy bombers were hanging in numbers low over Copenhagen, and the king noted: "I considered continued fighting pointless against such supremacy and ordered shooting to be halted and negotiations to be initiated."[4]

Fighting was suspended virtually before it had begun, and the government accepted the German terms "under protest." In essence Germany would take Denmark "under protection" based on three crucial commitments the Danish government extracted from the ultimatum that morning: The occupiers would respect Denmark's continued neutrality and not force Denmark into the war. Moreover, Germany gave an assurance not to "interfere with the Kingdom of Denmark's territorial integrity or political independence." This meant that in addition to Denmark staying out of the war, the 1920 border would be recognized for the first time, and Berlin would not interfere in the country's internal affairs. Democracy could remain.

That same day Prime Minister Stauning, together with his old coalition partner and the two democratic opposition parties, formed a national unity government that took responsibility for the resulting cooperation with the German authorities. The politicians labeled this construct "the policy of negotiation," indicating that henceforth every question between the occupying and the occupied countries was to be settled through negotiations between the two. Critics of this stance have tended to use the term "policy of cooperation" to indicate that the negotiation was based on the fiction of Denmark retaining its sovereignty and on the fiction of continued neutrality, both challenged by the fact that Nazi Germany kept the entire country occupied. The Danish government in fact acted under duress, and of course negotiations were conducted under the constant threat of imposing an all-out Nazi administration parallel to the development in Norway, where armed resistance and violent occupation exiled the constitutional government together with King Haakon VII and installed direct Nazi rule in collaboration with the Norwegian Nazi leader Vidkun Quisling.

The situation in Denmark thus rested on the unique understanding that Denmark was the subject of a "peaceful occupation." Germany had indeed occupied its neutral neighbor, but with a minimum of violence, without a state of war being declared and thus without Germany assuming responsibility for Denmark's internal affairs. There were many problems associated with this unusual design, but also benefits for both countries. From a Danish point of view, one of them was that a peaceful occupation preserved all fundamental institutions of democratic society and protected the country against the nazification enforced in other occupied countries. This also barred persecution of Danish Jews, who were fully integrated into Danish society. The Danish government consistently rejected special laws or provisions in relation to Danish Jews. On this and other key points the elected politicians were uncompromising, and their stance was reinforced by King Christian, whose support was decisive both because only he could endow a Danish government with constitutional legitimacy and because he soon became a popular symbol of hope for Denmark to regain its lost freedom.

As long as the war went Germany's way, Danish cooperation with the occupying forces became more and more proactive, actively seeking to ensure Denmark's production and exports within the zones controlled by Germany. In the summer of 1940 the national unity government was reshuffled with a view to becoming less "political" and more active in economic and trade cooperation. A veteran diplomat from the successful Danish policy of neutrality during World War I, Erik Scavenius, was recalled from retirement and once again appointed foreign minister, now in the critical junction between the German representatives and the Danish authorities. He was persuaded to take responsibility for the more active cooperation with Nazi Germany that the elected politicians felt necessary but knew would be highly unpopular with the electorate. Scavenius was reluctant to take on the role of a scapegoat, and he harbored no illusions as to the strength of elected politicians' spines. An anecdote relates that upon Scavenius's nomination a colleague asked Prime Minister Stauning whether the new foreign minister might not be too friendly with the Germans. Stauning is said to have replied: "Scavenius? He is not friendly with anyone!"

On September 18, 1940, as the successful German campaign in the west came to a conclusion and the Battle of Britain intensified, the king discussed the Jewish issue with Prime Minister Stauning. Christian refers in his personal diary to the conversation, which was based on the fear of a German demand for deportation of Danish Jews: "I interjected that after the Germans' past performance one might expect they would demand the expulsion of Jews who were present, and that such a requirement would definitely be repellent to me. The prime minister was of the same opinion and added that the question was once raised by the leaders in Berlin, but the president of the National Bank [former leading Social Democratic politician Carl Valdemar Bramsnæs] had rejected it saying that 'in Denmark, there was no issue in relation to Jews.' I pointed out that I had noticed that when we were determined, the Germans backed off."[5]

A few months later the king and the prime minister reverted to the issue in a private conversation, and according to his diary, Christian stated "that I considered our own Jews to be Danish citizens, and the Germans could not touch them. The prime minister shared my view and added that there could be no question about that."[6]

The Germans were aware that an action against the Danish Jews would mean the collapse of cooperation. Whenever the German authorities raised the issue, the politicians would in one form or another come back to the argument that their legitimacy, and thus their capacity to keep the machinery of society running, originated solely in their mandate from the electorate. If this confidence was betrayed, people would no longer respect them and follow their rules and instructions: The resistance would be pervasive, and the carefully structured design of peaceful cooperation would collapse.

The Germans largely bought this argument, not because of sentimentality or excessive respect for the Danish politicians' objections in relation to their voters. They bought it because they believed that fundamentally Danes would react exactly the way the politicians claimed. If the Germans pushed this point, the occupying power would have to take full responsibility for the community and run Denmark as they ran other occupied countries: with violence and force. That possibility always existed, of course, but there were important advantages for Germany in the construct of cooperation. Until 1943 the Wehrmacht needed hardly more than twenty thousand men in Denmark to maintain the occupation. This number, however, increased substantially with growing German fear of an impending Allied invasion on the west coast of Jutland, and it is estimated that the number of German troops in Denmark reached some 150,000 by the end of 1943, predominantly worn-out units or new ones undergoing combat training.[7] In comparison Germany kept 300,000–450,000 troops in strategically more important and geographically more challenging Norway.

In addition Danish industry and especially Danish agriculture were providing increasingly essential supplies to the occupying power. Both factors played into the discussions in Berlin. Perhaps a third consideration was ultimately the most important: The peaceful occupation of Denmark was in Hitler's lens the very model for how Germany could control Europe when the Third Reich had prevailed. While the areas and populations to the east were colonized and exploited—in fact mostly obliterated—in order to expand German Lebensraum, the northern and western European countries and populations held a more fortunate position. Denmark was a special case, both racially and because the government had chosen from the outset to base its policy on cooperation.

Thus the Danish design was not just practical and useful. It was also a confirmation of the new European order—the *Neuropa*—Hitler meant to create. Even more cynically, it made Denmark a living political laboratory for practical arrangements in a future Europe dominated by the Third Reich. But the sum of German interests in keeping cooperation alive at the same time gave Denmark astonishingly firm ground in its ongoing tug-of-war with the occupying power, which from the outset began to cut bits and pieces from what soon became known as "the promises of April 9."

The Policy of Cooperation

While King Christian could note the protection of the Danish Jews as one of the few accomplishments of recent years, the adoption by mid-1941 of the "Communist Laws" troubled him. Indeed, one of the most critical concessions made to German demands was the internment of Danish Communists after Operation Barbarossa, the German invasion of the Soviet Union, on June 22, 1941. The democratic parties harbored a deeply rooted distrust of the Communists, whose leader had declared from the podium of the Folketing, the first and dominant chamber of the Danish parliament, his party's willingness to take power by violence. This distrust was further fueled by the conclusion of the nonaggression pact between the Soviet Union and Germany in 1939, the Soviet Union's attack on neutral Finland later that same autumn, and Communist legitimizing of the German occupation of Denmark as a preemptive move to counter English and French imperialism. From this point on, the Communists were regarded as pariahs, feared and hated by many and together with the small Danish Nazi Party excluded from the common "us" of society. In this way those who chose to join the two nonparliamentary parties on the political extremes were ostracized by the strong national community that the four democratic parties celebrated.

Immediately after Hitler's surprise attack on the Soviet Union, the Germans demanded that "all leading Danish Communists" be interned. The Danish government responded by launching a police roundup after a Ministry of Justice order—based on lists of Communists the Danish police had already prepared.

By the end of July 1941 nearly three hundred Communists were interned, including several members of parliament. The Danish authorities chose a broad definition of "leading" and demonstrated a shameful zeal in carrying out the German requirements. Further arrests directed against virtually all known Communists were conducted in five waves over the following sixteen months.

Internment was legitimized—again with reference to emergency law—by an act of August 22, 1941, banning Communist organizations and activities. When Stauning presented this law to the king, the head of state according to his personal diary warned the prime minister to be careful in his approach to members of parliament, as these enjoyed special protection under the constitution: "One could sympathize or not with the party, but justice has to be respected in all matters and such arrests may backfire, also at a later point." Later, as Christian authorized the "Communist Law" in the state council, he noted that it "was precarious to touch on this issue as the constitution stipulated freedom of speech and the press, and even if Communists are subjected to general measures, one cannot change their personal attitude."[8]

Little doubt remains that the internments in general, and the arrests of members of parliament in particular, amounted to outright violations of the Danish constitution and thus encroached on the very foundations of democracy the policy of cooperation aimed to protect.

Another vulnerable group was also those from Nazi Germany who had sought refuge in Denmark, including both political refugees, mostly Social Democrats and Communists, and stateless Jews. The Germans gradually increased pressure on this group, and Danish authorities went further and further in accommodating these requests. This proved fatal for between 50 and 100 refugees, including 21 stateless Jews, who were individually exiled from Denmark to Germany, where the vast majority vanished in the camps.[9]

A direct consequence of the German attack on the Soviet Union was a request for Denmark to allow volunteers to join a special army group, Frikorps Danmark, established for the same purpose under the Waffen SS, and designed to engage in the "fight against Communism" on the eastern front. The arrangement was an example of the kind of compromises by which Foreign Minister Erik Scavenius kept the cooperation above the fray. In order to avoid Danish conscripts being forced to take part in Hitler's crusade against Communism, the unpleasant and ambiguous—but still much less harmful—opening for volunteers could satisfy the Germans. The government walked a thin line by allowing

Danish army officers to enroll without directly encouraging them to do so. The politicians also saw—but did not say—that those most likely to volunteer would be Danish Nazis, the majority of whom came from the German-speaking minority just north of the border. From a cynical perspective it was not unwelcome if individuals from this militant group went off to an unknown fate on the eastern front.

Though King Christian clearly also saw this dimension, he did not like one bit the idea of Danish officers fighting in German uniforms, and he did little to hide his contempt when a high-ranking German representative in August 1941 went to see him to give official thanks for the Danish contribution. According to his diary notes, he responded by declaring that "anyone could volunteer and I would recommend using those doing so in the front lines. They had chosen themselves to fight there, and it would save your own troops."[10]

To the stunned German officer the king further explained that to him the arrangement "would be equivalent to Germans fighting in British uniforms in the ranks of British regiments," and the German assurances that the volunteers would carry Danish demarcations on their uniforms did nothing to calm him. Over the following years six to seven thousand volunteers joined Frikorps Danmark; some two thousand died in combat.

In many other cases Denmark extended itself to accommodate Germany or improve its position in German-occupied Europe. With the discontinuation of exports to its main market in Great Britain, Denmark became economically dependent on its exports to Germany. Of particular importance in this regard was the country's substantial agricultural production, which, together with goods and foodstuffs from other occupied areas, contributed to keep the Reich running.

Step by step the unparalleled "peaceful occupation" of Denmark developed into a very special case within the Europe controlled by the Third Reich. On the one hand Denmark firmly rejected Nazism and the German war efforts, firmly upholding democratic institutions and the rule of law. On the other the constitutional government did cooperate with the occupying power, not least in economics and through exports, and it played its part in keeping the situation in Denmark calm, including arresting the Danish Communists. While Danish cooperation with Nazi Germany was pragmatic, unheroic, and sometimes humiliating, it was not without clear lines of demarcation. In the midst of its apparent powerlessness Denmark managed to force significant concessions from the Third Reich—even on points that were central to Nazi ideology. A central source of this surprising strength was the very unity hailed by the king. Despite all internal strife and rivalry, the elected politicians remained united, not allowing any elected representative who commanded the slightest popular credibility to join forces with the Germans or to drive a wedge through the Danish administration. With a mixture of delays, compromises, partial concessions, and references to democratic rules, applicable law, and public attitudes, the government in many cases managed to meet the Third Reich's representatives on a negotiating ground that was defined not just by Nazi logic but also by the Danish perception of what was right and wrong. Nowhere is this precarious balance more apparent than in respect to the question of the Danish Jews.

The German historian Peter Longerich points out in his compelling analysis of the Nazi persecution and murder of the Jews that the *Judenpolitik* was closely linked to the strategic alliances of the Third Reich with neighboring countries, and that together with economic policy and military security and cooperation it constituted one of the main axes of German occupation and alliance policy. Thus cooperation on this specific issue was considered key to the loyalty of the alliances Germany sought to forge with other countries.[11]

In this area cooperation was refused in Denmark, and the conversation already quoted between the king and the acting prime minister on September 10, 1941, only confirmed the complete agreement within Denmark to draw a line right there. While mass deportations were organized from Vichy France, Danish Jews were able to continue their daily lives protected by law and a complete refusal of Danish authorities to embark on even the first steps of the persecution—the naming and identifying of Jewish citizens.

Defiant Diplomacy

While there was ongoing friction within the cooperation, the basic construct came to its first tough test in the dramatic process that in November 1941 led to Denmark's signing of the reinvigorated Anti-Comintern Pact between the German Reich and Japan directed against that international arm of Soviet Communism. Germany insisted that Denmark join the pact, which was first and foremost a piece of propaganda designed to demonstrate support for the fight against Communism at a time when the German campaign in the East was getting bogged down. Since victories were not immediately apparent on the military fronts, they were now to be harvested with all the more fanfare on the diplomatic one. This posed a problem for the government in Copenhagen, because the pact came uncomfortably close to a linkage of Denmark to German war aims. Any hint in that direction would break the notion of Denmark's continued neutrality and, even worse, be a first step toward active participation in the war on the German side. The government, therefore, was inclined to refuse flatly German demands for Denmark's signature, even if doing so meant the collapse of the policy of cooperation.

Eventually Foreign Minister Scavenius persuaded the government that Denmark was best served by joining the pact. Scavenius, who was burdened with the unenviable task of bridging German demands and Danish reluctance, held out the possibility of compromise while raising in the politicians' minds the specter of total Nazi control as an inducement to make the concessions he found necessary. Scavenius believed that Denmark had a vital interest in continuing the cooperation, and that his country should go as far as was necessary to accommodate Germany—even when this appeared unfair and came close to compromising the promises of April 9. There would always be, Scavenius argued, a moment when Denmark needed the accumulated goodwill for more important purposes. Scavenius believed in realpolitik, which for him was based on the premise that Germany would always remain Denmark's big neighbor and that therefore Denmark could not afford being seen to side with Germany's enemies, not even in the event of war. He based his policy on two fundamental principles that were not easy to reconcile: On the one hand, Denmark had every interest in holding on to the three promises from April 9. On the other hand, it was crucial that the elected politicians explicitly back each concession given to satisfy the ever-more-arrogant backed. This attitude implied that the Jewish question was a line Scavenius felt Denmark could not and should not cross, because it would involve a flagrant breach of Denmark's political integrity.

It was not surprising, therefore, that Scavenius turned strongly against breaking with the Germans on the question of Denmark joining the Anti-Comintern Pact. If Berlin was anxious to reap a hollow propaganda gain, Denmark had to bend and secure compensatory measures where it really mattered. The compromise between Foreign Minister Scavenius and the elected politicians was that Denmark could join the pact while insisting on a set of reservations that would expressly state that the pact did not oblige Denmark to participate actively in the war against Communism—let alone against the Soviet Union. According to his diary notes, the king concurred: "I nourished my own reservations in regard to signing the pact, but faced with an ultimatum with unforeseeable consequences we had no choice." The wording of these reservations was negotiated and agreed with the German minister in Copenhagen, in order that every detail be settled before the hesitant politicians gave their final go-ahead.

At the last moment Scavenius traveled to Berlin to sign, only to learn upon his arrival that the Nazi leadership had no intention of accepting the agreed Danish reservations. Everything came to a head when the German foreign minister, Joachim von Ribbentrop, bluntly ordered Scavenius to appear with Hitler the following day at 12:05 for the signing ceremony at the Court of Honor in the new chancellery of the Reich and Scavenius refused outright on the grounds that he had no mandate to sign without the reservations. In that night's war of nerves between the Third Reich's foreign minister and his stubborn Danish counterpart, everything was at stake. But in the end a solution was found, and Scavenius got the Danish clarifications adopted, albeit secretly and in attenuated form. The drama suggested that the Danish negotiating position was stronger than one might have expected, even in direct confrontation with the Nazi leadership in Berlin: The appearance of Denmark's "voluntary" support for the pact was more important than a political concession, which in practice would be irrelevant when Germany had won the war.

Denmark had made countless concessions to the Germans before Scavenius's signing of the Anti-Comintern Pact. For an increasing number of Danes this appeasement was disgraceful, and Scavenius's signature in Berlin triggered the first demonstrations with public demands for "Norwegian conditions" rather than an unwilling drift into the German embrace, all the more so as the hard-won Danish "reservations" could not be made public. Were clarity and suppression not preferable to "voluntary" submission to injustice? Now the question was being posed directly, and the students in the streets adopted a resolution addressed to King Christian proclaiming that they "would rather share conditions with the Norwegian people than have Denmark submit without resis-

Foreign Minister Erik Scavenius in conversation with Adolf Hitler in Berlin on November 28, 1941, after Scavenius signed the Anti-Comintern Pact on behalf of Denmark. Both men had reason to smile: Hitler because he got the press photo he needed to keep alive the idea that a large group of civilized Western countries supported Germany's crusade against world Communism and the Soviet Union; Scavenius because he had managed to extract Germany's explicit assurance that Denmark would remain outside the war and would not contribute in any concrete way to the fight against Communism, either at home or by forced conscription of soldiers to the German campaign.

But these concessions remained secret, and the image of Denmark's foreign minister smiling with Hitler shamed the Danish public. When Scavenius came home he was met with demonstrations crying for "Norwegian conditions," implying that some would prefer an outright Nazi takeover to continued concessions to Berlin. By continuing to maneuver within the narrow margins of Hitler's "model protectorate," Scavenius became a symbol of subjugation greater than what the Danish resistance wanted, but not greater than what elected politicians of all democratic parties could support.

Scavenius's policy of cooperation did not reflect a lack of spine, position, or will, but rather a deep conviction that Danish democracy could be defended only in this way, and that a confrontation with Germany would place the most vulnerable in peril. Among them, no one group was more exposed than the Jews. Polfoto tance to aims that deeply conflict with our determination to live in a free and democratic Denmark."

Even if most citizens apparently continued to accept the government's answer that the lesser evil was preferable to the greater one, a small but growing minority disagreed. To them confrontation was necessary, no matter the cost. Still, it took another year to build up the first significant armed Danish resistance.

The demand for "Norwegian conditions" has continued to echo through later critiques of the policy of cooperation. But even if the Norwegian government and king, like the Dutch, were forced into exile after putting up a fight against the German invasion, neither the Dutch nor the Norwegians were spared the ugly dilemmas entailed in practical cooperation with the occupying power. King Christian—a brother of King Haakon—described those dilemmas in a secret letter he addressed that same day to the Swedish king, Gustav V, who was the father-in-law of his son Crown Prince Frederick. The close connections among the Scandinavian royal families, together with the intimate ties among the ruling Social Democratic parties in the three countries, served to enhance a sense of communality despite their very different fates during the war.[12]

A few weeks later Germany's major ally, Japan, launched a surprise attack on Pearl Harbor, the main base of the U.S. Pacific Fleet. The following day President Roosevelt declared war against Japan, causing Hitler to honor Germany's alliance and declare war against the United States. World War II was a reality, and at the turn of 1941–42, Prime Minister Winston Churchill and President Franklin D. Roosevelt met in Washington with their delegations and with those of the other countries at war with the Axis to forge the great alliance against the Axis powers and their adherents. The United Nations Declaration was agreed upon and formally signed as a formidable demonstration of the forces now uniting against Germany and Japan. Surely the war was far from won, but it was suddenly hard to see how it could end with anything but the ultimate defeat of the Axis powers.

At the Allied meeting Denmark was represented by its former minister in Washington, Henrik Kauffmann. At the occupation of Denmark, Kauffmann had been the only prominent Danish official to denounce cooperation and the very idea of the "peaceful occupation." A year later, he secretly negotiated and signed in Washington, on April 9, 1941, an agreement granting the United States the right to build military bases in Greenland, still a Danish colony and thus formally neutral. The Danish government regarded Kauffmann's action as high treason and issued an arrest warrant for the rebellious diplomat, who in turn was recognized by President Roosevelt as an independent envoy with power over the frozen Danish funds in the United States. It was in the latter capacity that Kauffmann at the beginning of January 1942 associated himself with the UN Declaration, stating that the Danish people shared the hopes and aspirations it expressed.

Kauffmann stopped short of signing this declaration of war against Germany, but he did bring Denmark into the curious position that official representatives of this small, neutral, but occupied country had within a few weeks participated both in Hitler's magnificent ceremony in Berlin against world Communism and in the Allies' conference to seal the war aims of the United Nations, including the Soviet Union. This contrast reflected Denmark's ambiguous position in the second half of the war, in which Germany did not relax but quite to the contrary stepped up its racial policies and its systematic effort to rid Nazi-controlled Europe of all Jews.

The "Jewish Question" in Denmark

Long before the rainy morning at Sorgenfri Castle on his birthday, King Christian had made clear his position in relation to the Danish Jews. Moreover, on this specific point his position coincided with that of the foreign minister. While Scavenius was in Berlin for the signing ceremonies of the Anti-Comintern Pact, Reichsmarschall Hermann Göring told him to his face that sooner or later the Danes would have to deal with the Jewish question. Scavenius had replied that there was no Jewish problem in Denmark, a view he repeated a few weeks later when he reported the conversation to the Swedish minister in Copenhagen. The Danish people would regard an attack on the Jews as a clear German abuse of power, and it would bring cooperation to a halt. In her classic book about the trial of Adolf Eichmann, the German American political theorist Hannah Arendt described this refusal to go along with the first initial distinction between Jews and other Danish citizens as critical. It had become clear to both the German and the Danish sides that this was a crucial test. The Israeli historian Leni Yahil, who in 1969 released her groundbreaking work about Jews in Denmark during the occupation, cast the implication in simple terms: "As long as the Germans, for their own reasons, were interested in honoring the agreement they had forced on the Danes, they could not touch the Danish Jews."[13]

Meanwhile, *Die Endlösung*—"the final solution"—was beginning to shape up under the supervision of the SS. It was not a plan or a program but a set of loosely defined aspirations, ideas, and actions aimed at exterminating the Jews from all areas controlled by the Third Reich. The deployment of special *Einsatzgruppen* ("operational units") on the eastern front in June 1941 marked the first operations to this effect. At the Wannsee conference near Berlin in January 1942, where German authorities organized the mass deportations and murder of the European Jews, the execution of the final solution in Norway and Denmark was initially postponed. The discussion is known through one single copy of the minutes, and it is not to be taken at face value as a reflection of what actually transpired at the conference. Adolf Eichmann transcribed the minutes from a stenograph that had been worked through several times by other participants in order to use them as secret operational guidelines to the units and institutions within the Nazi machinery commissioned to deal with the final solution of the Jewish question. In the Scandinavian states it was foreseen that "difficulties will arise if this problem is dealt with thoroughly and that it will therefore be advisable to defer actions in these countries. Besides, in view of the small numbers of Jews affected, the deferral will not cause any substantial limitation."[14] The postponement gave the Norwegian Jews a delay of ten months and the Danish Jews a year and a half.

This decision obviously was not known at the time, and the threat of an action against the Danish Jews hung in the air; it was also conveniently used whenever the occupation authorities needed additional leverage. It was tangible in September 1942 when the Danish-German relationship ran into a crisis caused by nascent acts of sabotage, and triggered by Hitler's rage over what he saw as King Christian's insultingly brief acknowledgment of the Führer's congratulations on the occasion of the king's birthday. Christian had simply responded, "I thank you," provoking the hard-liners in Berlin to convince Hitler that Denmark had grown intolerably defiant.

Resistance in Denmark was beginning to grow, however slowly, and the terms of the occupation became tighter. By virtue of its formal sovereignty Denmark was the only one of the occupied countries that was controlled by the German Foreign Office, and Foreign Minister Ribbentrop had no lack of enemies within the Nazi leadership waiting only to rid him of his authority over Denmark. In the wings Adolf Eichmann, together with the Gestapo, pushed for the imposition of direct Nazi rule on the occupied country, bringing it into line with Norway and the Netherlands.

As Hitler seemed to relinquish all notions of Denmark as the ideal protectorate, Ribbentrop was forced to take a harder stance and demand the deportation of the Danish Jews. But Hitler's first inclination that Denmark should henceforth be ruled with an iron fist as a hostile country was replaced with the decision to send two new representatives to oversee the German operations there and to impose a reshuffle to obtain a more acquiescent Danish government. Hitler instructed the newly appointed supreme commander of the Wehrmacht in Denmark, General Hermann von Hanneken, to take a tough line. Essentially, however, the general was to focus on preparing the Danish front to fend off the feared Allied invasion on the west coast of Jutland. This war aim was at odds with the soft occupation policy pursued by the German Foreign Office, jealously protecting its sway over Denmark. But the general had his priorities right—and they were military and strategic, not political.

On the civilian side, Hitler decided to make a more decisive political move by appointing the thirty-nine-year-old SS Gruppenführer Werner Best to become the new Reich plenipotentiary in Denmark.

Werner Best

Werner Best was to play a key role in the fate of the Danish Jews, but exactly what that role was is still debated today. It was as ambiguous as Werner Best's personal motives. It is not easy to figure out what was fundamentally going on in the mind of a committed Nazi and anti-Semite, and Werner Best is a case in point with plenty of confusing contradictions. Educated as a lawyer, he had been a member of the party since 1930 and had, as a close collaborator of then SS Reichsführer Heinrich Himmler and the head of the security police, Reinhard Heydrich, worked his way up to the number three position in the SS hierarchy as head of the Gestapo personnel and administration department, surpassed only by Himmler and Heydrich. After the invasion of

Poland, in September 1939, Best participated in the organization of the deportation of Jews into the new "Generalgouvernement" as well as in the "völkische Flurbereinigung," which was the Nazi term for "ethnic reallocation and consolidation," a shorthand for the initial steps in the organized mass murder. At this point, a deep conflict with Heydrich created turbulence in his career.

Best was sent to Paris in the summer of 1940 as part of the German occupation administration. Here, he issued the *Judenverordnung* setting in motion the deportation of non-French Jews, first to detention camps in France, then from there on to Auschwitz. In France he also tested and further developed his theories on how best to elicit cooperation in an occupied country with the minimal use of force, and his work helped to develop the Nazi leadership's thinking about how territories should be administered and organized in a German-dominated Europe. Best focused on how each nation could be impelled to voluntarily concede its sovereignty and submit to the German administration. In August and September 1941 he traveled to Brussels, The Hague, Oslo, Copenhagen, and Prague to study in detail occupation practices in those countries, including their official and legal framework and overall working methods. In this comparative study, Best reached the clear conclusion that Denmark was the country where the occupation costs to Germany were by far the smallest, partly because the civil administration was more effective than the military, even when it came to surveillance and security. A mere 89 German officials in the Danish governing authority were able to manage 3.8 million Danes, while the corresponding figures were much higher for the other occupied countries: 260 in Norway, 1,596 in the Netherlands, and some 22,000 in France.

The advantages for the Reich were obvious, and Heydrich's death in June 1942 paved the way for Best to return to Berlin, where he served for a while in Ribbentrop's Foreign Ministry before he was sent to Denmark as Hitler's special envoy to set things straight in the Danish protectorate. On October 27 he received his instructions from Hitler personally, accompanied at the audience by his predecessor, the career diplomat Cecil von Renthe-Fink, who ironically was sent to Vichy France to represent Germany there. This seems to confirm that Hitler had not denounced the negotiating line pursued by Renthe-Fink in Denmark. Rather, developments had convinced the Führer of the necessity to send in someone stronger to continue it, as the Danish side seemed increasingly reluctant to give the concessions demanded. That someone was Werner Best, who left Berlin not only as Hitler's personal choice but also with unique backing from both his old comrade SS chief Heinrich Himmler and Ribbentrop, who all seem to have endorsed the idea of allowing Best to practice in Denmark the ideal form of "administration by supervision" that he had been advocating.[15]

Best's bloody past was not known in Denmark at the time, although the underground Communist press retrieved and passed on Best's nickname, the Bloodhound of Paris. But the gentlemanly lawyer did not appear to be a brutal man. He was an anti-Semite of the "civilized" kind, who aimed to purge the Aryan people's body of the Jews but not necessarily the hard way. For him the Jews constituted a biological threat to the purity of the Aryan race. Therefore it was more about the separation and removal of the Jewish population than its eradication. With an intelligent and cultivated appearance, Best was able to instill confidence and foster personal respect, all the more so as he was a pragmatic and creative bureaucrat for whom the ends trumped the means. And Best's goal in Denmark was to maintain the peaceful occupation and its basic features, allowing Hitler to indulge in this unique vision of *Neuropa*, Ribbentrop to maintain his authority over this piece of the bigger European puzzle—and Himmler to avoid having to expend too many resources on that particular corner of his SS universe while securing most welcome provisions from Danish agriculture. In this way maintaining the status quo served not only Berlin but Werner Best's own standing as the central figure in the German administration of the occupied country.[16]

This position provided Best with a strong footing, also enabling him to resist pressure from the Danish Nazis aiming to take advantage of the arrival in Denmark of this leading SS officer to roll back the cooperative policy and gain direct access to power like their comrades in occupied Norway. It was a source of deep frustration to the small but radical Danish Nazi Party that the old elected politicians had successfully kept them out of any position of power—indeed of any position at all—as a key condition of "the cooperation." But Best had no interest in the Danish Nazi amateurs and deftly outmaneuvered their leader, Frits Clausen, who ended up having to heed his own call and join the few thousand Danes volunteering to join the Waffen SS on the eastern front.

For all these reasons Best was generally perceived in Denmark as a man of moderation and cooperation. Few realized fully that hidden behind the cultivated and pragmatic exterior, Best remained a devoted Nazi. Most Danes who got close to Dr. Best felt they could trust him.

The occupation force's two leading officials in Denmark, Wehrmacht general Hermann von Hanneken (left) and Reich plenipotentiary Werner Best, giving a military salute during a parade at the German soldiers' cemetery in Copenhagen in November 1943, one year after both had arrived in the occupied country.

Hanneken was deployed as commander of Wehrmacht troops in Denmark in October 1942, shortly before Best arrived. While Best seems to have had the backing of the Nazi leadership to continue the peaceful occupation of "Model Protectorate" Denmark, Hanneken had orders from Hitler to fortify the west coast of Jutland against the feared Allied invasion. The lack of coordination between these widely divergent instructions fostered a continuing power struggle between the two rivals.

The action against the Danish Jews was part of this complicated maneuvering, and each man tried to put the blame on the other. Best won in the sense that Hanneken failed to keep the Wehrmacht out of the action, which took place while the general was still enforcing martial law, giving him executive powers. But the Wehrmacht engaged without enthusiasm in what the general considered to be an unpopular police task.

General Hanneken was a veteran of World War I and an expert in strategic planning. Denmark was his first military assignment during the war.

von Hanneken family

And they were right in the sense that Best did not let his Nazi beliefs overshadow the moderation or the maneuvers that were necessary to preserve and consolidate Best's own position at the epicenter of the German occupation of Denmark. Best was also more open than most in terms of the problems Germany was encountering, and at regular intervals he published an information newsletter to all German service units in Denmark, in which he outlined not only how the situation should be viewed from the German perspective, but also in surprisingly direct terms how Germany's opponents assessed developments of German policy in the occupied country.

Best fully realized that only a trusting cooperation with the Danish authorities could ensure the status quo sought by Berlin and thus his own position. It was therefore not without foundation that many leading Danes saw in Best a bulwark against what was worse.[17]

Holding On, 1942–43

Through the short year from Werner Best's arrival in Copenhagen in November 1942 until the end of August 1943, Erik Scavenius and he fine-tuned the cooperation between the occupying power and the occupied country. It reflects Best's diplomatic ingenuity that in the first half of 1943 both Ribbentrop and Himmler praised his performance in Denmark—and that they and Hitler all accepted Best's first two decisive moves after his arrival in Denmark despite the fact that both appeared to be in direct contradiction of his instructions to solve the Jewish question and impose a more German-friendly government upon Denmark.

Best's predecessor, Cecil von Renthe-Fink, had tirelessly warned Berlin that any move on the Jewish issue would be deeply disturbing to continued cooperation with the Danes. Accordingly, no move had been made, except to employ Lorenz Christensen, a devoted Nazi and anti-Semite from the German minority in South Jutland, to work on "a research project" on the Danish Jews, including the compilation of a list of names and addresses of individuals within the community. With the increasing tension in September 1942 and the extraordinary displeasure with which Hitler reacted to developments in Denmark, both Ribbentrop and the Reich Security Head Office, responsible for overseeing the final solution, began to move.

But real action had to await the arrival of the new Reich plenipotentiary in November, and upon his arrival Best immediately realized that a continuation of a relatively elastic policy in Denmark, which he saw as his overriding mandate, was irreconcilable with a demand for the hand-over of the Jews living in the country. He also successfully negotiated a restructuring of the Danish government, not (as instructed) to become "apolitical"—that is, Nazi oriented—but with the significant adjustment that Scavenius, in addition to his key function as foreign minister, now also took over the prime ministerial responsibilities. [18]

Those moves helped construct the image of Werner Best as a man to be trusted. Twice, in January and again in April 1943, in telegrams to Berlin that continued Renthe-Fink's argument, he advised against action against the Danish Jews because it would poison the cooperation and thereby terminate the peaceful occupation. In June 1943 he traveled to Berlin, where he procured Ribbentrop's and Himmler's personal agreement to a further postponement of a resolution of the Jewish issue in Denmark. [19]

Norway was not equally fortunate. Maybe as a sort of compensation for the stalemate in Denmark after September 1942, Berlin pushed for the persecution of the Norwegian Jews, which was rushed through in the following months. Under Nazi rule, preparations for the exclusion of the some 2,100 citizens of Jewish origin were initiated shortly after the occupation, following patterns familiar from other occupied countries. More than 1,500 individuals had their personal papers stamped with a J and were also subjected to other discriminatory measures, such as removal from public service and confiscation of property. Discrimination was increased gradually and without provoking major protests from the Norwegian public. Throughout 1942 Quisling's ruling Norwegian Nazi Party stepped up its anti-Semitic propaganda, and in October the Reich Security Head Office decided to go ahead with the action. On October 23 Norwegian police received the order to prepare for the detention of the Jews. Three days later the arrest of all Jewish men between the ages of fifteen and fifty-four began, and 532 were deported directly to Auschwitz; on November 25 arrests of women and children followed. Further deportations occurred in November, in February 1943, and in 1944, bringing the total number of deportees to 772. Only 34 survived the German death camps.

Immediately after the action the Quisling regime passed a law confiscating Jewish property, and the regime actively cooperated with the German security police to secure the gold, silver, and jewelry of both the deportees and the refugees. In the ensuing period Quisling and his people followed up along German lines with tougher measures against "half and quarter Jews," which sparked a new wave of flight to Sweden.

Over time more than half the Norwegian Jews managed to escape to Sweden with the help of friends, relatives, and public institutions such as hospitals. In total some 1,100 Jewish refugees arrived from Norway, including 170 who were not Norwegian citizens.[20]

The developments in Norway caused the director of the Danish Ministry of Foreign Affairs, Nils Svenningsen, who in many respects operated as Scavenius's deputy, to confer with the Jewish community on the possibility of a "mild discrimination" against the Danish Jews, implying that they would no longer be appointed to top positions within the administration or appear in public, for example on national radio. The idea was to make the Jews as little visible as possible so as not to "provoke" the occupying power. The "problem" also came to the fore when in the spring of 1943 it became known that the security police in some cases were seeking information on citizens' racial background. As internal criticism was raised about this practice, Svenningsen warned that people were to proceed cautiously and not rock the boat: "In the interest of society as a whole and that of the Jewish community we have to accept some minor annoyances. This is consistent with our approach in the press office when we seek to prevent publicity in regard to various events and conditions in other countries in connection with the Jewish question."[21]

Like his boss, Scavenius, the forty-nine-year-old director believed that continued negotiations with the Germans and cautious concessions constituted the only way forward for Denmark, and indeed the only possibility to protect the Jews. In his younger days Svenningsen had been a legation secretary in Berlin, and he was, like most of his contemporaries among Danish diplomats, convinced that the balance of power in Europe meant that in any conceivable outcome of the war, Denmark would in the long run remain economically, politically, and strategically dependent on Germany. Given this perspective it did not serve Denmark to attempt daring plays in the arena of the ongoing war. No matter how much Denmark hoped for the defeat of Nazism, it could not risk joining forces with Germany's enemies. For Svenningsen and men of like mind, the Danish-German relationship was a strategic fact because at the end of the day no other great power would or could come to Denmark's rescue if it were to face Germany's fury.

The End of Political Cooperation

King Christian's confinement at Sorgenfri was the culmination of a difficult year. As the crisis caused by his disdainful telegram to Hitler culminated, on October 19, 1942, the king fell from his horse while riding alone through the streets of Copenhagen. Severely injured, he was forced to transfer executive powers to Crown Prince Frederick, and though the prince had handled affairs well under the guidance of the Scavenius government, Christian realized both that he alone commanded the authority to rally support behind the unpopular policy of cooperation, and probably also that it would be the worst of circumstances for the crown prince to take over full responsibilities. In a constitutional monarchy the transfer of power from one generation to the next is never trivial, and for the king there were good reasons to take upon himself whatever responsibilities the cooperation might ascribe to the head of state. Christian was therefore eager to resume his full executive powers, which he did in May 1943.

In January 1943, a secret meeting between President Roosevelt and Prime Minister Churchill with the Allied chiefs of staff was held in Casablanca. Here, the Allies agreed to insist on Germany's unconditional surrender. No partial or conditional peace settlement would be accepted. In February the Wehrmacht suffered disastrous defeats at Stalingrad, and a few days later President Roosevelt declared that those responsible for the war and for genocide would be held responsible. It was not good news for leading Nazis, such as an SS veteran like Werner Best. In early July, U.S. troops landed in Sicily and then began to advance through Italy after the fall of Mussolini later the same month.

The cooperation with the Danish government implied that even Best as Germany's top political representative in Denmark could not simply impose his demands, but had to negotiate terms with Prime/Foreign Minister Scavenius, seeking the appropriate mix of persuasion, threats, and direct pressure. This meant that Scavenius could also raise demands, as he did when in the spring of 1943 the constitutional deadline for general elections was coming up. Best and Scavenius managed to negotiate terms for the holding of the elections in March 1943. Notwithstanding the limitations arising from the occupation, the result was seen as a manifest confirmation of democracy, with record numbers of voters massively supporting the parties behind the policy of cooperation, and equally strongly turning their back on the Danish Nazis, who obtained a disastrous less than 2 percent of the vote. (The Communists, outlawed and hunted, were banned from running as well as from participating in the campaign leading up to the elections.)

Best's pragmatic line, and particularly his good interpersonal relations with Scavenius and Svenningsen, helped to keep the cooperation alive, although the Wehrmacht commander, General Hanneken, more and more insistently wanted direct military rule in order to curtail growing sabotage and reinforce fortifications along the west coast of Jutland.

During the summer of 1943 news from the war fronts encouraged optimism in occupied Denmark, where a wave of strikes and sabotage actions took hold in August, especially in major provincial cities. The spike in sabotage, strikes, and civil riots caused the occupying power to make nonnegotiable demands the government could not and would not accept, including the introduction of martial law and the death penalty. As the politicians met to consider the German ultimatums, Thorvald Stauning's successor, former prime minister Vilhelm Buhl, urged the government to reject the German requests outright. The possible consequences of a Danish refusal to continue cooperation under the new conditions were unclear. But the elected politicians felt they were already walking a thin line, and that their constituents would not understand if they conceded to requests that made yet another deep gash in the democratic foundations of Danish society. Maybe they also hoped that Germany was on the verge of giving up and that the war would soon be over. In any event, disregarding the risk of a violent and destructive German reaction, the government agreed to draw a line in the sand and to refuse the ultimatum with a simple no.

Although Scavenius was more inclined to attempt once again to ride out the crisis with some concessions, the king supported the politicians. On August 28, according to his diary, he received "party representatives at 2 p.m. and expressed my thanks for the unanimous consent that the parliament had given the answer to the German note. It is a serious step that we have taken, whose consequences cannot be overlooked. We have made these years bearable, and the longest period is perhaps over, but the main thing for me is that we stand united. With God's help we will also manage whatever is in store for the coming days."[22]

Finance Minister K. H. Kofoed, who attended the meeting, described in his diary how Christian, with tears streaming down his cheeks, thanked the ministers for having held out so long: "It has been a heavy duty loaded with responsibility. Thank you, everybody, and especially you, Prime Minister Scavenius, for the work you have done for your king and for your country."

With this the policy of cooperation came to an end as far as the elected politicians were concerned. The question was, What would replace it?

Early in the morning of August 29, 1943, the Wehrmacht responded by imposing martial law in Denmark and disarming the Danish forces, who until this point were still serving. Brief fighting erupted with Danish troops in several garrisons. Also, under the command of Vice Admiral Aage H. Vedel, navy crews succeeded in scuttling the vast majority of vessels of the substantial Danish war fleet, preventing it from falling into German hands—a strong symbolic gesture in a country proud of its navy. Within hours conditions in occupied Denmark changed and tension grew, with no direct contact points between civilian society and the Wehrmacht command. For many the developments seemed troubling—but also in their own way refreshing: Suddenly things seemed clearer and the air more transparent—Danes on one side of the line, Germans on the other.

It quickly turned out, however, that martial law was difficult for the Germans to manage. The occupiers were eager for the Danish politicians to take back responsibility for the workings of society. But the zeal of elected Danish politicians to hold on to power was now suddenly transformed into a stubborn rejection of any responsibility at all. The government was uncooperative to the point of not even executing its own resignation to clear the way for a caretaker government installed by the Germans. Formally the government had submitted its resignation, but in accordance with a prior understanding, the king refused to accept it. Hence the appointment of a new government with even a mere tinge of constitutional legitimacy was effectively blocked. The Germans could not find one single Dane with a mandate from the electorate to head a new government, and the king, confined under martial law at Sorgenfri Castle, claimed not to be in a position to provide any new government as his executive powers had been seized by General Hanneken. Scavenius, the Germans' last hope, refused to reenter the scene without the backing of the politicians, and disappeared into oblivion for the rest of the occupation.

Now it became a problem that Denmark was not formally at war with

Germany and thus not, under international law, considered to be a country under enemy occupation. The Germans had to respect the country's laws—and General Hanneken could not simply proceed with martial law without taking the full step of liquidating the remains of Denmark's continued "sovereignty"—which would do away with this token of Hitler's vision of the new Europe. The general had little appetite for such a move, even less as it would require more troops to keep the occupied country under control. By simply refusing any cooperation Denmark managed to work itself into a not entirely impossible negotiating position. The occupiers could of course choose to do what they wanted. But they could not impose direct military rule in Denmark while maintaining the image of a peaceful occupation. Soon the Germans were desperately looking for a soft landing, also regarding martial law. They tried with the creation of an "administrative council," an idea favored by both Scavenius and the president of the Supreme Court, but the king in consultation with the elected politicians flatly rejected the idea of such a "nonpolitical" government. To his refusal King Christian acidly added that as General Hanneken had taken over executive power in Denmark, the intervention of the king was unnecessary.[23]

The Germans were caught in their own net. As long as the Danes stood together, the occupiers had to choose between assuming full responsibility or handing a form of government authority back to the Danish side. While imposing martial law had at first seemed to be a major victory for Hanneken in his ongoing power struggle with Best's civil authority, the civil envoy now stepped back onto the scene in order to find a way out of the impasse. Though some in Berlin, including Goebbels, had lost confidence in Best and thought he treated the Danes too well, Best still enjoyed sufficient support in the Nazi leadership. He got the Führer's mandate to seek a political solution, and was more eager than ever to strengthen his own power resources in the form of German police units that could counterbalance Hanneken's Wehrmacht soldiers.[24]

The result was an evolving arrangement by which the nonpolitical permanent secretaries of the Danish ministries formed an informal council led by the Foreign Ministry's director, Nils Svenningsen. The outgoing cabinet ministers stayed in the wings and covered the permanent secretaries politically, the exception being Scavenius, who withdrew completely from politics. In this untested design Svenningsen was a sort of informal head of government, whose practical powers were shrouded in uncertainty. He was first among equals in the circle of state secretaries, and he thus replaced Scavenius as Best's direct counterpart. On issues of particular delicacy Svenningsen would consult discreetly with former prime minister Buhl, who in turn had contact with the Social Democrats' elected leader, Hans Hedtoft, and other party leaders. The trick was to maintain the advantage of Danish administration without drifting into a real governing council with executive powers and exposure to German demands.

Svenningsen, like his mentor, Scavenius, remained convinced that cooperation was the only sound choice, viewed both pragmatically and ethically, and he was the official willing to take personal responsibility for putting this policy into practice. Although he was careful and punctilious in many ways, he was also a devoted activist with a sharp eye for the lesser evil: better to take the initiative than leave it to the occupying power. There is no reason to doubt Svenningsen's motives or his sense of responsibility. But he had trouble figuring out the nature of what he faced in October 1943. For him, as for many of his contemporaries, Germany was still Europe's greatest cultural nation, and it seems that Svenningsen saw Best more as a representative of the Weimar Republic and German culture than as a Nazi criminal with blood on his hands.

For members of the Jewish community, however, developments around August 29, 1943, were ominous. To the occupying power the cost of finally addressing the "Jewish question" in Denmark would be substantially lower, as the price in the form of the resignation of the Danish government had already been paid. The question was whether the permanent secretaries could provide the same protection as politicians previously had. Uncertainty arose here, as reflected in Svenningsen's records of his own remarks at a September 25 discussion with the troubled leadership of the Jewish community: "It was quite impossible that the permanent secretaries would agree to implement provisions directed against the Jews, and if the Germans took anti-Jewish measures on their own, and put them over as a fait accompli, I was in no doubt that all the permanent secretaries would voice the most energetic protest to the German authorities."[25]

This was meant to be reassuring, but obviously it was not. It was highly unlikely that even the "most energetic protest" would have any effect at all. Previously, refusing any measures directed against the Jews had been a make-or-break cabinet question for the government. But now the government no longer functioned. At the meeting Svenningsen also felt he should warn the Jewish representatives against any illegal

The director of the Danish Foreign Ministry, Nils Svenningsen, who from September 1943 served as the informal leader of the Council of Permanent Secretaries.

Svenningsen played a key role after August 29, 1943, when the elected politicians handed in their resignations.

Although Svenningsen saw himself as the politicians' alter ego and remained loyal to the framework and borderlines established by them, he still felt empowered to act according to his own judgment whenever the cabinet ministers were prevented from doing so. As he regarded the ethics of a senior civil servant, his main obligations were to the constitution and the national interest as he perceived it. Seen through this lens, he, as an official, was not merely an instrument but an independent actor, someone who had the responsibility to execute his own judgments—and to vouch for them personally.   Polfoto

emigration of Danish Jews. The argument was that it could magnify the possibility of action against their law-abiding fellows who stayed behind. The leading members of the community held similar views and largely seem to have been convinced by Svenningsen's reports of Best's repeated personal assurances that the Danish Jews had nothing to fear.

The German Team

Best's assurances were a lie. In fact he had personally initiated action against the Danish Jews by sending a telegram on September 8, which went to Hitler by way of the German Foreign Office. The central section read: "A consistent implementation of the new course in Denmark in my opinion now entails a resolution of the Jewish . . . issue in Denmark."

Setting the avalanche in motion, Best clearly realized the danger of becoming one of its victims himself. To mitigate that danger, he immediately endeavored to push as much responsibility as possible onto the broad shoulders of his archrival, General Hanneken, who was already overseeing the precarious state of emergency. Now was the time to move, so that the action would be carried out while martial law was still in force and the general would be blamed for anything that went wrong. Moreover, by having the general still formally in charge, some of the resentment the action surely would provoke among the Danes would be directed against him. With all this in mind, Best continued his telegram: "The measures that this entails must be taken before the current state of emergency ceases, because at a later stage they will cause a reaction in the country that will lead to new emergencies, probably under less favorable conditions than at present. In particular, according to my information from many sides, any functioning constitutional government would be likely to resign, just as the king and the parliament would cease all further participation in the government. Moreover, one ought to count on the possibility of a general strike because the unions will cease operating and thus end their moderating influence on the workers."

The aim seems to have been to anticipate the negative effects of the action. It is likely that at this point Best had already realized that a new Danish government could not be formed, and that accordingly his focus was to reinforce his own position vis-à-vis Berlin, his Danish counterparts—and General Hanneken: "It is possible that [we] will no longer be able to form a constitutional government under measures taken during the current state of emergency, so that a management committee must be created under my leadership, while legislative power is exercised by me through regulations."

It was important for Best to prepare Berlin for trouble and for the widespread opposition that was to be expected in Denmark. At the same time he seems to have realized that the practical requirements of the situation could also be turned to his own advantage, because the action could justify the deployment of new police forces, which had long been at the top of Best's wish list: "For in one fell swoop to arrest and transport approximately 6,000 Jews (including women and children), the police forces, which I have previously asked to be made available, will be required. They will be deployed almost exclusively in Copenhagen's metropolitan area, where most of the Jews live. The commander of the German troops in Denmark [Hanneken] must provide reinforcements. Transport should probably first and foremost be by sea, so ships should be directed here in good time."[26]

The telegram can best be explained as the expression of a delicate balancing act. Best knew the request for an action was under way following the breakdown of the cooperation. Anticipating these orders, he went ahead, but in a way that aimed to consolidate his own standing in Berlin, to strengthen his position in relation to Hanneken, and to forestall Adolf Eichmann in Berlin by acting toughly and energetically. At the same time it was critical for Best to keep cooperation going with the Danish permanent secretaries. Best was a man of action, and by taking the initiative he played an important card in relation to his rivals in the Nazi power apparatus.

At the German legation in Copenhagen, housed at Dagmarhus, overlooking the Town Hall Square, Best worked closely with forty-three-year-old SS Brigadeführer Paul Kanstein, who was his deputy and old acquaintance. Kanstein had been in Copenhagen since the first days of the occupation overseeing internal security, and he was well versed in the delicate cooperation with the Danish authorities. A third member of the team was a thirty-nine-year-old expert in maritime affairs, G. F. Duckwitz, who was to play a legendary role in the fate of the Danish Jews.

Paul Kanstein had long been a party member, but from the late 1930s he had also had connections to the German military opposition. Had the plot to assassinate Hitler on July 20, 1944, succeeded, Kanstein was supposed to have been appointed to head the new German security police. Starting in the summer of 1942, Kanstein had worked actively in Berlin to get Werner Best to Copenhagen, and it was also he who cautiously introduced Duckwitz to the German opposition against Hitler. Unlike Best, Duckwitz had a thorough knowledge of Denmark, where he had spent extended time before the war. He spoke Danish and had good contacts, in particular with the leading Social Democrats, including the young party chairman, Hedtoft, and the former prime minister, Buhl, who held the reins in Danish politics. During the dramatic days in August when riots were spreading in the provinces, Duckwitz had persuaded Hedtoft, Buhl, and other leading politicians to visit Best for an intense exchange on the future of the cooperation.

From the outset Duckwitz had been a confidential adviser to Werner Best and his teacher in the noble art of understanding the Danes. The relationship between the two men went beyond the purely professional, and Best's and Duckwitz's families also socialized privately—often in a context that gave Best the opportunity to meet Danes in convivial settings. A surprisingly trusting relationship seems to have prevailed among Best, Kanstein, and Duckwitz, although there is no evidence to suggest that Best realized, let alone sympathized with, the opposition activities secretly pursued by Kanstein and Duckwitz. Still, it's hard to avoid the thought that Best may have sensed more or less explicitly that his two closest advisers at the German legation were both active in the opposition to Hitler. Considering Best's cunning mind, it is not at all unthinkable that he both sensed this and realized that knowing without knowing might in a given situation come in handy and be to his advantage. Be that as it may, both Kanstein and Duckwitz survived the wave of arrests after the July 20, 1944, attempt on Hitler, which suggests that if Best suspected his collaborators were involved, he kept quiet.

Although Duckwitz entered the party in 1932, he gradually distanced himself from the Nazi mind-set. While retaining his party membership, he moved to New York to work in the shipping business. In 1939, the Foreign Office requested his shipping expertise and sent him to the legation in Denmark, a mission mandated by the military intelligence service, Abwehr, though his exact mission is unclear. On his way back to Europe, Duckwitz wrote notes illustrating that at this point he still shared many of the Nazi ideas in regard to the damaging role of Jews in Germany. Duckwitz was a shrewd operator with direct access to the German foreign minister Ribbentrop, who as part of the power struggle within the Nazi leadership was seeking to build up his own intelligence network in the Nordic countries. Although parts of Duckwitz's work and mandate remain enigmatic, it is obvious that he and Best worked closely together, both on the implementation of the action against the Jews and in attempts to fend it off. The two men were not necessarily driven by

*Georg Ferdinand Duckwitz was the maritime expert of the German lega-
tion in Copenhagen, where he was one of Werner Best's closest confidants.
He came to play a key—though not entirely clear—role in the rescue of the
Danish Jews.*

*Duckwitz had a professional background in Copenhagen in the shipping
business, and he spoke Danish. He also had a wide personal network, which
included leading Danish Social Democratic politicians. It was his warning
and personal credibility that finally convinced prominent Danes, including
the leadership of the Jewish community, that the threat was real.*

*Duckwitz was a conservative German patriot, and in the early 1930s he
joined the Nazis. He shared the prevailing negative attitude toward the
Jews in Germany, and there is no evidence that he distanced himself from
the party before the war. But gradually he began to look more critically at
Nazi practices. In late 1942 his colleague at the legation in Copenhagen,
Paul Kanstein, connected him to the German opposition. Duckwitz worked
closely with Best to maintain and develop "the policy of reason" that aimed
to continue cooperation and avoid an escalation of violence in the occupied
country. Duckwitz called Denmark his "chosen fatherland" and shared with
close friends in the Social Democratic Party a deep distrust of the Communists and their engagement in the Danish resistance. At the same time
he resented German fanaticism and violence and worked with Best against
Wehrmacht demands for military solutions to problems Duckwitz saw as
political. Likewise, he turned against the Gestapo terror after August 29,
1943. As a strong advocate for a peaceful occupation, Duckwitz became a
crucial liaison between Danish politicians and the German authorities.*

Frihedsmuseet

the same motives, but both wanted the cooperative policy in Denmark to be continued, and both realized that a brutal action against the Danish Jews would undermine it. If things went wrong, everything would be at stake—including their own lives. It is from this perspective that one must try to decipher Best's double game and Duckwitz's role in it. Best believed that Berlin expected a move for an action against the Danish Jews—or at least that his enemies could use it against him if the initiative did not come. But for Hitler it also weighed heavily that cooperation with the Danes did not collapse. Here Duckwitz could play a key role. The two incompatible goals had somehow to be reconciled through a series of improvisations played by political ear. And the one thing Werner Best and G. F. Duckwitz surely had in common was exactly that: a political ear. [27]

Preparing for the Action

Three days after Best's telegram calling for the action against the Jews to be initiated, Best and Duckwitz agreed that the latter should travel to Berlin to attempt to influence the decision-making process there. Duckwitz flew on September 13 and later explained that his goal was to prevent the telegram from reaching Hitler—which makes no sense. But given the tense gambling it was of great importance to the legation in Copenhagen to have a clear picture of how the matter stood within the complex power games in Berlin, and to put in a word where necessary. Duckwitz noted in his diary from Berlin that a friend offered him a new post in Stockholm. It was tempting to get away but obligatory to stay. Duckwitz stayed, and on September 16 he had a long conversation with Werner Best on which he noted in his diary: "The Jewish question is simmering, and I have warned him of the consequences. . . . [h]e secretly agrees. Deep down he's decent."[28]

On September 17, Best's telegram triggered the expected order from Hitler on the implementation of the final solution in Denmark. German police forces were made available, but while the practical preparations for the raid progressed, the plan was subjected to surprisingly strong criticism from within the Nazi administration, spurred also by Best, who made a point of emphasizing in his reports to Berlin that the action would likely lead to a very significant deterioration of the political situation in the occupied country. Clearly it was not consideration for the

Jews that led to doubts about both the advisability and the feasibility of the planned action, but rather whether the operation would upset the fragile cooperation with the Danish state secretaries, which now seemed the most likely avenue toward maintaining some degree of continuation of the policy pursued since the beginning of the occupation.

On September 19, Duckwitz, according to his own report, was informed that the order was now in motion. That day he wrote in his diary: "Now I know what I have to do. Who can take responsibility for such an act?? An unprovoked, hazardous game for which the instigator is ultimately responsible."[29]

The instigator was Best, even if he already had begun to maintain that his telegram to Berlin had not been intended to provoke the order. On the same day the new head of the German security police in Denmark, SS Standartenführer Rudolf Mildner, arrived in the country. He would be in charge of about three hundred Gestapo operatives who would be responsible for the implementation of the action against the Jews. But Mildner's overarching mandate was to combat the armed resistance in Denmark. Mildner had worked in Poland since 1941, and he was known to have been a tough head of the Gestapo in Katowice. Mildner's responsibilities included Auschwitz, where he conducted courts-martial. He was thus well versed in the mechanics of the final solution and in the fate in store for those deported to the camps.

Immediately upon his arrival in Copenhagen, Mildner began the practical preparations for the action. But not many days passed before he hesitated and, supported by Best, recommended to Berlin that the entire operation be canceled, or rather postponed, probably because he considered the job almost insoluble in a situation where the Jewish population was already highly alarmed by rumors about an impending action, and where the population as a whole could not be expected to provide any support for it. If the Jews went underground, it would require close cooperation with local Danish police to root them out of city and country. This cooperation was very unlikely to materialize, and even worse, both Mildner's and Best's highest priority was to build a future working relationship with the Danish police. Both men realized that an action against the Jews would poison that possibility.

But even Mildner couldn't stop the train now, and a few days later he flew to Berlin with Kanstein to put the last practical details in place. Still, Mildner's hesitation seems to have raised some concerns in Berlin, because a few days later, Adolf Eichmann's deputy, Sturmbannführer

Rolf Günther, also arrived in Copenhagen with two more men. They were sent to administer the action and see to it that the matter would be pursued with sufficient zeal.

In this way multiple layers of mutually highly suspicious German police were responsible for the action's practical organization. On the hard end was Rolf Günther, who established his own office and got his own Gestapo people attached to it. The first lists of 1,673 Jewish families in the metropolitan area, about 33 in the provinces, and 1,208 families from Germany, had already been compiled with the help of Lorenz Christensen working under Best. The lists were presented to Mildner, who relied heavily on Best's local knowledge and contacts. Eichmann's people were not only up against deep Danish resistance, whose impact spread to the Danish authorities' outermost parts, including the Danish police. They were also up against a sluggish, passive resistance by the local German authorities and also the new head of the security police, Dr. Mildner.[30]

The hesitation of the German authorities reflected the two sides' mutual interest in the continuation of cooperation, even in the reduced form of the state secretaries. The German administration in Denmark realized that an outright, brutal deportation of Danish Jews to the death camps would make it impossible to continue cooperation with the Danish authorities. Maybe another consideration also played a role for the Nazi officials in Denmark. Many must at this point have realized that Germany was going to lose the war, and that once that happened everyone in the Nazi executive would need whatever "good deeds" could be collected to save their necks. On the other hand, it was far from risk-free for prominent Nazis to take a moderate approach when it came to one of the party's highest objectives, namely the extermination of the Jews. Yet it is undeniable that even hardened Nazis in Denmark went out of their way to soften the blow. In the operational planning, Mildner pushed the point that German police must not break into Jewish homes with a violent show of force. Günther was fuming but could not change the decision. The argument was that breaking into apartments could easily lead to looting, which would put the action in an embarrassing light and give Germany a bad name among the Danes. Regardless of the reason, the guideline was that the police-soldiers should knock on doors when the action was launched but not force their way in if nobody opened them.

On September 20 Hanneken got wind of Hitler's order, prompting an immediate protest to Berlin that if the Wehrmacht were to be involved, it would harm its prestige and burden the young recruits. Therefore the action should be postponed until martial law was lifted. According to the general, a deportation of the Danish Jews would also ruin the relationship with the Danish authorities, including the police, and slow deliveries from Denmark—precisely the arguments that had caused the entire Nazi apparatus to hesitate. The general was hammered into place by his superiors, but it was without any desire or willingness that he called his soldiers to action.

The next day in Copenhagen, Duckwitz discussed with the Swedish minister, Gustav Dardel, the possibility of legal emigration of Danish Jews to Sweden. Dardel, according to Duckwitz, "made every effort. He already regards Denmark as a German province." The following day the minister reported to Stockholm that the Germans were preparing—probably moderate—laws against the Jews in Denmark.[31]

On September 23 Foreign Minister Ribbentrop personally took up the matter with Hitler. But this further attempt to postpone was to little avail. The ball was rolling, and Hitler's order could not be countered. And yet the Führer conceded that the operation had to be carried out while martial law pertained and not, as Hanneken preferred, afterward. Even more important, Ribbentrop also made the specific proviso "that every effort should be made to prevent unnecessary incitement of the Danish population."[32]

The duality that characterized Best and Duckwitz—and other prominent representatives of the occupying power in relation to the action against the Jews in Denmark—thus was present all the way up to the pinnacle of the Nazi power apparatus. This is critical to any understanding of the fate of the Danish Jews: Even Hitler's most trusted men, who were deeply engaged in the final solution's murderous logic, were challenged by the occupied country's clear rejection of this very logic. The circle around Hitler had realized that they could impose the operation on Denmark, but not force the Danes to make it their own. Thus, the execution of the final solution in occupied Denmark came at a real cost to the Third Reich. This price was not high enough for Hitler to call off the operation—but high enough to soften the blow.

Denmark's Jews

The Jewish population in Denmark was complex. Three major groups stood out. There were old Jewish families who had come to the country as early as the seventeenth century. They were deeply integrated, and many of them occupied prominent positions in society's upper echelons from business, research, and medicine to politics, the press, and the civil service. Most were not religious. The Meyer, Hannover, and Marcus families belonged to this group, as did the chairman of the Jewish community, Supreme Court attorney C. B. Henriques. According to Henriques, the men served as representatives to the community board "because they were Jews, not because they had any particular interest in Judaism, the Jewish religion, culture or history." The board was, in other words, anything but a religious assembly.

Shortly after his arrival in Sweden, Poul Hannover described his own relationship to his Jewish origins: "I am a Jew—brought up in a rather secular home, where religion was seldom spoken of. I remember that the first time I was to go with my father to church, I asked him which church we were going to. I didn't take religion classes at school or confirmation instruction in 1911–12. My father told me that his father, who was as secular as my father and I were, went to the synagogue each year on the eve of Yom Kippur, not because he understood what he was hearing, but rather to show that he was listening to it. I'm quite sure that Father, who had learned a little Hebrew, did the same for the same reasons. I can easily say that I went once a year as well for quite the same reasons, without much enthusiasm, because I'm not much part of it, I didn't understand it, and took no great satisfaction from it."[33]

As an adult his son, Allan Hannover, reflected the same basic vision:

Both of my parents were Jewish. My grandparents and all of my ancestors were Jews, however they weren't Orthodox. We didn't follow any strict Jewish rules, either about the food we ate or about celebrating the Sabbath and Jewish holidays. My father only participated in the High Holidays at the synagogue in Copenhagen. We celebrated Christmas at home with the Danish traditions of a tree and presents.

I think it's accurate to say that we felt more Danish than Jewish, and speaking for myself, I can say that as a boy I never had the feeling that I was different or treated otherwise than my friends and classmates. My impression is—and it may be naïveté—that my classmates never gave my Jewish background a second thought. I learned later that they were amazed when they heard I'd suddenly left for Sweden and understood the reason for my disappearance.[34]

Around the turn of the twentieth century new groups came from Eastern Europe, fleeing poverty, pogroms, and war. About three thousand took up residence in the country, where they were known as "Russian Jews." Many of them had a more traditional relationship to Jewish traditions and rituals, and most spoke Yiddish at home. They had originally settled in Copenhagen's poorest neighborhoods, but by 1940 many had gained a better social foothold, and quite a number had become prosperous and well integrated. Their relationship to the old Jewish families in Denmark was not harmonious, however, and it was only in 1937 that the "Russian Jews" succeeded in getting a member elected to the board of the Jewish community.

At the same time a new wave of Jewish refugees reached Denmark. Despite the fact that Denmark followed an increasingly restrictive refugee policy, about fifteen hundred German, Austrian, and Czech Jews fleeing Nazi persecution managed to obtain residence permits in Denmark, though they were not recognized as political refugees. Most were socially disadvantaged, they had little or no funds, and their status was uncertain. The group also included the already mentioned Jewish agricultural trainees with Zionist goals and refugee children who had arrived in the country at the behest of Danish volunteer organizations; taken together these added up to almost 650 young people.[35]

This diverse group totaling more than seven to eight thousand people—the Germans' lists calculated the figure at around six thousand—was then subdivided. Some were married to non-Jews, others were children of interfaith marriages of one degree or another, and it remains impossible to identify the various groups as Danish authorities made a point of not asking citizens to declare their faith—let alone keeping registries based on descent or religious beliefs. Some had retained to a greater or lesser extent part of their Jewish faith and heritage, while others carried their Jewish origin only half-consciously. Some—particularly men—were easy to identify as Jewish because of their family names. Others, especially women whose non-Jewish Danish married surnames, appeared less Jewish to the surrounding community.

No precise definitions existed—or were called for. But who could tell how the Germans would decide who should be deported and who should not? Far more than the approximately seven to eight thousand who were directly subject to the operation were uncertain and felt threatened by what lay ahead.[36]

The underground press was naturally aware that the question of the Jews would come to a head now that "the state of emergency is the most normal thing in our country," as one illegal paper put it. On September 23 *Free Danes* reported an episode that reflects both the resistance movement's strongly critical attitude toward Danish police cooperation with the occupying power and especially the vulnerability of the Jews who had come to Denmark as refugees from Nazi persecution: "Two officers from the coastal police, No. 3208 Larsen and No. 230 Sergeant Nielsen, are to blame that two Jewish families with their children—a total of 11 people—who have lived in this country for years, but who had emigrated here because of the Nazi seizure of power in 1933, will be deported to Poland, where children and adults alike are sure to meet a horrible death after great suffering.

"We wonder if the screams of these people will reach the 'Danes' No. 3208 Larsen and No. 230 Nielsen from Poland and haunt them for the rest of their lives? We believe it—and how these un-Danish coastal cops deserve it! We loathe the idea of even calling these two guys countrymen."[37]

The first part of this article is true. According to a laconic police report, Danish police on September 21 requested the coastal police to investigate the harbor of the small fishing village of Sundby. Here, officers with drawn guns had arrested a group of Jews in full traveling gear in the cabin of the motor vessel K575 *Lis*, moored at the northern pier. Two fishermen were also arrested, under suspicion of having assisted with the planned escape. Fortunately, however, it is not accurate that those arrested were deported to Poland. They were presented at Police Headquarters in Copenhagen before the state attorney for special afffairs. This implied Danish jurisdiction, and according to standard procedures in such cases the suspects were released pending later trial for attempted illegal immigration. Most likely the defendants disappeared before they could be taken to court.[38]

At the editorial offices of *Politiken*, one of the leading newspapers, Vilhelm Bergstrøm, the hard-bitten crime reporter, followed the growing panic with ironic distance. The offices of the paper overlooked Town Hall Square, and thus also faced Dagmarhus, the German headquarters. Bergstrøm knew his way around occupied Copenhagen and was a well-informed observer. From his lookout post on the square he saw and heard much that was complemented by his work as editor of *The Crime Squad Magazine*. What's more, he wrote it all down in a detailed diary, which has been preserved as the unique testimony of a sharp and sarcastic observer who experienced day-to-day events during the occupation without the layers of rationalization that invariably characterize later memoirs. Bergstrøm had no special connection to the Jewish minority, but he took the temperature of Copenhageners' experiences and conveyed the power of rumors and reports, which were part of daily life. Nobody knew anything, but everybody had heard a lot. What should one think? On what basis should one make decisions that could prove disastrous for the entire family? Bergstrøm couldn't use the hindsight of posterity to sort through everything that proved extraneous or of no value. He wasn't a witness to truth, but a true witness to what was thought and said, person to person, in occupied Copenhagen. Bergstrøm was an utterly unheroic patriot who despised everything the occupation forces stood for, but who preferred to express his views only in the diary that he kept assiduously, which together with his clippings from the underground press and much more fills no fewer than 207 binders.[39]

Bergstrøm shared many of his contemporaries' prejudices about Jews and was, as will be seen, not a great fan of what he called "Jewish lineage." Initially he found it hard to take the toss seriously. But he recorded in his diary that others did, as demonstrated in an excerpt from September 24: "Næsh [a colleague] mentioned that 8–14 days ago the Germans had seized the addresses book of Jewish émigrés up at Chief Rabbi Friediger's, while he was on vacation. Now the entire city's Jewish stock shook over what would happen. Miss Ventegodt came rushing. She was very excited, cheeks aflame, then she was off, an errand, she would not say what it was about. Later it came out. She is of Jewish genealogy on her mother's side. She had been out to say good-bye. These Jews were dead sure that they would be picked up in the night and must therefore say good-bye. The protectorate would come upon us, and we would get laws against the Jews."[40]

Dr. Meyer and the Uncomfortable Rumors

The well-known pediatrician Adolph Meyer sat on the Jewish community's advisory board and was a prominent member of Copenhagen's cosmopolitan and liberal bourgeoisie. He had five adult children, including thirty-four-year-old twin daughters, Kis and Inger, who were happily married: Kis's husband was a five-years-older merchant, Gunnar Marcus, who ran an agency in textiles and knitted fabrics, and with whom she had a daughter, Dorte, nine, and a son, Palle, six. The family lived in Charlottenlund, a well-to-do suburb north of Copenhagen not far from Lyngbyvej and Søholm Park, where Inger lived with Poul

Hannover, twelve years her senior and the managing director of the machine factory Titan. They also had two children, son Allan, who had just turned thirteen, and daughter Mette, who was four years younger. The two families were close and confidential with each other. The Hannovers were better off than the Marcuses, who were comfortable without being wealthy.[41]

On September 26 Dr. Meyer detailed in his diary the developments he was made aware of that day, which he immediately realized would have a dramatic effect on the Jewish community. Since he was a member of the board, it weighed on his mind to explain and justify for himself and history the basis on which he and his colleagues had consistently sought to calm the unease among fellow Jews: "After April 9, 1940, when Denmark was occupied, there were often fears among the Jewish Danes that the Jewish laws of Germany would be imposed. But time and again assurances were given that the 'Jewish issue in Denmark' had been shelved by the Germans until after the war, which they naturally expected to win. Therefore the Jewish representatives also adopted a resolution that it was up to the Danish government to undertake what it felt was in keeping with Danish well-being and dignity. When, on August 29, 1943, the state of emergency was introduced, and several hundred prominent citizens were interned—among others Chief Rabbi Friediger, the superintendent of the synagogue Axel Margolinsky, the president of the Jewish community C. B. Henriques, . . . and several others (in total, I believe, only 10–12 Jewish Danes), anxiety increased among the Jews."[42]

The Israeli historian Leni Yahil also describes the Jewish community's grasping for normalcy as the only way out: "The members of the executive committee felt in the spring of 1943 that the foundations of the law were about to crumble beneath the feet of all Danes, and they were in the dark as to the people's attitude toward them in the absence of a stable rule of law. They knew no other way than to continue to cling with all their might to that same law and to place their trust in the 'preservation of law and order.' "[43]

One of the common arguments against early escape was the danger that it could provoke retaliation against those who remained in the country, which was also pointed out by Nils Svenningsen to the Jewish representatives. In a sense this made all the Jews hostages to one another, and the threat that the escape of one might lead to the deportation of another paralyzed the entire community.

In his contemporaneous report Dr. Meyer explains further how the

German theft of address lists from the offices of the Jewish community gave notice of what was coming: "In September, the representatives held many meetings in the president's office. On August 31, I think, the Germans arrived at the secretariat, and having clipped the phone wires, forced the two women present, under threat of a gun, to hand over the ministerial ledgers and some other records [that contained lists of members, among other things]. A notification to this effect was sent to the criminal police and to the foreign ministry."

This holdup at the community's secretariat was conducted under the direction of a Danish anti-Semite, Paul Hennig, who worked for the Gestapo at Dagmarhus in a small unit responsible for collecting and processing information on the Danish Jews.

Dr. Meyer continues:

Later in September, on the seventeenth, a Friday morning, the Gestapo came to Ny Kongensgade 6 [the address of the Jewish community offices, where the community's archive was also located], sought out the librarian, Fischer, under threat of a gun against the porter, Petersen, who led the way to his apartment. Mrs. Fischer opened up, and the apartment was searched. When Mrs. Fischer said that Mr. Fischer was in the synagogue, the Germans drove there with the porter, went into the synagogue, and took away Fischer, who was about to pack his things. . . . They drove back to Ny Kongensgade and searched the house with Fischer and the porter, asked to see the library, which they ransacked, and took a number of books, among other things, everything of biographical interest and genealogical lists, as well as an earlier genealogical table, also an earlier lodge minutes, a vocational guidance book, and a recently begun manuscript of the lodge's history. Then they went to the community's office, where they took an old marriage register and inquired about the society's wealth, which of course is in deficit. Axel Hertz, the treasurer, asked one of them in German: "By what right do you come here?" He answered: "By the right of the stronger," to which Alex replied, still in German, "That is no good right." They were polite, but surrounded by armed soldiers.

This brief exchange of words in the Jewish community's office stands as a concentrated expression of the countless communications in which Jews met injustice. The treasurer's question was in all simplicity what a law-abiding citizen had to ask when he, without resistance, chose to give in to thugs and disclose documents that were entrusted to him: "By what right do you come here?" In Axel Hertz's world the question was vital, neither humble nor polemic. It was the issue of the rule of law, on which democracy is founded, and it remains fundamental and urgent for one who has to yield to what he perceives as injustice. The Nazi's answer was full and honest. They came by the right they believed in, which formed the basis of their ideology: the right of the stronger. Not as a slogan but as a genuine expression of the idea that a society dominated by the stronger, cleaner, and more insightful would be a better and more powerful one. There were necessary costs, in the Nazi worldview, associated with the establishment of this new order. The eradication, or at least expulsion and elimination from society, of the inferior races, along with weak and deviant individuals, was one such cost. But this was justified in a world where the ideal was the right of the stronger.

In this perspective Axel Hertz's brief rejoinder is all the more significant. It is not the crime committed against him and his colleagues he objects to, let alone opposes. It is the very idea behind it that he rejects. Axel Hertz in his own way was a courageous man. He did not speak up only for himself and other members of his community. He expressed a simple fact within his world: The right of the stronger was no right at all. Elsewhere in Europe an Axel Hertz would barely have survived the visit and most likely not such an exchange. The fact that it took place and was told and retold within the community's leadership testifies to the Danish Jews' insistence that the rule of law was their best defense. This may seem a dangerous illusion, even a self-deception, given what ensued. But it is not that simple. It was a strategy that helped solidify the view of Danish society, as a whole, facing a threat that went much further than those first in line, the Jews. What was at stake was the very foundation of the rule of law, and therefore of everything Danes had fought for and built over decades. Thus, if society gave way to the idea of the right of the stronger, the entire nation was threatened.

In this situation Axel Hertz was personally powerless. But rooted in his simple observation was precisely what made the implementation of an action against the Danish Jews so difficult: Few felt it was necessary, fewer that it was right. And even injustice needs a semblance of law. That is hard to find when the entire society denies the right of the stronger.

Hannah Arendt is quoting Leni Yahil when she says that "for the Danes the Jewish question was a political and not a humanitarian question." Axel Hertz confirms that thesis. He did not react as a victim but rather as someone who rejected the political rationale behind the Nazi atrocity.[44]

Dr. Meyer continues his account:

> Through the Foreign Ministry the representatives learned that the investigation was caused by "an indication of sabotage." Dr. Best still assured the Foreign Ministry that no action against the Danish Jews was intended. Rumors swirled, and they assumed more and more certain form after September 22, but through Bishop Fuglsang-Damgaard and Mr. Nils Svenningsen, and also through the outgoing prime minister Scavenius and Trade Minister Halfdan Henriksen, we still got soothing assurances, originating from Dr. Best, the German Reich representative, and from General von Hanneken, the head of the German Wehrmacht. I acted in good faith, therefore, when I denied the rumors.

Leni Yahil summarizes, in her historical retrospective, the situation after the government's resignation on August 29: "With the annulment of Denmark's democratic institutions, in reality, the Jews' protection was also repealed as a constituent part of legal society."

What Yahil overlooked, Erik Seidenfaden—a Danish journalist, resistance fighter, and leader of the Danish Press Service in Stockholm—noted. In a book written under a pseudonym and published in Sweden shortly after the Jewish operation, he explains why the Danish Jews had their sense of relative security confirmed during 1943, rather than the opposite: "It had become clear that persecution of the Jews was unthinkable as long as Denmark's king and legitimate government functioned, and the Best period showed many signs of a strong German desire to maintain to the end 'the Danish form of occupation.' The impression that the prevailing conditions could be preserved had gradually been reinforced. When persecution of the Jews began in Denmark, it came suddenly, and it seemed all the more violent as the German strongmen went directly to deportations, without preparing the Danes gradually through the Nuremberg Laws, Jewish stars, and individual pogroms."[45]

It is against this background that one should understand the confidence with which Dr. Meyer accepted Werner Best's assurances. Of course the action against the Norwegian Jews in October and November 1942, and the rumors about what was going on elsewhere in Europe, were deeply troubling. But despite all fears, Best had turned out to work for the stabilization of the situation in Denmark. After all, since his arrival elections had been held, and he had assured that no measures would be taken against Danish Jews. Thus Best had built up considerable trust among leading Danes, including the Jewish community. But after August 29 anxiety spread, intensifying by the end of September to deep concern, as is clear from notes Poul Hannover, Meyer's son-in-law, made the same day:

> I called up Knud [his oldest brother]—he spoke very carefully on the telephone, but I understood that he had received the same warning as we did, just not from the same source.
>
> Sunday afternoon two people came from the factory, neither of whom I had anything to do with at all on a daily basis, to warn me. In addition, a man who is married to Inger's cousin came to give a warning. When the children were out we went over to Kis and Gunnar. They were very nervous. Eventually we went home, but on the way back we met a police officer whom we knew. He reassured us—though he had certainly heard some of the rumors—but definitely did not think that the Germans had enough people to do anything to the extent that was being talked about. But he did promise to warn us if he noticed anything. For safety's sake I went over to an old friend who has a house in the countryside north of Copenhagen to hear if I might borrow it if need be—but I didn't find him. Eventually I went home—but I spent the night away—and got Inger and the children to do the same, although Inger shook her head. But as the children had a day off from school the next day they just considered it exciting.

Thirteen-year-old Allan Hannover now also began to register that something was wrong. With his uncle and aunt he had been to a concert downtown at the Odd Fellows' Palace on the occasion of the king's birthday, and when he came home by trolley, he asked his mother if there were any other plans for the evening. She said she didn't know yet, but the boy understood from her tone that "there was something afoot" and noted in his diary: "A little later, when I came up to the bedroom, I saw that some suitcases were packed." Allan was told that he should spend the night with a friend in the Søholm Park neighborhood where they lived. The neighbors there, after the imposition of the August 29 curfew, had built small stepladders, so that they didn't have to walk on public thoroughfares after nightfall and could move around in the neighborhood unimpeded, through each other's gardens. The family now sought refuge with neighbors or acquaintances living nearby, where they spent the night.

Poul Hannover's sister-in-law, Kis Marcus, describes the turmoil in her diary, and her sister and brother-in-law's visit that Sunday afternoon: "We got visits in the afternoon, first from Erik Schottländer [a friend] and then from Poul and Inger, who advised us to go away for the night. We then went down to Erik and Elsa Nyegaard, who had agreed last week that we might live in their little guesthouse if it became necessary."

Erik Nyegaard was vice president of Automatic, a telephone manufacturer. He lived with his wife, Elsa, in a villa on Strandvejen 184—not far from Kis and Gunnar's own residence. The Nyegaard and the Marcus families had close ties, and apparently Erik Nyegaard had early connections with a non-Communist resistance group, "Holger Danske," named after the legendary Danish warrior and knight in Charlemagne's army—though little is known about Nyegaard's precise involvement in armed resistance.

Within the Jewish community everyone sat tight. But it is clear that on Sunday hopes were still that the anxiety would pass and that soon things would calm down again.

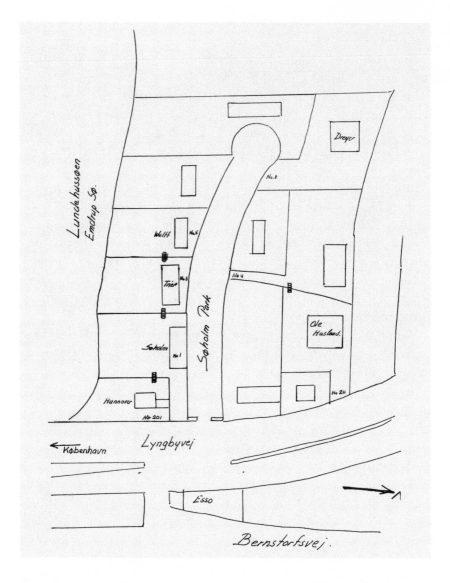

Allan Hannover drew a sketch of the Søholm Park neighborhood. He
depicts the houses and gardens, and also the small stepladders the family
fathers had built in order to be able to move freely between houses during
the curfew. The brief account written by the boy in the days before his family's departure reflects how the entire community rallied behind them, each
seeking in his or her own way to help out and find a solution. The implicit
assumption is that everyone was threatened and that no one at Søholm
Park could be indifferent.
Private family collection

CHAPTER 2

MONDAY, SEPTEMBER 27

AT HOME

Beliefs and Doubts

The next morning it seemed to be over, like a nightmare that disappears at the break of day. Daily life restarted, and they had, using Poul Hannover's expression, "almost the impression that there was a relaxation of the situation. Possibly it was because one could not stand continuing the excitement. We were home at night." Kis and Gunnar also took it easy, now that Sunday's stir had subsided. Kis writes: "The next morning we went home. I had an ironing day, and hired a new maid to begin Friday, October 1. We were home that night and thought again that it was all rumors."

Young Allan reports that the maids who had stayed in their house overnight reported in the morning that everything had been quiet at night. The family returned home, unpacked their suitcases, and the children were sent to school as usual. It all seemed to be a tempest in a teapot, and on Monday night everyone slept safely at home as if nothing had happened. So did Dr. Meyer, who "spoke optimistically" to anxious friends. He also went to bed at home, but noted the rumors: "It was said that a raid was to be conducted on the Jews and that there were ships in the 'Free Port' to take the Jews to Germany or Poland, etc."

For most people it was hard to believe that it really could come to an action against the Danish Jews, the majority of whom were fully integrated into society. A contributing factor was that the threat of an action against the Jews was included as a standing item in the more-or-less explicit threats the occupation authorities resorted to whenever they wanted to pressure the Danish politicians and authorities. After August 29 in particular, when martial law was imposed, and rumors swirled about the Wehrmacht or the German security establishment taking direct control of Denmark, it was widely perceived as part of the Germans' usual campaign of intimidation to scare the Danes into place and form a new government more to the liking of the occupying power. This fooled many politicians and indeed many Jews.

Most Danes simply could not bring themselves to believe that it could happen there. A short note from Vilhelm Bergstrøm's diary for September 25 illustrates the mood: The husband of the famous cabaret singer Lulu Ziegler, the actor and stage director Per Knutzon, was among the hostages the Germans had taken on August 29: "Lulu Ziegler every other day storms against 'Dagmarhus' to free her husband, Per Knutzon. She is on speaking terms with the people there. She asked if there would be any Jewish laws in this country, but they didn't think so."[1]

A few days later, on September 27, a source within the police tells Bergstrøm that something is not right: "Bjerring [the police commissioner] said there were probably 500 to 600 Gestapo up here at the moment and that the police general [Kurt] Daluege himself had been here and seen the situation. Bjerring observed that the news from Russia sounded kind of strange. Was there anything left out? The Germans had retreated almost too willingly. We talked about a possible Russian victory and its consequences. It was by no means pleasant if we got Russia too close. It was just about the worst thing that could happen."[2]

Bergstrøm voted for the Conservatives, but his view of Russia closely reflects the policy the Social Democratic and Center Liberal Party coalition government had also followed for more than a decade: The danger came from totalitarian thought itself. Nazism, Communism, and persecution of the Jews all originated from the same totalitarian mind-set. One evil was no less dangerous than the other; Communism could not be fought with Nazism or vice versa. This view made the Danish politicians deeply skeptical of early armed resistance because it originated mainly from the political extremes, especially from the well-organized Communists who had gone underground in 1941 after the German campaign in the East and the subsequent Danish arrests. For the ordinary citizen—like Bergstrøm—this perspective was so fundamental that it overshadowed most other political views. The nation's existence was threatened by the rise of totalitarian ideologies that also entailed the degradation and elimination of people because of race, creed, or political conviction. This was the front line that separated the "them" and the "us." It was also the line that the Danish people somehow had to defend.

Meanwhile in Sweden

There are many similarities in the development of the Danish and the Swedish attitude toward Nazi Germany. In both countries the electorate overwhelmingly rejected Nazism as well as radical anti-Semitism. Both countries stood out as firmly anti-Communist and both sought to remain neutral in regard to what the Social Democratic Swedish prime minister, Per Albin Hansson, called "the war of the great powers."

Sweden and Denmark also pursued largely the same restrictive policy, attempting to stem a feared wave of refugees as Germany, in the lead-up to the war, sought to expel its Jewish population. Both countries kept a firm focus on their own internal social stability, and in both the authorities sought to discourage critical press reports on events in the Third Reich and, after the outbreak of war, in regard to atrocities committed by Germany. As in Denmark, a coalition government spanning political parties was formed in Stockholm, where significant voices on the Right favored active and far-reaching cooperation with Germany. In general the extreme Right in Sweden was stronger and more radical than in Denmark, but the dominating Social Democratic Party held firm control of most government institutions.

Sweden maintained extensive exports of strategic goods to Germany and provided concessions that pushed the government to the edge of its declared neutrality, including a controversial access that allowed transit to Norway of German troop contingents. After the occupation of Norway and Denmark, public opinion in Sweden grew more and more hostile to Nazi Germany, and the attitude to refugees from the Nordic countries was favorable. Opinion in Sweden in the fall of 1942 turned increasingly against the policy of concessions pursued by their government. It was not only the changing fortunes of the war but rather the increasing press reports on Nazi repression in Denmark and, in particular, in Norway that had a decisive impact within most of the Swedish population.

Still, the action against the Norwegian Jews in the fall of 1942 took Sweden by surprise, and efforts to intervene came too late, provoking widespread criticism. This taught the Swedish authorities a lesson that came to good use in Denmark in 1943, and again in 1944 as Sweden intervened to help the Hungarian Jews.

Gradually Sweden became more defiant in relation to Nazi Germany. As the danger of an outright German attack on Sweden seemed more and more remote, the need to demonstrate vis-à-vis the Allies and the other Nordic countries a will to resist the Reich seemed more pressing. In the summer of 1942 Sweden, for the last time, returned German deserters to the Wehrmacht in Norway, and that same fall the press was granted more freedom. By the spring and summer of the following year efforts by the Swedish government to control the news ceased.[3]

After the August unrest in Denmark, anxiety in Sweden grew over the fate that now awaited the Danish Jews. Up to this point only a total of some hundred Danish resistance fighters and other refugees had managed to escape illegally to Sweden, but in the first week of September the refugee flows increased dramatically and quickly reached six hundred people. The fugitives were primarily Danish military personnel who fled to safety or who wanted to proceed to Britain and volunteer for the fight against the Germans. But about sixty were Jews who already felt the earth moving underfoot.

On August 31 the Swedish foreign minister, Christian Günther, told the Danish minister in Stockholm that Sweden would do everything possible to help the Danish refugees, and that a castle in southern Skåne, not far from the Øresund, the narrow strait separating Sweden from Sjælland, the island on which Copenhagen is situated, had been prepared as a reception center. At the same time the Swedish minister at the legation in Copenhagen was instructed to issue Swedish visas with a considerably freer hand than usual. Minister Gustav Dardel, who was a committed activist, did everything in his power, but in practice the acquisition of a Swedish passport was a viable option only for the very few Danish Jews who already had manifest personal ties to Sweden. The first days of September intensified the stream of rumors, and the minister tried through interviews with Danish authorities and Dr. Best to clarify how much was true. Best assured him that he would prevent the action, but Dardel did not believe him, probably partly because the same day Duckwitz indicated that an operation was indeed under way.

Duckwitz traveled to Sweden on September 21—by all accounts with Best's blessing, maybe even at his request. The next day he reached Stockholm by train, where on the evening of September 22 he met with Prime Minister Albin. We know nothing from Swedish sources about the content of their three-hour conversation, but judging from Duck-witz's brief notes the conversation focused broadly on Swedish-German relations. They also appear to have agreed that a Swedish diplomat, Nils Erik Ekblad, was to join Duckwitz on his return in order to step up Swe-den's efforts to issue papers allowing Danish Jews to travel out of Den-mark legally. There is nothing to suggest that the meeting in Stockholm changed the Swedish position. But it is reasonable to assume that it fur-ther strengthened the Swedish government's decision to prepare for a German action against the Danish Jews and the possibility that it would trigger an influx of refugees into Sweden.

When Duckwitz returned to Copenhagen and talked with his Swiss wife, Annemarie, he noted in his diary: "Everything I do, I do fully con-scious of my own responsibility. Here, I am assisted by my rock-solid belief that good deeds can never be wrong. Therefore, I need to get to work and to muster all my courage. . . . It's good that Annemarie thinks exactly as I do. So there is no retreating from the path once chosen. Only once in a while the responsibility seems unbearable. But those moments pass. There is still a higher goal. I bow to this."[4]

The double game between Best's soothing assurances and Duckwitz's alarming messages helped create the myth that the Jewish operation was Berlin's project, which Best and Duckwitz opposed with all their might. Of course the action was instigated by Best himself, but for those directly concerned there was great uncertainty and confusion. Rumor flourished both in Copenhagen and Stockholm, causing prominent members of the Jewish community to rush to the Swedish legation to get it to issue visas for, among others, the stateless Jewish agricultural students, who were in a particularly vulnerable position. Minister Dardel, however, could not bend the rules that far, despite all good intentions. The Swedish legation could not help the Jews in such large numbers.[5]

Kis Marcus biking in the streets of Copenhagen with her children, Dorte and Palle, early in the 1940s.   Private family collection

Opposite, top:
Gunnar Marcus in his home in Charlottenlund, autumn 1943.
Private family collection

Opposite, bottom:
The Hannover family shortly after their arrival in Sweden, October 1943.
Private family collection

THE MESSAGE

Fading Hopes

Werner Best received the final order to launch the operation on Tuesday, September 28, and the same day he informed Berlin that it would take place on the coming Friday night. At *Politiken* Bergstrøm sensed that something concrete was now about to happen: "Up at the paper I met Schwartz [a colleague]. He looked very worried. How was the situation going? He spoke of the many German policemen who had poured into the country. Was an action against the Jews about to be carried out? I knew as little as he. The police, the Danish ones, know nothing. Schwartz probably has some Jewish acquaintances that he is worried about."

For those immediately impacted it became increasingly hard to make sense of the normal business of daily life, and Poul Hannover's notes from that Tuesday show how he suddenly began to single himself out from his colleagues, and how senior members of the Jewish community now began to discuss among themselves how to deal with the many rumors:

Tuesday I was at a meeting of the board of directors within the Manufacturers Association—and apparently none of them thought anything but that there is peace and no danger. Later I was called into a meeting with the [president of the Jewish community] Supreme Court attorney C. B. Henriques. In addition to him Director Karl Lachmann was present and Max Rothenborg and Sophus Oppenheim. It was agreed that it may only be a war of nerves, fomented by the Danish Nazis, and that it was not worth letting them destroy our lives for this—but the two gentlemen from the board asked us, that if something should happen to them, we three would take action—and of course we promised. So I left again for the office.

In the office there was a message that Jørgen [his brother-in-law] had been there—and when I called him, he asked if I could come by. I did—and he asked me immediately if there was anything new. I told him what I had heard at the meeting—and I thought that life would be quite unbearable for all of us if we mutually went around scaring one another—so I had nothing more to say. I could not, however, help asking him if he had heard new rumors. Yes—he had—namely, what hadn't happened in the previous week would happen in this one. I was not impressed by his source—but called, for safety's sake, my one friend in the Foreign Ministry and asked him if there was anything new lately—he said definitely not—there was peace and no danger—Dr. Best had reportedly traveled to Berlin and had not returned yet. I called Inger's cousin's husband again—he too thought it all overwrought—only there was something with the police he could not understand, but that he would give me an update the following day. I went home quite reassured.

The Warning

During the day Duckwitz rang up Hans Hedtoft, the Social Democrats' elected leader, who had been ousted from politics by the Germans, and asked for an immediate meeting. Duckwitz would also try to set up a meeting between Werner Best and former prime minister Vilhelm Buhl, but Buhl refused categorically to meet with the occupation's first man, undoubtedly because he feared Best would try to sandbag him into supporting the formation of a new Danish government. Instead Hedtoft asked Duckwitz to come to a meeting in a discreet "cabin of trust" in the Workers' Assembly Building, where the Social Democratic executive leaders awaited him: In addition to Hedtoft and Buhl, several other leading Social Democrats also attended. Shortly after the war Hedtoft recalled the message Duckwitz delivered to the group of prominent politicians: " 'The disaster is at hand,' he said. 'Everything is planned in detail. Ships will anchor at the mooring off Copenhagen. Those of your poor Jewish countrymen who get caught by the Gestapo will forcibly be brought on board the ships and transported to an unknown fate.' He was white with indignation and shame."[1]

Hedtoft relates that the party members divided the tasks among themselves: "Through a clandestine police connection we got cars provided and drove off in all different directions. I went first to the president of the Jewish community, Supreme Court attorney C. B. Henriques's villa in Charlottenlund. I shall never forget this meeting with the Danish Jews' leading man. We didn't know much of each other in advance, but had met a few times. . . . I asked to speak to Henriques face-to-face, and when we were alone, I said, upset, nervous and unhappy as I was: 'Henriques! A major disaster is about to begin. The dreaded action against the Jews in Denmark is coming. It's going to be executed by the Gestapo on the night between October 1 and 2, seeking out all the Jews in their homes, and then transporting them to ships in the harbor. You must immediately make every effort to warn every Jew in the city. It is clear that we are prepared to help with everything."

According to Hedtoft, Henriques answered with two words: "*De lyver!* [You're lying!]" After he was convinced, he kept desperately repeating: "I do not understand how it can be true. I've just been at the Foreign Ministry with Director Svenningsen, and he reassured me and said that it is his belief that nothing will happen." Hedtoft insisted that Svenningsen had spoken in good faith and only reported what the Germans said—but also that the Germans had lied. The action was imminent.

In the following hours the message spread through a large number of channels. Parallel to networks within the Jewish community, the Social Democrats used their dense web of political contacts, conveying to their local party chairmen in the capital information of the planned action, with instructions to ensure that all concerned were alerted. It was more difficult in the provinces, where the warning emerged later and spread more slowly.[2]

After his conversation with Hedtoft, Duckwitz also went to Dardel, who immediately informed Stockholm that this time it was for real. Evidence suggests that both Best and Duckwitz were eager at this time to send the signal that they would do everything in their power to prevent or limit the deportations. There is an unmistakable element of public diplomacy in the zeal with which Duckwitz spread the message both before and after September 28. Earlier notions that he did this in spite of Best and without his knowledge do not seem likely, although Best, in a telegram to Berlin, expressed surprise at how the Danish Jews could have gotten hold of precise information about details of the upcoming action. During those days Best and Duckwitz worked closely together, and both of their later testimonies also confirm Best's explanation that "the Jews were warned with my knowledge and in accordance with my wishes."[3]

The Decision

The message spread like wildfire, and it also reached Poul Hannover the same day, just after he had returned to his home:

> When the time was well half past six I was called by a friend of mine: Poul, take a car and come out here immediately. Fortunately I got a car right away—met with one of Knud's friends out there and got the message: Three men, one of whose source in particular was utterly convincing to me, had just been with him to alert him that it was definitely under way and would happen—to cut it short all Jews in the country would be rounded up during the night between Friday and Saturday and would be taken down to the ships that lay in the harbor—the old would be transported to Theresienstadt by way of Vienna, the others to Poland if they were not liquidated en route.
>
> Yes—so this was the message and nothing else. I got Knud's friend into my car—as soon as I got home, I called my brothers over. Knud was very little inclined—although he came—I told them, asked the eldest to inform Kis and Gunnar and Knud to inform mother. Then the whole family disappeared out of the house for the night between Tuesday and Wednesday.

The precise information about the plan in Poul Hannover's diary suggests that Duckwitz had been more detailed than Hedtoft gave him credit for, and proves that it was the direct contact with the country's top politicians that finally convinced the doubters that it was serious.

Poul Hannover's son, Allan, reports in his diary that he sat down with his mother and did homework after his father left for the hastily convened meeting. It wasn't long, however, before Inger Hannover called her father, who was visiting her older sister, Ada. She got a message to immediately pass on to her brother, Hjalmar, who lived nearby. While his mother bicycled over, Allan went out and played with the neighbor's children.

When they returned later to the Hannover family's garden, Allan noticed, standing in front of the house, three bicycles he recognized as belonging to his father's three brothers. The boy realized that the four brothers were meeting to confer with one another, and that something serious was going on.

On the same evening Kis writes: "Tuesday Johanne Kruse was with us for dinner. We got a call from Flemming, who wanted to warn us, but I reassured him that we ourselves were reassured. While Gunnar and Dorte followed Johanne to the trolley (Palle was already asleep), Aage Hannover came over, very upset and said: 'You must hurry away from here; The Gestapo has been with Hjalmar. I have heard from a reliable source that we are to be taken tonight and sent to Poland.' I rushed to pack our bags, and when Gunnar came home, we woke Palle and walked through the woods to our refuge. I had stupidly called down there to say that we were coming, and we were afraid that the conversations had been intercepted, and that they would come and pick us up during the night."

While Duckwitz's warning spread in the family, Dr. Meyer seemed not to have received a clear message. On the other hand his son had some alarming news that ensured that the pediatrician would not sleep in his own bed: "Tuesday September 28, Hjalmar came to me and told me that while he had been out in town, three Germans had been in his office, one by the kitchen stairs, and two on the main stairs. As he was not there, they asked when he had last been there? The answer was: Not in the last few days. They forbade anyone to inform him about their visit, stood and stared into his office, and left. As soon as he came back the staff at the other offices told him about the Germans' visit. He and his family have been in hiding since. As it occurred to me they might come looking for him at my place, I went over to Honoré [a colleague] and spent the night there."

For Poul Hannover it was a harrowing night. He was no longer in doubt about what was to begin: "I do not think I will ever forget the night that followed, while I lay awake and wondered what was going to happen. I wouldn't have thought that this could happen—but I didn't dare disregard it, given the source it came from—and for this very reason it became clearer and clearer that it would not help to take refuge in the countryside. If this was real, then there was only one option—we had to leave the country."

Adolph Meyer during the first part of the occupation. Dr. Meyer was part of the well-off Copenhagen bourgeoisie and also had a close connection to the leaders of the Jewish community.
Private family collection

Erik Nyegaard, who was instrumental in helping both the Marcus and Hannover families, and later Dr. Meyer, in their escapes. The photograph dates from the 1950s.
Scanpix

CHAPTER 4

WEDNESDAY, SEPTEMBER 29

DEPARTURE

Which Way?

The next morning, Wednesday, September 29, the day before the Jewish New Year, there was an early-morning service at the synagogue on Krystalgade, where warning of the impending raid spread through the congregation and from there along countless roads to almost all Jews in Copenhagen and to most in the provinces. But the community did nothing to organize a unified response, let alone help members to escape. Everyone was left to himself and his family and friends—or to the scattered private initiatives to organize flight and temporary hiding. It proved fatal for the most vulnerable groups, among others, for the so-called Aliyah-children, who did not necessarily have any contact with other Jews, and also for some of the old people at the Jewish nursing home in Copenhagen who had not been evacuated by their relatives.

The same day several senior police officers arrived from Germany, including the aforementioned special command of experts from Berlin under the leadership of Adolf Eichmann's deputy, Sturmbannführer Rolf Günther. It was also Duckwitz's thirty-ninth birthday, and though he celebrated much of the day together with his Danish friend Hans Hedtoft, he noted gloomily in his diary: "Everything looks bleak and hopeless. Preparations for the Jewish action are rapidly being made. New people have come—experts in this sordid business. They will not find many victims."[1]

But for the team of professional German police who were now deployed, the goal was clear: The trip had finally begun for the Danish Jews, and the German administration in Denmark drifted rudderless toward the disaster it had caused.

On the same day Danish foreign police told the Germans at Dagmarhus that the Swedish legation had tipped the scales when it came to the issuance of visas to Sweden for Danish Jews. As mentioned, the Swedish minister, Gustav Dardel, stretched the rules to the extreme and probably beyond them. The lawyers at the foreign police now thought this to be too much, especially with the long string of temporary passports. Best promptly responded and informed Berlin that he would stop the traffic. Despite attempts by the Danish Foreign Ministry to ease up again, it was clear that the road to Sweden by way of a massive issuance of passports and visas was open to only a few. Most had to find other ways.[2]

For Poul Hannover the decision was already made. It was also his a birthday. He turned forty-six and was not going to sit still and wait until he and his family were collected by the Gestapo: "I told Inger about my determination—she could not help but hope that maybe it was a false alarm—and that one did not need to flee the country, but could come back little by little. In the office I announced my plan to my immediate entourage—they could only agree with me that there was little else to do. One rushed out to explore the possibility of getting away from Skovshoved or Tårbæk [harbors north of Copenhagen], but found out that both were equally impossible. I immediately set off again—beginning with an old friend, but did not find him—then proceeded to get a visa—on to Louis's office, where I both wanted to warn an emigrant they have there, who had previously considered escaping, something I have so far advised against—and partly because I wanted to hear from him if he knew any way out."

Amid the feverish preparations for flight, Poul Hannover also tries to attend to his daily business, which on this day included a meeting of the Industry Council. Suddenly the minor everyday squabbles are seen in a glaring light by someone who knows that he and his family face an unknown fate: "An almost perfectly ridiculous meeting about whether the Danish authorities should protest to the German authorities in the Netherlands and Belgium as they appeared to be standing in the way of exports from Danish companies that were run by Jews. I advised them to take care of the issue—I could not tell them it probably would have lost its topicality before it went forward."

Poul's day continues with hectic but also perplexing activity: How could the family get away? Illegal avenues were not obvious for the law-abiding businessman who preferred to engage friends, colleagues, and employees to explore various options. At the same time the warning was confirmed by several sources: "I met Annalisa on the road—she called me to give me a message: 'Poul, you know, you must not be home. I just came from the minister—he's giving a strong warning."

The message had gone through but the practical difficulties piled up rapidly:

> I continued on to the office on Bredgade—which had been notified that our passports also required visas, but we were going to have to go out ourselves and sign them at the Swedish travel agency. I telephoned to Inger to take her bike and meet me at Titan—and cycled out there myself. . . . Inger and I got a car and left for the central station. The genial manager of the travel agency had been alerted by the minister—he immediately asked me if I was aware that the situation was extremely serious. As it turned out, we needed photographs—it all took time. We met a couple of acquaintances . . . but there was not much to say for mutual comfort. When the practicalities were done, I left Inger to wait for the passports and proceeded to Erik Birger [a friend] who in every detail confirmed what I already had learned—though he held the view that after a certain time, maybe 3 weeks, it might calm down somewhat as by that point in time they wouldn't be too eager to keep searching. He promised to let me know if he heard of any ways out. . . . Finally Inger came—she hadn't money enough to pay for the passports, so we had to return to the bureau and pay—then out to Titan where we loaded the bicycles onto the car and continued home.

A common feature of the entries of these first days was that the family sought help and advice from anyone who might be able to provide it. The thought that among the large circle of friends, acquaintances, and colleagues who were involved, there might be someone who would turn the family in, or try to lure it into a trap, seems not even to have occurred to Poul Hannover. On the contrary, his fellow citizens were his natural allies. This is also reflected as he returned home: "Svend Aage Holm was waiting—the other man from Titan had investigated conditions in Skovshoved and Klampenborg—both hopeless—he was about to proceed to his house in order to see whether there were any possibilities from there—he had already promised to put the house at my disposal if need be. In addition, one of Ludvig's staff was there—they knew of nothing yet—but worked on it and it was agreed that I would look for one of them at 3:30 at Østbanen [East Station] . . . "

Small and large concerns are getting mixed up—all under the general theme of utter confusion: "At home everything was breaking up. Inger had begun packing—a small bag for each, but as we had no idea of how long we were going to stay . . . it was rather random—we didn't dare not to bring a few towels—though they were bulky, but we might end up needing precisely just them. Gunnar was there—we had decided to go together. I hardly managed to eat two bites—then went on to see Herbert [Jerichow, the vice president of Titan]. He was in despair—promised to see whether he could do anything—we agreed on a telephone code—then home again to begin packing. Thank God, Mom had given me a tennis bag ideally suited for the purpose—I took that one and Inger her equivalent."

The apparent confusion is also due to the fact that Poul Hannover, in typing up his diary notes, is trying to reconstruct the details a few dramatic days after the events: "The more I write the more I realize that I'm not getting it all down. I had agreed with my brothers the preceding evening to try and get Mother with us. I called her from Bredgade in the morning to tell her that I would send someone to collect her passport—but she said she was already on her way to the countryside. I didn't even think to thank her for my birthday present—and she did not congratulate me."

Still considering himself a good citizen, Poul Hannover is not in the least uncomfortable with seeking assistance from the police: "Just as I was standing there, Carl Holbøll, the policeman whom I had met on Sunday, came by—like an angel from on high. He had found a way we could get away—to an address in Gentofte [north of Copenhagen]. He, Gunnar, and I immediately went out there. No one was home. Gunnar was told that he should call there every quarter hour—I went to Østbanen—at nearly half past three as I came in I ran into my old friend who had moved from the country to Vedbæk. He was immediately willing to entrust his house to me, but regretted that there was no bedding or space—so I had to abandon the idea. Just before he came, Louis's man arrived—he now had an address, but did not know if it could help—it was very busy, but when they heard my name, they had expressed their willingness to talk to me."

On the same day Kis Marcus writes of her doubts and confusion: "We went home again the next morning when everything seemed to be normal. I spoke with Inger on the phone and since we could not speak freely, I asked Gunnar to drive by Lyngbyvej and hear the news, on the way to the office.—Meanwhile Joanna [a friend] called and we agreed that she should come out right away to pick up some things, including my jewelry, which she had offered to keep for us. Gunnar came home again. We were now aware that something was cooking. Inger was going to town to meet Poul, and Gunnar was to go there again at 1 o'clock to hear what they would do.—I took care of lunch for us (none of us had any appetite), and so I took care of some things in the house and packed our bags, but afterward I realized that I was not thinking enough and therefore we didn't have with us what we could have had."

Kis is struggling to deal with the prospect that they are about to leave their home, possibly for good, with no more than they can carry by hand. The sense of the whole thing being unreal is also supported by the fact that nothing has actually happened. It was all in the air, all based on hearsay: "Gunnar telephoned to say we had to go immediately, and we cycled back to Erik and Elsa Nyegaard. The children played there all afternoon, and I walked around nervously and began to worry about Gunnar, who had said that he would come within the hour. Then Johanna Kruse came again. She thought we were gone, but now promised to go look for Dad. It was his birthday, and when I called there in the morning, Line [his maid, Miss Oline Henriksen, also known as Line] had said that they were waiting for us in there with hot chocolate. Johanna fetched a wastebasket that Dorte had made for Father, and then went to see him. Later in the day she came back with greetings from Father, who thought it was sensible for us to go to Sweden, and with the message that he would hide in Denmark. Once he was assured later that all his children and grandchildren were saved, he would go over himself."

The Final Doubt

Dr. Meyer had the day's third birthday. The aging physician's report confirms his daughter's, but also sheds light on the considerations and intelligence brought to the Jewish community's leadership, still finding it hard to believe what was about to happen, and that they had made a fundamental error about Werner Best's credibility and the Germans' plans: "I got up on September 29 at 7 a.m. and went home, where there were flowers from the girls. It was my 72nd birthday. And what a day it became. I telephoned to congratulate Poul, where I was to go for dinner. 'We'll see each other at dinner,' I said, but he responded with a maybe. I heard nothing from Else and Knud, nor from Kis and Gunnar. Through the girls I heard that Poul and Inger, Kis and Gunnar, and the children had left. . . . I cycled to the clinic as usual, received congratulations. At 9:45 a.m. Mrs. Hermansen presented cake and champagne (Mumm), I gave my little thank you speech. . . . When Allan and I left, Leif Henriques [a nephew of C. B. Henriques] was waiting for us below and said that 'now it is going awry.' Pihl [a friend] had been at Henriques's office and told of the planned raid. . . . At 11 a.m. I was already at C.B. [Henriques]'s office, he and Lachmann came down the stairs to a waiting car to drive to the Foreign Ministry, and I drove with them. C.B. had a confirmed message (from a German source) about a raid on the Jews."

It is Hedtoft's dissemination of Duckwitz's warning that materializes here, and that has lit a fire under the community's leadership. But it's hard to look the worst straight in the eye, especially when you are afraid that by doing so you will exacerbate it. Dr. Meyer reports on the visit to the Foreign Ministry: "We saw Director Svenningsen instantly; he was ashen at the message, which was a surprise to him. He promised to summon the permanent secretaries to meet at 2 p.m. He admitted that the outgoing government would have resigned over the Jewish question. As we drove away at approximately 11:30 Lachmann said, 'I still don't believe it,' and I too found it unthinkable."

With hindsight and with our knowledge of the horrors of the Holocaust it can be difficult to understand the reluctance of the Jewish community's foremost representatives to believe what was now written in letters flaming as *mene tekel* on the wall. After the war Karl Lachmann tried to explain the refusal of the leaders to engage in planning for an escape, "since it was agreed that one should refrain from it as 6,000 to 7,000 people could not go into hiding. Any action would require help from non-Jewish countrymen, a request one could not make, or expect to be honored." This does not explain what is perhaps difficult to understand today: Accepting that the threat was real was arduous for those directly concerned. Even so cynical an observer as Vilhelm Bergstrøm still doubted the whole thing was more than much ado about nothing: "I had a bunch of people who wanted to know what was going on with the persecution of the Jews. They would not believe that I knew as little as they. They thought that the police must know something. Alfred Olsen came and told me that today several large Jewish firms had paid staff three months' salary in advance.

"Several had fled to Sweden, and many just abandoned their homes. There was a general fear in Jewish homes. All sorts of stories are told and believed. There are supposed to be ships ready in the 'Free Port' of Copenhagen to take them away. In short, panic. There may now be something else behind this. The Germans would like to have a Danish government, and they are pushing. Pressure on the Jews could be a way."

Bergstrøm was right that the Germans had deliberately played on the fear of an attack on the Jews, using the threat as leverage in the wrestling with the Danes, currently for a new pro-German government. The cry of "Wolf!" had been heard many times before.[3]

A report written by a young woman, Lise Epstein, in 1944, reflects the shock and confusion that prevailed in many families: "We met in the hallway—Mother wailed, fully dressed to leave the house, with a face that was red and swollen from crying and despair, and in a half-choked voice stammered that Mrs. Storm . . . had been informed by a reliable source that raids on Jews in Denmark would start this night. We should dress and leave house and home as soon as possible as we were no longer safe in our own home. Mother told me that she had called Father, and we expected him momentarily. . . . When Father came home, he said, surprised: 'You almost frightened the life out of me on the phone. What happened? What happened?'—'Poor man, poor man! Don't you understand? Now the Nazis are coming. Get your clothes and run away.' Dad stood confused and stammered: 'What should I do? What should I do?' "[4]

The daughter notes her parents' shock, fear, and confusion. That the mother broke into Yiddish reflects that the family belongs to the so-called Russian Jews who had emigrated from Eastern Europe, and for whom pogroms were more recent memories than for the "old" Jewish families in the country. For her it was not the Germans who were coming, let alone the Danes; it was the Nazis.

There was great difficulty in reading the Germans' real intentions in Denmark. From the end of 1941 one of the country's first and leading resistance men of a Conservative persuasion, the industrialist Erling Foss, prepared short intelligence reports, "The Week," on conditions in the occupied country for use in the free world. These reports were sent by courier via Stockholm to London, where the information was included partly in the BBC's news programs, including those broadcast in Danish, and they were also used by the British authorities to assess developments in Denmark. Foss had good contact with other resistance fighters and a broad knowledge of the illegal press, in addition to his personal contacts with leading Conservative politicians. Even with this solid start, Erling Foss also had trouble figuring out what was at stake, and in his weekly intelligence report on September 29 he writes: "Copenhagen is extremely alarmed today by a persistent rumor that all Jews will be arrested and be carried south by ship. There is also talk that room has been made for two thousand in the prisons. Some famous half-Jews are said to be on the list. The announcement comes from undoubtedly well-intentioned and well-informed sources, so there are only two possibilities. Either it is true, and if so the arrests will happen overnight on Friday or Saturday. Or maybe it's the Germans who have deliberately put the message into circulation, either because something less bad is coming, or because they want the Rigsdag* to bow before them and establish a new government."[5]

Foss is aware that the leading Social Democratic politicians believe the warning. But have they allowed themselves to be led by the nose? Have they let themselves be used in a cunning German intrigue? The doubts gnawed. And Foss was far from alone in seeing the rumors now being spread by the Germans from this perspective. One of Denmark's leading industrialists, Gunnar Larsen, had been serving as a cabinet minister since the summer of 1940. He was co-owner and CEO of Denmark's single largest company, the major construction firm F. L. Smidth & Co., pursuing enterprises throughout the world, and as a strong ally of Erik Scavenius he shared the desire to find a way for cooperation with the Germans to be resumed after the August events. Larsen kept a diary, and his notes from September 29 reflect a long conversation he had that day with a former transport minister who was a leading member of the Farmers' Party and agreed with the need to resume the cooperation in some way involving the elected politicians. To Larsen the fate of the Jews was among the prime arguments: "I did not consider it advisable to leave things alone, as this would entail taking on a very serious responsibility to answer for the future in several regards, including also the fate of the Jews."[6]

---

*Denmark's bicameral parliament, Rigsdagen, was abolished after a 1953 referendum when the dominant first chamber, Folketinget, became the singular legislative body.

Erling Foss was by no means a typical Danish resistance fighter. He was one of the very few who went into active resistance early, and he was Conservative, but outside the National-Conservative wing that was hostile toward parliamentary democracy. In 1941 Foss initiated contact with Danish military intelligence. As a businessman he could legally travel to Sweden, bringing documents and microfilm to the leader of the Free Danes in Stockholm, Ebbe Munck, who served as an intermediary for the British secret service. It was this military intelligence that Field Marshal Bernard Montgomery, at the liberation of Denmark, complimented as "second to none."

Foss participated in the negotiations between the leading resistance fighters, resulting in the formation of Denmark's Freedom Council in September 1943. The council functioned as a kind of internal government in exile with representatives of the Communists and other leading opposition groups—but no prominent politicians.

Erling Foss was arrested in December 1943, but he managed to keep the scope of his illegal activities undisclosed and was subsequently released. In February 1944 he escaped to Sweden after an attempt on his life.

Frihedsmuseet

These leading political figures had not realized that this logic cut both ways, and that the imminent raid was closing the door to any further cooperation on the political level.

For those directly concerned, the practical questions were pressing. The aforementioned librarian of the Jewish community, Josef Fischer, who was born in Hungary and thus was one of the more recently arrived "Russian Jews," had three adult daughters. One of them, thirty-three-year-old Ella Fischer, who worked as an assistant in a bookstore, was admitted to the municipal hospital for treatment. In her diary she recounted how the warnings that came via her sister were presented exactly the way Duckwitz and Best wanted: "With the politicians Alsing Andersen and Hans Hedtoft as the sources, it was announced that there were personal orders from the Reich chancellor that the Jewish issue in Denmark should be resolved before week's end. The German Reich agents in Denmark, Dr. Best and the commander of the German Wehrmacht in Denmark, von Hanneken, were against it, but you dared not assume that they could exercise their influence. . . . Father, Mother and Harriet would go up to Hornbæk, and Edith would go to Miss Raastöff. It was about everyone getting away from their residences, of course, if they were raided."[7]

Dr. Meyer also realized after meetings with the leaders of the Jewish community and at the Ministry of Foreign Affairs that staying at home was no longer an option:

> From C.B.'s office I bicycled home, it was teeming with flowers, letters, telegrams, gifts. It was terrible, I did not have time to open the letters. As I recall, ate lunch with Ada who said that she and the children would go away, wanted me to, but I did not want to because I did not know anything about the others. . . . During consultation time called Medical Association, and was read a message from the Danish Medical Association that there would be a raid against the Jews, and that any Jewish doctor had to hide privately, in hospitals or in the country, would probably only need 4–5 days. Now there was no more doubt. At 2:15 I rode my bicycle with my attaché case to the Farmers' Bank and emptied my box. 2:45 I was sitting with C.B. (called from there to Dr. Keller to come to me regarding admission to the hospital, he promised to come at 4 p.m.). . . .
>
> Present at the meeting with C.B. were also Lachmann, Mogens, and I . . . , Arthur Henriques (with wife) and the Supreme Court attorney H. H. Bruun, to whom the representatives gave power of

attorney to act on their behalf. At 3:30 p.m. we said good-bye to one another, and I rode home with my papers. There had been various people with gifts. Mrs. Kruse came with a wastebasket from Dorte and with a message about Kis and Gunnar's plans. . . . I wanted to go up to Ada, who had said that she would go on the train at 5 p.m. but she now took the 4:20. We met in the hall and embraced each other and the kids, sobbing. . . . I asked [a colleague] by phone to cover my practice during my absence, of which I also put notice on a poster outside the front door.

It is characteristic of all reports that the fugitives are doing whatever they can in haste to ensure and prepare their return. This is achieved, among other ways, by making provisions for their business's continuation in their absence, which they obviously see as quite temporary. The warnings now come with a force that convinces almost everyone that escape is necessary. But not emigration. It is loaded with symbolism that the pediatrician puts up a poster about the clinic's continuation in his "absence." Dr. Meyer's poster is not only a practical measure. It is also a manifesto with the message that the occupation will not last, and that the Danish Jews will return home as soon as possible. Like many others Dr. Meyer sought hospitalization as a cover while he saw how things developed:

Dr. Keller came at 4 p.m., in the meantime having secured a room on the maternity ward, he was overwhelmed, wrote a hospitalization note for prostatic hypertrophy [difficulty urinating]. I actually had the thought last week to seek him out again because of certain urinary inconveniences (perhaps part of the nervous nature). Then I spoke to Honoré, as far as I can recall, I had asked him to come to my home, I asked him to write to Dr. Hart in Ruds Vedby to ask him if he could possibly house me, he should ring me up the following day (the 30th), but only say yes or no. Line and Miss Rigmor Eriksen, my faithful domestic workers, were distraught and upset; they packed my red suitcase, and after dinner I left. Hjalmar came earlier and announced that he thought he could get away in a couple of days. . . . It was probably about 7 p.m. when I drove to St. Joseph Hospital, the girls would be sleeping out (they did at least a few nights). I did not answer the phone for fear of wiretapping, Mary [Goldschmidt, Adolph Meyer's sister-in-law] insisted that she must speak with me, but I said I could not because of wiretaps (probably not justified).—At the hospital I was admitted to a private room on the maternity ward under an alias. An intern took my medical history, and I went to rest, using bromisoval [a common sedative] to sleep.

A Danish Initiative? First Attempt

As Director Svenningsen had promised the representatives from the Jewish community, he summoned the permanent secretaries to a meeting at the Foreign Ministry at 2 p.m. At the same time he informed King Christian's cabinet secretary of the unfolding events. Maybe the king could be brought into play? It appears from Christian's personal diary that he had already been informed by his pastor before the message reached him through the formal channels.[8]

At the permanent secretaries' meeting Svenningsen explained the situation: "From various reliable sources almost-certain information indicated that an action against the Danish Jews was imminent. Nothing official was available, but the rumors and information were of such a nature that one had to give them credence. . . . There was talk particularly of the night from Friday to Saturday."

The permanent secretaries' leader did not hide the seriousness of the situation: "The king had previously stated that he considered himself to be the protector of the Danish Jews, and it was a given that a constitutional government would have resigned if confronted with a demand for an action against the Jews. The question was: Can we do something, and then in what form?"

Svenningsen now laid out for his colleagues the terrible dilemma of trying to do something or disclaiming responsibility for the crime. An illegal mass exodus seemed impossible to carry out, but it was advisable that the Jews should make sure not to be home on the night the raid was conducted. The main question was what the permanent secretaries could do to avoid the disaster. The Justice Ministry's permanent secretary, Eivind Larsen, threw out the notion that perhaps they themselves should offer to intern the Jews in Denmark. The idea had been discussed with Jewish representatives, who according to Svenningsen had said "that any such measure would be seen as welcome aid in the given situation." That discussion was the one Dr. Meyer also participated in. His brief diary entries are the only contemporaneous account from the

Jewish representatives, and they do not mention the startling proposal about Danish internment. Immediately after Denmark's liberation C. B. Henriques repudiated the permanent secretary's claim that he or his colleagues had accepted this proposal. It had been presented, but Henriques emphasized that it "won support neither from me nor from the later summoned cabinet secretary to the king," and he demanded a retraction, so it would appear that "such a thought had not been supported by any responsible Jewish side."

The issue was controversial for the Jewish representatives in 1945, but since neither Henriques nor Lachmann left written records of the actual conversation, we have only Svenningsen's claim that the three guests endorsed the plan—and Dr. Meyer's silence on the subject.[9]

According to Svenningsen the Jewish representatives considered "providing a larger sum of money as security from the side of the Jewish interests"—that is, payment of a kind of ransom. But the plans for internment in Denmark provoked several questions from the Jewish representatives: "How would it be possible to arrest Danish citizens, and what was the crime for which ransom should be paid? Would one accuse the Jews of sabotage?" Svenningsen's answer had been a clear no: The goal was to bribe and soften. But their questions could not be conjured away.

For Nils Svenningsen and Eivind Larsen what stood out first and foremost was that the reality that awaited the Jews after deportation "was so terrible that the heads of administration must consider it a duty to do their utmost to prevent this from happening." Svenningsen added that "it was hardly imaginable that something like this could be a reality in Denmark" before he turned to the head of the Department of Statistics with the words: "I cannot help but express our sympathy for our colleague Einar Cohn." Everyone understood that the issues they were now discussing could mean life or death for Cohn and his family. According to the minutes the participants rose in silent sympathy before negotiations continued.[10]

The discussion that followed between the permanent secretaries was intense and penetrated to the very core of the dilemma of cooperation. The arguments for and against, and the entire terrifying moral quandary, were stunningly clear to the permanent secretaries that Wednesday afternoon. How far could they take responsibility for injustice if the goal was to avoid the worst? A protest letter from the bishop of Copen-hagen, on behalf of all of Denmark's Lutheran bishops, was read.* Also one from the dean of the University of Copenhagen, again an urgent protest. But to what avail?

While Larsen and Svenningsen argued for active engagement, most of the other state secretaries opposed it. Hakon Jespersen, the state sec-retary for the Ministry of Economy and Trade, who took detailed notes of the discussion, explains why: "I expressed the view that the heads of the administration, as an expression of public opinion, had to make specific objections against persecution of the Jews. This was one of those extreme measures about which there had always been agreement: The administration would not and could not be part of it. It had to be empha-sized that such measures would sharply conflict with the Danish sense of justice and complicate the maintenance of peace and order, which was a prerequisite for a satisfactory Danish administration."

Jespersen would protest. The others would, too, just as protests began to arrive from all parts of Danish society. He would also point out the decisive breach of trust such an action would represent, and refer to its consequences. But the protests were not the issue. It was as if the perma-nent secretaries were acting in a kind of self-defense. Larsen expressed it clearly in his support for Danish internment based on "realistic con-siderations." He did not believe that either protest or argument would have any impact whatsoever other than causing irritation. The order came from "a place we could not penetrate with arguments. The task was to find ways to avoid the worst, namely deportation." Svenningsen supported him without reservations. "He was not afraid of the conse-quences for the permanent secretaries . . . because it was about saving people from the irreversible, from death and horror and destruction of human life in a cruel manner."

Although the Holocaust's systematized consistency was not yet known in all its ghastly details, Svenningsen's remark reflects a very precise idea of the fate that awaited Jews who were deported to Germany or German-occupied Eastern Europe. Svenningsen had to balance this knowledge against his own limited ability to prevent a disaster. It says a lot about human psychology that when faced with this almost unbear-able dilemma, he chose to cling to the hope that he could, after all, rely on Werner Best, whom he knew as a reasonable man. If Best could be

---

*In the Danish Lutheran state church all bishops are equals. There are no archbishops.

persuaded that it was better for all parties that the Danish authorities themselves intern the Jews, it would be a way out that could avert the impending disaster. It was all about gaining time: Bureaucratize the matter. Make it the subject of negotiation, wrangling, and mutual promises. Give concessions where necessary to avoid the worst: deportation. Seen through Svenningsen's eyes, there was no way around it: The permanent secretaries had to take the heavy responsibility. And they had to rely on Werner Best.

This mind-set was endorsed by an increasing number of state secretaries. Even Jespersen swung over, with the essential caveat that he did not think there could be any possibility that Danish authorities themselves would be responsible for the internment: "You could probably defend agreeing to receive Jews arrested by the Germans in Danish internment camps, as this would be better for the Jews than to sit in German camps, but in my view you could not in any form actively contribute to getting Jews gathered in internment camps."

Jespersen had a strong feeling that the permanent secretaries were out on a limb with a decision that went far beyond their competence, and he appealed for consultation with politicians from the newly outgoing government to share responsibility for this most unusual step: "I considered the present question to be an extremely important issue and a matter outside the administrative tasks that were assigned to the state secretaries. I necessarily felt it appropriate that the issue be presented to representatives of the parliament—if one could not connect with more, at least Minister Buhl as chairman of the Committee of Cooperation."

Larsen replied that the Danish plan was hardly feasible if the Danish authorities did not also engage in the internment: "The greatest asset in the Danish counterproposal lay in the fact that from the German side, it could and of course would be used as propaganda. We had to provide something in return for the rescue operation, and this might be that we provided for the Jews ourselves, although formally it would be done in collaboration with the Jews themselves. You had to ask for a guarantee from the German side that they didn't subsequently do what we by our actions had just intended to avoid."

Larsen was obviously aware of the danger: that the Danish authorities interned the Jews and the Germans then, despite all their promises, deported them. It had to be avoided at all costs—but the only guarantee was ultimately a promise from the occupying power—from Werner Best. The discussion continued, but it was clear that the majority were in favor of internment. If it concerned the secretaries' self-interest they had to refuse, but now the central message was that it had to be done for the Jews.

At this point Einar Cohn made his views clear. He had already spoken out in support of any steps that could mitigate deportation, and now he declared "that it would not cause any misunderstanding if the Danish authorities helped to capture the Jews, as the intention was very clear." This would be "far preferable," and "people would not misunderstand it."

The prime minister's permanent secretary, Andreas Møller, stated that the permanent secretaries could not escape responsibility by turning to the politicians. They had to carry it out themselves. The result of the discussion was that Svenningsen and Larsen were mandated to go to Dagmarhus as soon as possible and seek an audience with Dr. Best to demand assurances and a more solid basis for any Danish decision to offer to intern the Jews.

Best had already been visited at Dagmarhus by the director of the Danish Red Cross, Helmer Rosting, who came on his own initiative. He, too, had heard the rumors, but for the distinctly German-friendly Rosting, the situation opened new opportunities, which he presented to Best. Rosting wanted to use the internment of the Jews as an opportunity to release those Danish officers and soldiers who since August 29 had been detained in their barracks as protohostages. The release might mitigate public reaction to the internment of the Jews. Best jumped at the suggestion and even developed further an idea to use the Jews as hostages in the fight against sabotage, whereby fifty to one hundred Jews would be sent to a concentration camp for each act of sabotage. He immediately sent the proposal to Berlin, but it was rejected by Ribbentrop, who did not want the action against the Jews to be protracted but implemented once and for all.

That afternoon Best sent another brief telegram to Berlin. He accepted an invitation to come to a meeting in Posen (now Poznan), Poland, to meet with SS Reichsführer Himmler on October 4, together with other senior members of the SS, and asked for official permission to travel there for the occasion although the action against the Jews was imminent. To be present in Posen was important for Best not least because it would provide him with the opportunity to discuss directly with Himmler the issue of the German police in Denmark, which was crucial to Best's own position. Whatever his motives, it was an essential meeting Best now signed up for.[11]

The two leading permanent secretaries, Nils Svenningsen and Eivind Larsen, were received by Werner Best on Wednesday afternoon at 5:30 p.m. According to his own records, Svenningsen began by underlining that he normally would not heed hearsay: "But the rumors had now assumed such a form, and appeared with such persistence and in such detail, that we felt compelled to consult with Dr. Best. If this issue were really to be raised and implemented as reported, it would have an incalculable impact in this country. The anticipation was currently immense, and conditions would deteriorate if the action was carried out. This question was of enormous importance to the general population, to the official stance, and to the permanent secretaries."

Svenningsen spoke in no uncertain terms, but if he had hoped that Best would change course at the last minute, he was disappointed: "Dr. Best answered evasively, asking a variety of questions such as: 'What then do these rumors say?' 'What is it all about?' 'Where do they come from?'"[12]

Despite Svenningsen's confidence in Best, it was obvious that the German was avoiding the issue and giving no hint of assurance that the action would not take place. Thus the plenipotentiary of the Reich in fact confirmed the permanent secretaries' worst fears. The conversation ended with Best promising to telegraph Berlin to ask "whether he was authorized by the Foreign Ministry to deny the mentioned rumors." The maneuver was slick because it both achieved a delay and instilled in Svenningsen yet another false hope—and perhaps most important, it helped to reinforce the impression that the order came from Berlin while Best himself was floating in the dark and—apparently—working to prevent its implementation. And Svenningsen took the bait. He had already told his colleagues that afternoon that the action "was due to a higher order from Germany," thwarted by Best, and when, the next day, he summoned the permanent secretaries again, he said that the conversation with Best had left the impression "that the issue was acute but not definitively settled," and that "there was an attempt to stave off the action." It was Wednesday evening, two days before the planned attempt to arrest and deport the Danish Jews to Nazi concentration camps.

·   ·   ·

That same day a discreet meeting was held by a group of prominent politicians from the parties supporting the policy of cooperation. Since August 29 the country had been without functioning constitutional bodies, and the politicians maintained that they were unable and unwilling to assume responsibility, either formally or informally, as long as the state of emergency was maintained. The leading elected politician, former prime minister Buhl of the Social Democratic Party, summoned senior members from the other democratic parties to deeply confidential discussions, partly to ensure the continued support of the permanent secretaries and the entire administration, and partly to monitor and prevent any move that could be the germ of something the Germans could present as an interim Danish government under their control. Policy was discussed at "Buhl's group" at a time when the politicians agreed that it was crucial to have no policy at all.

The Buhl group had hardly been established on a regular basis when it gathered that Wednesday at 1:30 p.m. The politicians spoke in support of the permanent secretaries as long as they "acted just as before, without German control." This meant that they were not supposed to turn into some sort of de facto government under German auspices. Best had given his support to their functioning on an independent basis, but he again kept Berlin in reserve with the comment to Buhl that his colleagues there would perceive the Danish refusal to form a proper government "as a sign of defiance and resentment." At their meeting the politicians also long debated whether the Folketing should open on October 5 as prescribed in the constitution. In the end the majority opposed that, but some argued in favor, and the discussion seems to have been quite heated.

Buhl also told his colleagues that "one credible source had informed him that an action against the Jews would be conducted any day now." It concerned six thousand Jews, and eighteen hundred Gestapo men would arrive in the city to do the job. The scribbled notes by a participant in the meeting are almost illegible, but it seems as though Buhl also passed along the reflection of Best's resistance and of the pressure from Berlin. However, there is nothing in the notes to suggest that at the time Buhl or the other politicians were aware of the permanent secretaries' discussions regarding a possible Danish internment of the Jews.[13]

Vilhelm Buhl was, after Thorvald Stauning's death in May 1942, the most prominent Social Democratic politician, even though the much younger Hans Hedtoft was chosen as the party's new chairman. Hedtoft, however, with his pronounced anti-Nazism, was unacceptable to the Germans, and it was therefore the former finance minister, Buhl, who became prime minister. Buhl was convinced of the cooperation policy's necessity, but he was painfully aware of the limits that had to be adhered to. Within the government he usually opposed Foreign Minister Scavenius's quest for more active cooperation with the Germans.

During Buhl's six months—May to November 1942—as prime minister, the situation deteriorated almost by the day, not least because of increasing sabotage that caused the Germans to threaten to take over law enforcement. Buhl saw no other way to avoid this than stepping up the Danish effort against sabotage. In this context, on September 2 he gave a radio address that became notorious for his urgent warning about the devastating consequences of sabotage, which he labeled to be against "the fatherland's interests." What seemed most offensive was Buhl's request that the public help by turning suspected saboteurs in to the police.

For Buhl and like-minded politicians, armed civilians conducting their own policy—namely, the armed resistance—constituted a danger to the rule of law and thus to upholding democracy. Even worse was the prospect of direct German law enforcement, provoked by the resistance. Therefore, to him it was imperative that the Danish authorities retain full executive powers, including the police, and when the German ultimatum issued on August 29, 1943, compromised this principle, it was Buhl who formulated the clear Danish rejection, just as it was he who kept Scavenius and the other politicians firmly on track in opposing any attempt to form a new Danish government. At the same time Buhl, like other leading politicians, deeply distrusted the Freedom Council, which he regarded as a threat to parliamentary democracy—the crucial frontier that had to be defended at all costs.

Despite the skepticism of the Freedom Council, on May 5, 1945, Buhl was appointed prime minister of the liberation government, formed with the equal participation of former politicians and resistance fighters, and backed by the Allies. Arbejdermuseet

International Interests

On Wednesday, the Swedish minister to Copenhagen, Gustav Dardel, sent a telegram containing the main elements of Duckwitz's warning to Stockholm. Shortly thereafter the minister personally summoned C. B. Henriques to the Swedish legation, partly to ensure that the warning had reached him, partly to announce that "Sweden is open. Many have already fled to Sweden. Sweden is open to them all." Dardel offered to make a boat available for Henriques himself, but the leader of the Jewish community refused. He still had a lot to do, including spreading the message that Sweden would open its coast to the Danish Jews. Dardel hardly had a mass flight in mind, however, which was entirely outside the scope of current imagination. Yet the Swedish gesture was important because it encouraged the Jewish representatives to spread the word that anyone taking resolute action had a chance to escape the fate that was intended for them.

In Stockholm the telegram presented the government with the dilemma of what Sweden could and should do. It was obvious that they should raise the issue in Berlin through a diplomatic démarche, and this had already been prepared. Besides the urgent protest, the planned démarche contained a proposal that Sweden would undertake to intern all Danish Jews—in Sweden. But as the relationship between Sweden and Germany had deteriorated rapidly over recent months, and Swedish words had lost weight in Berlin, the Swedish minister there, Arvid Richert, warned that a Swedish intervention would not lead to anything good, precisely because the Germans already perceived Swedish public opinion and press as being so hostile it hardly could get worse.

Richert discussed the issue with his Danish colleague in Berlin, Otto Carl Mohr, who was slightly out of the loop in Danish-German relations, which were being handled mainly in Copenhagen directly by Werner Best and his Danish counterparts. Thus Mohr misunderstood the whole situation, and he saw the rumors of the pending action as part of the Nazi effort to force a new, pro-German government upon Denmark. To Mohr the lifting of martial law was the main concern, and he was afraid that a Swedish démarche in regard to the Jews would only serve to complicate matters and further irritate the Germans. Therefore Mohr supported Richert in his rejection of the démarche. The strong reservations on the part of the ministers in Berlin made an impression back in Stockholm, and the planned démarche was shelved for the time being.[14]

Rumors of the impending raid against the Danish Jews also reached the United States. On the same day the permanent secretaries met in Copenhagen to discuss a possible Danish action, James Waterman Wise, on behalf of the World Jewish Congress in Washington, sought out the independent Danish envoy there, Henrik Kauffmann. They had first made contact to discuss how to help the Danish Jews as early as September 9. Kauffmann now told Wise that he had decided to provide financial support to all political refugees from Denmark who arrived in Sweden, and who did not have the means to get by. He also made it clear that he would readily consider all Danish Jews who fled to Sweden to be political refugees—and thus eligible for help. On the same day Henrik Kauffmann also informed the U.S. secretary of state that he would commit himself to cover all costs that any government incurred as part of their efforts to rescue Danish Jews and other victims of Nazi persecution.

In a conversation with the Swedish minister in Washington, Kauffmann proposed that Sweden present a special offer to Berlin in regard to detention of the Danish Jews in Sweden—very much in line with the démarche the Swedish government already was about to undertake there. Kauffmann also stated that he was willing to bear all costs Sweden would incur if this plan was to unfold—an offer similar to a pledge made by the Norwegian government in exile to cover costs on behalf of Norwegians fleeing into Sweden, including Norwegian Jews.

Kauffmann could make such financial guarantees because, with formal recognition by President Roosevelt, he had been provided with full power over frozen Danish government assets in the United States and thus was single-handedly able to dispose of significant resources. Kauffmann sought to use this leverage to demonstrate to the free world that, unlike the authorities in Copenhagen, cooperating with the occupying power, he was free and thus the true representative of "free Denmark." Contrary to his colleagues in Copenhagen—and the Danish minister in London—Henrik Kauffmann fully realized that the war was permanently changing the American role. Henceforth the balance of power among the old nations of Europe would be impacted by a newly emerging player: the United States. No matter the outcome of the war and the arrangements in postwar Europe, the United States had come to stay. Therefore, in Kauffmann's eyes, it was strongly in Denmark's interest to balance its traditional ties with Berlin—and with London—with an equally strong transatlantic relationship. Here the perception of Denmark among the American public was of crucial importance. The fact that Denmark had not put up a proper fight against the German invasion on April 9, 1940, was no help in this regard. Nor was the seemingly smooth cooperation between the Danish government and German authorities in the occupied country. Kauffmann's Greenland treaty with President Roosevelt in April 1941 had helped a lot, as had the fact that Danish sailors continued to man the Danish merchant fleet, volunteering to sail for the Allies. More than six thousand Danish seamen contributed to maintaining the vital transportation links in Allied convoys—and close to one thousand never returned. Now a determined effort to save the Danish Jews would be another important token that despite the ongoing policy of cooperation, Denmark was not on the side of Nazi Germany but very much aspired to become once again part of the free world.

Things, however, did not work out the way Kauffmann planned. Neutral Sweden also had considerable political interests in helping the Danish Jews—and the Swedes rejected Kauffmann's offer courteously but adamantly. Sweden needed all the goodwill its efforts for the Danish Jews could generate. In addition the Social Democratic government in Stockholm was concerned with cooperating directly with the leading Danish Social Democratic politicians. They shared with their Danish comrades a fundamental skepticism in regard to militant resistance groups, in particular those with Communist leanings. The advance of the Red Army was encouraging to the extent that it broke the neck of Nazi Germany. But it was frightening for the Nordic democracies to the extent that it could connect to Communists as part of an armed resistance within occupied Denmark and Norway. The Social Democrats together with other democratic political parties wanted to return to parliamentary democracy and not to a sort of Communist-backed "people's democracy." This implied that while the Swedish government was eager to help, Prime Minister Albin wanted to direct the help to the victims—or if possible to channel it through his party colleagues in occupied Denmark. The leading Social Democrats fundamentally suspected that a strong Communist armed resistance might not be on the side of restoring parliamentary democracy at the end of the war.[15]

London felt roughly the same way, even if there the crucial alliance with the Soviet Union inspired more subtle tactics in regard to the armed resistance in Denmark. Undeniably, Communist groupings continued to play a crucial role in the armed resistance encouraged by London. At the same time even the Special Operations Executive, the British World War II body in charge of sabotage in occupied Europe, wanted "the old politicians" to dominate the endgame in Denmark in order to curb Communist infiltration in the occupied country.

Bad Omens

Permanent Secretary Einar Cohn had a nephew, a thirty-seven-year-old lawyer, Bernhard Cohn, who also kept a diary during the critical days from September 29 to October 5. A few hours before the department secretaries' Wednesday meeting the nephew visited his uncle, to see if he had any updates about the swirling rumors: "But Einar was Einar. He didn't know a damned thing. . . . He was going to a meeting in the afternoon and promised to call me around 4 p.m. Of course he didn't call. I then turned to make a new call and was referred to a secretary, who informed me that he had greetings from Einar who said that he had nothing he could convey. So I was aware that it was for real. . . . I rushed home to find it in wild disarray. . . . 7:15 by car to the Mission Hotel in Colbjørnsensgade, where we went to bed very early.—I promised Ella that if something happened—the Germans would never get me alive. I do not think she understood what I meant. At night, the air-raid sirens, which didn't add to the enjoyment."[16]

Poul Hannover also describes extensively in his diary for Wednesday, September 29, the many worries and the trial and error that filled the day, as he desperately tried to find a way to get to Sweden with his family. His diary also touches on a theme that was an inevitable part of the refugees' concerns: money. It was clear that illegal transport to Sweden would cost money, and that there could be a need for a large amount of cash for the whole family to get out. How much was not known. But getting hold of cash was urgent.

For the wealthy another consideration was how best to cope with companies, investments, and personal assets. How could one protect, in haste, the family's valuables? How much should be cashed in, and how much was transferable? To whom? And who should be authorized as caretaker during an absence of unknown length? How could one fulfill obligations and personal commitments in order not to default on future demands? The future was suddenly completely unpredictable, and it was vital to ensure the necessary liquidity—without resorting to a fire sale of anything that was easily marketable. Poul Hannover articulates these concerns, which in turn reflect the fact that the refugees remained responsible citizens: "Again off to the office—I deposited money to pay my bills—even to pay my taxes—agreed to meet Erik Birger [a friend] again on Østerbrogade, where he came by car with his brother, sister, and his mother. Again an address—that *maybe* could be used—so I went to the place Ludvig's contact had recommended. It was more than amazing. The lady I spoke with was afraid that all places were already taken on the first night—and the price, which had previously been 500 kroner per person, had risen today to 3,000 kroner. I thanked her but dared not accept. So I went home."

This first offer for the crossing, in total twelve thousand kroner for the four members of the family, was no small sum. The monthly salary of a skilled worker was approximately four hundred kroner, and nearly half of the Danish Jews had income levels corresponding to those of the working class. A new fishing boat cost between fifteen and thirty thousand kroner. The crossing was considered extremely risky, even for helpers, but a single trip could earn a new boat in hand, and still more.

Poul Hannover continues: "When I came home, Inger had sent the silverware away. We had already brought some clothes to our friends—but only very little. . . . We packed up cigars and cigarettes, so they could be removed. We were having roast goose—I could barely eat anything—I had literally not slept for several nights, and the day had been horrible. Suddenly Gunnar came with his friend Erik Nyegaard—he had stayed with him the last nights. Since we had parted, Gunnar had called the agreed phone number in Gentofte every quarter hour . . . and had finally gotten through. He had rushed over there with Erik Nyegaard and was told that it was likely to be possible—we were to leave the next day for Nykøbing Falster on the express train."

It may seem surprising that the family decides to head for Falster, a southern island close to the German coast, and anything but the shortest route to Sweden. But this was, for the first time, a concrete possibility that seemed worth trusting. And what else could they do? The hours were passing, and they could not stay much longer. If there was a prospect of leaving by way of Nykøbing Falster, that was where they would go. They had to take the chance: "Erik went in to buy tickets—I went down and picked a bottle of our best wine—we had to have something to strengthen our spirits. . . . Erik came again. He had not been able to get us all tickets on the express, and had even been told that he should provide names and addresses to get the tickets. So he had taken tickets for the slow train. That suited me better—I thought we were less exposed. For safety's sake, he had even bought return tickets—though he had taken an express ticket for himself.

"We had been told that the trip cost 1,500 kroner per person. Gunnar had about this amount—I did not—During the day I had deposited no less than 27,000 kroner—with different people, so now there was not much left. I wrote Erik a check for 6,000 kroner—which fortunately was still available . . . and we agreed that he would cash it and come down and meet us in Nykøbing."

Apparently Poul Hanover had mobilized his available funds, which together amounted to just about 33,000 kroner. He had entrusted 27,000 to various contacts and business associates—probably to spread the risk. When he had to raise 6,000 kroner to pay for the crossing, he pulled out the last free capital he owned. Erik Nyegaard was mandated to collect this sum in Copenhagen the following day and follow the family to Nykøbing Falster. Gunnar Marcus had apparently already raised an equivalent sum in cash, so the two families together had at least 12,000 kroner. The question was whether it would be enough. Hannover continues his description of the day: "The Swedish professor—our old family doctor's son, called to invite us to stay at his hospital, our friend Esther, who wanted to put her house outside Tisvilde at our disposal. Herbert Jerichow had also been to our house to offer advice. We gave the maids a last message, said good-bye to our faithful Pless [their maid], and went to stay with our friends."

Hannover's son, Allan, also had an eventful day, but it began normally with his father's and grandfather's birthdays and a regular school day. When he came home from school he was told that they would have to travel that night, and that he should get ready. He gathered the necessary items and packed up his electric train and hid it away. He notes that his father did not come home for dinner, but that the guests stayed and ate with the family. Poul Hannover came home during the meal, as his son recounts, but he did not know what they should do. Allan learns about the plan to travel via Nykøbing Falster, and gives his account of how the family gathered their luggage and some belongings after dinner and carried them, by ladders in the garden, over to a neighbor who lived a few houses away in Søholm Park.

Poul Hannover ends his diary from the long day: "We put the kids to bed—just sat and tried to collect our thoughts—it was not easy. Around

Politikens *crime reporter Vilhelm Bergstrøm, who had been at the paper since 1928, was socially conservative, with a sharp eye for the common man's condition and the vanity of rulers. He had tried his luck as a novelist in the 1920s, but his strength lay in reportage, and at the outbreak of war in 1939 he set out to keep a comprehensive diary documenting events big and small. The idea was, as he himself put it, "to preserve every day in a jar," and his record from occupied Copenhagen includes more than four thousand pages supplemented by a gigantic amount of documentary material. The diaries reflect the time without any gloss, and also provide a unique insight into prevailing views—including prejudices about Jews thriving within parts of the Danish population.*

Following the German invasion on April 9, 1940, Danish telephone and telegraph connections with the outside world were cut. The Germans demanded that the Danish media not be allowed to publish or broadcast information that could harm German military interests. Censorship was also introduced to prevent anti-German propaganda. The Foreign Ministry established the necessary force to control the media, building on experiences from the 1930s when the government had systematically applied pressure to avoid "provocations" of Hitler's Germany, which had become ever more sensitive to criticism and satire.

Censorship could take several forms, from banning specific articles to injunctions against others. From time to time the Germans demanded that a specific journalist or editor be removed from his or her respective columns.

Although censorship and self-censorship were widespread, in practice the press had a fair amount of room to maneuver. Editors quickly learned to send clear signals marking which articles were German plants, and to disseminate views and information in forms overlooked by the censor. Still, the legal press—unlike the underground one—assumed that the basic premise of the cooperation policy was preferable to direct Nazi rule.

Mediemuseet, Odense

half past nine an air-raid siren went off—I went with Ole [a neighbor]. He gave me a strong sleeping pill—I could use a little sleep. I fell asleep and slept for half an hour—the rest of the night I lay awake."

Not far away Kis Marcus also heard the air-raid siren that evening:

Gunnar finally came back. He had met the police officer Carl Hol-bøll with Poul and he had given them the address of a man who got people to Sweden from Nykøbing. Gunnar and Erik then went to the station and bought 8 return tickets to Nykøbing on the slow train for the next morning. There was only one ticket left for the fast train and you had to give your name. Erik took this ticket, as it had been agreed that he should come down to us with more money as we did not have enough for the boat. Gunnar several times called the number he had been given for the man with the boat. His name was Talleruphuus. Finally there was a connection, and he and Erik set off. At 6:30 p.m. we all ate, Johanne also had dinner with Elsa. Erik came back at 8, as he had other things to do.—Afterwards I put the kids to bed, and we sat for a while and talked with Erik's neighbor, Mr. Busch-Petersen, who happened to be going hunting the next day with his brother on Falster. He was taking the same train as Erik and offered his help if it became necessary.—Then we went to bed.

A chance encounter with a neighbor, but one that would prove to be more important than Kis Marcus could imagine. In a macabre coincidence the annual hunting season traditionally opened on October 1. In many families it was customary to gather on the farms that day to eat a festive meal. In many places a game of cards in the evening, accompanied by an aquavit or two, was also part of the order of the day. That was also the case at the Busch-Petersens', and Kis Marcus would soon find out that the family farm was not, as she assumed, located on Falster, but on the nearby island of Lolland.

But that evening Kis Marcus didn't give much thought to all this. She finishes the day's entries: "We took something to sleep, like the previous nights, and slept fairly well. I was the only one who heard the air-raid warning during the night. We had previously heard that they had an air-raid warning in Oslo when they rounded up the Jews, so I did not say anything about the alarm to Gunnar."

CHAPTER 5

THURSDAY, SEPTEMBER 30

THE ESCAPE

The First Leg of the Journey

Poul Hannover also noticed the air-raid alarm—but did not notice when it stopped: "Did not know until the next morning that it had been called off—and lay there imagining all sorts of horrors that the air alarm had only been a pretext to begin the attack against us. At 6 a.m. I got up—I woke Ole—and he got up too. We gathered at Mads's [their housekeeper]—she gave us breakfast with real tea and eggs. Then our maids came in with packed lunches—and we left with them, half crying—off by tram—divided between the main and second compartment—accompanied by Ole, Grethe, and Mads. They even bought tickets to Valby and followed us. In the distance we saw Kis and Gunnar with their family on the platform—but we traveled separately until Næstved. So we got in—the train left—and we were on our way. We said good-bye to our friends in Valby—they were absolutely magnificent. They promised to go home immediately and to empty out as much as possible from our house—I think they succeeded."

Kis Marcus also gives her account of the trip's first step:

After a lovely breakfast of bacon and eggs we said good-bye to our good friends and rode the tram from Charlottenlund to the main station. Poul and Inger were on the platform with Allan and Mette. . . . We kept clear of each other on the train as well, until Poul and Inger's compartment was empty of other travelers. Then we moved in there and enjoyed having someone to discuss the situation with, while the children were playing nicely with Mette and Allan.—We ate lunch, which the others had brought for all of us. At around 11 a.m. we were in Nykøbing. Talleruphuus was not at the station, as agreed, but in a restaurant, Gunnar recognized him from a photograph.

It turned out that he did not know we were coming, and the boat, which we almost had the impression was in "regular service" to Sweden, had not yet been over at all, and he did not know yet if he could arrange anything at all. It was a disappointment, but we still hoped that something would turn up. We went with all the luggage (we had 3 small bags and Inger's family had their own—in addition we had our traveling blanket) to a hotel: Stad Nykøbing, where we had coffee. Meanwhile Erik had come to join Talleruphuus, who was going to Gedser to talk to a fisherman who might sail for us.

When we had drunk our coffee we dragged our luggage back to the station where we put it in the cloakroom. Then we all went for a walk. Later the men went back to the station to be in contact with Talleruphuus. Inger, the children, and I waited in the town square, where we were cold and tired and it felt like a long time. Poul and Gunnar finally came, and we ate dinner at the Industry Café.

Poul Hannover's diary describes the same sequence of events through his own eyes:

I think it was in Næstved that the others joined us. I hardly need to say that it was all a big question mark—we knew nothing. We ate our packed lunch—or at least part of it, but we didn't have much appetite. We came to Nykøbing. The idea was that a man whose picture Gunnar had seen would meet us by the express train. We saw a few other refugees—a lawyer and a judge. Where they went, I do not know—we couldn't even give any information ourselves—they probably couldn't either.

Gunnar found Talleruphuus. Frankly, he didn't know much. He could only say that the original plan had failed—but that he would take the express south. It did not sound good. He went on the same train that Erik Nyegaard came on. We went to the hotel he had indicated—it was a good distance from the station—I was not happy to lug our baggage over there. We drank some coffee—Erik, who hadn't any food, ordered a chop. The host sat a little away from us—and a German soldier came down and talked with him—apparently he lived there in Stad Nykøbing—and spoke Danish. I was aware that we had to get away. When we had eaten, we dragged the luggage back and put it in the cloakroom at the railway station—and then went for a walk. There was a cold wind—and the children couldn't help being tired. There was little hope that Talleruphuus would come back on the next express—it was over half an hour late—but he was on the train. Unfortunately things had not been arranged—but perhaps there was hope somewhere else. It was 21 kilometers away. We began to feel seriously troubled. Erik offered to go with him—in a car. We agreed, and the rest of us went down to the Industry Café and ate.

The situation was already untenable. Two families traveling to Nykøbing with their essential belongings and a large amount of cash, only to find out that their contact, Talleruphuus, who is completely unfamiliar to them, doesn't have a clue and barely knows where to look for one. The day passes, the children are restless and tired, and confusion spreads. They do not dare stay at the hotel. What to do?

Poul Hannover continues: "Now I must interject something different: While Kis and Gunnar lived with us—or rather with Erik—they had talked to his neighbor—coincidentally he went down to see his brother and go hunting on the same day we left home. The brother owned some property at Lolland. Erik and his neighbor had been on the same train to Nykøbing—and Erik had explored with him the possibility of us hiding at his brother's farm if we did not succeed in getting over at once. The neighbor promised to find out, if we called. We were told that taxi cars were not allowed to run after 8 p.m. It all started to pinch—my head was bursting with speculation. I must say that the children were magnificent. I had said to Allan not to ask questions that day—it was hard, but he managed."

One can immediately understand both of their positions. The father, who is still in the dark and utterly unfamiliar with the situation, has to make fateful decisions on behalf of the family. He cannot stand the questions. He does not know the answers himself. The adolescent boy who tries to follow as best as he can, who is bursting with questions, who understands that things are all wrong but only halfway why. Who would like to share responsibility with his beleaguered parents but gets the message: Do not ask questions. Not today. Keep your spirits up, but do not ask questions. He accepts that this is his contribution, and he

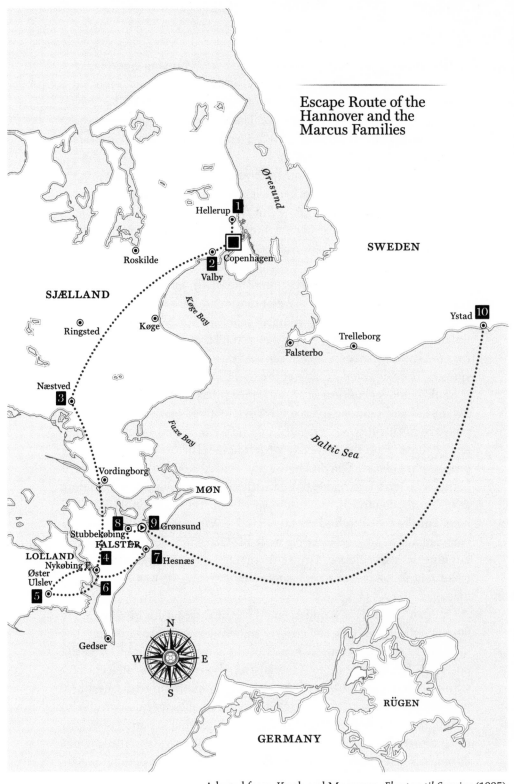

Escape Route of the
Hannover and the
Marcus Families

 Øresund

Hellerup 1

SWEDEN

Roskilde

Copenhagen

2

Valby

SJÆLLAND

Ringsted

Køge

Køge Bay

Ystad 10

Trelleborg

Falsterbo

Næsted

3

Baltic Sea

Faxe Bay

Vordingborg

MØN

8 9 Grønsund

Stubbekøbing

FALSTER

7 Hesnæs

LOLLAND

Nykøbing F.

Øster
Ulslev

4

5

6

Gedser

N

W   E

S

RÜGEN

GERMANY

Adapted from: Kreth and Mogensen, *Flugten til Sverige* (1995).

restrains himself, while the secure world he knows collapses in front of his eyes—with no questions asked.

His father continues his account: "I realized that we couldn't keep the kids calm. I called our representative in Nykøbing. I didn't dare say my name—and as he knew nothing about the whole thing, it was hard to persuade him to come down to us. In the meantime I called Herbert Jerichow to see if there was anything new. He was somewhat surprised to hear where we were—I had to give a false name, when you said who was calling—he asked me to call again the next day, as he had not yet acquired space for us. Then Gunnar rang up Erik's neighbor, Busch-Petersen—who said we were welcome even if they did not have much space. We would have to manage. Then my representative came—he was thunderstruck to see us. I asked him if he could possibly make room—no beds, just room for us."

The Titan Machine Factory's chief executive stands on the street in Nykøbing with his family and, under a false name, gets his representative to come only to ask the astonished man for shelter. Initially the representative took Kis Marcus and the kids home so they could rest. But the situation is still in flux, as evidenced by Poul Hannover's entries: "Erik came back again. Nothing new—he doubted that it was possible to get us over—but now Talleruphuus would go to Gedser again, and Erik suggested that I go along to talk to the man with the boat, so I could see with my own eyes if I believed in it or not. Inger opposed it, utterly determined. Erik was willing to go alone with Talleruphuus. I called our representative to take the kids down to the station where the clothes were—and we all met there, got a big car and drove around 30 km out in the country."

Kis Marcus describes parting from the representative: "We were urgently asked to go to the station again, kids with pockets full of pears and apples.—From the station we went on in a hurry with the car out to Busch-Petersen's brother's farm, as they could only drive up to a certain time in the evening. The farm was about 30 km outside the city. While this was going on, Erik was in Gedser with Talleruphuus, who earlier in the day had made various unsuccessful attempts to get us a boat."

It's a long drive from Nykøbing Falster to Busch-Petersen's farm just outside Øster Ulslev on Lolland. The farm by the pond is perhaps a good hiding place—but far from the most obvious starting point for embarkation. The families could hide there, though they could not escape from there. Poul soon realizes this: "We came to nice and good people—but they were certainly ignorant of everything that was going on. There was not too much space, but Busch-Petersen immediately gave up his room—and they had another. In one room there were two beds and a cot. Palle got the cot, Allan one bed, and Mette and Dorte lay at opposite ends of the second—using the same quilt. For us it was even worse—there were two beds—in one lay Kis and Gunnar at each end—in the second Inger and I in the same way. We quickly got the kids to bed, and then just sat and talked."

It was becoming clear to this little traveling group that the step from legitimate travel to the illegal crossing was not as easy as they had hoped. They had not yet taken part in any illegal activity at all, and no special measures had been announced, let alone taken, in relation to the Jews. But the feeling of insecurity and vulnerability had taken hold, and the presence of an observant German soldier was now more than enough to drive the family to flee. Something that just the day before would have been quite obvious, such as calling Titan's representative in Falster, was suddenly shrouded in secrecy and difficulty. Everything seemed uncertain and threatening. When it came to the actual situation, the fear of eavesdropping and "disclosure" might have been exaggerated—but who dared to run even a small risk that could cost the family's life? And when it came to the next step, they were on shaky ground having to decide on a crossing that still seemed unlikely. Whom could they trust? What was possible? What would it cost?

"The good thing was that we were probably fairly well hidden—but we quickly realized that we could not stay there for a long time—and then there was the problem that the connection back to Falster went over a bridge—and the next connection from Falster toward Copenhagen over yet another. All this was not reassuring. I pondered and pondered what to do the next day—but I was determined that we must at least cross the first of the bridges. I also saw with some horror that the distance to Sweden from down there was great—you could hardly expect less than 6–8 hours—and the wind was not calm."

Poul Hannover's diary begins to reflect the thought that the situation might not find an immediate solution. Their next moves had to allow for flexibility if it turned out to be impossible to cross the water. Strategic considerations began to emerge. The boundary between law-abiding citizen and persecuted refugee loomed ever closer: "It was probably half past eight p.m. when a car came—it was Erik who despite the curfew had gotten his driver to drive him out there. He had been in Gedser and talked to the man—and he could at least say that he trusted him. He had explained to him that this was a life-or-death situation for us—that he could not play with our lives—and the man had said that his boat had been out of order—but he expected to be able to sail either Friday or Saturday. That relieved us, and we went to bed. Of course we slept terribly, or not at all. Mette was crying because she was cold, so we had to swap quilts—and since we could not use our blanket to black out the windows—they didn't have blackout-curtains—we didn't dare turn on lights, otherwise we would have found out that if we took off the duvet cover the quilt became somewhat bigger."

Kis Marcus's version reflects the uncertainty spreading in the precarious circumstances:

At the Busch-Petersens' we were welcome, and we all had places to sleep. All the kids in one room with Dorte and Mette in the same bed. In another room we 4 adults slept, also 2 in each bed, while Mr. Busch-Petersen gave up the room and slept downstairs.

At approximately 8:30 p.m. Erik came by car. He persuaded the driver to drive out there despite the driving ban after 8 p.m. He believed the fisherman in Gedser could be trusted. His boat had been out of order, but he expected to be able to sail on Friday or Saturday. We discussed a lot about what we should do next day. Inger preferred to stay in Denmark, possibly at Herbert Jerichow's house on Møn.—The rest of us wanted to go to Sweden. One thing we agreed: We could not stay where we were, because if the Germans began their raids, we would not be able to get over the bridges back to Sjælland. There was also talk about going down to Poul's representative's house, but we didn't dare, since a Nazi lived nearby. We would only be here 1 to 2 days until the boat came. In any case we had to wait to make any decision until the next day, when we would get a telephone message around noon confirming whether the boat could go that day.

From Irony to Indignation

The many Jewish families who had been set in motion were visible especially around Copenhagen and along the coastline stretching north along the Øresund. It was noticed that people of Jewish origin suddenly disappeared or did not show up at their jobs or at prearranged meetings. It didn't take a Sherlock Holmes to understand what was going on. At Rådhuspladsen, the Town Hall Square in central Copenhagen, Bergstrøm commented sarcastically: "It was reported from the court of Frederiksberg that a Jewish defense attorney was absent and a Jewish clerk as well. Herbert Steinthal [a German-born colleague affiliated with *Politiken* as a book reviewer since 1936], himself a Jew, heartlessly amused himself over all the Jews he had met the day before with bewildered expressions and a suitcase in hand. The Jews are on their way out to the countryside. . . . Mrs. Lassen entered. She spoke of a Jew who should have been assessing a doctoral thesis but had made himself invisible. An Aryan professor had replaced him on one day's notice. She was also aware that many Jews had disappeared from their homes these days."

Although rumors of the impending action were now on everyone's lips, nothing had happened yet. On the contrary, the authorities continued to deny categorically that anything was in the wind. There were therefore no special restrictions on travel or movement, and the many Jews who ventured forth traveled quite legally—but with nagging uncertainty about when the occupation forces would strike. This meant that they were already making an effort not to attract attention or seem obvious. This was hard, because often entire families traveled in groups with their jumble of possessions. Most were utterly unaccustomed to any illegality, and strangers to the idea of standing on the wrong side of the law. For the same reason the German security police did not intervene: Everyone insisted that everything was perfectly normal. And yet no one believed it.

A few days earlier these travelers had been ordinary citizens who were completely assimilated into society with their fellow citizens. As a group nothing special united them to or separated them from colleagues, friends, and neighbors. Now, suddenly, they were aware that they *were* something special. They were brought together into a common destiny with others who happened to be of Jewish origin, who saw their lives and future threatened—and who needed help from the surrounding community.

For those citizens who did not feel directly threatened, the development was equally incomprehensible. It is characteristic that Bergstrøm, who was hardly plagued by excessive sentimentality, still found it hard to believe that things really were that bad. Together with a colleague he still finds the commotion and panic slightly ridiculous—the point being that the person he's trading ironies with is himself a Jew, even one of German descent, who apparently fails to realize that the looming disaster could affect him personally. But the little exchange between Bergstrøm and Steinthal also reflects what made it so difficult to implement an effective action against the Danish Jews: Regardless of whether people were personally affected, the grim ideas driving the Nazi actions were completely foreign to them. It was a tremendous strength that these ironically inclined colleagues could meet at *Politiken* and find amusement in the fuss—together. This was not something that concerned one more than the other. It was something they shared. The distinction between "them" and "us" did not separate the two journalists, only one of whom was a Jew. Instead it separated the Nazis from the surrounding community. The gentlemen journalists traded ironies simply because they could not believe that something so insane could really be happening. But the distance from irony to indignation is only a short one.

We have no way of knowing whether the Busch-Petersen family at the farm in Øster Ulslev also tended toward irony. But we do know how they reacted when their telephone rang and the fate of unknown refugees was suddenly bound up with their own. We can only imagine the visiting brother from Charlottenlund explaining about his distant acquaintances now asking for refuge just as the annual hunting party was gathering at the farm. Apparently there was no hesitation, no reservation, and no conditions. They were welcome, all eight of them. Perhaps this seems obvious, given the fate of the European Jews. But the Busch-Petersens did not know what we know. On the contrary, they knew that so far no measures had been taken against Jews in Denmark, and no threats directed against them. The easy response would have been to defer the issue. It must also have occurred to the Busch-Petersens that if a German action against the Jews really did materialize, it would be most dangerous to be housing a large group of refugees. What to do with them? And for how long? Yet here, as in so many other cases throughout the country, the refugees were welcomed into private homes. There wasn't much room, but the farmer and his wife vacated their own bedroom to make room for the families.

Leni Yahil concludes after countless interviews, "Even where the request came from the Jews themselves, these were never refused. . . .

Institutions also opened their doors. For short stays schools were placed at the disposal of the refugees, but it was clearly impossible to keep many people in them for any length of time without attracting undesirable attention. Among other institutions which took in refugees were the hospitals."[1]

The crucial point is that the refugees could count on their countrymen and engage friends, colleagues, and neighbors, as a matter of course, in their efforts to find a way out. Not even necessarily those who were known to be involved in the armed resistance or those who were particularly vocal in their loathing of Nazism or the occupation forces. Rather, a wide array of ordinary citizens took their first step into defiance by helping fellow citizens. They did so because they perceived the impending action as an attempt to break the spine of the society they felt part of. Hence the action, even before it was launched, triggered the very reaction the Germans feared in advance: the transformation of the general—passive—public into a self-aware citizenry determined to stand up against injustice.

Of course there are examples of doors being kept shut. And of course cowardice, betrayal, and greed can be indentified in specific situations. But the Danish democracy had mobilized itself to protect the values on which it was based. With its decision to extend the final solution to Denmark, the Third Reich had aroused the strongest force in any country: the common popular will.

Admitted to Hospital

No one can say how many Danish Jews slept at home that Thursday night. We only know from numerous reports that the warnings spread in ever-larger circles and with increasing weight. Still, some refused to believe it—and others wouldn't try to escape, even if they did.

A small number, typically among the most recent arrivals, never got the message. But the vast majority heard, and generally they decided to make themselves invisible. It was not very difficult to leave home or to find somewhere to spend the first night or two. After all, no action had been directed against them yet. But from there the difficulties began. Where would they go next—and how? Who could they trust, and which way should they take? And what about family and relatives? Who was to take care of them and of what was left behind?

Some, including the young Hannover and Marcus families, chose to act early and decisively. For them the flight was already unfolding. Admittedly their rapid departure had brought them into a situation and a place that were far from optimal. But at least they were on their way and had gained the first hard-earned experience, even before the threat became reality. Others still hoped to wait it out. Among them was Adolph Meyer, the twin sisters' father, who had now overcome his doubts and acknowledged that an operation was under way, but had difficulty realizing how fundamentally this changed a position that, after a long life, he took for granted. Dr. Meyer had both a large family and many professional and personal acquaintances who cared deeply for his welfare. Meanwhile his adult children each took their own steps, independent of him. Their determination helped give him a feeling of greater security, and probably also encouraged him to stay put in order to be able to help if any situation arose where his children or grandchildren were in need.

It appears that Dr. Meyer felt relatively safe once admitted into the hospital—but also that he did not yet fully realize the radical nature of the threat. Clearly he assumed he was somewhat protected by his social status, still in a position to pull a few strings if necessary. Key members of society—including some who were prominent in the Jewish community—were accustomed to being able to negotiate tolerable terms with the occupying power. It was tempting to believe that in spite of everything reason would eventually prevail, and that ultimately the top representatives of the occupation forces could be trusted to prevent the worst. After all, they were men of some honor. Or at least so it still seemed to many leading Danes, including those of Jewish origin. They were yet to discover that contrary to all their previous assumptions, this was a fatal error.

In sharp contrast to his daughters, Dr. Meyer still lived in the relative security of the old world order, and as a patient he noted events that Thursday in his diary:

The next morning, blood was taken to determine blood urea, and my blood pressure (150/90). I had some fruit that I had received as gifts, grapes . . . and some large apples . . . brought to me a few days before. It was nice to be able to treat the nurse and the sisters. Dr. Keller came and said that he was going to go away for a few days, but that Dr. Freudenthal had been informed. During the night I had decided to contact my lawyer, Frans Bülow, and Keller promised

The illegal Danish cartoon from 1942, "The Cold Shoulder," illustrates how most Danes felt about—and acted toward—the German occupiers. With the choices Denmark made upon the German invasion on April 9, 1940, and the understandings between the occupying power and the Danish government that developed during the following months, the Danish community on the whole continued to function on its own terms. Both parties had a mutual interest in maintaining the fiction that Denmark was still a sovereign and neutral country. In the eyes of Hitler and his henchmen Denmark was a friendly country inhabited by Aryans. But this was not the perception of the majority of Danes, who had no friendly feelings toward the intruders. The prevailing attitude in Denmark was to sit it out, or, as Prime Minister Stauning put it, "to play for time and to avoid . . . major disasters."

Meanwhile workers in the cities experienced a sharp decline in real wages and social conditions, and some of the hard-won social gains achieved through the 1930s were rolled back. But the society held, and few opposed the policy pursued by the national coalition government. A wave of patriotism swept the nation. Countless citizens participated in popular rallies, joined in community sings, and wore a national emblem with the king's monogram. For them this was all part of a passive resistance, as demonstrated by the "cold shoulder" attitude by which most Danes sought to avoid any social contact with the Germans. But critics said that the Danes clenched their fists in their pockets, as the country increased economic cooperation with the Third Reich and put up little active, let alone armed, resistance to the occupation.

Ever so slowly, from 1942 resistance grew and began to bite in 1943. But this did not put an end to the cooperation, which actually expanded over the last years of the occupation, even as the government stepped down in August 1943.

After the action against the Jews in October 1943, sympathy for the resistance grew stronger, but probably most people at the same time maintained their support for cooperation, wanting both to uphold normality as much as possible and yet also to get rid of the occupants as soon as possible.

Museet for Dansk Bladtegning

DEN KOLDE SKULDER   Tegning af Østerberg.

to attend to this. My maids visited me in the morning, as well as Honoré, who brought confirmation from Dr. Hart that I could stay with him in his summerhouse in Ruds Vedby. Bülow came by in the afternoon, and I gave him full power of attorney over my property and belongings, we went through my papers, and he got the inventory and the little red notebook. . . . Honoré had received my 3 best paintings for storage, a canteen of silverware had gone to Miss Eriksen's aunt, a few paintings to Mrs. Poulsen on the 4th floor—I believe she eventually got 7 in total. My summer clothes were left with Miss Albrechtsen. Bülow got the inventory of all my furniture I had drawn up in the summer, and he got my savings-bank books and the lockbox with the key from the built-in cabinet, this latter on October first.—In the evening I was moved from the maternity ward to a room in another department, slept there.

A Danish Initiative? Second Attempt

At midday on Thursday representatives from all branches of commercial life in Denmark gathered one by one at the German headquarters at Dagmarhus. It was an impressive group, ranging from the Employers Association and the Federation of Trade Unions to the Confederation of Industries and the Agricultural Council to the Provincial Chamber of Commerce, the Shipowners Association, and the Merchants Guild—in short, everyone who had a say in Danish production and in the labor market. Each of them came with his own mandate and on his own initiative, and each made brief declarations stressing the adverse effects any action directed against "fellow citizens" would have on "peace and order," the sense of justice, and on productivity. The message could not have been stronger or more deeply anchored in the Danish economy. But it did little to help. Werner Best refused to receive the deputations and only advised Berlin of it a day later, when the action was already in motion.

Shortly after 3 p.m. the permanent secretaries resumed their discussion from the day before. But Einar Cohn did not show up. Like thousands of others, his daily duties had given way to the very pressing issues of escape and survival for himself and his family. At the meeting Nils Svenningsen and Eivind Larsen reported on their conversation with Best the night before, and the discussion within the group intensified as the impression was confirmed that an action was imminent. Several hesitated. Others argued for the urgent adoption of the proposal for an internment initiated by the Danes. Even so, opinions differed. Most important: Should Danish police engage in the arrest of innocent citizens—and even take the initiative to prevent the Germans from doing so? And should a final decision be subject to approval by former prime minister Buhl and other politicians?

According to the contemporary notes of several participants. the discussion was sharp but unfocused. Everyone realized that people's lives, and the personal legacy of the permanent secretaries, were at stake. And they were painfully aware that their decision could also have a far-reaching impact on the outside world's view of Denmark and the perception in the free world of its position under the German occupation. But this awareness did not necessarily produce a clear—let alone a common—conclusion. Which was worse? Risk initiating a Danish action that, if it went wrong, would help the Germans deport the Jews? Or sit idle in a worthless protest while a crime was committed against innocent citizens?

The sharpest opponent of the idea of detention was J. Wilcke, the permanent secretary in the Ministry of Agriculture. He had not participated in the discussion the day before and would not budge an inch from basic principles: "It will come back to Denmark in a bad way that we already agreed to intern the Communists, and it will be even worse if we also take the Jews. We must stick to the rule of law."

Svenningsen was not convinced. It wasn't a "question of infringement of a legal principle, but of a purely humanitarian initiative. If we interned the Jews, it would be by their own choice and only to help them. . . . It was not right to involve the politicians in this case. If they were consulted, their advice would have to be respected. But this would also be dangerous in relation to the Germans, who might then get the impression that ultimately the politicians were still in charge."

Wilcke, however, held firm: "The plan for internment of Jews by Danish measures was opportunism and a flagrant violation of The Hague Convention. It would hardly help the Jews, because it could not ensure that the Germans wouldn't still take them and deport them. If on the other hand the permanent secretaries put the entire administration's continued cooperation on the line, the Germans would likely hold back in order not to expose themselves to the chaos that would result. They could not afford that."

Wilcke thus again raised the question whether the permanent secretaries should make the implementation of the German action a sticking point and threaten to resign if the raid was carried out. Svenningsen had rejected this idea the previous day, when the Jewish representatives requested his opinion. Too much would be at stake if the permanent secretaries left the administration of the country to the Nazis. Vice Admiral Vedel, who attended the meeting, rejected Wilcke's idea as wishful thinking. The Germans both could and would do whatever they estimated to be in their own interest. He readily agreed with Svenningsen. But Permanent Secretary Jespersen did not. He was "of the view that an active involvement in the round-up of the Jews—despite the best intentions that lay behind the idea—would be completely erroneous and harmful. It would, in my view, be an ineradicable stain on our country if the Danish administration participated either directly or indirectly. Such collaboration could potentially cause incalculable consequences internally, destroying the civil respect and trust that were the necessary foundation of the official Danish administration."

Jespersen also had an eye out for the further implications in regard to the balance of power between the permanent secretaries and the occupiers: "To go along with breaking the rule of law ourselves was not only a serious violation of principle, but also a decisive operational move. Because if we are seen to be ready to abandon the rule of law when threats are directed against Jews, then in reality we signal that we are ready to do whatever they ask when we have a gun at our chest."

Also Jespersen felt strongly that only politicians could make such a radical decision: "If I want the politicians—and preferably a broader range than Minister Buhl—involved in the case, it is not to exempt officials of responsibility, but because issues that are vital for our country were meant for the people's representatives to consider, and they in my opinion are in a much better position than the appointed officials to make determinations in accordance with the people's desires and view of the law."

With this one might think that the plan was abandoned. Not so. The majority still felt that something had to be done on purely humanitarian grounds, and that the plan was the best option they could think of. As one put it, saving thousands of people was more important than the question of principle. It was not about contributing to injustice, but preventing and mitigating that which was coming from outside. And in addition, since the Jews' most prominent leaders agreed, one need not consider whether assistance would be detrimental or beneficial. (Clearly the state secretaries took the support of the Jewish leaders for granted. It was only after the war that argument erupted as to what was actually said at the crucial meeting between the leaders and Svenningsen.)

At this point Wilcke declared that he would resign if the majority advanced the internment proposal. Immediately this notion was forcefully rejected by his colleagues: None of the permanent secretaries could act individually. They had to remain united. It was all for one and one for all. No one could make the case for an individual decision. It would paralyze the administration and open the country to dark forces. It was now clear that the permanent secretaries would not resign collectively. The majority also opposed involving the politicians. This was not a political step, but an act of compassion. No one other than the permanent secretaries could take responsibility. Politicians could not or would not cover them. They were left to make the awful decision on their own.

Late in the day, when Svenningsen had already left the meeting, Andreas Møller of the prime minister's office attempted to sum up a conclusion: Svenningsen should seek out the envoys from Sweden and Finland to learn where they stood. He also must sound out the views of politicians "without binding effect." Behind these concrete decisions was an unspoken understanding that the permanent secretaries, if deportation became an imminent fact, would intervene for Danish detention as a last resort. The country was en route to a domestic plan for the internment of the Danish Jews.[2]

While the permanent secretaries struggled to reach a common position, Gunnar Larsen, the former minister of public works, went to see Prime Minister Scavenius at his home. The two ministers, who were part of the government that had handed in its resignation but had not had it accepted, explored the possibility of getting a new Danish government up and running as they both felt this would be the only tenable solution to the government crisis that had prevailed since the end of August. But according to Larsen's records the same day, Scavenius now took a skeptical view: "It was getting late, and as developments unfolded, the Germans moved farther and farther, so that the way back was increasingly difficult, especially if now the Jewish question also was effectively messed up, the way back would no longer be open."

Scavenius's assessment is interesting because it reflects not only the understanding that a new Danish government could not uphold the protection of the Jews, but also the perception that a German action against the Jews would definitely make future cooperation at the political level impossible. From one of his former collaborators later that day Larsen got a full report on the dramatic negotiations among the permanent secretaries: "The meeting had been quite moving, and some of the permanent secretaries, among them apparently Jespersen and one or two others, stated that if such a thing happened, they would resign. The majority, however, had gone against this idea, as they were aware that it would only create further chaos, and it was felt that that ought not to happen."

Larsen had also had word of Svenningsen's conversation with the representatives of the Jewish community and of the internment plan, which seemed to be supported by the majority of permanent secretaries, even though they realized the risk of "being denounced as traitors, even more so than members of the Scavenius government had previously been." Larsen's informant had himself supported the proposal "as he did not think one could think only of oneself."[3]

Stockholm Intervenes

The rumors of the Danish internment plan reached *Politiken* and Bergstrøm's vigilant ears that same day. It was Herbert Steinthal who had intercepted the proposal, and he realized at once how fatal it could be: "Herbert said that Svenningsen and Eivind Larsen . . . had been or were about to go to Dr. Best with a proposal that would create a big Jewish concentration camp guarded by Danish policemen. A really strange thought. You put all the Jews in a sack."

Bergstrøm shook his head and later that evening went to the nearby Hotel Kong Frederik, where he slept when he worked late at the newspaper and could not get home because of the curfew. Again he encountered hearsay: "I strolled in to 'Kong Frederik.' The clerk asked if there was anything new with the Jews. He knew some. He was 100 percent Aryan himself, he said. I had rated him at least 75 percent Jewish, and I did not change my assumption after I looked closely at him."[4]

Fear and uncertainty about the Germans' intentions were already impelling individuals to try to avoid being among those who were selected as scapegoats.

The resistance activist Erling Foss now was also convinced that the threat was genuine. In his report of September 30 to Stockholm and

London he outlines the situation: "There is hardly any doubt, after all information obtained yesterday, about the impending arrest of the Jews. Information from the circle of permanent secretaries indicates that the local Germans, both Best and also Hanneken, are unhappy about it, but the order came directly from Hitler. This also explains why the message has been circulated. . . . Some permanent secretaries are contemplating a Danish effort to arrange for the internment of the Jews. This is a dangerous position, because there's no guarantee that immediately afterward one will not be forced to hand them over.

"As the road to Sweden is hardly open for more than a minority, there is only one sensible way left. The Jews must flee from home and change their names. It won't then be possible for the Germans to find them. The Danes then have to sabotage any attempt by the German side to convey a message that Danes are not allowed to house Jews or foreigners. . . . The Danish people will be able to stand together in such a passive defense against the extradition of the Jews. An immense wave of indignation is already beginning to sweep across the country."[5]

Foss bought Best's deception, which places responsibility for the debacle in Berlin, and, like everyone else, he doesn't see a possibility for many Jews to seek refuge in Sweden. The only chance seems to be for them to remain in hiding until the end of the war. But this would be extremely difficult for entire families with no prior experience of secrecy and illegality. Maybe Foss's most important observation is the last, dealing with the mood of the Danish population. The wrath about the impending action was building in a great wave. The first response came in the form of protests from all sectors of society. But what would happen if the protests were not heard? How would the Danish population react then? And how would Stockholm respond to the reports now pouring in on the impending action in Denmark?

Despite resistance from Swedish minister Arvid Richert and Danish minister Carl Otto Mohr in Berlin, time was on the side of a Swedish intervention. Svenningsen spoke late Thursday evening with Dardel, who had prevailed on Stockholm to instruct Richert to get moving in Berlin. Dardel informed Svenningsen about the wording of the proposed Swedish démarche, which emphasized to the German government the deep indignation a deportation of Danish Jews would engender in Sweden and at the same time presented the "offer that Sweden would receive all Danish Jews to intern them there for the duration of the war."

Although the Swedish legation in Berlin was reluctant to hand over the démarche, which now became known in Copenhagen, Svenning-sen got permission to divulge its contents to Best first thing the next morning—again in the vain hope that he would seek to persuade Berlin to stop the action. But Best was far beyond that point. In fact that same day he managed to get Berlin to send orders for General Hanneken to make his Wehrmacht troops available for the action. No Danes knew this, of course, and Best's duplicity kept the situation fluid.[6]

That evening Foss wrote an additional daily report to Stockholm and London. He recounted Duckwitz's warning, but uncertainty still loomed: "It is not possible to be certain whether something will happen." There were reports, according to Foss's information, "that Hitler, against even Himmler, has demanded the arrests," and in this connection Foss con-veys an interesting rumor: "If they get just a few hundred and the rest disappear, this would satisfy and no more would then have to be done because it would be assumed that Hitler would calm down and forget about the matter."

But doubts still rankle: "Thus far one can get an overall picture, and the warning provided fits into it, but it isn't at all certain that the picture is right." Moreover, in Foss's eyes the considerations of the permanent secretaries were completely misguided: "C. B. Henriques has been to the ministries and suggested that Danes themselves should intern the Jews. The permanent secretaries showed their political incapacity today by meeting—first error—and then by agreeing to send notification to the Germans—second error. The Germans rejected the 'offer'—however it was shaped—and didn't want anything to do with an internment. They have still denied that the story is for real. It's pretty strange, after all that has happened, that one should attach any credence to a German promise not to touch the Jews, whom the Danes themselves had gathered. That the Jews themselves cling to this last fragile straw is more easily under-stood."[7]

Foss was well informed, but he misunderstood some important details. The permanent secretaries had not adopted their proposal—let alone submitted it to the Germans. But the rumors flew, both about the Jewish leaders' call and the secretaries' discussions, and we are no closer to the truth about what Henriques and his companions had actually proposed to Svenningsen. There is little doubt that Foss's information about the conversation comes from the permanent secretaries and not from Hen-riques himself.

In London the Danish envoy, Eduard Reventlow, wrote in his diary

The Fischer family in 1937.
Paula and Josef seated in front
with their three daughters,
standing from left to right,
Ella, Edith, and Harriet.

Danish Jewish Museum

Bernhard "Bubi" Cohn and his
wife, Ella, at the beach early
during the occupation.

Danish Jewish Museum

that day that his colleague in Washington, Henrik Kauffmann, had sent the U.S. government a note, "concerning his willingness to help with money if anything can be done for Jewish refugees from Denmark. So far, however, no actual Jewish persecution has been initiated, so that it seems to me a bit premature."[8]

At this point the arrests were to begin within twenty-four hours.

CHAPTER 6

FRIDAY, OCTOBER 1

THE ACTION

An Agenda of Uncertainties

On Friday, October 1, 1943, U.S. forces broke the last resistance in Naples and took the city: The significant Allied victory sent waves of hope across the troubled Continent, where many prayed and some believed that the war might soon be over—a vain hope, as we now know.

In Copenhagen the rumors were of the Jews. At *Politiken* Bergstrøm noted in his diary how he experienced the fateful hours filled with false alarms: "Heltberg said before he left that he had heard from reliable sources that the hunt for Jews would begin tonight and continue for the next 10 days. Someone came and told me that Seedorff, who had good connections, had said that the German interior minister Himmler would come here. We didn't think that sounded probable. Amid the serious mood were flashes of gallows humor. Herbert [Steinthal], who is more than a tad Jewish himself, said laughingly that yesterday he had seen a myriad of obvious Jews on the street and all of them were equipped with suitcases."

Bergstrøm and his Jewish colleague see the irony in the emerging panic over a danger they still do not believe is about to materialize. Nothing was confirmed, and many refused to believe that it could become a reality. But for others flight was already a fact of life. At the municipal hospital Ella Fischer received a visit from the hospital's priest. Judging by her account, it was not an edifying meeting: "In the morning the hospital priest, pastor Hejlesen, came to our room and gave a little sermon in which he repeatedly denigrated the Jews and in particular said that Christians should not follow the bad message that came from the Jews: an eye for an eye and a tooth for a tooth. Afterward he came to my bed, and I told him that I was a Jew, which he said he had been well aware of, and we talked a little about the situation, which he knew in detail, although he seemed to have scant sympathy for us."[1]

Few Danish Jews celebrated the Jewish Day of Atonement and Yom Kippur in their homes. Most were already on the move and many spent the beginning of Sabbath Friday evening with Christian friends and acquaintances. The final preparations fell into place on the German side, and in the morning Best announced to Berlin that the action would commence the same evening. The deported would depart by ship from Copenhagen and on special trains from Jutland and Fyn. The capacity was great and could easily accommodate all the estimated six thousand people thought to be directly affected. Best's telegram to Berlin also establishes that he did not intend to mention the action in public and that he had decided to leave the deported Jews' property untouched—and finally that he, in agreement with General Hanneken, was going to announce that the release of Danish soldiers detained in August was about to begin.[2]

The Wehrmacht now had instructions to engage, and Best conferred extensively with Hanneken about practical implementation. Best affirmed Dr. Mildner's orders that the police soldiers [a special German police unit] should not force their way into houses and apartments where no one answered the door. Berlin was informed of the many protests that had been received from all quarters, and not least about the warnings that the action might have a negative impact on Denmark's production and exports.

Best was clearly seeking to reinforce the impression in Berlin that the operation was very delicate in regard to the future cooperation with the Danes. Neither he nor other senior German officials in Copenhagen nourished any doubts that the action could develop into a huge fiasco. It was hard to imagine that many Jews were waiting patiently to open their doors and let themselves be arrested and deported by German police.

In the Farmer's Bed

At Hulebækgaard, Busch-Petersen's farm in Østre Ulslev on the island of Lolland, the two refugee families woke up to a day filled with confu-

sion and doubt—but also with a determination at least to cross Guld-
borgsund Bridge to Nykøbing Falster on the way back to Sjælland. The
eight uninvited guests and Erik Nyegaard constituted quite an invasion
on the small farm, but everyone pitched in to make it work under ad hoc
conditions. The diaries show that the Copenhageners were adjusting, but
also that they felt uncomfortable about the way they had barged in on
strangers. Poul Hannover notes: "The next morning we were eventually able to wash ourselves. Our hosts were terribly nice, though we
had barged in like a bull in a china shop—it was the first of October, the
day hunting begins. It was a tradition that his brother came down there,
and that they went hunting with a neighboring landowner—and that he
and his wife came for lunch—and now we, 9 people, had to be included.
They had a painfully spartan bathroom—eventually we each got a kettle
full of hot water—and it was lucky that we had towels—we could have
never expected them to provide us with them. One by one we washed
and shaved—even hung our wet towels to dry in the kitchen—Inger and
Kis helped out a little."

Hannover has decided to seek refuge at his colleague's summerhouse
at the nearby island of Møn and also invented a plan to get the message
across in coded language: "I called our agent and asked him to call Herbert Jerichow and tell him that the man from Copenhagen had received
an order for 8 engines to be delivered to his property down here—and
thereby provide me the address. It worked perfectly, and I got a message that showed that it was understood and that we—at least within
a few days, could seek refuge in the house—he would personally take
care of this. I also asked the representative if I could borrow his summer
home—but that wouldn't work—there were some 'unfriendly' people
around—instead he proposed a guesthouse near Marielyst. I was not
happy about that."

Poul Hannover had made progress in his short career as an illegal. He
became more security conscious and began to plan for a contingency
in which the group could not get an early transfer to Sweden. Herbert
Jerichow's summerhouse could be a safe haven. Now what mattered was
to avoid a breakdown or discovery before they could get there. While the
eight refugees on the farm desperately searched for ways out, life continued around them with an almost unreal normality. Poul Hannover continues: "Erik went on the hunt—he shot really well—and around noon
the four gentlemen came home—and lunch began. It was a real hunting
lunch with schnapps galore. In the middle of lunch, Talleruphuus rang

Erik—we had to meet him at a certain place—but we could not get a clear message about whether they would sail or not."

Kis also recounts the awkward lunch: "At noon the men came home from the hunt, and lunch began. It was a real hunting lunch with piles of food and schnapps, it was a bit difficult for us, who were not in the mood for celebration. In the middle of the meal Talleruphuus called. Erik came back from the phone and nodded encouragingly to us, and we were happy at the thought that everything was in order."

Those who fled had to constantly stay on the move. They could not remain at the farm, and even the smallest chance was better than nothing. Especially when it pointed back toward Falster and further toward Sjælland. Poul Hannover obtains transportation: "I decided to take a car—and we all climbed into it, although we were too many. . . . So we left. There was no talk of my paying at the farm—the farmer said nicely: 'We hardly feel the impact of war—we only see that we earn a little better, so we are only happy to be able to help out.'—We gave the girls 10 kroner each—I gave Erik a card so he could requisition a box of my cigars, which he could send the man as thanks for his help—and a box for himself—so we loaded everything in the car—we were 9 people, as we now had Erik along. The driver was concerned—and not without reason. A few kilometers before Nykøbing one tire exploded. We reached the town—I met our representative . . . —and he wished us God's help in crossing over to Sweden. I dare say we needed it."

A Danish Initiative? Third Attempt

Others were also in need of help that Friday. Starting in the early morning Svenningsen sought out Best's right-hand man, the head of internal security, Paul Kanstein, to talk about his conversation with the Swedish minister the night before and about the forthcoming démarche, whereby the Swedish government would announce to Berlin that Sweden was ready to intern the Danish Jews there. Kanstein promised to inform Best, and Svenningsen hastened to contact the Danish minister in Berlin, Otto Carl Mohr, by phone, in order to impress upon him the urgency of the démarche. Mohr informed Svenningsen that Richert had not yet delivered the message to the Germans, and that both he and Richert had recommended that it be dropped for the time being. Richert in his telegram explained to Stockholm that the postponement was due to a lack of confidence that the démarche would have the desired effect: "Numerous Swedish press organs are considered here to have gone so far in their hostility to Germany that they've used up their ammunition, which means that further denunciations are unlikely to persuade the German decision makers to take special account," he sourly explained as the clock ticked away.

Svenningsen strongly rejected Mohr's interpretation and resumed contact with the Swedish minister, Gustav Dardel, who via Stockholm managed to get things moving. Reinforced instructions arrived in Berlin, and the same afternoon Richert delivered the Swedish offer, which indeed was not well received in the German Foreign Ministry. Richert was met with hot air from a subordinate official, and his dry report back to Stockholm states that "the connections to Hitler's headquarters, where decisions are made, often completely bypass the Foreign Ministry." It did not matter whether officials there did not know what was going on, or whether or not they would tell. The result was the same: There was no way the action could be stopped through diplomatic channels.[3]

On Friday morning, while Svenningsen worked intensively to get the Swedish démarche delivered in Berlin, he ran into the speaker of the parliament, Hans Rasmussen, a staunch Social Democrat. Svenningsen took the opportunity to raise the issue of internment by Danish initiative with Rasmussen, as instructed by his colleagues at the meeting the day before. Rasmussen responded positively, but a few hours later sent Svenningsen a letter that greatly modified his initial support: "Continuing our conversation this morning regarding the possible detention of . . . I wish here to clarify that my support is to be understood to mean that *there cannot be* . . . any inference of commitment or obligation on our part with respect to the search for any of the relevant group of people."[4]

It seems obvious that Rasmussen had in the meantime discussed the idea with political colleagues who had not endorsed the proposal. If the permanent secretaries decided to act, it would be without political backing.

That same afternoon at 4 p.m, they met for their third discussion of the matter. Svenningsen outlined what had taken place during the course of the morning, and also mentioned the many protests to Dr. Best that were pouring in from the country's most influential organizations, now joined by bishops and the university, the Danish Women's National Council (with more than one hundred thousand members), the Lawyers

Council, and the Supreme Court. The women appealed to Best "not to take steps that would persecute innocent people because of their religion or race, as this would arouse deep and lasting bitterness and go against all that is right."

From Sorgenfri the king had also issued a protest, which Svenningsen, after the meeting, would present to Best. Christian "felt compelled—not only out of humane concern for my country's citizens, but also for fear of further consequences for the future relationship between Germany and Denmark—to emphasize to you that specific measures with respect to a group of people who for more than 100 years have enjoyed full civil rights in Denmark could have the most serious consequences."

According to the king's diary that day, he got "a message that Bishop Fuglsang-Damgaard had sent a message to the German envoy Dr. Best to waive the arrests of the Jews. The Industrial Council had forwarded a similar request. In line with these requests, I today sent Dr. Best a similar note protesting against the arrest of Jews who for centuries had been obedient citizens."[5]

Meanwhile several of the permanent secretaries had discussed the situation with "their" former ministers, among whom there seemed to be widespread sympathy for a Danish action. But this was far from a consensus, and it remained unclear whether the alleged support also included the idea of Danish authorities arresting the Jews. The urgency of the situation provoked a sharp disagreement among the permanent secretaries as to how far their mandate could be extended. The group had only acted as a kind of emergency government for a few weeks, and the individuals did not have a common understanding of how far their authority went. The more traditional side, led by Jespersen, maintained that as civil servants they were not entrusted with governmental authority "once and for all," as it had been "explicitly pointed out that it was only under certain specific conditions that officials could exercise legislative functions and the like; this excluded the undertaking of anything that was in violation of Danish law—and for me there was no doubt that was exactly the case here."

Jespersen also still argued that the politicians should be involved, and he warned that the group "could not take active steps in violation of Danish concepts of justice that could provide a basis for the impression in the outside world that we were anti-Jewish."

Time was running out, and the permanent secretaries felt the pressure of the situation. They hesitated to take an active part in the internment of innocent citizens, but also had a hard time satisfying themselves with protests no one believed would have any effect. Jespersen and his peers were more inclined to disclaim any responsibility for an action they feared would damage both the Jews and the country. But their colleagues kept arguing for the overarching necessity of remaining united. Ultimately Jespersen gave in—almost: "In response to the statements that we had to make every effort to achieve consensus ... I expressed my agreement that we had to come together, as far as possible, and to that end, of course, we also had to demonstrate resolve—but when the talk turned to decisions that ran counter to an individual's conscience, the majority, in my view, could neither bind nor justify any individual to act against his conviction when what was at stake for the country were crucially important political decisions."[6]

Andreas Møller finally came to the conclusion that "the action against the Jews was an action by Germany, while the Danish counterproposal was a relief measure, which would be obvious to everyone." Maybe. But the permanent secretaries' conclusion sounded more like a prayerful incantation.[7]

The notes of the secretaries' intense debate reflect the fact that they fully realized the impossible dilemma of the situation and that they were prepared to assume the heavy responsibility, although it was obviously more convenient not to. The men shared a profound concern about the impending action and despair at their own powerlessness, and an almost unbearable responsibility—knowledge of what was coming—had been placed on their shoulders. In the end they came to a decision. Although they reached it after thorough discussion, with open eyes and with the best intentions, we can now see that it was all wrong. If the permanent secretaries had been successful in reaching a quicker decision and in persuading Best to let the Danish authorities be responsible for carrying out the action, events might have proceeded entirely differently than what transpired next.

However, even with the benefit of hindsight it is hard to condemn Svenningsen and his colleagues for deciding to make the offer. The permanent secretaries' offense was not their plan—disastrous as it may have been. It was their lack of understanding of their own limitations. They failed to see that in this situation there were possibilities completely beyond their ken. That they themselves didn't possess the tools that could avert the disaster did not—as they lulled themselves into believing—imply that no option existed. In this way the plan became a confirmation of the truth that one of man's most dangerous limitations is the inability to recognize those very limitations.[8]

The next step was now up to Svenningsen, who thought he had a workable mandate from his colleagues. He had agreed to meet with Best at Dagmarhus that same afternoon at 6 p.m. He would offer to intern the Jews against a German guarantee that they would not be deported. It was urgent. No one knew when the Germans would strike. But the rumors were pointing to that very Friday night.

By Friday the rumors also reached London, where Reventlow was informed of both the impending action and the Swedish note that had been delivered in Berlin the day before. He noted the facts in his diary with the comment that Kauffmann's initiative from Washington the previous day had accordingly not been premature. But little if anything could be done.[9]

This was confirmed on Friday by an unexpected source. Helmuth von Moltke, an expert in international law at the Wehrmacht high command in Berlin, stopped over in Copenhagen on his own initiative in order to secretly warn Danish friends of the standing orders to launch the action against the Jews. Knowing nothing about the actual situation in Copenhagen, he imagined that he might be the first to pass on the vital information. As it was, Moltke's personal courage had no practical importance for the fate of the Danish Jews, beyond the memory that there were prominent Germans who opposed the action for reasons other than their narrow personal or bureaucratic interests: They were simply utterly against the ideas on which it was based. Moltke was one of the founders of the secret opposition group known as the Kreisauer Kreis, and after the July plot against Hitler, he was executed in Berlin-Plötzensee on January 23, 1945.[10]

On the Beach

Poul Hannover resumes his narrative on the same afternoon the families were leaving Nykøbing Falster heading for Hesnæs on Falster's eastern tip, 20–30 kilometers from the town: "As I dared not go on with the overloaded car, I got an additional one—I think we hired them for about 600 kroner in those few days—and started again—off to the east. When we were 1½ kilometers from the agreed place, I dismissed one vehicle—we shouldn't have too many witnesses—allowed part of the company and luggage to continue with the other, while some of us walked until the car returned. I did notice that we passed a large van by a farmhouse along the way—but now we had a small wagon, all our luggage on the coast—not so particularly smooth or confidence inspiring—now what?"

His sister-in-law Kis also doesn't have an answer: "So then we were all out in the woods with our luggage and glanced out over the water, which looked pretty scary, it was cold and windy. . . . Either we could drive around 4 kilometers into the countryside, where there was a small hotel, but then we probably couldn't get a car, if we were to sail, since this one is supposed to be back home before 8— The other option was to stay in the woods. We did this, although it was not encouraging to think that perhaps it would be for the whole night. We were told that there was an empty holiday camp nearby, which we might get into."

Poul Hannover is plagued by doubts that are only confirmed when the group meets other refugees in the forest:

> A moment later—it was almost 6 p.m.—the second car rolled up— out came Talleruphuus with a gentleman I had seen at the station in Nykøbing the previous day. His name was Goldstein. He asked me if I trusted Talleruphuus. I answered honestly that I wasn't sure if I did or not. It turned out that they also did not know whether we would leave or not. The skipper, who was about to sail, had unfortunately gotten a hernia from lifting a cupboard—and as he had previously suffered from this affliction, and was afraid that something bad had occurred, he now wanted to go to the hospital to be examined. It sounded so crazy that you almost had to believe it. So they were waiting for a 7:30 p.m. message to know if we would get away or not. In the meantime we could either wait here—in the woods—or go 4 kilometers inland, where there was a small hotel—but where you were not sure you would be able to get a car—or rather it was almost certain you would not be able to get a car since it would have to be home before 8 p.m.

Hope fades that they can get to Sweden that evening, and the family has to think about where to spend the night. They don't dare go to the hotel—and four kilometers is a long way with children and luggage. At the same time they are afflicted with doubt: Was Talleruphuus trustworthy? What to think of the fisherman with the strange story about the hernia? Where would it leave them if it was not true? In just two days the two families had made the journey from a safe world north of Copenhagen to a cold and dark night on the open beach without shelter or a firm plan for what to do next. And all the fuss had been triggered by a threat that had not yet materialized. Maybe the whole thing was a false alarm and they had simply overreacted?

The same day Adolph Meyer at last decided to make the next move. As nothing was occurring yet, and he was relatively unconcerned about the danger, the pediatrician simply went home to make the last practical arrangements. Meanwhile, German military police made their final preparations for the planned operation that evening. Meyer noted:

> Decided next morning to go to Hart . . . , checked out, paid in the office, and went home by bus # 3. The train would depart at 1:25 p.m. It was now Friday, October 1; at home I asked that several paintings be removed, had all my clothes packed in the steamer trunk, Uncle Moses' suitcase, my leather suitcase, my red suitcase and a new suitcase that the girls bought, and my attaché case and my oilcloth bag with my eiderdown blanket. . . . I arranged with Bülow that he should pay my taxes and rent, and terminate the apartment and give my trusty maids one year's salary and one year of expenses. He would sell 50,000 kroners' worth of bonds. I had approx. 5,500 kroner on me and in Honoré's box which he brought me, 11,000 kr was deposited on September 29, which he brought home to me October 1. I kissed the girls good-bye at home. They drove the suitcases and my bike to the station, whereas I took the tram and tickets to Ruds Vedby. I arrived at 4:30 p.m., . . . Went up to Hart, who had been waiting for me since Thursday. I lived there under the name Dr. Madsen until the fourth of October.

Dr. Meyer felt relatively safe, comfortably installed at his colleague's house in the countryside. But his sense of security was quickly mixed with growing anxiety for the rest of his family and relatives, including his sister-in-law, Mary Goldschmidt. Everyone was afraid to call and communicate directly, and all the secrecy opened many possibilities fraught with misunderstanding: "They were immensely gracious to me. I immediately said that I would be a paying guest. I was very sad I knew nothing about my children. Despite my pseudonym, Michael knew me from last summer, so did the housekeepers. I knew, or thought at least that I knew, that Mary had a connection to Dagmar Christensen and I wrote to the office head, to ask if Mary would get in touch with me. The Harts had offered to have her to stay with them. Later in the evening, I asked Dr. Hart to telephone . . . to say that Mary was welcome at the Harts and could get there Saturday by the 13:28 train from Copenhagen. I would not have done so if I had known that she was with [relatives] in Ålsgarde, waiting for a boat that they had bought together. She thought, in turn, that I, who was alone, wanted her to come over to where I was, and in her goodness she left the others, which is why I have also felt great responsibility for her since."

For very wealthy people, fleeing presented an additional problem, since they had to dispose of their assets at short notice, so they—hopefully—could be recovered after the war. This was true whether the individuals in question were being pursued, or whether they simply feared it. One example was the prosperous Supreme Court lawyer and art collector C. L. David, who was publicly known as a Jew, and was vilified as such in the local Nazi press, although strictly speaking he was, according to the Nazi concept, "half Jewish" and therefore not yet in the Germans' spotlight. But dared he trust this? David doubted it and sought the advice of his personal friend, the respected lawyer H. H. Bruun, who with great thoroughness sought to clarify the question of whether David could safely stay or not. It is interesting that the seasoned lawyer, according to his own handwritten notes, went directly to the primary source in the form of the German consul general, who on Friday, October 1, before the action was launched, carefully explained to Bruun the German arrangements in regard to half and quarter Jews.

Even more interesting is Bruun's subsequent calming advice to the frightened David. In the midst of the madness both men seemed to still have great confidence in the soothing assurances of German officialdom. So David stayed on.[11]

Messages to Best

In a short note dated October 2, Nils Svenningsen outlined his attempts to get in touch with Best the previous evening. The frustration is apparent, as is the dual purpose of the account—to serve also as life insurance when, in the fullness of time, questions are asked as to his role in the critical hours, history is written, and responsibility established: "On Friday, October 1 at 4:30 p.m., an appointment was arranged . . . for me to be received by Dr. Best at Dagmarhus at 6 p.m.

"Dr. Best's secretary called at 5:45 p.m. to cancel the meeting. Dr. Best was suddenly called away. The secretary did not know where he had gone and did not know when he would be back. It would hardly be possible for me to be received in the course of the evening."

With the mandate obtained from his colleagues, Svenningsen went to Dagmarhus anyway to talk to Best's staff, who turned out to be polite but impenetrable. Everybody claimed total ignorance. Svenningsen delivered the king's letter and the Supreme Court's appeal and otherwise continued to look for Best, who actually got the note from the king, as can be established from the fact that he telegraphed it to Berlin at 7:30 p.m., confirming what Best had already warned, namely that the intense rumors of the impending roundup would "impede the action, as many Jews will not be in their own apartments." The action would start at 9:00 p.m.[12]

At approximately 8:40 p.m. Svenningsen received a message through the Foreign Ministry—actually dispatched from Dagmarhus, where he was still waiting—informing him "that in the course of the night arrests would be made of a number of 'individuals hostile to the Reich.' Dagmarhus asked that police across the country be informed in order to avoid clashes between the police and the German authorities who were carrying out the action. Notification to this effect had been sent to the police by telex."

This was the signal that the action against the Danish Jews had been launched. The following day Svenningsen noted subsequent events at Dagmarhus, where his colleague from the Justice Ministry, Eivind Larsen, had joined him: "Shortly after, the phone lines were cut. Partly as a result of this it was not until 11:15 p.m. that I managed to get an audience with Dr. Best. Permanent Secretary Eivind Larsen accompanied me. I referred to the conversation on Wednesday and said that I had wanted the opportunity to talk about the case with Dr. Best earlier in the day. However, this evening we were informed that there would be the arrest of a number of individuals hostile to the Reich, and we understood that it meant the Jews, which Dr. Best confirmed. He also confirmed, on inquiry, that those concerned would immediately be taken to Germany on Saturday morning. Those fit to work would be put to various tasks, while the elderly and unfit would be taken to Theresienstadt in Bohemia, a city where Jews had autonomy and lived under decent conditions. From there they would be able to correspond with the outside world, including also with their relatives in Denmark."

Svenningsen was not persuaded by Best's reassuring references to German concentration camps. He was aware that the worst was now at hand: For the permanent secretaries this was precisely the situation in which their offer of Danish internment had to be made immediately as a last resort:

> After Dr. Best had thus confirmed that this was about immediate deportation, I presented a proposal for internment by Danish authorities in this country, as I delivered a handwritten letter with the following text [in German]:
>
> "Tonight I have . . . received notification that German authorities intend tonight to arrest a number of individuals hostile to the Reich. I understand this message to mean it is about the arrest of Jews. Since I was not able to get the opportunity to speak with you personally about this matter today, I send you these lines, despite coming at the last hour, to ask whether any possibility exists to at least avoid *this*: The deportation of those concerned. *If* it really is about immediate deportation, Mr. Eivind Larsen and myself stand ready to do everything possible to create an arrangement whereby the persons wanted by the German side would, by Danish initiative and by our own authorities, be interned together here in Denmark. I ask you to ensure that a further exploration of such a solution is not prejudged."

Svenningsen's draft of the handwritten letter has been preserved. He must have written it that night while he and Larsen, with mounting fear, were waiting for an audience with Best, who repeatedly avoided direct confrontation with his Danish counterparts while the raids rolled on. By his own admission Svenningsen pushed as hard as he could: "I asked Dr. Best, in light of the Danish counterproposal, if he could delay the transports and obtain new orders from Berlin. Best stated that it was quite impossible for him to stop the transports, since he could not make any decision in this case. However, he would immediately forward my letter by telegraph to Berlin and ask for instructions."[13]

Again Best deftly played the sympathetic innocent who does what he can to halt the action. This was hypocrisy. But the strong Danish reactions had nevertheless already had an important effect. Best and other

Dagmarhus, the German headquarters at Copenhagen's Rådhuspladsen (Town Hall Square).

"Peaceful occupation" meant that Denmark in principle maintained both its sovereignty and its neutrality. Therefore official contacts between Denmark and Germany went through the German legation, which expanded its staff and moved to larger offices at Dagmarhus, where Werner Best also had his headquarters. It reflects the paradoxical situation in occupied Copenhagen that the German legation was a neighbor to the "Jew-newspaper Politiken" and also shared the building with the Dagmar Theater on the ground floor—the stage for some of the day's most popular revues, which specialized in poking fun at the Germans in subtle ways that escaped the censors' rigor.

A master of this genre was the writer and architect Poul Henningsen, who created a number of iconic items of Danish design, including the classic PH lamps. Just before the German invasion he wrote a hymn to free love, but when the censors found it too frivolous, he revenged himself by slightly altering the phrases, turning the song into an evergreen manifesto for freedom:

> They chain our mouths and hands,
> but they cannot tie our thoughts,
> and no one is imprisoned when the spirit runs free.
> We have an inner fortress here
> that is strengthened in its own worth,
> as long as we fight for what we believe.
> He who keeps his soul erect will never be a slave.
> No one can govern that
> which we determine ourselves.
> We promise with mouth and hand,
> in the darkness before dawn,
> the dream of freedom shall never die.

The popular revue was performed some 395 times in twenty-six cities, and audiences stood up at the last stanzas. Henningsen was amused since "the conservatives in this country had to swallow a lot of modern sexual morality before they were allowed to give themselves over to the patriotism of the last verse." The German authorities tried several times to get the Danish government to silence the talented Henningsen, but it was ultimately an attempt on his life by Danish Nazis that made him flee to Sweden.

Dagmarhus survived the war, and the distinctive functionalist building is still the setting for both offices and a popular movie theater.

Frihedsmuseet

prominent German representatives in Denmark had long warned Berlin about massive rejection by the Danish population, which could eventually damage the continuation of the policy of cooperation to which the Nazi leadership attached such importance. It was these warnings that caused Ribbentrop to emphasize that the operation should be carried out as cautiously as possible.

Even wrongs need a figleaf of legitimacy, and even an assailant needs to justify his assault. Thus the Nazi persecution of the Jews also needed grounds and legitimacy, bound up in anti-Semitic stereotypes, prejudices, and lies that made it possible to present the Jews as troublemakers, saboteurs, and enemies of Germany. The individual Jew had to be suspect, and the group associated with a larger conspiracy. Where the Jews had previously been part of society, they now had to be separated. In Denmark such complicity was explicitly rejected. Except for declared Nazis, not one single organization—not a church or congregation, not a single institution of society—expressed an ounce of understanding of, or even sympathy with, the roundup of the Jews. The occupiers were left with the full responsibility for the assault and had to carry the entire burden of the crime. This turned out to be decisive, both for the Germans' lack of enthusiasm and zeal in the implementation of the action, and for the fate of the Danish Jews.

Best's response to Svenningsen was quickly communicated back to the king, who in his diary noted that "Dr. Best had said that he personally could do nothing but would send my letter by telegram to Berlin."[14]

In many ways Best couldn't have had it better. Everyone seemed to accept that it was not he who was to blame but Berlin. The risk to him now was that his Danish partners would draw the unwanted conclusion that he was no longer the key person in the Danish-German equation. So this was only the first round. The next was to do damage control and get back into operational mode with the Danes again.

For Duckwitz the action's implementation was a low point that he had hoped until the end to prevent. In his diary he notes late on October 1: "Restlessly busy day. Worked tirelessly to prevent the worst."[15]

Although Svenningsen only slowly and reluctantly came to realize what was under way, he understood the people's feelings, and he shared and expressed them himself. This was not the Germany Svenningsen knew and, despite everything, trusted. To cope with the dichotomy between the impossible and what was now unfolding before his very eyes, Svenningsen had to distinguish between Berlin and Best, between the radical Nazis in the capital and the personal partner he knew so well. Best played this sentiment skillfully and was careful always to appear as the one striving to prevent disaster. According to Svenningsen's minutes of the interview with Best late that Friday night, this was also true when it came to the scope of the German raid, which concentrated on "the arrest and deportation of 100% Jews. Excepted were Jews or Jewesses in a marriage where the other party is Aryan. I asked if further measures against the Jews were supposed to be taken, such as property seizure or similar. Dr. Best did not think this would be the case."

Best now brought up his attempt to mitigate the Danes' response: "Finally Dr. Best reported that the question of the release of the detained Danish troops would be resolved in connection with the Jewish action. Repatriation would now take place in accordance with a plan that had been set."[16]

With the German authorities' lukewarm commitment to the action, they vied for the honor of linking the arrest of Jews with the release of Danish soldiers. In a telegram on the evening of October 1, Best emphasizes the importance of the link, pointing out that it "hereby would be made clear that no one from the German side, as has been alleged here in the last days, will equate the sons of Danish farmers with Jews and deport them like such." Handwritten annotations in the margins of the telegram show that General Hanneken, Heinrich Himmler, and the Führer had been briefed and endorsed this barter.

The Danish reaction brooked no misunderstanding: This was an assault on innocent citizens. Germany went from being a neighboring country that for strategic reasons had occupied Denmark under favorable terms to being an assailant perpetrating violence against the Danish people.

The idea of linking the release of the soldiers with the arrest of the Jews demonstrates how far the Nazi leadership was from understanding the mind-set of the country it had occupied. It is also possible that the proposal served primarily to reinforce the impression in Berlin that Best was hands-on and able to keep the occupied country under control. Given his exposed position it was important for Best to appear tough and uncompromising on ideological issues—while at the same time taking an accommodating line with the Danes. How the two lines were to be reconciled was of no concern to Hitler. Best had to figure that out for himself. He was, as Leni Yahil has put it, "the prisoner of the regime he served, and of his own tactics."[17]

At about the same time the roundup of the Jews was launched in Denmark, Best's old mentor, SS chief executive, Reichsführer Heinrich Himmler, wrote a short letter to his protégé in Copenhagen. The precise date is uncertain and is disputed, but the letter seems to have been written on October 1. It reads:

> October 1943
> Headquarters in the field
>
> My dear Best,
>
> First, thank you for your various letters and telegrams. I have monitored overall developments in Denmark, which in recent times have not been entirely happy in every respect. The solution that Frits Clausen has signed up as a doctor for the Waffen SS I find very good. The promotion of the Schalburg Corps [a corps of Danish SS veterans used to terrorize civilian populations] is important. The Jewish action is also rightly done so. It will raise dust for some time, but all in all it gets the worst saboteurs and main agitators out of the way. With the repeal of martial law, SS Gruppenführer [Günther] Pancke will be appointed as higher SS and police chief. I am deeply convinced that the cooperation between you both will be most harmonious, and I have the strongest confidence that thereby many things will become considerably easier. Have the greatness of heart not to be sorry that I have not placed the higher SS and police chief as your subordinate. The form of organization is better this way.
>
> Yours, Heil Hitler! [no signature]

The letter seems to confirm that the initiative for the Jewish action emanated from Best, who receives the advance compliments. But Himmler's real objective is clear from the last part of the letter. Best had long been asking for reinforcements of German police in Denmark, and Himmler was clearly aware that he had hoped to get full command over them. A note from the meeting the previous morning confirms that Best still at this point believed he would be in command of the police troop reinforcements. Now Pancke was being elevated to a level equal to Werner Best and Hanneken, the reason probably being Himmler's desire to have direct command over one of the three leading Germans in occupied Denmark. Over the following days Best tried several bureaucratic contortions to avoid Pancke's involvement. But he failed, which many interpreted as an expression of Himmler's dissatisfaction with the outcome of the raid in Denmark. But the chronology indicates that Best's bureaucratic defeat had nothing to do with the implementation of the Jewish action—rather, it was part of the power play in Berlin between Himmler and Ribbentrop.[18]

The Summer Colony

That evening, while Nils Svenningsen and Eivind Larsen waited in Dagmarhus for an audience with Werner Best, the Hannover and Marcus families stood idle on the beach not far from Hesnæs on the eastern point of the island of Falster. They waited for a boat that didn't arrive, and for a fate they feared. They didn't yet know that the action against them was about to be launched, and though they feared the worst they did not realize that from that night on they were to be hunted in their own country. But they knew they had to act, and set a course, as Poul Hannover observes as the families head for the nearby Abildvig summer camp, supposedly a kilometer inland:

> I learned that a summer colony lay nearby—we went there—and Erik began to break in. He demolished a big set of shutters, broke two windowpanes and opened the windows so we could get in. I didn't dare go back to any hotel, and so we stayed. We carried the baggage over a kilometer up to the summer colony, while Talleruphuus and Goldstein drove away again. We found a petroleum lamp that could provide a little light, as well as some used candles. There wasn't any water—not that we could find—and of course no toilets either. There were some beds without mattresses. We took the latch off the door, closed the window, went inside, and hung what was left of the shutter back up again. If anyone came past it could have been fatal. We covered the beds with our coats for the children, but it was far from enough, in addition to my winter coat and raincoat, and I, who had brought both my cotton coat and my winter coat, went around without a coat. Around 8 o'clock Talleruphuus came back alone—he still had not received any message. There was no specific agreement where to meet—there was a little jetty—I didn't know if a ship or even a dinghy could come in there. The day before he had already

spoken about how one possibly ought to give the man some money in advance—I had given Erik money to take along—1,000 kroner that was to go toward the dinghy. One could easily suggest that it was done on flimsy grounds—considerably thinner than I usually spend 1,000 kroner for.

We let the children eat the food we had—I had obtained lunches from the farmer's wife at Hulebækgaard—but unfortunately it wasn't very much, and we didn't have anything to drink. It was an awful night. We kept watch—in part to see if any of the others would come—in part to see if the ship would arrive, but no ship came. We tried to sleep, sitting in a chair—we got maybe a half hour's sleep, but the children slept tolerably well.

To Poul Hannover, the break-in at the summer colony represented a threshold he had a hard time crossing. Even under the difficult circumstances, he found it troubling to resort to criminal trespass. The small group had only begun to get used to being outside the law, but the illegality was getting under his skin, just as it got under Kis's:

We got the children settled down with our coats and the blanket, which we were glad we had taken with us. They were now a bit sad. Dorte cried because Grandfather wasn't with us, and when I comforted her she said, "Well, it's so hard." I thought that myself, but I had to get the children to sleep, which I was finally able to do. Before the children went to sleep they had some sandwiches, which we had received from the Busch-Petersens. We adults got one piece of sandwich each but there wasn't enough, so the men didn't get anything, and there also wasn't anything to drink. I was sad they told Palle, as he became so thirsty, and he cried because he couldn't get anything to drink. Well, in the end all four children fell asleep in their scary rooms with a candle on the table. We kept watch in the beginning, in part to see if the others would come, and partly to see if the boat would show up, but we saw nothing. Talleruphuus was also with us during the night, but he mostly walked around the forest, probably because he was freezing, as he had given me his coat. We were freezing and hungry, but we comforted ourselves as best we could, lay across two chairs and tried to sleep a little, either on a bench or sitting down. Erik, Inger, and Poul tried to play bridge with the cards Gunnar had brought but realized it wasn't much fun and quickly stopped. Now and then we went out to warm ourselves up, and we smoked a lot of cigarettes. The children slept pretty well until the morning.

Poul Hannover is tormented by speculation about what is the right thing to do now:

> I don't know what made the night worse—was it the horror of having broken in, which could be discovered—was it the uncertainty about what was to come—was it the anxiety about whether the children could handle it? We had to be perfectly clear that this was just the beginning, and that what was to come could be much, much worse. And who was this Talleruphuus anyway? The man we were so confidently entrusting with our lives? During the night I mentioned, when I spoke to him, that at least he had a chance to earn some money due to this affair. Apparently he became very indignant about this, but was his indignation genuine? There were plenty of questions one could ask. And then we were here without a radio—perhaps the planned action was accelerating now, as the news of it ran from mouth to mouth—maybe the Jewish law was now in place, turning us into outlaws and overwhelming any desire to help us with the threats they would certainly face if caught. It was not easy to appear optimistic. It was lucky that the children slept fairly well—I had to sometimes go out and walk—sneak a little stroll—it just cleared my thoughts a bit—which would otherwise probably be very confused.

The Action

The same evening, October 1, 1943, the sole duty officer at Police Headquarters in Copenhagen sat as usual, noting the so-called minute reports, which record the brief telephone, radio, or telex reports from the various police stations and posts. They were typically about everything from drunks to bicycle thefts to regular burglaries and other serious crimes. The log from October 1943 still exists, and the laconic reports depict the tragedy then unfolding:

> 20.00: 20 large German vehicles are driven from Frihavn [the free transit port in Copenhagen] in a convoy. More is not known, but the radio car is keeping in touch with it and will keep reporting.

20.40: German cars from the barracks in Herluf Trollesgade forming a convoy in front of the barracks apparently ready to move out. It appears they are making preparations to man the vehicles.

21.10: In Frihavn 20 German vehicles were observed driving to Ny Carlsbergvej, where they are being manned by German military police.

21.25: About 20 vehicles manned by green uniformed military police driving through Strøget . . . It is believed that this is about the Jews.

21.30: It is now believed that there are 50 vehicles. There are also vehicles along Købmagergade.

21.37: All exit roads are now occupied by the Germans, and all vehicles stopped and searched.

21.38: 18 large trucks driving along Vestre Boulevard toward the city.

21.40: A cop says that several German vehicles are near his residence.

21.43: On Sølvtorvet 32 trucks are observed with canopies, fully staffed by German soldiers near Trianglen.

21.45: All phone lines have been cut.

21.59: Tanks have been driven onto Kgs. Nytorv.

22.00: German vehicles are stationed on Værnlandsgade.

22.03: Telex messages sent from the National Police Headquarters that the local commanders must go immediately to their stations, and that Danish policemen must NOT assist in any arrests initiated by the German side.

22.10: The action started in Købmagergade. There's a chain blocking the street, and a few small groups [of German police soldiers] go into the buildings and come back with civilians. A German major in the 4th District told a Danish policeman that this is a German affair, and that Danish policemen should not interfere with it.

22.15: 2–3 shots were heard from the Trianglen, but it can't be confirmed.

22.30: There are no tanks at Kongens Nytorv. It is probably a misunderstanding.

22.55: Telex message [from Police Headquarters]: In the places where German soldiers are carrying out operations, Danish police should stay away.

00.15: Police director and deputy director at Police Headquarters. Survey of districts indicates quiet everywhere.

00.40: Loud shooting at Højdevangs School. Station 4 is ordered to send a small car out for observation. Orders NOT to assist the Germans.

00.50: Phone lines reopened.

00.55: Frihavn guard heard loud engine noise along Langelinje [at the main harbor].

00.55: Langelinje quay is open, and there is loud engine noise in the steamer *Wartheland*, located there.

03.15: German guards are posted out by Grønningen, on the road to Langelinje.

08.00: The German guards at Grønningen are withdrawn. Since the ship at Langelinje dock hasn't sailed, Station 3 has blocked Langelinje quay from the barge channel and the high promenade.

08.05: Prison commander Kaj Jensen communicates that notification has come from the Horserød prison camp that the German authorities are currently in the process of moving the interned Danish Communists. It involves an estimated 150 prisoners, and the prison camp is very eager to know where they are being taken. A radio truck will follow and observe.

09.15: 8 German transport vehicles with German soldiers and civilians have been observed on Lyngbyvej by the city. A radio truck will observe where they drive to.[19]

Three times during the evening and night messages are sent from Police Headquarters to the police units on duty not to engage. The orders are clear: Stand by, observe, but do not engage—let alone assist—in the arrests. For the individual policemen, appalled by the German action, these orders must have been understood to mean that they had their superiors' support to at the very least passively assist the Jews if they could. This was what Danish police did in numerous cases.

From his base at *Politiken* in central Copenhagen, Bergstrøm reported the same events in his diary: "At 10 p.m. the phones were disconnected. At the same time I was told that lots of German vehicles were seen on the street, the large ones covered with canvas. So that's how the raid would begin. When you couldn't use the telephone, it was because they didn't want the Jews to talk to one another. At the same time, it affected us all. One had a strange prisonlike feeling of being cut off from the outside world. I tried the phone again and again. It was and stayed dead. But the radio played in full force. First a song with an Armageddon-like character. Later patriotic tunes. There was a strange contrast between what was going on and what one heard. I said jokingly to Flemming: 'What is a home without a father (the embroidered piece in many small homes) and what is a reporter without a phone.' One could not be sure, of course, that the Germans would not also pay visit to *Politiken*, which was always being accused by the Nazis for being a Jew newspaper. Therefore I ate a solid meal as a precaution. You never know."

The action breathed new life into some of the painful questions that had plagued Danes since the surrender of April 9, 1940. Why didn't we put up a proper fight? And was it right for politicians to have cooperated with the occupying power? Didn't the assault now show that the Germans were not to be trusted, and that the Danish authorities had been duped? There were no easy answers, and still no one could point out what it was that the government should have done on April 9 or before. The war had amply demonstrated that even much larger countries could not stand against Germany. And it showed the brutality and the terrible devastation that was the result of even futile resistance. So was it wrong, after all, that Denmark had avoided such a disaster?

These issues, too, end up in Bergstrøm's records: "Some of the young people came, and the issue of defense was again debated. In regard to defense they still asked the question 'To what avail?' and I thought it would be irrelevant to discuss what we should have done when we were doing nothing. I slept a little in the chair. The watchman came. He said that the Germans had tanks and guns on the city's periphery, as if they were awaiting a rebellion. Plenty of cars drove through the streets, and Jews were being arrested everywhere. They were driven to Alsgades School.

"Soon there was a full house. One of the watchman's friends, whom the Germans had told to lock Jews up someplace, ran away through some backyards. He wouldn't do it. It was past midnight. The phones were still down."[20]

The resistance fighter Erling Foss also put his observations that night into a report sent to Stockholm and London a few days later, including his intelligence on the embarkation in the harbor: "The scenes at the loading of the two vessels are said to have been heartbreaking, as told in the city from the cordoned-off neighborhoods where the prisoners were embarked. Whole families were taken. Two cases were mentioned of women over 80. There was talk of suicides prior to the action, including one for sure—Manager Poul Dessau. There are reports from those released—who are afraid to speak for fear of harassment—that they were roughly treated, including being kicked in the legs."

In the same report, dated October 4, Foss backtracks in regard to the role of the permanent secretaries: "The message that the permanent secretaries met and decided to give the Germans an offer to intern the Jews was somewhat premature. They refute that anything like this happened, as several permanent secretaries would not agree to facilitate the work of the executioners."[21]

It is unclear whether someone deliberately lied to Foss about the Danish offer or—more likely—whether he talked to some of the permanent secretaries who opposed handing over the Danish offer. If that is the case, it reflects that at least some of those directly involved had already gotten cold feet and absolved themselves of responsibility for the failed Danish internment plan, while Svenningsen and Larsen stood by it. It may also reflect some confusion as to what precisely was decided and presented to the Germans.

Today we know more about what actually happened that night than Bergstrøm could know on Rådhuspladsen while the events were unfolding, or what Foss subsequently gleaned. During the night German military police, helped by Danish SS volunteers and the Schalburg Brigade, carried out a comprehensive action across the entire country, but most intensely concentrated in Copenhagen, where the majority of Danish Jews lived. The action was well prepared and well staffed, and it was implemented consistently and brutally. It is estimated that there were thirteen to fourteen hundred German policemen in Denmark—enough to carry out a full-scale action, all the more so, since in the provinces there were Wehrmacht soldiers available to assist. The order was that all "pure Jews" and "half Jews" married to Jews were to be deported. There is no doubt that the goal that night was to arrest as many people as possible. Yet the result of the raid in Copenhagen was meager, with fewer than three hundred out of the German estimate of six thousand Jews arrested. This was due first and foremost to the fact that the vast majority had fled from their homes, but also because of the order not to break into houses and apartments if the owner did not open the door. A grim exception was the Jewish old people's home in the synagogue courtyard. Many there had not been warned or evacuated, and about thirty of the residents were taken during the operation and deported.

The raid was completed at 1:00 a.m. and the arrested were immediately brought on board the cargo ship *Wartheland*, which had sailed to Copenhagen for this purpose. The ship could hold up to five thou-

Ekstra Bladet's front page on October 2, announcing the release of the sol-diers, at the bottom lower left, and—subtly—also the purge of the Jews.

The last thing the Germans wanted was publicity about the action against the Jews in Denmark. At the same time, some explanation had to be provided. The result was the announcement that the Danish soldiers who had been held hostage since August 29 were now being released, as the Jews who had instigated the sabotage were removed from society. The attempt to blame the sabotage on the Jews, and to link the much-wanted release of the hostages to the rounding up of Jewish citizens, only served to fuel public anger and contempt for the Germans.

Even if Werner Best noted in his reports to Berlin that the action had not been met with violent demonstrations or protests, and that the release of the soldiers had served its purpose, it is clear that the German authorities in Denmark were well aware of the profoundly negative impact of the action on relations with the Danish authorities and the Danish public. No German wanted to be responsible for a further manhunt, and though a notice about further efforts to arrest the Jews was drafted, it was never made public. The Germans wanted to proceed to other matters.

The legal Danish press, thus, made no reference to the stunning fact that overnight some seven to eight thousand people had vanished into thin air or to their obvious efforts to escape to Sweden. Nor did the press step up anti-Semitic rhetoric or direct further accusations against the Jews or those coming to their aid. The issue simply disappeared from the press—except in Sweden, where the free papers reported in detail on the percecution of the Danish Jews and on the stream of refugees landing on the Swedish coast.

Mediemuseet, Odense

REDAKTION
AADHUSPL. 33, KØBENHAVN.
KONTORTID 7—17½ — TELEFON 1114
Telegram-Adresse:
EKSTRABLADET COPENHAGEN

TATSTELEFON 146. CODE: WESTERN UNION

EKSPEDITION
AADHUSPL. 37, KØBENHAVN.
KONTORTID 8—17 — TELEFON 8811
POSTGIROKONTO 1199

Ekstra Bladet

KORRESPONDENTER I PARIS, LONDON, BERLIN, ROM, WIEN, NEW YORK, BRUXELLES, ATHEN, OSLO, STOCKHOLM

ABONNEMENTSPRISER

	I alt I Periode	København og Provinsen	Udlandet + Sverrig	Sverrig Finland Tyskland
Uge i samlet Forsendelse)...		1.50	1.25	
Maaned	3.15	6.15	5.15	
Kvartal	9.00	18.00	15.00	

Løssalgspris:
15 Øre over hele Landet

AVNEOMRAADET
NEAPEL RØMMET AF
E TYSKE STYRKER

fter Bortflytning af alle krigsvigtige eholdninger og Ødelæggelse af Anlæg, er kunde være til Nytte for de Allierede

arde Kampe paa begge Sider Vesuv

Berlin, 1 Dag.
ternationale Information meddeler
ET spanvere Havneomraade i Neapel blev i de tidlige Morgentimer
ne efter flere Maaneders grundig
lytning af alle krigsvigtige Behold-
er og Ødelæggelse af snadanne An-
Byen og Havne, der kunde være til
e for Englænderne og Amerikanerne,
net, uden at de amerikanske og en-
e Divisioner havde været i Stand til
ingge Hindringer i Vejen for Rømnin-

lve Byen havde allerede lidt over-
tlig haardt under de talrige heftige
k-amerikanske Luftangreb, og det
aer gaaet ud over Boligdistrikterne

ampene omkring Vesuv

llierede Angreb, der blev brudt ved haard tysk Modstand

Berlin, 1 Dag.
internationale Information meddeler
ng Aften om Situationen i Syd-

ORDVEST for Salerno foretog britiske og amerikanske Styrker i
det forudsete Forsøg paa at til-
ge sig Bevægelsesfrihed paa begge
af Vesuv i Retning af Neapel. Efter
den foregaaende Dag havde fundet
kehaben paa Sletten ved Neapel i
den foregaaende Dag havde fundet
Havel og paa Landsiden ved Vulkan-
siven paa haard tysk Modstand, som
rods gentagne Angreb ikke formaaede
rede nogetsteds.

store allierede Tab ved
Kysten

den smalle Kyststribe i Torre-Omraadet
de saa store blodige Tab, at de endnu
Hermiddagens Løb ikke formaaede at
optage deres. Angreb. Paa dette Tida-

punkt forsøgte engelsk-amerikanske In-
fanteriafdelinger, der stottedes af Kamp-
vognsafdelinger, at aabne Bjergvejen mod
Nord ved Vesuvs østlige Rand. For at ud-
ligne de betydelige Tab, de ogsaa led her
ved Angrebet nærved van Styrker, der
fortes frem fra de nærliggende Omraader
ved Scafati og Pompeji. Efter Tabet af de
fleste Kampvogne, nemlig i alt 7 Sherman-
Vogne, der i øvrigt kun viste sig paa langt
Skudhold og efter at to Nygrupperinger
var blevet sprængt af de tyske Batterier,
der sattes ind fra begge Sider, traak Englænderne og Amerikanerne sig ogsaa tilbage her.

Alle Omringningsbevægelser er mislykkedes

Derved er alle de sidste to Dages Gen-
nembrudsforsøg og Englændernes og Amerikanernes Omringningsbevægelser i det
vestlige Kystafsnit fuldstændig mislykke-
des. Amerikanernes Tab af Mandskab i
og ost for Avellino-Omraadet oversteget
de britiske Tab, fordi disse sidste i flere
Dage holdt sig forsigtigt tilbage i den
nordlige Bue af Salerno-Bugten, medens
Amerikanerne aabenbart havde faaet
Ordre til at foretage en Fremrykning fra
Øst, (R.B.)

LØSLADELSE AF
DE INTERNEREDE
DANSKE SOLDATER

Løsladelsen paabegyndes de nærmeste Dage og vil finde Sted i det Tempo, der bestemmes af de tekniske Muligheder

Officielt meddeles:

EFTER at Jøderne, som ved deres tyskfjendtlige Ophidselses-
virksomhed og deres moralske og materielle Støtte til Terror-
og Sabotagehandlinger, hvilket i væsentlig Grad har bidraget til
Skærpelsen af Situationen i Danmark, ved de fra tysk Side trufne
Forholdsregler er blevet udskilt af det offentlige Liv og hindret i
fortsat at forgifte Atmosfæren, vil der som Opfyldelse af det Øn-
ske, der næres i videre Krese af den danske Befolkning, i den nærmeste Dage blive paabegyndt Løsladelse af internerede danske
Soldater, og Løsladelsen vil finde Sted i det Tempo, der bestemmes
af de tekniske Muligheder.

Vu falder Træerne
i Østersøgade

KOMMUNALBESTYRELSEN har be-
sluttet at Beløb til Ombytning af de
ule, mer eller mindre defekte Træer i
astersøgade, og i disse Dage er Gartnerne
i Gang med Arbejdet. Først kappes
nevene af — som man er paa Billedet —
bagefter falder Træet for Økerns Hug.

Gigtdagen

er hurtigt blevet populær, takket være en
energisk og maalbeidst Propaganda, og
efter i Aar tog Københavnerne godt imod
de smaa og store Sælgere, som fra Mor-
genstunden prægede Gadebilledet. Her ser man en ung Dame, der ikke alene be-
synes sig selv, men samtidig køber et Mærke til sin firbenede Ven: Ogsaa Hunde
kan jo komme til at lide af Gigt, ma hvorfor skulde "Trofast" ikke give sit Bidrag
til Dagen?

5 ALLIEREDE BOMBEMASKINER
SKUDT NED AF TYSKE JAGERE
UNDER LUFTKAMPE OVER ALPERNE

Fem andre Maskiner blev saa alvorligt beskadiget, at de maatte forlade deres Formation

Berlin, 1 Dag.

DNB erfarer, at fjendtlige
Bombemaskineafdelin-
ger ved Middagstid i Gaar fløj ind over
de østlige og vestlige Alper. De blev angrebet af tyske Jagere og forfulgt. Ifølge
de hidtil indløbne Meldinger blev 5 fire
Motorers Bombemaskiner skudt ned over
de vestlige Alper og 5 andre saa haardt
beskadiget, at de maatte gaa ud af For-
nationen. Under disse Operationer fløj
de fjendtlige Maskiner gentagne Gange i
flere Bølger ind over schweiziske Omraade. Ogsaa over de østlige Alper kom det
til heftige Luftkampe. RB.

En Maskine skudt ned af det schweiziske Anti-luftskyts

Bern, 1 Dag.
Britiske Bombemaskiner krænkede ifølge
D. N. B. Fredag Middag paa ny Schweis'
Højhedsomraade, i en officiel schweizisk
Meddelelse hedder det, at de i forskellige
Dele af Østschweiz og i Graubünden ned-
kastede Bomber. Det hedder videre, at der i
disse Omraader efter Luftkampe mellem fi-
remotorers amerikanske Bombemaskiner

tyske Luftjagere er styrtet Flyvemaskiner
ned. Antiluftskytset traadte i Virksomhed,
og det er med Sikkerhed observeret, at det
har beskudt en firemotorers Bombemaskine.
Ifølge de hidtidige Meldinger er der anrettet materiel Skade ved Bombenedkastnin-
gerne. RB.

ET TYVERI FRA
FRILANDSMUSEET

Et Par værdifulde Museumsgenstande stjaalet ved højlys Dag. — Sandsynligvis er Kosterne ført bort fra Museet i en Barnevogn

PAA Frilandsmuseet i Lyngby er der
for et Par Uger siden begaaet et dri-
stigt Tyveri, hvorved et Par uerstattelige
Museumsgenstande er blevet stjaalet.

Det drejer sig om en antik Tinkande
og en Tallerken. Kanden, der er blevet
stjaalet fra Østenfeldtgaarden, er en
Pibekande med buet Underdel og slank,
cylindrisk Hals. Den er 26 Centimeter
høj, og Bundens Tværsnit er 11,8 Centimeter. I Laaget er indgraveret Navnet
Jacob Selck og Aarstallet 1770. Kanden
er desuden forsynet med tre Tinstempler.

nemlig tre Taarne, to Bogstaver — vist-
nok R. B. — og Christian VII's Krone og
Navnetræk.
Tallerkenen var halvdyb og med glat
Kant.

De to værdifulde Genstande er fjernet fra Museumsom-
raadet i en Barnevogn, da det er forbudt
at tage alle Slags Tasker med ind paa Museet. Du skal aflevere ved Indgangen.

Man har hidtil ikke villet meddele Of-
fentligheden noget om Tyveriet af Frygt
for, at Gerningsmanden skulde blive smeltet
om af Forbyderne, men efter at Kriminal-
politiet nu forgæves har søgt efter dem hos
Marskandiserre og andre, har man ment
det bedst at offentlyse dem.

Det maa siges at være en uslminedelig
utilladelse Handling at berøve Museet
disse Skatte. Metalværdien er kun nogle
faa Hundrede Kroner, men Museumsvær-
dien er naturligvis en ganske anden. Det
veriet betyder et smerteligt Tab for Frilandsmuseet.

6000 TONS HVEDE
TIL DEN GRÆSKE
CIVILBEFOLKNING

Athen, 1 Dag.

DE svenske Dampere "Bardaland" og
"Tamara", der sejler for det internationale Røde Kors, til Middelhavet blev
fra autoritativ Side, oplyser D.N.B., an-
komme til Saloniki med 6000 Tons Hvede
og andre Levnedsmidler fra overgtiske
Lande. To andre Skibe er undervejs til
Piræus. Levnedsmidlerne er udelukkende
bestemt for den græske Civilbefolkning.
R.B.

SIDSTE

Bukarest, 1 Dag.
I Nat fløj fjendtlige Flyvere if. D.N.B.
ind over rumænsk Omraade uden dog
at nedkaste Bomber. I Departementerne
Ilfov, Arad og Timisho-rantal blev der
nedkastet Flyveblade. En Premierløjtnant
og en Løjtnant, der var sprunget ud med
Faldskærm, blev taget til Fange. De har-
de store Mængder rumænske Penge, Læ-
gemidler og Levnedsmidler paa sig. R.B.

*

Berlin, 1 Dag.
I Nat fløj britisk-amerikanske Bombe-
maskinestyrker ifølge D.N.B. ind over
den rhinsk-westfalske Omraade. Det tyske
Luftforsvar angreb straks de fjendtlige
Maskiner, der opererede under Beskyttelse
af et tæt Skydække, og splittede dem,
da de ikke kunde gennemføre et planlagt
koncentrisk Angreb. I rhinsk-westfalske
Byer, der ligger langt fra hverandre, blev
der anrettet Skade paa Bygninger, og Ci-
vilbefolkningen led Tab. R.B.

BRITISK FARTØJ
SKUDT I BRAND
VED BOULOGNE

Berlin, 1 Dag.
Internationale Information meddeler:

KORT før Midnat blev et britisk Far-
tøj, der havde nærmet sig Boulogne
Havn skudt i Brand. Efter at være blevet
ramt af Granater drev Fartøjet omkring
for Havnen ude at Stand til at ma-
nøvrerere. Andre britiske Fartøjer, der-
blandt Hurtigbaade, der ligeledes blev beskudt, drejede af og forsvandt. (R.B.)

TYSKE U-BAADE HAR UNDER
10 DAGES ANGREB PAA TO
KONVOJER SÆNKET 10 SKIBE

Blandt de sænkede Fartøjer er tre Krigsskibe

Amsterdam, 1 Dag.

EFTER hvad der ifg. D.N.B. meddeles fra en By ved Canadas Østkyst,
har tyske Undervandsbaade sænket 10
allierede Skibe under et heftigt 10 Dags

Angreb mod to Konvojer, der var undervejs til Canada. Angrebet begyndte den
19. September, og der tilføjedes de allierede haarde Tab. Blandt de sænkede
Fartøjer var tre Krigsskibe. R.B.

BRYLLUP I DAG

I Gentofte Kirke vies i Dag Frk. Jytte
Liz Østrup, Datter af afdøde Fuigtemei-
ster Østrup, til Landinspektør Haukur Pje-
tursson fra Reykjavik, der er knyttet til
Geodætisk Institut. Vi præsenterer her det
unge Brudepar.

HERREGAARD SOLGT

Uldkræmmeren, der blev Herremand

Hjørring, 1 Dag.

FABRIKANT J. Krøjgaard, Herning,
har solgt den gamle historiske Herre-
gaard "Høgholt" ved Sindal til en Kon-
sortium fra Frederikshavn for ca. 500,000
Kroner. Herregaarden, som har et Areal
paa 505 Td. Land, blev overtaget af Fabrikant Krøjgaard for to Aar siden og ko-
stede da 430,000 Kroner. Overtagelsen fin-
der Sted i næste Uge. "Høgholt"s Historie
gaar tilbage til Tiden før 1340. Fabrikant
Krøjgaard, der nu har solgt Herregaarden, er i Halvtredserne. Han er født i et
fattigt Husmandshjem paa Heden ved Herning og var i sine unge Dage ved Land-
bruget, men slog sig senere paa Uldhandel
og var i en Del af sine Ungdomsaar om-
vandrende Uldkræmmer. Han er Hernings
største Skatteyder.

AGERHØNS:

Der er mange Agerhøns i Aar, saa
mange, at man haaber at faa lov til
at plumbere nogle for at sikre dem til
Jagt-paa de haarde Agerhøns. Markmaur-
prisen paa de gamle er 3.00 pr. Par, Høns
og gaat Nøb, de unge er gulnrøde og
Nabenes sorte. Saa er De orienteret og
at følge den unge Damer Eksempel!

sand prisoners. Paul Hennig, the leading Danish Gestapo man, was aboard cross-examining those arrested to establish whether they should be deported according to the given criteria. This procedure led to the release of nearly a third, who were not rated as pure Jews, leaving 202 individuals to be deported. To these were added some 150 Danish Communist detainees from Horserød, brought to the ship that night. In the provinces eighty-two Jews were arrested and placed in three of the forty waiting freight cars destined for Theresienstadt in the present-day Czech Republic.[22]

It was already clear from Duckwitz's warning and later from Best's information to Svenningsen in the evening that the detainees would be taken to Theresienstadt. According to some of the initial information, the deported would be divided by age and ability to work, but it seems to have become clear very quickly that all the Danish internees would go first to Theresienstadt. The camp was used partly as a collection camp for older prisoners, partly as a transit station from which thousands were sent on to the extermination camps. Thus, although Theresienstadt was not an extermination camp, the key factor was whether prisoners remained under the relatively orderly conditions there, or whether they were sent to death camps.[23]

After the raid thousands of Jewish refugees went underground, in many cases whole families with their elderly and children who traveled together, particularly in Copenhagen and the northern part of Sjælland. Where earlier they had been on the run from an action they feared would come, now they had become hunted and critically dependent on help from the surrounding community.

CHAPTER 7

SATURDAY, OCTOBER 2

THE TRANSFER

After the Storm

That morning, a brief, laconic telephone message from the police summed up the situation: "German patrols seen tonight in numerous places leading entire families with children and suitcases. They're moving in the direction of Langelinje. Besides that nothing is known."

When Vilhelm Bergstrøm brought his bike into *Politiken's* courtyard, the worried guard asked him: "Are they allowed to do just anything?"

In the harbor the *Wartheland* was ready for those to be deported. Jesper Trier, who went with his ninety-year-old father to the ship, reported: "The climb to the ship up a high, steep and very awkward ladder took place under brutal shouts and blows. A few German military police officers stood behind the railing equipped with long bamboo rods, bent into a hook at one end, with which they caught the neck of victims and dragged them up, if their ascent did not go fast enough."

At 10:00 a.m. the steamer left Copenhagen heading for Swinemünde on the German Baltic coast, just east of today's border with Poland. The eighty-two arrested Jews from Jutland and Fyn were picked up by one of the special trains departing from Aalborg at 11:10 a.m. The purpose of the trains was revealed only shortly before their departure, and the report from Danish Railways noted that "railway staff was very shaken by what they witnessed, however they performed correctly."[1]

To many the action against the Jews was a humiliating negation of the cooperative line the elected politicians had promulgated. The indiscriminate exercise of power against innocent citizens, which the politicians had been so resolved to deter, was now a reality and confirmed the worst fears of August 29 that the introduction of martial law, the internment of Danish forces, the application of the death penalty, and deportations were only the beginning. Despite all protests the Germans had not hesitated to carry out an operation that lacked even the flimsiest legitimacy. This was Nazi ideology in its purest form, deeply threatening to a society that had hitherto been remarkably successful in avoiding such abuses in daily life. Bergstrøm met a friend who told him in a frightened whisper: "It is good that we are not Jews." But Bergstrøm, who had now understood the bigger picture, could not reassure her: "We mustn't rejoice too soon. Our turn could be next. And in any event, it is a very sad story."[2]

For the families in the forest, Bergstrøm's perspective was already an urgent reality. The restless night at the cabin had not lessened their problems. On the contrary, they were now more perplexed than ever even if they had no idea of the wider events of the night. Uncertainty and responsibility weighed, and Poul Hannover began to question the decisions they had already made, and the blind alley in which the family seemed to find itself. If one wants to travel from Copenhagen to Sweden, Falster is neither the straightest nor the most obvious way. On the other hand, it was not so easy now to begin to head north again. They were also hungry, thirsty, and tired.

Poul continues:

We wondered just how early we could risk going up to a farm the next morning—and when it was 7 o'clock, Talleruphuus went on the road—Erik and I—we had seen a paradise apple tree [a kind of crab apple] in the forest, less than a kilometer from the holiday camp—we went down, and Erik shook it like crazy, so that we downed a good dozen small apples—those we ate to clean our mouths. At last Talleruphuus came back—he had been calling about a car—and he said something about the ignition, which had blown, so that the boat could not make the trip. It did not sound encouraging. We cleaned up as well as we could—and after having packed the family out the door, we put a new latch on it—went with our flashlights back to the window we had broken into and crawled out of—and hung the broken shutter up again—and grabbed our bags. It was not so easy to carry them a good kilometer. When we got to the place where the car had left us the previous day, we put down

the bags—and Gunnar and I walked on—it was our intention to go
to Horbelev, approximately 4 kilometers away, as we were aware
that the car could not possibly take all of us.

The families had decided to go to the town of Stubbekøbing, ten
kilometers north of Hesnæs, partly to solve the problem of the hungry and thirsty children, partly to find further transport. Panic is kept
in check, and the cottage is left as decent people would do. But everything is suddenly very difficult, and even getting a few kilometers up
the road entails great challenges and risks: "When we had gone some
way, the car passed—it came back somewhat later with all of them and
the luggage—when it stopped, the nice driver gave us a lift and we went
off—toward Stubbekøbing. I sat in front with Mette and talked with the
driver—although he didn't say anything, he knew what was going on.
Later I was told that the police had called him and asked where he had
been the previous day. I'm pretty sure that they did it to help us—but of
course we saw ghosts everywhere. A forest ranger cast a long look after
us—who would expect to see a dozen people with suitcases come out
of the woods? The driver had answered the police that he had been in
another small town—and he detoured to bring us as directly as possible
to the hotel."

Meanwhile in Copenhagen, Dr. Best sent his first report on the night's
action to Ribbentrop. Best chose to go on the offensive, but he did not
mention the number of detainees. Instead he chose to build on the
overall objective, which was fulfilled. The Danish Jews had evaporated:
"Starting today, Denmark can be considered cleansed of Jews [*entjudet*]
as no Jew can legally reside or work here anymore." Best skillfully tried
to push the responsibility for continuing the search over to General
Hanneken, who according to martial law still held the executive power
in the country. Best thus continued his efforts to tie the Wehrmacht in
to the action, and in his early reporting to Berlin he quoted an official
statement supposed to be published later that same day to the effect that
all Jews had to report to the authorities and that anyone who helped the
refugees would be "punished according to the laws of war." Curiously,
the announcement was never released—a fact Best subsequently blamed
on Hanneken and on Dr. Mildner. The fact is that no one within the
German top brass in Denmark wanted to get his fingers dirty, and that

everybody was seeking to avoid direct responsibility for the continuation of the search. Still, in relation to Berlin they all had to play it subtly and be seen as doing neither too much, nor too little.

While the proclamation threatening anyone helping the Jews was never issued, the German authorities explained the action in an official announcement on Saturday morning, published in newspapers and broadcast over the radio: "Whereas the Jews, who by their anti-German agitation and their moral and material support for terrorism and sabotage have contributed significantly to the radicalization of the situation in Denmark, have been removed from public life by the measures taken by the German side and thus are prevented from continuing to poison the atmosphere, the authorities will meet the demands from a wide circle of the Danish population and in the next few days begin release of the detained Danish soldiers."[3]

If Best believed this reasoning would play well with the general public, he was utterly wrong. Most parts of the population, already deeply traumatized by the events of the night, felt that the statement added mockery to injustice, and even if the wish to have the detained soldiers freed was indeed widespread, linking their release to the arrest of innocent citizens was met with anger.

This reaction was not surprising given the mood of the general public in the lead-up to the action. What is more surprising is the fact that no enthusiasm can be traced to any of the leading representatives of the German occupation authorities. Everybody seems to have been busy disclaiming responsibility for the consequences, while trying to protect themselves against criticism of the night's meager catch. An example is Major General Erik von Heimburg, who was commander of the German Order Police in Denmark, and who summarized the situation that Saturday in a secret report to Berlin: "The consequences of the action against the Jews could be decisive for the entire situation in the country. Generally, there is fear of an increase in anti-German sentiment, which is already strongly influenced by the enemy radio propaganda, which still can be received everywhere here with impunity."[4]

It was still quite unclear to most Danes how many Jews had been interned during the night. But all had their own experiences, and rumors swirled, as revealed by Bergstrøm's notes from arrests in the apartment house where he lived with his wife and young daughter: "Last night at 10:30 p.m., the caretaker heard the tramp of ironclad boots in the yard, and he thought that it was the housekeeper, who had put the Germans onto him. His wife had been very nervous. But it was not the caretaker the Germans were after, but some Jews who live in this building. . . . However, they had left several days ago. . . . I went up and told Elsa the news. She was deeply disturbed. . . . She had read the notice in the newspaper about the Jews' situation. It had affected her so strongly that she felt sick in her chest. She said that no Jews had been for the dancing lesson last night. . . . They had vanished. When she and Tusse [their daughter] left the dance, they met a Jewish family outside, who had come over with suitcases from the Terminus Hotel. Their sons used to be part of the dance classes. One of them wanted to take a look inside, but the father said: 'Oh good heavens, that was the way it was!' So they went on, rigid and petrified. The woman had no fur coat—she was in a light worsted jacket. Where were they going? Elsa felt so sorry for them."

There is still some way to go before the hardened crime reporter's own heart starts to ache. But the irony is abating, supplanted by human sympathy. At the same, just like Heimburg, Bergstrøm predicts that the action will permanently change the relationship between occupiers and occupied: "This step now taken by the Germans will destroy much. Pressure is bound to produce counterpressure, and since we are the small ones, there will probably be hell to pay."[5]

The same morning Werner Best's second-in-command, Kanstein, telephoned Nils Svenningsen at the Foreign Ministry. The Germans were still fending off Danish authorities with talk, and Kanstein told him that no reply had come from Berlin about Svenningsen's offer of the previous evening, that Denmark itself was ready to initiate the detention. He explained further that the Jews who were interned during the night would be sent to Germany very soon, by ship. He gave assurances that there would be no new actions like that of the night before and asked Svenningsen, in a conciliatory way, to ensure that the deportees' apartments and property would be taken care of. The director of the Foreign Ministry was of two minds. On the one hand one "could expect a reluctance on the Danish side to deal with anything whatsoever concerning this case." Conversely "a protective measure" might warrant consideration.

It did not take long before Svenningsen overcame his reluctance to have anything to do with it. On the contrary, he now wanted to involve the Danish authorities to ensure that no half Jews or other "fraction Jews" were accidentally deported—as had already happened. Svenningsen therefore asked for permission to "send representatives to the place where the Jews were held to check if there might be more mistakes."

This request was the first sign that the permanent secretaries were about to change horses. If the deportations could not be stopped, it was important that the Danish authorities now engage as much as possible. The more closely Danish officials followed the deportees, the greater the chance of saving at least a few—and also the chance of holding the Germans to their commitments that the deportees would not be treated badly. This initial attempt at Danish involvement in the fate of the deportees evolved over the following days, weeks, and months into a comprehensive effort to keep track of individual Danish deportees and to ease their conditions where possible.

During the conversation Kanstein also told Svenningsen that a large group of Danish Communists—the last of those arrested by Danish police on the orders of the Danish government in 1941—were also being deported to Germany. This was extremely embarrassing as those arrested and now to be deported had been held in violation of normal legislation and, according to the prevailing view, in breach of the constitution. The attempted protection extended by Danish society toward its citizens of Jewish origin was not mirrored in the situation of the Danish Communists who were arrested in 1941 by Danish police: They were held under a sort of protective Danish control and repeatedly reassured that they would not be handed over to the Germans. But on August 29 the Germans had simply taken over the camp—and now some 150 detained Communists were being deported to an unknown fate in German concentration camps, excepting only about 90 who had managed to escape in the wake of the dramatic events on August 29.

Werner Best needed the Communists to pump up the numbers of deported, and when Svenningsen inquired it turned out that the steamer *Wartheland* had already left Copenhagen. All attempts to get Danish officials involved were in vain. The troubled Svenningsen was assured that the 150 Communists "would be placed in a camp and would get light work. There was no reason for concern about their fate." Nothing could have been further from the truth. The Danish Communists were taken to Stutthof concentration camp near Danzig, present-day Gdansk, where six of the deportees perished during the following sixteen months, nine others in January 1945 during the death march from east to west, ordered because of the advancing Red Army, and another seven after liberation as a result of maltreatment and abuse.[6]

Frey's Hotel

While Danish and German officials maneuvered in Copenhagen, the overloaded car on Falster arrived safely in Stubbekøbing with the whole family tired and worn out after the night in the summer colony. Unaware of the night's events, they decided to disregard security and go into the city hotel to recuperate, wash, and get something to eat. The idea of fried eggs overcame fear, and they headed straight for the city's finest hotel, right on the main street and a stone's throw from the harbor. It could have been fatal.

Poul Hannover writes: "Arrived in town—again with a big car bill—and went straight in to get some breakfast—we had ordered a lot of bread and 2 fried eggs for each—Kis and Gunnar had gone to wash themselves—when the radio suddenly came on—well, I can't remember the exact wording, but it was the announcement that since the Jews were behind all the sabotage and unrest, the German authorities had made arrangements to have them removed from public life."

The German communication was so unbearable that Poul and Inger Hannover initially decided to keep the alarming news to themselves: "It was read twice—luckily Kis and Gunnar hadn't heard it—and Inger and I were immediately aware that if it could be avoided, neither they nor the children should hear about it. As soon as we had eaten—it went quickly—I looked for Goldstein [the adult son of another Jewish family, who was also at Frey's Hotel, and whom Hannover had met by chance the day before]. As his group consisted of a total of 9 people, I was aware that they might occupy several rooms, and in order not to attract too much attention, I asked him if we could borrow a few of them—in particular that our children could get some rest. Although they had slept, it had been a tough night for them—and what was worse, the next night would hardly be better. We had room no. 10. I took the bedspreads off and put each child on his bed and told them to sleep. It was difficult—of course they could feel that our nerves were completely on edge—Kis and Gunnar got one or two other rooms—Dorte and Mette asked to be together, but I was strict—and refused. Palle even had a little cold and a small earache—but they got some powder for him—and fortunately he got better again."

Kis wrote her own version of the arrival at the hotel and the difficulties with finding additional transport: "The first fisherman whom Talleruphuus tried was willing to sail, but it was not certain that his wife would let him. There was also talk about someone on Bogø [an island near Stubbekøbing] and a Swedish steamer, which was said to be in the harbor. Erik ran around and tried all the available options. The host at the hotel and the waiter were completely with us, and the host had told the Goldsteins that he wouldn't send any notice to the authorities about them before they had left the hotel.

"The local priest and the bank director offered their help. The idea was to stay with them if we did not manage to depart—as we dared not stay at the hotel. Afterward we found out that Poul and Inger that morning overheard the radio announcement about apprehending the Jews, as it was they who were behind sabotage and unrest. Inger, who up to this point would rather have stayed back home, now no longer doubted that we had to leave. Still, it was obviously going to be difficult to get someone to sail for us."

In the course of the few hours at Frey's Hotel the family's situation is becoming both clearer and more exposed. They are wanted, and the last doubt about the necessity of escape is swept away. At the same time it becomes clear that it is not so easy to find passage to Sweden, even for the assembled families who were prepared to pay considerable sums for the crossing. The Danes around them, from the hotel owner to the local officials, are all willing—even eager—to help. But the crucial link is the fishermen and their boats. Can and will they take the risk? For the refugees there is no choice. But for each fisherman it is a big decision that involves his whole family: A large profit is in the balance if things go well. But no one knows what the consequences will be if they go wrong. Arrest? Seizure of the vessel—the basis for the welfare of his entire family? Or even worse: sinking in the open sea, armed pursuit, deportation, torture, execution? No one knew.

The situation forces the refugees together in a community. In addition to the Hannover and Marcus families, three other families had sought refuge at Frey's Hotel. The Goldsteins were accompanied by the Ledermann family, and by a young man, Mogens Margolinsky, all of whom were unfamiliar to the newcomers. But that changed at Frey's Hotel, where they quickly realized that they had a shared destiny and therefore had to stick together and try to reach a joint decision. The group was far from socially homogeneous. When each accounted for their financial situation a few days later, Poul Hannover declared an annual income of 100,000 kroner, Abraham Ledermann 40,000 kroner, Gunnar Marcus

Frey's Hotel on the main street of the small town of Stubbekøbing, around the beginning of World War II. The building no longer exists.

Postcard from local archive, Stubbekøbing

Allan Hannover shortly after his arrival in Sweden. The boy struggled to keep aloof from events and wrote his own diary notes. Mostly they follow his father's, but Allan himself understood the grim dilemma his family faced as they sought escape to Sweden.

Private family collection

14,000 kroner, while the Goldstein brothers declared annual salaries of 1,200 and 1,500 kroner. These last declarations are somewhat confusing considering that both were educated and one of them held a position as engineer that at the time would normally generate an annual income of some 5,000 kroner. In any event, paying several thousand kroner for the passage was quite a different issue for Poul Hannover than it was for the Goldsteins.[7]

In his refuge with Dr. Hart in Ruds Vedby in the western part of Sjælland, the twin sisters' father, Dr. Meyer, had also heard the German message on the radio. It made him more indignant than scared: "Next morning . . . I heard on the radio the infamous, vile announcement that 'by the German Wehrmacht's action the Jews had been separated from public life because of their acts of sabotage and aversion to Germany, and after they had poisoned and demoralized the population. In turn the military internees would be released!' (As is well known, General Gørtz [supreme commander of the Danish army] announced later that the Danish military did not want to be released as a consequence of vio-lence against their countrymen.) On Swedish radio I heard the offer of Sweden to receive all of the Danish Jews. The day before I had been on a little walk to Vedbygaard, but I have kept inside since, only twice a walk in the garden, because there were a few Nazis in the town. At 1:28 p.m. I picked up Mary, who brought most of her securities, otherwise only a small bag. She got the name of Miss Mary Gotfredesen."

For years Dr. Meyer had taken care of his elderly and fragile siser-in-law, Mary Goldschmidt. Now, owing to a set of misunderstand-ings, she had left the north coast, where she, like thousands of others, had fled to find passage to Sweden, to travel back to Ruds Vedby to join Adolph Meyer. Although Meyer was not in a hurry, he slowly realized that he, too, had to cross the Øresund and go to Sweden. And he also felt a special responsibility for Mary, whom he had inadvertently sum-moned, and who now shared his fate.

In Copenhagen, Bergstrøm and other outsiders tried to get an overview of what had happened during the night—and the guesswork concerning the Germans' next move raced on:

On the street below *Politiken* I met Jacob [his colleague, Johannes Jacobsen, known as Jacob]. His wife came soon after. . . . Jacob told a story about how his daughter had been taken last night in her home in Vestersøhus. They thought she was a Jew, because the name Jacobsen was spelled with a *c*. They had dragged her to the synagogue on Krystalgade, which was the collection point. It was only there that they became aware of their mistake. Through the whole thing she stood tall and proud. At home she had various illegal resistance writings, but the Germans had not seen them. Up at the paper I heard that a ship with Jews had departed. This was confirmed by a night watchman who had heard "screaming and yelling" of women and children from the same quarters.

Nielsen came home from Police Headquarters, where he had served as a "listening post."... [Police Commissioner] Stamm had said that the search for Jews would continue. The general [Hanneken] had argued in favor of leniency. He had therefore stressed that the doors could not be forced. They had to make do with knocking. A ship with Jews had sailed, which would bring them to a camp in Bohemia. Each of them had to provide food for 8 days (how?). Between 600 and 1,000 Jews had already been taken.

Permanent Secretary Svenningsen, on behalf of all his colleagues, had been to see the general and protested against the persecution of the Jews, but the general had lamented: He had orders from the highest authorities. The German soldiers had been very sad to execute the task that they had been charged with.... Sweden had protested in Berlin; the rumor yesterday, then, had not been a lie. The empty apartments left by fleeing Jews would immediately be occupied by Christians. It was to be expected that the telephone disruption would continue.

In the Swedish legation Gustav Dardel was better informed. Shortly after midday he summed up the night's events in a telegram to Stockholm: "Yesterday at 9 p.m. 1,000 Gestapo and Danish Frikorps moved out—as the Danish police had refused—and arrested a large, as yet unknown, number of Jews who were brought to a vessel. The phones were cut across the country. Himmler seems to be in Copenhagen. Today the newspapers maintain, under the headline 'The soldiers released,' that this is made possible because the Jews are now separated from public life and can no longer continue to poison the atmosphere."

There were intense rumors that SS Reichsführer Heinrich Himmler, who was also head of the German police, was secretly in Copenhagen to oversee the operation. Just hearing the name caused most people to shudder—but the rumor was not true. Nor was the estimated number of deportations reported by Dardel in the course of the afternoon: "The Danish police inform confidentially and provisionally that approximately 1,600 full and half Jews have been taken and abducted."[8]

Meanwhile Bergstrøm comments on the German attempt to make the Danes accept the arrest of the Jews as a precondition for the release of the soldiers: "Commander Westermann told the sailors in a speech: 'Now we are released, but only in exchange for a really dirty deed.' He was referring to the Jews. And the sailors had loudly shouted: 'Shame!' There was widespread outrage in the city at the treatment [the Jews] had received."[9]

Uncertainty about what really had happened led many to fear the worst. The art collector C. L. David, who as mentioned had been in the sights of the local Nazi press, did not know what to believe, or whether being half Jewish protected him. Deeply worried, on October 2 he wrote a farewell letter to his friend and adviser H. H. Bruun:

Dear Bruun,

The possibility that I will be arrested seems, unfortunately, substantially closer than it seemed during our conversation yesterday. If I am deported, I do not see the possibility that I will ever live to return. I hope that you will monitor my business, as long as there is hope that I can return. When that chance can no longer be considered reasonable, my business should be run—not sold. I refer you here to my will, which is in the safe in my living room.

You will do what can be done, both for me and my business. Thank you for this and for many years of friendship.

With the heartiest greetings also to the whole family—not least to Libbe.

Yours CLD

The farewell letter has a brief addition reflecting David's distress, and surely that of many others, at the deliberate attempt to question and undermine their personal credibility and honesty. For a man like David this humiliation was almost harder to bear than the fear of deportation and death—as is also reflected in Poul Hannover's difficulty in coming to terms with the family's intrusion into the deserted vacation colony. Like most citizens these men nourished a deep skepticism in regard to the armed resistance movement, which at this time was still seen to be dominated by Communists and other radical forces whom the pillars of society considered threatening, as they did other criminals. Not because of sympathy with the Germans or as a reflection of cowardice, but because most accepted the premise that Danish society's best defense against Nazism was to unite under the prevailing social order. Therefore the Nazi accusation that the Jews were behind the sabotage was not only wrong, it was also insulting. This is why David felt the urge to add the following short postscript to the letter: "I do not need to assure you, with your knowledge of me, that I have never done anything that would in the least way motivate my arrest. On the contrary I have, always when I had the opportunity, as strongly as possible, tried to make people understand that any illegal activity had to be condemned."[10]

The Open Door

The message about the night's action reached the Swedish Foreign Ministry in the morning, and shortly after lunch Foreign Minister Christian Günther called the German minister over to protest, and to propose that the ships transporting Jews to Germany be diverted to Swedish ports instead. Although the first reports were that there were sixteen hundred detainees on board, Sweden was ready to receive them and to provide whatever help was need to alleviate their situation. The minister was not impressed. Sweden had no right to interfere in the Danish-German relationship, and he could therefore only receive the bid for help. Moreover the foreign minister's reference to the bad effect that the action would have on Swedish public opinion left little impression. The German minister noted acidly that the Swedish press's posture toward Germany was already so hostile that it could hardly get worse. In this he was wrong.[11]

Neither the politicians in Stockholm nor the Swedish legation in Berlin nourished any illusion that Nazi Germany would allow the Danish Jews to seek refuge in Sweden. The proposal served other purposes. The Swedish government wanted to demonstrate to the troubled Swedish public that it was doing everything possible to help in this desperate situation. The Free Danes in Stockholm were also drumming up public support and encouraging the Swedish government behind the scenes to take an active line in its efforts to help. The most prominent Free Dane in Stockholm, the journalist Ebbe Munck, who served as a liaison between the Danish resistance and the free world, worked persistently to put maximum pressure on the Swedes, who the courageous activist thought were moving too slowly. So did the world-famous Danish nuclear physicist, Niels Bohr, whose mother was Jewish, and who was in Stockholm for some weeks after his escape in September. Bohr had contacts with the government and the Swedish king and crown prince. He too deployed intense efforts to get the Swedish effort into gear.

Though both men lobbied throughout the Saturday, it was hardly the Danish activity that triggered the Swedish advances. The door to Sweden was already wide open, and Sweden also had a strong interest in demonstrating to the free world that after its extensive cooperation with Germany during the first years of the war and the halfhearted effort to save the Norwegian Jews in November 1942, the country was now ready to take action for the Danish Jews.

Like all the other players in the complicated diplomatic game, the Swedish government also figured that the end of the war was in sight, and that Germany was losing. Building the relationship to the victorious powers was now crucial. By August 1943 the transit agreement with Germany was discontinued and, under growing pressure from the Allies, Sweden now also sought to limit its exports, particularly of iron ore. Sweden was fully aware that the slightest hesitation in regard to the Danish Jews would be judged badly, particularly in Western Allied capitals. At the same time the German assault on civil society in Denmark provoked a violent feeling of injustice deep in a majority of the Swedish public, much the same way as it did in Denmark.

Thus, on Saturday, October 2, the Swedish Foreign Ministry, contrary to all diplomatic convention, decided to publish the contents of the démarche that the Swedish legation in Berlin had handed the German Foreign Ministry the day before. The head of the Foreign Ministry's press office argued for publication, which he felt in relation to the expected media frenzy could help to lift the newspapers' comments to "a higher level" and give them "a firmer basis." Foreign Minister Günther agreed, and the chief press officer held an international press conference on the afternoon of October 2 at the Grand Hotel in Stockholm. That evening at 7 p.m., the declaration was read aloud on the Swedish radio—in a version that was a little stronger than the one the Swedes had given directly to Germany: "For several days information had been provided to Sweden that actions against the Jews in Denmark were being prepared, of a similar nature previously implemented in Norway and other occupied countries. Upon instructions, Sweden's minister in Berlin, on October 1, has highlighted to the German authorities the serious consequences such actions would provoke in Sweden. In this context the minister made an offer from the Swedish government to receive all Danish Jews in Sweden."[12]

The journalists at the Grand Hotel asked pointed questions about the implications of "serious consequences," but the press officer responded circumspectly. He knew as well as anyone that Sweden could not or would not do anything to block the actual deportations. But Sweden was mobilizing its capacity to act as a safe haven ready to receive those who might miraculously be able to escape from Denmark to Sweden. This turned out to give major encouragement to the many Jews now hiding in Denmark, where Swedish radio broadcasts were easily heard (as noted also by Dr. Meyer). The Swedish declaration nourished a new hope—even if no one at this point imagined that the number of Danish refugees would be counted not in the hundreds but in the thousands.

"Half Jews" and "Full Jews"

In Copenhagen the permanent secretaries met at noon. It is tersely noted in the minutes from their meeting that their colleague Einar Cohn "was unable to be present." He was on the run. But a nephew of his, Bernhard Cohn, had until the same morning been of two minds about the rumors. On one hand he was determined not to let the Germans take him alive, on the other he didn't really believe they were coming after him. He had moved in with his friends Bjørn and Laila for a couple of days, and he took the fuss fairly calmly, at least if his own handwritten notes from those days are to be trusted. He drank some cognac with his friends, and he read the announcement that Sweden was ready to accept the displaced Danish Jews as an indication that the operation would be suspended. On Friday he had also sought out friends who were preparing for flight, encouraging them to stay. It was, he wrote, "silly to go" when one is "only a half Jew."

By Saturday morning the seriousness of the situation became apparent even to Bernhard, who had slept well overnight:

The next morning there was nothing noticeable. Bjørn got hold of the newspaper, big headlines declared that the detained soldiers would be released. I called Thomsen [his landlord]. I only reached

Mrs. Thomsen. When I asked her if there had been anything, she confirmed that the Germans had been there. As Laila and I looked more closely at the newspaper, we discovered something quite different. In the article on the released military, it was noted that the soldiers were freed because Denmark had now rid itself of the Jews, who were behind both the physical and moral acts of sabotage and other such lies.

Laila bicycled out . . . to hear what had happened, and she learned that they had driven around all night with human cargo. She was completely shocked and offered that I stay with them. To test Laila's strength, I asked her what she would do if it was made a capital crime to house Jews? "I don't care" was Laila's response.—I neither could nor would stay. I had previously heard from a chauffeur that a fisherman in Rørvig [a harbor some sixty kilometers northwest of Copenhagen] might be able to sail me over to Sweden. I intended to ride up there on my bike. When I came to Harry's summer home, I went in. Only Jeanette was at home. She said that Harry had gone to the dentist! She had heard nothing. I asked her to run down to the Fønns'. After half an hour she came back and told me that the Germans had taken Mama.[13]

Bernhard's mother was the sister of the head of the Foreign Ministry's statistical department, Einar Cohn, who had now made himself invisible. While he and his nephew struggled to find passage to Sweden, the permanent secretaries tried at their meeting to get a grip on the rapidly evolving situation.

Nils Svenningsen told his colleagues of his conversation with Best late the previous evening, including Best's assurances that the deportees would not be sent to Poland but to Bohemia, where they "would not have to suffer." (The notion that the intention for the Danish Jews was permanent detainment in Theresienstadt already seems to have taken root.) Svenningsen reported that, faced with the imminent German action, he had presented the proposal for a Danish internment; he also reported Best's lukewarm reaction to the Danish proposal. He transmitted Best's statement that the action concerned only the "full Jews, and even these were immune if they were married to an Aryan. There was no provision for the confiscation of Jewish property." Svenningsen also conveyed Kanstein's impression "that there were relatively few Jews who had been taken," and quoted his assurance that "it was ruled out that a new action would be launched."

With no way of knowing whether this would hold true, and without means to halt the deportations, the permanent secretaries began to focus their attention on the possibilities for mitigating the consequences for those directly affected. This was achieved partly by doing everything within their power to keep a line open to those who had fallen into German hands. As a first measure the Foreign Ministry insisted on involving itself in the efforts to avoid the deportation of "half Jews" and Jews married to Aryans, as opposed to "full Jews," while in parallel a special effort was made for those who were actually deported.[14] Svenningsen and his colleagues were about to change course to catch up with the situation now at hand. In London, the Danish minister, Reventlow, who was Director Svenningsen's predecessor at the Foreign Ministry, noted in his diary on October 2 upon the news of events in Denmark: "Poor Svenningsen. I think a lot of him, the best man of our foreign service."[15]

The authorities also decided to take care of the homes and belongings of those who disappeared, regardless of whether their owners had fled or been deported. Permanent Secretary Hans Henrik Koch of the Ministry of Social Affairs announced to his colleagues "that he had directed the Copenhagen Social Services, in cooperation with the police, to ensure a degree of supervision of the Jews' apartments, to the extent they had been abandoned without caretakers," and Svenningsen thought "that we should appoint a legal guardian for each case." It was the Foreign Ministry that got the Social Affairs Ministry started, but Koch was instrumental and from the outset involved the municipality of Copenhagen, which was home to the vast majority of Danish Jews. Initially the problem was that the Danish authorities simply did not have names and addresses of those affected, as no register existed of Danes of Jewish origin. The task was entrusted to a special entity, the "Social Service," which took care of various inquiries from caretakers, individuals, or the tax authorities. When there was a presumption that the issue related to the property of a refugee or a deported person, special staff from the Social Service went out to inspect the apartment and register the household possessions. Staff often called for assistance from various volunteer corps or staff who took care of cleaning up, housekeeping, and removing spoiled food that had been left in haste. Edible food was donated to charity. Valuables, bankbooks, or cash found at the apartments or houses were taken into custody, to be returned later to the rightful owner. This is not the place to describe in detail this vast operation pursued jointly by authorities and neighbors. Suffice it to note that the vast majority of refugees who returned after the war found their homes taken care of and their valuables protected, although obviously there are exceptions to this general picture.[16]

In his book *Golden Harvest* (2011) the Polish American historian Jan Gross described the greed that helped to drive the genocide of Europe's Jews, citing the Israeli historian Saul Friedländer: "The catastrophe of European Jewry came about because genocide, which in time became the cornerstone of Nazi occupation policies, was given a kind of consent, manifested in a variety of ways, by many societies, in countries that had been conquered. As Saul Friedländer has put it: 'Not one social group, not one religious community, not one scholarly institution or professional association in Germany and throughout Europe declared its solidarity with the Jews (some of the Christian churches declared that converted Jews were part of the flock, up to a point); to the contrary, many social constituencies, many power groups were directly involved in the expropriation of the Jews and eager, be it out of greed, for their wholesale disappearance. *Thus Nazi and related anti-Jewish policies could unfold to their most extreme levels without the interference of any major countervailing interests'* "[17] (italics added).

The plunder of Jewish property was a common experience in most German-occupied territories, that is to say: it was a rule which knew such exceptions as Italy and Bulgaria. And although this resistance only spurred the leading Nazis in Berlin to put even more emphasis on the extermination of Jews and on engaging the occupied territories actively in the genocide, this strategy did not work everywhere. Once the deportations were initiated, their scope depended, as the German historian Peter Longerich has pointed out, to a significant extent on the practical cooperation of the occupied country or territory. This meant that the deportations in a number of countries did not reach the desired volume.

In the spring of 1943 the German desire for mass deportations met a growing, if not open, opposition, even in Slovakia, where many were already deported. The image in each region and in each country is different, and the specific circumstances of each place are hard to compare. What is important is that local involvement in mass deportations was not a given in 1943. Rather, this involvement in each of the occupied countries was a key factor in their delicate and evolving relations with Berlin.[18]

A reflection of this diversity is also found in the Holocaust statistics collected by the Yad Vashem museum in Jerusalem. Large differences appear in the proportion of the Jewish population of each country that became victims of the genocide. While up to 70–90 percent of the Jews in Hungary, the Netherlands, Latvia, Greece, Lithuania, and Poland perished, the corresponding percentages in Estonia, Belgium, Norway, and Romania were 40–50, and around 20 in Italy and France. In Bulgaria and Denmark fewer than 1 percent of the Jews were killed.

The story of the rescue of the some fifty thousand Jews living in Bulgaria was only fully told after the end of the cold war. After Bulgaria's accession to the Axis powers, in March 1941, Jews were deprived of all civic rights. When in 1943 it became known that the Bulgarian government of the annexed territories Thrace and Macedonia was preparing deportations, parliament members, church leaders, and other public persons in Bulgaria proper immediately started to put pressure on the king and his government. The plan to deport 48,000 Bulgarian Jews was never executed.[19]

Denmark and Bulgaria are small but significant exceptions to the general picture outlined by Gross and Friedländer of the involvement in the genocide from all parts of the society in the occupied countries. These exceptions are important reminders that history does not run in an inevitable pattern. Denmark is a case in point. Here, each of the groups cited by Friedländer—and many more—manifested their support of the Jews, and after their escape or deportation, citizens generally made a determined effort to protect the property and interests of those who had been driven away. This counterpart to the overall picture is not unimportant, even if it concerns only a few of the Nazis' many victims. It demonstrates that public involvement in the atrocities was not a given but depended on many factors, including the policies pursued in the individual countries. The Danish exception shows that the mobilization of civil society's humanism and protective engagement is not only a theoretical possibility: It can be done. We know because it happened.

Blind Alleys

At Frey's Hotel in Stubbekøbing the two fleeing families now joined forces with the other refugees at the hotel. Poul Hannover is especially relieved about the two young members of the Goldstein family, who are energetic and hands-on: "Goldstein and his brother filled me in on the situation. There were various options—and they were in the process of investigating them all. There was one fisherman in particular—the one Talleruphuus had recently sought—but not taken—he did not seem to be unwilling—now it was just a question of whether his wife would let him go. I hardly know what other options there were—one was on Bogø—a third was a Swedish steamer that was said to be in the harbor. Erik, who was able to move around without great risk, took off—so really there was nothing for us to do. I had anything but happy thoughts. I was aware that if we did not get going, I had to try to get over to Herbert's place—I just wished I had followed my original instinct and gone to Rødvig. Our present situation, however, entailed one advantage. We were not alone. I was quite aware that the money would come to play a certain role—and obviously we were better off being 17 than if we were only 8."

Hannover's view was simple and undeniable: In the end the escape depended on whether a fisherman or boatman was willing to put his boat, and maybe his life, on the line to sail them over. Seventeen passengers could pay more than eight, thus increasing the likelihood that someone could be persuaded by the prospect of a large financial gain. Hannover continues: "Goldstein almost betrayed this morning's news to Gunnar—by the skin of his teeth—but it was avoided—I hauled him out of the room before anything happened. The main advantage that we got the message was that I, for my part, was quite sure that we had to leave . . . and Inger, who had been unable to free herself of the idea that maybe it was unnecessary to go, was now quite aware that it was the only way."

It is difficult to understand that the Hannover family, in their precarious situation, still tried to hide from the Marcuses how serious the situation had become with the raids the previous night and the radio broadcast of the occupation's denunciation of the Danish Jews. The desire to spare their traveling companions hearing the Nazi message may perhaps be explained by their extreme discomfort with the intimidation and suspicion that were now publicly addressed toward all Danish Jews. In any event, Poul Hannover did everything in his power to keep the ominous knowledge to himself, even though his son, Allan, also had the news directly from the radio. The teenager wrote: "We drove to Frey's Hotel in Stubbekøbing, where we met Samuel Goldstein, who had gone back to Stubbekøbing the previous evening to bring us news.

At the hotel we got a solid breakfast. While we sat in the restaurant, we heard on the radio the Danish/German controlled announcement that 'the Jews had been separated from public life that night.' I was later told that it was crucial for Mother, who had hitherto been in doubt as to whether it was necessary to leave the country. Now she knew for sure that it *was* necessary."

Soon the families faced a fresh dilemma as outlined by Poul Hannover: "At a certain point—it was along about 12—a lady came—Mrs. Goldstein—and asked me to go in to Director Ledermann. . . . They told me what other people who were working on our behalf also confirmed during their brief visits to our room, that many were now engaged in finding a solution.

"Thus the hotel was apparently seeking to help—both the host and the waiter who told Goldstein that he would wait to submit notification of who was at the hotel for the evening—and it was the impression that the police were also being helpful. A group of leading citizens—including the local vicar and the bank manager—had also offered their help—and they asked me to go down to the latter to thank them and discuss how we could possibly be helped. I did it—accompanied by a young man, Mogens Margolinsky. The residents were obviously aware of the danger and immediately offered to take care of and hide our children. I thanked them very much—but asked, in case we didn't manage to get away, whether they could provide hiding for us all, because I was quite aware that we could not risk staying at the hotel at night—and this was in line with the hotel's view."

The short record of the exchange between the refugees and their Danish helpers in Stubbekøbing reveals choices that loomed large. Both the people of Stubbekøbing and the fugitives had to imagine a situation that could develop in ways that might require a more lasting accommodation. Entire families could be hard to hide—but the kids, perhaps. Maybe it would be better to split up the families, and the Germans might content themselves by taking the adults, if the children had previously been separated. And who could know whether such a split might offer the kids the best chance of survival?

From the local vicar, Niels Lund, who came with the offer, there is an undated report, probably written somewhat later, that adequately reflects the bewilderment of the local helpers: "Some Jews, who a few days before had fled from Copenhagen, were staying in town at Frey's Hotel when the German radio announcement came about the action.

They came here hoping to slip unnoticed over to freedom's Promised Land on the other side of the Sound.

"On Saturday, October 2, attorney Ernst Thomsen, bank manager N. P. Jensen, and I spent all morning making plans about how we should help these people. One proposal after another was rejected, and when we finally got completely stuck, we did what we should have started with: We walked into the hotel, greeted them, and offered our assistance."[20]

It must be at this point that the offer to take care of the refugees' children was made. It was well intentioned, but for the parents the idea of leaving the children and then rallying against an unknown fate must have been almost unbearable. And yet we know that it was a reality for many Danish Jews. Only very recently a group of surviving children has come forward with their stories. They represent widely different fates and family circumstances, but each had the essential experience of loss and of emotional deprivation. Overall at least 149 children were left in Denmark when their parents fled. This is roughly one in ten of the children who were involved in the action, and it's estimated that one in five of the youngest children (under the age of five) were hidden in Denmark. Fewer than half of them subsequently came to Sweden, while the rest were separated from their parents until Denmark was liberated in May 1945.

Both the children and their foster families came from all professions and walks of life, and the path to each relationship was purely coincidental. In some cases public authorities were involved, but most were strictly private arrangements. The children were not physically hidden as in other European countries. They became open foster children with a secret identity. Even though there are examples of middle-aged couples with adult children who from one day to the next acquired school-age foster children, there are no recorded examples of such astonishing developments causing a stir for any of the children or families. The local communities kept quiet.[21]

A Swedish doctor who examined refugees upon their arrival in Höganäs on the Swedish coast notes in his diary how traumatic it was when families were separated during the escape: "Many had left their young children to benevolent people who had undertaken to take care of them, but the grief over the little ones was horrible."[22]

The bottleneck was still the transport. As the hours went by, Poul

Hannover grew more desperate and hence more willing to take chances: "It seemed that it was very difficult—if not impossible—to get someone to undertake the journey—the said fisherman apparently wasn't allowed by his wife—time marched on—when Erik returned around 2 o'clock, he came in pretty exhausted and asked me: 'Poul—you can sail a boat?' I said it was impossible. He said he thought it was the only chance—and he had just bought a boat for 20,000 kroner—plus the same amount to he paid after the war.

"It was a terrible question to be faced with. I was aware that we had to go at any cost—but first, I had no concept of sailing—partly, I tend to get seasick—partly, I barely understand engines. Inger supported me—it would be certain death. On the other hand, I knew only too well that to stay might also mean certain death. The predictions from Max Rothenborg [a member of the Jewish community] in terms of the action had proved to be true—why shouldn't the rest be right, too?"

Poul Hannover held a senior position as the director of a major company. He was used to making decisions and to acting in difficult situations. But this was not a question of an order or a business challenge. The question was whether he would take the responsibility for sailing his family to Sweden knowing that he had no concept of either sailing or navigation. Seen in reverse, could he defend *not* assuming this responsibility? How would he, and others, judge his hesitation if in a few hours the family was divided and on the road to deportation and a terrible fate in German camps? Was there really another option than to do it and try to cross when the first opportunity presented itself? And all the more so, as a significant part of the family's cash was now about to be invested in the boat, which currently represented the best—and only tangible—opportunity to get to Sweden. While Poul Hannover ponders yet another impossible choice, his son, Allan, puts on paper his perception of the crucial discussion between his parents: "In order not to take up additional rooms in the hotel, we borrowed the Goldstein family's room to wash ourselves and rest. We did not know if we would sleep a wink the following night. While Mette and I rested, Erik Nyegaard and Goldstein came back and repeatedly told us that now there was a chance. Erik Nyegaard announced that the city's police chief had promised to keep the coast guard ships away and to reveal where the German patrols were. Later Erik Nyegaard reported that he had bought a boat that Dad had to manage because the fishermen would not go, but Mother was strongly opposed, and therefore it was dropped."

The Scarlet Pimpernel

Poul Hannover continues his account: "In this terrible moment, the door opened and someone—probably one of the Goldsteins—asked me to go down with them. We didn't go into the restaurant—but into a fairly large room in the back. There were a good dozen people in the room all gathered around a man—apparently about my age—with the national emblem in his buttonhole—and he took the floor right away: 'You don't know me—and who I am, I cannot say. Suffice that the Germans know me—I've been in their claws twice. I've arranged it this way: At half past seven tonight there will be a boat at Grønsund's ferry berth. How to get out there is your own problem—but no crowding or anything of the sort—you must get out there individually and in random order. I've got the fisherman to make the trip for you for 15,000 kroner, but he doesn't have to receive it before the trip—he just has to see the money. But I have three refugees somewhere else that I need to get away—and they have no money. Therefore I am making it a condition that you must give me a further 5,000,—to get them off too.' "

The Grønsund ferry berth is situated in the countryside some seven kilometers east of Stubbekøbing, providing the ancient critical link between the islands of Falster and Møn. It was to be closed, as earlier in 1943 a ferry service had been established from Bogø to Stubbekøbing. Poul Hannover goes on:

> It was a tough decision to make, but there was no choice. We knew that if we gave this man our money—most of what we had—and he failed, we were lost. But against all the other hopeless options, what should we do? The man—let me call him the Pimpernel—for it *was* vividly the Scarlet Pimpernel—continued calmly: "If one of you meets me at the place and gives me the money there—I don't want to deal with collecting the money, you'll have to figure that out between yourselves—but I'll take care of the rest. I cannot tell you my name—but I can mention a name"—and he named a young sculptor—I asked if it was him—but it was not—it was probably his family—but it was just one of his acquaintances, not himself. It was our own matter to get the luggage out there. The trip out there was approximately 7 kilometers—and no one was supposed to drive all the way there. He asked me if I was in—and there was no choice.

He disappeared again, just as suddenly as he had come—I said to the others, to come to our room within 5 minutes and pay me—it was 1,200 per person—even a little cheaper than had been promised us by others.

Within 5 minutes I had the money. As I had promised to be there very early—after only an hour and a half, I immediately ordered dinner for us—Erik ate with us in our room. What about Talleruphuus? The others were of a mind to hide it all from him. Erik felt that was wrong. We agreed that he should come to an agreement to cover their costs—obviously they had already received the 1,000 kroner from me and apparently also something from the others. Erik also believed that he had to give the man whose boat he had purchased some small compensation. He found another young fisherman who was willing to drive down to the ferry in a closed grocery truck with our bags—the guy, a brilliant young man, just wished he'd had his boat and had been able to take us over.

The Goldsteins had been in contact with the police—and it appeared that they had promised to stay away from the place of departure—even trying to give us the position of the patrol boats. Things really began to brighten.

I gave Erik the 400 kroner, as I had received too much for the tickets, besides 600 of my own—so there should be plenty considering that I have paid 1,000 kroner in advance—if the man didn't demand that we had to pay for his burst head gasket. There would even be a few hundred kroner left over—which I asked him be sent to the vacation colony as compensation for the break-in.

Allan keeps track of the timetable—perhaps for the teenager an attempt to bring an element of order into a process that is at once frightening and fascinating. There *is* an element of adventure in the dramatic events, so far removed from the everyday, which had been interrupted just a few days ago. And yet the boy, if not in quite the same way as the adults, grasps the deadly seriousness of it all. The solid breakfast also helped his mood: "When we had rested and washed ourselves, Mette and I went into another room and played with Dorte and Palle. While we were playing, Moritz Goldstein came and announced that he had gotten hold of a boat. At 1:20 p.m. a whole lot of men came in to Father. The one who had arranged the whole thing gave Father the message to collect money from everyone who would travel and be at the old Grønsund ferry berth at 3:30 p.m. and pay him the money. The other travelers would be at Grønsund ferry berth at 7 to 7:30 p.m. He also informed us that the boat might come a little earlier and circle a bit.

"At 1:30 p.m. we ordered some food, but it only arrived at 2:15 p.m. The idea was that Erik Nyegaard was supposed to take all our suitcases to the embarkation point by car, but while we waited for the food, a fisherman came and offered—free of charge—to take the suitcases out in a grocery truck. It was decided that Erik Nyegaard should take care of our and Kis & Gunnar Marcus's suitcases, while the fisherman should take those of the Goldstein family."

Kis Marcus later inserted the name of the unknown Pimpernel, August Jensen. He was forty-five years old, living in Klampenborg, the director of an insurance company, and an active airplane pilot. His further connections to resistance work are not known.

Kis Marcus mentions another episode that, in a few words, reveals how the refugees' desperate situation exposes an individual's character in a way that rarely happens in everyday life: "I will not fail to quote a beautiful trait of the young (light-haired) Goldstein. Gunnar met him that afternoon in the hallway, and he told Gunnar not to be nervous. They would not go alone, even if they had the chance, they would only go if all of us could go.—That was generous, and I do not know if we would have said the same."

All three accounts reflect that the two young members of the Goldstein family were better prepared for the situation than the Marcuses and Hannovers. Mrs. Goldstein was traveling with her two adult sons, one of whom was an engineer. In addition, the youngest, Samuel Goldstein, apparently did not look typically Jewish, and therefore felt less exposed. Kis Marcus's brief acknowledgment of Goldstein's assurance that they would not leave the two families in the lurch reflects more than her natural gratitude. It also contains an important insight about themselves: Would they—with responsibility for their young children—have shown the same solidarity if the possibility of escape had been presented to them alone? It is extremely difficult to answer how you would behave faced with a decision that could mean life or death for both yourself and your loved ones. And it demonstrates how deeply Kis Marcus is affected that when she writes her account of the family's escape, she is so brutally honest with herself that she remembers the doubts that assailed her. Samuel Goldstein assured her that they were all for one: Would she have said the same? The question has no answer. But it was the same choice thousands of hapless citizens throughout Europe faced when Nazi persecution hit them. And elsewhere few escaped to make such decisions. Regardless of the circumstances, each person who faced such a dilemma lived with the terrible choice between trying to save themselves and their loved ones, perhaps—or sticking together in a larger group with less immediate chance of surviving. The variations on this theme are endless but all cruel—and in many cases the executioners deliberately played on the devastating effect of making the individual face such choices. The Danish refugees were spared many if not most of the effects of such decisions. But no one was spared facing themselves at this critical juncture.

Poul Hannover tells about the plan's execution. The first step was to get the family fed. They didn't know when there would be another opportunity for a meal—and the previous evening and night at the cabin without food and drink had made a strong impression on the refugees:

I would not say that we had much appetite—nor for a meal in the small room where there was barely room for us, which was not particularly cozy—we did not think it right for us to show up in the restaurant. But it also had to go fast, since we were the first to set off. And then we went—at full speed. Thank God that our children are healthy—for it was a fast pace we had to keep up—and with pretty warm clothes, and each with an additional coat. The weather was almost warm—but the wind picked up—and there were dark clouds on the horizon. We marched a good kilometer in 10 minutes—well done for the kids—as we approached the ferry berth there were only a few people to see—mostly trucks that drove the sugar beets to the ferry. Ten minutes before the final destination, Inger and children lay in the forest—I went out past the customs officer's house—and met the Pimpernel and a woman—both on a bike.

Quietly—as if it was a perfectly ordinary event—he directed me to where the place was—where one could be sheltered—where the boat, whose number he gave me, went at 6 p.m.—its captain came while we stood and talked, and the Pimpernel talked to him—all while the beets were weighed near the departure point, but that would probably stop around 6 p.m. So I gave him the money. He counted it—then asked if he could get an address where he could return the 5,000, if there turned out to be no need for it. That sounded reassuring. He asked how things were with the others. I said that our children had done well—but I was afraid that it would be a predicament for Palle—even though they have twice as much time as we did. Indeed, it was a long trip. Jensen's wife said: "I think I'll take him on my bike." They asked if there was anything we needed. I had ordered a quantity of sandwiches and asked Erik to ensure that we had mineral water—but I had forgotten fruit. All right—she would take care of that.

And then he said good-bye—and he did so in such a way that from that second I was aware that he was quite simply and completely the right one. We both wept—and they rode away.

I didn't turn to look after them—I went out—as far as possible unseen by the beet diggers—and sat in a ditch. I had probably been sitting there for an hour when I saw a cyclist approaching. I jumped up, delighted—it was the Pimpernel's wife—and Palle sat in back—so merry. I took him to my ditch, wrapped him in their travel blanket which he had been sitting on on the luggage rack—and gave him something to play with. We probably sat there a good hour or so, when Kis and Gunnar and Dorte came—I was later told that the Pimpernel had taken Dorte on his bike and brought her out to Inger. And a little later—when it was almost 6 p.m.—Inger came with Allan and Mette.

Kis, who together with her family formed the rearguard, also mentions the helpfulness they encountered: "Well, we started on our walk out of town. The weather was very mild, and we were all wrapped to sail in all our woolens and the warm clothes we had, so it was not long before we were sweating, and I also had to lug the children's clothing and Gunnar our rug."

What Kis could not know was that the refugees at Frey's Hotel had been denounced to the German police and that a raid on the hotel was conducted shortly after she left with her children. The Germans found the hotel quiet—no refugees were there. Meanwhile the family continued on:

We had not gone halfway before Palle began to get tired, and Gunnar had already had to carry him on his back. Suddenly an "angel" arrived in the figure of a woman on a bicycle. It turned out to be Mrs. August Jensen, and she greeted us from Poul and asked if she should run Palle the rest of the way for us, which both Palle and we were happy about. A little bit later, Mr. August Jensen came and took Dorte. As we came closer to the ferry berth we met both Mr. and Mrs. August Jensen, who were heading back toward the town again. We said thank you and good-bye to them, and all four of us were nearly in tears. They were a fine pair of people!

A little further along the road we had a glimpse of Inger, who together with Allan, Mette, and Dorte was hidden in some bushes. We continued with Dorte past the ferry landing, where we saw Poul and Palle. There were a lot of beet carts being driven onto the ferry, and we did not want to attract attention, so we remained in the shelter of some bushes. Soon after, Inger and the kids came out there and we sat on the rug while the children played around.—We ate the packed lunch and then it started to rain, so we went to shelter in the bushes.—When it was just past 7 p.m. we approached the ferry berth. The others began to come, and at 7:25 the grocery truck drove in with Erik riding on the footboard. I spoke a moment with a young man, Svend Otto Nielsen, who was a friend of Goldstein's. He was definitely also a special kind of man.—He had been taken and tortured by the Germans, but when I suggested to him to come with us, he replied that he should, but that they couldn't all leave the country, because there had to be some to help those who were left behind—I was told later that when he left the main station in the morning with 2 revolvers in his pocket (we should have had one, but didn't because he did not think it was wise), he had been searched by the Germans, but he had a fake police badge, which saved him. On the whole it felt very good, in those days, to feel the kindness, helpfulness, and dedication so many of our countrymen showed, and also the camaraderie that existed between all of us who by chance were "in the same boat."—We were 21, Poul, Inger, Allan and Mette, Gunnar and I with our 2, Mrs. Goldstein with engineer Moritz and Samuel Goldstein, Director Ledermann and his wife, 2 daughters, and 1 son, Mogens Margolinsky, and Adolph Dannin with wife, son, and daughter.

Poul Hannover continues the story from the ditch in which the families sought shelter:

It became more and more windy—it rained on and off—we huddled to shelter ourselves as best we could, but it was still pretty wet.

Grønsund ferry landing at the time of the escape. The landing was small and located in a remote part of the island, with no nearby farms or houses except the ferry house. Local archive, Stubbekøbing

Mette Hannover shortly after her arrival in Sweden. Private family collection

We ate a little of the food we brought—and when the time was just past 7 p.m., we approached the ferry dock. Then the others started to arrive. A car had driven the weakest out some way from the spot—and when the time was 7:25 p.m. a covered food truck came chugging along—where Erik stood on the footboard. . . . A traveler, whose name I did not know, came up to me—it was the one who had come at the last minute. Adolph Dannin was his name—we had gone to a dance together God knows how many years ago.

A few fishing boats sailed past—one had rattled around a little when it suddenly landed—and in less than 2 minutes we were all aboard—most tucked into the cabin—luggage lashed on board—we made quick farewells—"Erik!" I shouted—"Long Live Denmark!" shouted Dannin—and we were already out—after all holding hands and having said their farewells.

The parting is brief and unsentimental. Everyone is aware of how little they know about what else the night will bring for them.

On Board

By many detours Bernhard Cohn had ended up in his friends' summerhouse along the Strandvej, north of Copenhagen. Earlier in the day he had been told that his mother was taken during the night's action, and he was now looking for possible ways of getting across to Sweden. He described his efforts this way:

I was in the summerhouse for a few hours and didn't know what to do. The Gestapo would not get me alive. On the other hand, I definitely did not intend to go down without a fight. I had once jokingly said to Pusse [his nickname for his wife, Ella] that the Germans would not get hold of me, and I would do my best to keep this promise.—Jeanette said it surely would be possible to travel with Harry on Monday. He (or his friends) had paid 10,000 kroner for this joke, but then the trip would be absolutely safe! Jeanette contacted Erik Petersen. She told me that one of the police patrol boats went from the beach, and that Erik knew everything about it. I did not trust Erik, but he could be quite fun to talk with. I cycled . . . over to Erik. He was not at home, of course. After an hour where I raged like a wild animal, Willy came. He told me that Erik was down by Kaj Nielsen in the office.—Willy asked me in passing if I would like to go to Sweden! He did not think, incidentally, that it was all that bad, etc.

He has always been an idiot.—He put me in touch with Kaj Nielsen. Kaj, as the upright figure he is, said it would be taken care of. Gradually the house filled up, [and] I decided to go to . . . with whom I could always be and sleep at night. I had barely come inside before Kaj Nielsen called and asked me to come over to his office, but it had to be now. After some difficulty we got hold of a car to get us to town. I lay in the bottom of the vehicle. . . . Up at Kaj Nielsen's was a Mr. Wulff, who seemed to be a decent guy. . . . Wulff and I were to go down to Havnegade, where there was a schooner. It was to sail the next morning for Horsens [in Jutland] at 6 a.m. It would anchor somewhere off the Swedish coast and take us ashore from there using a dinghy. Wulff and I sneaked onboard the ship by 8 o'clock in the evening. We were well received by a mate who made a good impression. The skipper would soon come, and in the meantime we sat down in the captain's cabin.[23]

While Cohn and his friends were waiting to get going, Poul Hannover describes the circumstances on the boat they had awaited with so much longing:

I sat down—after a short bout of convulsive weeping—and was together with, I do not know how many, nestled down in the engine room—into a corner where I had as much space as if you were put under your own desk. I lay there for the first hour—and talked to the others, who didn't have it any better. I spoke mostly with the engineer Goldstein—a brilliant guy.

It might now—though it is unromantic—be the place to say who was on the boat—in addition to the three magnificent people who helped us over—and hopefully are now home again. . . . Given the four late arrivals who joined us, the price should go down—it was Samuel Goldstein who took care of it—but as he, like me, had a lot of uncertain costs, we agreed with him that if there was any surplus, the money should go to young Margolinsky, who apparently had little means for the future.

Let me also as an explanation say that Mrs. Goldstein, who was born in Russia, had already had to flee her country once. She was widowed early—had gotten through by sewing and had thereby educated one son as a civil engineer with a very fine degree—the other son they could not afford to educate—so he became a foreman instead at his uncle's factory. It was he who was engaged to Ledermann's daughter.

Yes, so the ship went. There were said to be three ship berths in the cabin—no, bunks, I should say—and I had reserved them so that the kids got them—whether they did, I hardly know—I was not even in the cabin—they had it terrible down there. When we had been out for half an hour, the boat began to roll terribly—and it did that until we set foot on Swedish soil. I suppose I do not know how bad they were—so let me just tell a little of how I was and felt through the night. It goes without saying that it was a night I will never forget. Even if one in the beginning lay down somewhat carelessly in the oil-stinking engine room, hearing the machine's monotonous but energetic stamping—it was probably more because we now had cast our die—there was no turning back—the only thing was to pray that a merciful providence would lead us the right way. The men on board gathered around as if it was just a joke—they put the luggage aside—I could at least see that we had gotten it all in. But I soon realized that I could not bear to be down in the engine room. I had to get up. I squeezed out of my awkward position and went up through the narrow control room—and out onto the deck, where I sat on the machinery's housing. There I was—virtually without moving for 12 hours. In the beginning it went fairly well—later I had to grab onto a rope—not to be thrown overboard. I talked with Gunnar—and I told him what he had been spared hearing on the radio. Also, that this had got Inger to master her reluctance to leave, which she had felt until the last—now she was clear that there was no other way. . . .

I also talked to Moritz Goldstein—and his brother, who was great at keeping our spirits up. Thankfully Gunnar was completely untouched by the sea—I can say that I did scarcely more than hold myself up—and he was able to run around and begin to distribute food, fruit, and drinks. Samuel Goldstein even had some real chocolate—it tasted so wonderful.

It wasn't going very well in the cabin. A few of the occupants came up eventually—first Miss Ledermann—Goldstein's girlfriend. She had been ill with pneumonia shortly before—this was hardly a good cure. Allan came a little later. The boat had a quantity of fishnets on board—which covered most of the deck—but you could use this if you were discovered by a patrol boat, as you could set the nets to fish. They were placed on top of this—there was even a lady—it later turned out to be Mrs. Dannin—young Margolinsky lay on the other side. They covered themselves in some sail—and the fishermen on the whole were wonderfully helpful—they picked them up and held them when they were sick—they helped them with a small bucket when it was needed—and they helped set the mood now, which was really needed. For example, one suddenly said: "It's probably best that my wife doesn't know that we're flopping around here, "or when he talked about how he had sailed the accompanying boat for our swimming competitions. He heard that I had not been able to take along my father-in-law, but that he was in the hospital, and I was nervous about him being there. The fisherman offered to bring him down to stay with him—if I would just give him the address, he would take care of it.

We saw a lot of light. They thought it was the lighthouse on the island of Møn—others were herring boats that were out—we certainly knew nothing. When we asked them if they thought we had passed the patrol boat, they answered no. We sailed without lights—but the engine's thumping could probably be heard quite far away.

If the previous night was terrible—it was nothing compared to this one. I do not know what time it was—but it was probably toward midnight when we observed something with a green light to the south—it was the patrol boat. All light in the cabin was instantly turned off—a blanket hung over the window to the wheelhouse—all sound ceased—it was as if we hardly dared to breathe. We were almost required to lie down flat—those who could clambered down into the cabin again—while straining our eyes mightily to see if the boat came nearer or became more distant. Luckily the wind blew the sound away from the boat—but anyway—it looked as if it was approaching. The fisherman then ramped up to full speed—the engine hammering away—as our own hearts pounded for our lives. In the cabin they hardly suspected what was going on—but the excitement is not easily explained. Even the fisherman's good humor seemed to fade—even though he consoled himself by saying that he had enough fuel to speed up—it takes a tremendous amount of fuel—and we anxiously looked on to see how it went.

I do not know how long the hunt was on. I would think it was the best part of a half hour, and particularly in the beginning, it was not possible to find out if the boat's lights were approaching or were getting more distant. Well—of course you might say that we were not positive whether it was actually pursuing us—it did not use a searchlight—but that initially it was moving in the same direction as us—there is no doubt. At last we could see that the distance was increasing—the danger seemed over this time.

Poul Hannover and the three fishermen were not hallucinating. But they had trouble figuring out what it was they saw. It was widely known that German patrol boats policed Danish waters, but how many there were and how aggressively they approached no one knew. There had not previously been an attempted mass escape across the Sound.

Allan's account is short and precise: "After half an hour we were allowed to come up on deck, which most did, except Kis, who put Dorte & Palle to bed, and Mom, who put Mette to bed in the cabin. During the night we saw light once, which seemed to be from a German patrol boat that pursued us for about 10 minutes. Fishermen went full speed, and we got away. Later in the night there was terrible weather, and the boat was blown off course, and we came so far south that we could see the lighthouse on the island of Rügen [off the northern German peninsula].

"Eventually everybody was seasick, and one after the other vomited. It wasn't nice to be on the deck where it rained and stormed. I was together with a few others under a sail, but it was pouring down, and the water washed over the deck, so I was soaked to the bone. Dad, who was on deck with me, stayed standing through the night holding on to the mast."

Kis Marcus has a more complete version:

At exactly 7:30 p.m. the fishing boat left, and we went on board after having said good-bye to Erik, who had proved himself to be a true friend. It all went very quickly. We were unloaded into the cabin, where we had counted on immediately putting the kids in the 2 bunks that were there. But there was a whole lot of stuff on the bunks, and I could not pull it off, and then all the female passengers came down there, plus the older Mr. Ledermann, and we could not move. Inger and I got ourselves to the bench with the kids. It soon became too hot.

We did not know that many of the passengers would later go up, so it looked pretty hopeless. Allan, who lay or sat facing me said: "This was not what we had in mind!" And as soon as they opened the door to the deck, he hurried upstairs along with most of the others.

The young fisherman named Arne came down and helped us get the kids to bed, and besides Mr. Ledermann, only Inger and I were in the cabin. We all took seasickness powder that Inger had taken along, but it did not help so much. The kids (Mette and Palle in one bunk—Dorte in the other) did fall asleep fairly quickly, and the first part of the night was not so bad, though it really rocked and I was the first to throw up in a bag, which we had from some fruit. It was dark most of the time in the cabin, as no light should be seen, and we had a little opening to the deck to get some fresh air. Suddenly I realized that I was lying on a lot of pears that had been crushed.

The Helpers

The amazing thing about the network of escape routes that was built after October 1 was both their effectiveness and the fact that a few days earlier there had been nothing. Only a few hundred Danes had fled across the Sound in the past three and a half years, and the resistance was as unprepared as the authorities to organize a mass escape. There was no organization, no coordination, no supervision, and no training. What worked instead was a myriad of initiatives and the ingenuity of the fugitives themselves and of the countless helpers who, from one moment to the next, engaged and undertook to do what was necessary.

We have little contemporary testimony from individual Danes at the time of their gradual transition from spontaneous helpers of distressed countrymen into organized and committed relief workers. Generally they did not write, they acted. A pair of them, Associate Professor Aage Bertelsen and his wife, Gerda Bertelsen, from Lyngby, north of Copenhagen, came to play a central role in building one of the most important circles, known as the Lyngby Group, which helped about one thousand refugees find passage to Sweden without a single arrest. A few years after the war Bertelsen wrote a book in which he tried to recollect the emotion that made helpers gather the very night the action was executed. At the time of publication the book was translated into a number of languages, and it has been many foreigners' first exposure to the Danish rescue work whose spontaneity Bertelsen aptly describes in his preface to the Danish edition from December 1952:

> The small crowd that gathered in Lyngby on the night of October 2, the night of the raids, with the decision to send the endangered Jews to Sweden, knew nothing about the means and opportunities, and what they thought they knew turned out to be wrong. Both for them who met that night, as well as anyone who later joined the group, it is true that they lacked almost any objective prerequisites to carry out the task they had undertaken. We lived inland, far from a suitable embarkation point. We had no special knowledge of the coast, knew nothing of sailing, had no connections among the fishermen and skippers, no money to pay, and not so much as a dinghy to sail with. The Germans had long since ordered all boats not used for business purposes removed from the coasts. The legitimate government had been ousted, the country's institutions of executive authority were under German control, and despite their best will, we could only count on the police for limited support. Our only real asset in the fight against the Gestapo, the world's cruelest and best-organized police force, was our will to help the persecuted. On every page of my presentation you will find testimony of our ignorance and incapacity in relation to the task at hand. Everyone can easily point out how the transports of Jews, at least in the early days, were a chain of improvisations, coincidences, misunderstandings, and amateurish blunders. But one thing is certain as the evidence of all of this is presented: If the helpers of the Jews had no other prerequisites, we were at least united in wanting to help those people.[24]

It remains one of the most fascinating dimensions of the events unfolding in Denmark that this force, described by Bertelsen, proved to be stronger than anyone previously expected it could be—let alone would be. Although helpers came from all walks of life and professions, two groups played a special role: doctors and students of all kinds. Most Copenhagen hospitals served as collection centers, and many practitioners were involved in the rescue work. Students took action and contributed at all levels of assistance, ranging from efforts to track down the hidden and transport them to safe shelter to the critical phase of shipping them out. The crossing was, from first to last, the crucial point where the capacity was lacking.[25]

Escape Routes

In the days after October 1 several transports left the Grønsund ferry dock. The collection center was Næsgaard, midway between the woods on Hesnæs, where the Marcus and Hannover families had spent a restless night, and the ferry dock, which for several days became the center of a lively traffic of everything but beets. Most refugees got away directly from the Copenhagen area, but many were looking to North Sjælland, where they gathered in the small fishing villages along the coast waiting for a boat. Unfortunately a number of them ran into the arms of Criminal Adjutant Hans Juhl, known as Gestapo-Juhl, who was the German security police representative in Helsingør (Elsinore) with an office in the ferry port. On Saturday, Juhl learned that a steamer had picked up some Jews who were found floating in a rowboat west of the Swedish island of Hven. The steamer was now outside Helsingør, and the captain had asked the Danish pilots to ensure that the shipwrecked Oppenheim family was handed over to the Danish police. It was not that simple. Juhl demanded that the pilot sail him out to the steamer, where he boarded with his people and arrested a total of eight Jews, including two children. The whole family was deported to Theresienstadt.

Gestapo-Juhl, who had previously been a chauffeur for German foreign minister Ribbentrop, was the exception to the general sense that the German authorities did not actively try to stop the mass exodus. Several accounts place him in a class by himself, and he is the only ranking German police officer who is reported to have been zealous in pursuit of the fleeing Jews. It was Gestapo-Juhl who was behind the most dramatic—and tragic—events in the North Sjælland fishing villages where he roamed.[26]

It was extremely difficult for the refugees to get an overview of the situation and the relative dangers of the various escape routes. Information on the Germans' movements was highly contradictory and difficult to interpret. An impression of the rumors that were circulating, and that many latched on to, could be acquired through broadcasts from the Danish Press Service in Stockholm, which was formed immediately after August 29 to gather news from Denmark and communicate it to the world press. From there it also filtered back to Denmark via Swedish radio and via the BBC from London, which included daily news-service bulletins to occupied countries.

On the evening of October 2 the Danish Press Service from Stockholm denied rumors that Danish SS volunteers were stationed along the coast of the Øresund. It was reported, however, that German guards stood at one-hundred-meter intervals guarding the North Sjælland coast from Copenhagen to Hundested—and particularly the ports. This was all wrong, of course. But the Danish Press Service was one of the few sources for the facts in Denmark not controlled by German press censorship.[27]

On Saturday afternoon one of the best-informed underground newspapers, the independent *Information*, ran a fairly accurate description of the events of the previous day: "With the raids last night, hundreds of Danish Jews along with individual immigrants and about 150 communists were dragged away from their homes and led to ships to bring them south, probably to Poland. . . . From the Danish side it is still far from clear how successful the Germans were in their manhunt. From the best-informed source in Copenhagen it is estimated that about 1,500 Jews have been taken."

Information was also able to give the vital details that Best "has announced through the Danish Foreign Ministry that there would not be more raids taking place beyond tonight," and that "the German authorities in this country have been eager to spread . . . rumors, whether this has been to threaten (to form a government) or to warn of the consequences of the Berlin sadists' impending excesses. Still, of course, it was mainly the more affluent who had slipped away from their homes—some very few of them, even to Sweden."

Information gives a detailed account of the action's culmination the previous night, including harrowing scenes from the inner city: "At Vesterbro, a predominantly poor neighborhood in Copenhagen, the captured Jews were gathered in groups. These Danish Jews were bound together like members of slave transports, many of whom suffered incredibly brutal treatment during the arrest, having been first gathered around Frihedsstøtten and elsewhere. Here they had to endure a wait of up to several hours. Children cried, and many women screamed continually from fear."

The underground newspaper is also aware that this image is contradicted by other information "later in the day," such as "Raids in some places have been a decided failure. Thus a German soldier of South Jutland ancestry reported that he was at twenty-five different locations, and that they did not get a single Jew. They had all made themselves invisible."[28]

That same evening, as Denmark was taking in the events of the night, the steamer *Wartheland* arrived in Swinemünde with its cargo of deported Communists and Jews, who were kept separate during the transfer. On the quay the prisoners were organized into two distinct columns. As the guards hurried the prisoners down the steep ladders, hitting and pushing the elderly who hesitated, the deported, according to several later accounts, stood silently awaiting their fate. At this point one of the Communists stepped out from his column and loudly addressed the Jews: "Countrymen, stand tall!"[29]

Cooking the History, Round One

While Jewish refugees lived through an awful night of uncertainty and anxiety, and the underground newspapers tried to deliver reasonably accurate information about what had happened in Copenhagen, Werner Best worked intensively to interpret the action as a success. He was obviously aware of the disparity between the three hundred Jews who were deported and the six thousand on the Germans' lists. The question was whether it should be seen as a problem or not. Best didn't think so: "So far, the first day after the action against the Jews manifested that the announcement of the impending release of the detained Danish soldiers has resoundingly made up for all the adverse reactions to the Jewish action within the Danish population. There is complete calm in the country."

Fear that the action would lead to unrest, perhaps even insurrection and rebellion, in the Danish population contributed to the moderation of Best and Mildner, and Best's report was a sigh of relief. He himself had proposed the notorious linkage of the *Judenaktion* with the release of the Danish soldiers, embraced and endorsed by Hitler. Now he made every effort to highlight this as a decisive and clever idea, instrumental for maintaining peace and quiet in the occupied country.[30]

But Best was also a man who was at home in the unique dual reality in which the Third Reich's most powerful men found themselves. On one side the extermination of the Jews stood above all other goals. The Holocaust was carried out with a zeal that, beyond all its human horrors and crimes, in many cases was given surprising priority over more pressing strategic objectives of direct military relevance. On the other hand, both Hitler and his closest associates—at least occasionally—had a good idea of what it took to conduct the war, including stability in Denmark and a steady supply of foodstuffs from the occupied country. Though Hitler hardly bothered to refer to this dependence, but rather to the "model protectorate" that Denmark was in his eyes, the upshot was the same. In relation to Hitler, it was therefore essential to show that the action against the Danish Jews had been successfully implemented, while at the same time ensuring that it did not mean the end of the peaceful occupation or adversely affect the steady flow of Danish supplies.

It was hardly a coincidence, therefore, that the action against the Danish Jews was carried out on the eve of the conclusion of the annual bilateral supply agreement between Germany and Denmark. Negotiations were under way through the same days that the last pieces of the action fell into place. While the permanent secretaries discussed the Danish internment plan, and German security authorities the plans for the Jewish action, parallel negotiations continued in regard to Danish supplies to the Third Reich. The two sets of talks were not formally interrelated, and yet Best was not ashamed to link the two issues directly. On Saturday afternoon, in the very same telegram in which he proclaimed the subdued Danish response to the action, he boasted of the successful trade negotiations. Himmler and Hitler had to be spoken to in clear language: They had gotten what they wanted. No Jews in Denmark—but continued supplies to Germany. The German trade delegation even managed to wring more out of the occupied country than in the previous year—which had already been favorable. From this perspective what actually became of the Danish Jews would perhaps be less critical to Berlin. If the Nazi leaders insisted on conducting a manhunt in Denmark, they could create major problems for the continuation of vital supplies. Best was a cautious man who had done what he could to take out a life insurance policy.[31]

Similarly, in the days following the action the new head of the Gestapo, Dr. Mildner, was deeply involved in negotiations on further cooperation between the German security apparatus and the Danish police. The goal was a continuation of the cooperation that had existed during the first years of the occupation. In this context the action against the Jews was an obstacle to be overcome as quickly and painlessly as possible. Otherwise many more men might be necessary to control Denmark.

Cooperation and Complicity

Part of the Danish public has had a hard time coping with the image of a country that continued to supply Germany, particularly with foodstuffs, and whose police continued interacting with the occupation forces for almost another year after the action against the Jews. Critics of the continued policy of cooperation undertaken by the permanent secretaries point out that Denmark thereby helped to prolong the war and thus indirectly made the ongoing Nazi atrocities possible. From this perspective the unique assistance provided to Danish Jews is seen in the context of continued agricultural exports that helped the Nazi regime to survive and continue the war. In the same vein it is argued that by maintaining security in the occupied country Danish police relieved German forces to fight elsewhere. By not picking an open fight, or at least discontinuing all cooperation with the Germans, was Denmark then not responsible for the deaths of countless victims throughout Europe? The question keeps being raised, and there is no simple answer.

Although it is estimated that Danish agriculture covered more than a month per annum of use of foodstuffs such as butter, bacon, and meat for about ninety million Germans, the supplies are not considered to be crucial because even without these supplies Germany would still have been at the upper end of European per capita calorie consumption. Also, there is no evidence that getting hold of provisions from Denmark was part of the rationale for occupying the country in the first place. Those reasons were purely strategic and closely related to the German push toward Norway. The possibilities inherent in Danish agricultural exports became apparent only gradually, and it is probably true—as several researchers suggest—that, while substantial, these exports primarily played a political role in German-Danish relations—a role whose significance grew in the occupation's later years.[32]

Part of the terrible reality is that *all* occupied countries and regions helped to keep the German war machine running, either through forced labor, looting, cooperation, or collaboration—or an ugly mixture of them all. It was not an option for any occupied country to avoid providing for the Germans. But the terms of the occupation and of providing supplies were very different, and no place obtained more favorable terms than Denmark—except if they were more or less directly allied with Germany. Until the action against the Jews, the situation in Denmark was more similar to that of its unoccupied, neutral neighbor, Sweden, than to that of occupied Norway or the Netherlands, where Germany had inserted a Nazi regime.

It is also part of the picture that it was the very cooperation that provided Denmark with the means to balance the German pressure against it with a countervailing pressure that proved surprisingly strong in key situations. With its firm control of the country and the rejection of any move to let the Nazis get a foothold—and thus a semblance of legitimacy—in a Danish government, Denmark succeeded in bringing about a situation where the occupier had something to lose: namely the cooperation and the advantages it provided. This position gave Denmark room to maneuver and the ability to shield the Danish population, among them Jews, from the worst of Nazi atrocities.

The ongoing trade negotiations gave Nils Svenningsen an opportunity to test Best's standing directly with other high-ranking German representatives. The action against the Jews had shaken Svenningsen's trust in Best, all the more so as Best claimed that he had tried to stop it. If that was true, the obvious conclusion had to be that Best and his people at Dagmarhus did not have the influence with the Nazi leadership that had been previously assumed by the Danish side. Svenningsen used the presence in Copenhagen of a senior German diplomat, Hilger van Scherpenberg, as a back door to explore Best's standing in the German Foreign Office. At the same time Svenningsen was sending a clear warning to Berlin that a continuation of the action against the Jews would have direct consequences for the Danish supplies. Scherpenberg first completely refused to deal with the action, let alone to discuss it, but as a dutiful officer he then noted carefully everything Svenningsen said in their confidential conversation, and sent the report to his superiors in Berlin—exactly as Svenningsen had expected.

According to Scherpenberg, Svenningsen pulled no punches. From now on Germany must expect to meet rejection and resistance, even from circles that had previously been willing to cooperate. Scherpenberg asked if that meant strikes or work stoppages. Svenningsen could not say; the situation had not yet stabilized. But even if he did not consider strikes to be likely, one could expect increased sabotage in the future. Deportation of the Communists posed a particular problem. While the Germans were solely responsible for what had happened to the Jews, the Danish government felt directly accountable for the arrest and deportation of the Communists.

Svenningsen made it clear that this situation undermined the efforts of the permanent secretaries to establish an administration. To avoid further problems, quiet now had to prevail: No further intervention in Danish conditions! According to Scherpenberg, Svenningsen repeatedly came back to this last point "in the most forceful way."

At the end of the conversation Svenningsen launched a trial balloon, though it is hard to say whether it was sincere or rather intended as an indirect warning to both the German Foreign Office and Dr. Best: Would it be possible, Svenningsen ventured, that there might be an opportunity in the near future to get the status of Denmark further clarified by a direct discussion with the competent German authorities—be it at the Foreign Ministry in Berlin or at the headquarters?[33]

Svenningsen was playing with fire. All of the special arrangements for Denmark stood or fell on Ribbentrop's success in keeping Denmark in the foreign policy domain—with Best as his local representative. Svenningsen's implicit message was that a continuation of the action against the Jews could tear apart the whole fragile construct of cooperation. It would be hard for Denmark—but likely even tougher for the leading Nazis, whose positions depended on the continuation of a peaceful occupation. Probably part of Svenningsen's bet was that the top Nazi echelon in Berlin would consider the meager results of the night's action as a failure. Now he wanted to send a warning not to let this failure provoke a manhunt in Denmark.

Even if contemporary sources do not document the reaction in Berlin, a postwar account confirms that Adolf Eichmann and his deputy Rolf Günther were indeed furious—but impotent in their rage. In the "Sassen conversations" with Eichmann, recorded in 1957 while he was still in hiding in Buenos Aires, and excerpted in *Life* magazine in 1960, he volunteered, "Denmark created greater difficulties for us than any other nation. The king intervened for the Jews there and most of them escaped." On the Sassen tapes Eichmann is more explicit in regard to what he calls his failure in Denmark. It was bad enough in Belgium, but worse in Denmark where Eichmann was unable to execute the deportation program as planned. "The result was meager. . . . I also had to recall my transports—it was for me a mighty disgrace." There are reservations as to the nature of these talks that were held with one of his admirers, a Dutch fascist and former Waffen-SS man, but they seem to confirm the general impression that the Nazi leadership considered the action in Denmark a failure. They also suggest that King Christian's protest was duly noted in Berlin, although it could not stop the roundup.

Be that as it may, the king himself cherished no illusions. At the end of this sad day he noted the cruel facts in his personal diary. He did not know the number of deportees, but was aware that the elderly were going to a camp in Bohemia. Still, he feared that the younger Jews would be sent to labor camps.[34]

That evening, October 2, C. F. Duckwitz, who more than any other German had worked to prevent the action, wrote in his diary a laconic status report of its implementation: "Tonight the Jewish action was carried out and a ship with the valuable cargo of 200 (!) old Jews sailed. In this way we have thus destroyed everything in this country, in this way, we have, as von Dardel told us today with tears in his eyes, finally closed the door to Scandinavia. For this—alas!"

The esteemed Danish historian Hans Kirchhoff, who through a lifetime of research has attempted to unravel the tangled threads about Duckwitz's role in the Jewish action, has reached the conclusion that Duckwitz acted with sincere motives—but also that he acted in close collaboration with Werner Best both in terms of the warning and in the efforts to minimize the impact of the raid. The two men—and Paul Kanstein—complemented each other well, both facing Danish society while covering their backs vis-à-vis Berlin. Whatever their respective motives, they remained mutually loyal, even as they faced justice after the end of the war.[35]

CHAPTER 8

SUNDAY, OCTOBER 3

YSTAD

In the Depths of Night

On board the small boat that had departed from Grønsund earlier the same evening, the twenty-one refugees clustered together through a night that seemed without end. The fear of minefields and German patrols had thrown the cutter off course, and the skipper was apparently not aware of where they were—or where they were going. The idea was horrifying. From the waters south of Falster it is not far to the German coast. If they got stranded there, the journey was bound to end in a bad way. Poul describes the night:

> The wind grew stronger and stronger—sometimes we had to stop the engine so that they could take depth soundings—and the boat pitched quite terribly—it was a great solace when it started up again. Then we heard airplanes—apparently a whole lot. It made sense that British airplanes were over Germany that night—we saw flares being dropped—and we saw antiaircraft fire—where it came from, we had no idea. All in all it was only guessing about what you saw—we had no idea.
>
> After a while, also to the south, we now saw a lot of light—later we were told that it was believed to be the lighthouses on the German island of Rügen. We also saw at least one boat—but if it was a patrol boat, or whatever it was, we had no idea. The fishermen did not think we were outside the patrol boats' range—they also didn't think so when the clock neared 5 in the morning—but the storm would steadily grow. We changed direction—apparently more

northerly. While we had previously had the wind roughly with us, it now came almost diagonally from the front—just about the worst place you can have it. The waves were over the deck—now I had to seriously hold on tightly—those who moved on deck almost had to crawl, if one of the three sailors didn't help them. A few sought shelter in the wheelhouse—I remained sitting on the deck. It was not easy to comfort everyone—we had no idea where we were, or anything else—and I cannot say that when we talked with the fishermen we got any particularly safe feeling that they knew either. Yet another danger—there is a provision that if a fishing boat stays out longer than a certain time—much shorter than we were out—it must be called by radio. They must have taken some precautions in this regard—perhaps it was the Pimpernel again who had been at work?—and I wonder if it was also he who had arranged that while our boat, which incidentally was not based in Stubbekøbing, left this port, another—equal-sized boat—probably the one that Erik had bought for me—left the harbor and sailed in the opposite direction—so no one could know who was out on the big trip.

We saw a stronger lighthouse—they said it was Falsterbo. We were supposed to go to Trelleborg—so it did not sound completely wrong. At last—the time was close to 6, we saw another light—that must have been land. It was not—as it later turned out—but Gunnar, whose mood was certainly not high, flew into the cabin to encourage them. They surely weren't having a good time down there. Strangely enough, the children, although seasick, were fairly good-natured. On the whole, they used buckets—but far from 100% had made it. The different coats showed clear traces of that when we came ashore—they looked terrible. Dannin, who was standing straight up the whole trip by the entrance to the cabin, had been down there a little—he had—without knowing it—stood with his leg in the bucket for 15 minutes. What he had been looking for, I don't know—he even stood with his briefcase in hand.

The light we thought was the land was not quite what it should be. It was red on one side—but if we came far enough to the left, it was white. We tried to steer by it—it was literally impossible to stay on course—time and time again we were blown off. And what was at least as bad—you had the impression that the distance to it—which was otherwise impossible to judge, increased rather than the opposite.

We saw a large steamer—there was no question of sending an

SOS—first we had nothing to send it with—and it would of course be picked up as well by the Germans—and there was still the risk of being captured—we were quite aware that we were not within territorial waters—however, if only we could be sure we were heading towards Sweden. We tried to read the depth—I don't think they got much out of it. The sea was coming right over the deck—those who were on it almost in a huddle under the sails were swept out along the railing—but the railing was fairly high, so it seemed relatively safe.—I had one wave after another crash over me. I was soaking wet through my thick overcoat—through woolen clothes, shirt, and underwear—since I only had a quite new pair of leather gloves which were in my inside pocket, I did not dare put them on—and I had to hold on so as not to be thrown overboard. I had the feeling that the fishermen had no idea where we were. They did mention Ystad—but they also mentioned Kalmar—so it was hard to know what was right.

Here the geography of the southern Swedish coastline must be taken into account. While Ystad is far to the south, it is almost 250 kilometers farther up the Baltic Sea to Kalmar, on the landward side of the island of Øland. It's a distance no fishing boat can reach in a single night. Perhaps the skipper mentioned Karshamn, which is about midway, but still very far to the east. Whatever the skipper thought, Poul had good reason for his suspicion that the crew had completely lost their bearings. Poul continues: "We tried to follow the big steamer's course—but it was clear—it would simply not be possible. So they turned to the east relative to our northern course—we did not know if we would get there."

If you consider the map, you understand Poul's concern. To the east lies the deep Baltic, with the island of Bornholm like a stopper in its mouth. To the north is Sweden. Once you've come past the island of Møn and the Øresund, a northerly course is far preferable to an easterly one—if you want to go to Sweden: "It began to get light—a lantern was mistakenly lit and then just as quickly put out again—still in fear that the Germans might see us. Finally it really looked like there was land. Admittedly it was the break of day and one could no longer see the light—but there was something on the horizon—was it Sweden—or . . . Yes—it was land—its shading came through a bit more by now—and in a single direction, not far from our course, it looked like there was a city. Indeed—it was Ystad."

Kis spent the same hours below deck and recounts the chaotic conditions in which the strangers suddenly became closer than any of them wanted:

I have no idea at what times the different things happened. Inger and I got some sleep, but later (I think around 4) the swells were terrible. Mette woke up and was seasick, and she threw up over Palle, who wept because he was wet. I could not get up, so I only tried to comfort him. We got a bucket down there, and we kept it going from hand to hand. We were happy when Arne and later Gunnar came down so they could take care of the kids for a while. Palle and Dorte held out the longest, but threw up in the end, Palle several times, and Dorte got much better again right after. Inger handed the bucket over to them, and I admired her for it. Mrs. Ledermann came down and sat on the bench, and Mrs. Goldstein stood on the stairs up to the deck.—Finally we could not manage to get the bucket around, and we told the kids that they should just throw up. Mr. Ledermann, who was spending the night on the floor, sprang up—he was lying just below Dorte. When I leaned forward to comfort her, he stumbled into me, and I got my head struck. Inger also hit her leg, and we were in pain. Mr. Dannin came down one time, and when Mr. Ledermann didn't move from his place to make room, he said to him: "You lack refugee culture, damn it." Once, when Inger had to pick up the bucket she couldn't shake it loose, and it turned out that Mr. Dannin was standing with one foot planted in it.

When it doesn't help to cry, you may as well laugh, and they also tried that below deck:

Another time the bucket overturned, but in the end we were almost indifferent to it all, although we thought with horror about how our clothes and other belongings looked; nevertheless we could not help but laugh, although it was actually all pretty hopeless. By now it was well over the time when we should have been in Sweden. We started to get a little anxious about what might be wrong, but we only found out later what horrors they encountered on deck. I must say that except for the one time when Palle wept, which you certainly couldn't blame him for, both he and Dorte were very sweet and brave that night, just like Inger's children; and they were also praised for that, and we promised them a reward when we arrived in Sweden.

We were supposed to go to Trelleborg, and the fisherman's chart only reached that far. . . . They saw flares and antiaircraft fire from the deck, which indicated a British attack on Germany that night, and they heard the sound of the engines. We had passed several German patrol boats, one of them was very near; they had seen the red and green lantern and were terrified at the thought that it would discover us. Fortunately the wind carried the sound away from the patrol boat and the fisherman picked up his pace, so we avoided the danger. Toward 6 a.m. Gunnar cried out that they could see a lighthouse that was signaling from Sweden. It turned out later that it was not, but we were encouraged, however little. It began to get light, but we were not yet in Swedish territorial waters, which of course was dangerous.—We kept asking if we would soon get in, but they still could not see land, and the boat went off course again and again.

Ystad is situated some fifty kilometers farther east than Trelleborg on the Swedish coast, so it is no wonder that the travelers on board found the sail time long. Allan's version is short but vivid: "By morning we did not know where we were. The skipper kept saying that there was only half an hour now until we arrived, and after the half hour, there was another half hour. Finally we saw land, and now it was important to find a port where we could go. We found one, but did not know if it was Trelleborg, Ystad, or Kalmar. It turned out to be Ystad."

Kis's account is from the cabin: "Finally the message came that we had waited so impatiently for. There was land in sight, but the fisherman didn't know where in Sweden we had reached. He believed Kalmar, while Arne said Ystad.—Those who had been on deck had frozen and had been soaked by the seas, which crashed over the deck. They had to hold on tight, so as not to be swept overboard. Most had been seasick, but Poul and Gunnar did very well."

The relief on board was palpable, and Poul tells how different passengers each reacted as it brightened and there was land in sight:

I must tell a little episode—one of those which almost seems like a parody. Before we were even sure whether it was land or not, something suddenly rose out of the pile of sails on deck—a lady asks me if I have a match. I thought I was dreaming. I considered those who were there, completely destroyed by seasickness. I had been able to keep track of Allan—he was really very sweet and brave and was content to say that he didn't feel great—it was the understatement of the day. Little Miss Ledermann was alternately crying and yelling, although her boyfriend had done everything to cheer her up, but Mrs. Dannin—incidentally, the only non-Jewish passenger among us—I had not even seen her the day before. It was partly that I didn't have a match, and if I did, it would never have burned—everything was soaking wet, but the lady survived, after all, and had nerve enough to ask for a match for her cigarette. She hadn't been sick—but just was not able to bear being in the cabin, where there was a lot of vomiting, and where all perhaps had not been equally considerate. She came up to me when we had come ashore and thanked me, because I had been almost the only one who had kept the peace on deck—and had only encouraged and comforted.

In the stuffy cabin Kis and her twin sister are so exhausted that they hardly dare to believe that it's over: "When we were told that we were almost in, the children and others who were in the cabin went out on deck. Inger and I could not bear to lift ourselves up before we were inside the pier. We each took a sip of cognac from a small bottle Inger had saved for this moment, and it healed us immediately. We were in Ystad."

The Well-Box

At around the same time the refugees from Grønsund sailed into the port of Ystad, Bernhard Cohn came in for an unpleasant surprise. He had, together with a handful of other refugees, spent the night in the port of Copenhagen in the captain's cabin of the schooner, which was supposed to depart early the next morning, headed for Horsen but planning to land the secret passengers on the coast of Sweden along the way: "I had slept on the ship, covered by the captain's filthy comforter. Wulff lay on a bench. We were up by 5 a.m. We were informed that we would lie behind the storeroom. The skipper couldn't put us in the cargo hold, because he did not trust his crew. It was impossible for all of us to be in the storeroom. The tailor was then placed under a bunk, where he lay comfortably. Wulff refused to climb down into the storeroom, he could

It is no wonder that very few authentic photographs document the escape of the Danish Jews. For the fugitives it was life or death—and their helpers attempted to leave no trace that could lead the Gestapo back to them or be used as evidence.

Among the few contemporary photographs of the escape are those taken by young Mogens Margolinsky of his fellow passengers on the cutter sailing from Grønsund to Ystad with the Marcus and Hannover families.

Above, the child who lies under the sails appears to be a boy, probably Palle Marcus, the young son of Kis and Gunnar. Below, at the bottom of the photograph, standing in profile seems to be Poul Hannover, while the man on the right with the pipe could well be one of the enterprising Goldstein brothers. The man behind him with the cap is apparently one of the fishermen.

The pictures were taken in relatively calm water and in daylight, probably just before the entrance to Ystad. The jacket photo on this book is from the same series. Private family collection

not stand the smell. It didn't bother me. However the skipper declared that I could be discovered, and we all had to go ashore. That was the whole kettle of fish. I got so angry that when I jumped over the ladder I twisted my left leg."[1]

There was also fear in the hours before dawn that Sunday morning in a small fishing boat in another part of Copenhagen harbor, in Christianshavn's Canal next to the German barracks, where Leo Schüstin, a professional wrestler and the son of Russian immigrants, was hiding with his family. Shortly afterward he wrote a brief report, reflecting the situation of a refugee with much less means and connections than many from the "old families." Against this background, he did not need many warnings to understand what was coming or what it could mean. He and his family had already gone into hiding by mid-September, and on Saturday, October 2, he had been on the run for ten days, staying with friends and acquaintances without returning to his home. During that evening he "got hold of a fisherman, a man of the right kind, he was from Frederiksværk, and he took us aboard at Ovengaden oven Vandet, next to the German barracks. Then we sat in the boat all night. It was the longest night of my life. My nerves were on edge, we could not eat or drink. We were just waiting to leave. We would sail on Sunday at 7 a.m. when it was light."[2]

Now the family waited with foreboding for daybreak and the fishermen who would take them to Sweden. At every moment they feared the worst: "It was 5:30 a.m. when the fishermen came. They wanted to make coffee for us, but we refused. We did not feel like it. Eventually the time was late, so we had to be packed down. My mother and wife were crammed into a well-box that was nailed shut and put down in the hold."

(Before shipboard refrigeration, fish were primarily kept alive in water. Well-boxes, still found in ports and canals, are large, flat wooden boxes whose sides and bottom are completely pierced by finger-size holes so that water can flow freely through them. The well-boxes are supplied with hatches, so that fresh fish can be easily placed inside and then caught again with a net on a handle. That was the kind of well-box on board the fishing boat, in which the two women were now confined. A very uncomfortable place to be—and fatal if the well-box somehow got into water.)

Leo Schüstin did not get better conditions himself: "I myself was laid under the wheelhouse, just above the shaft. There was just room to lie curled up, but since it was life or death to do it, it was done. Otherwise it would have been impossible. When this was done, each of the fishermen took a big, thick, knotted stick and told us that the Danish police were not bad, but if the Germans came aboard, they would be killed. Before leaving, we had agreed that when he turned the engine off and stamped 3 times on the floor, we had to be quiet. Three minutes after departure, the engine was turned off. The police came on board, and we were quiet as mice. It all lasted about 5 minutes, but for us it was an eternity.

"Everything went well, and most of the danger was over. We sailed past the German observation boats. Everything went smoothly, we came off Barsebäck, where we saw and waited for the Swedish marine police to come out. They did not."

At this early stage fishermen apparently believed that it might be unsafe or dangerous for them to enter the Swedish port, so the refugees were transferred at sea from the Danish fishing boats to the Swedish naval vessels. The idea of turning back at this point must have been unbearable for the fugitives: "Then the fishermen made a decision to enter, no matter what it cost. We were taken by the police. The fishermen's papers were also taken, but it was not long before they were allowed to sail again. There was an interrogation of us in Barsebäck. We got coffee and tea. Everyone was so nice to us. We were then driven by car to Gævlinge, where there was questioning. Everything went smoothly and we were driven by car to Malmö, where the third interrogations were held. Then we got ration cards and were sent down to the Jewish community, where we each got 25 kroner and were assigned a fine room at Södra Förstadsgatan 36."

After the hardships, the small family had landed, and relief exudes from Schüstin's brief notes. For his family, as for other refugees, it's also a question of finding connections so they can leave the camps and go out into Swedish society: "In the evening we went to our good friend Gustav Lindstrand, who is chairman of [the sports club] 'Sparta' in Malmö. He lives on Skolgatan 7, where he has a fine fur business and the entire house. When he heard what had happened and how, he put his whole vast apparatus in gear. He has done everything for me, for which I personally cannot thank him enough. He and his wife have proved themselves to be the most helpful people I've ever known."[3]

Tout Paris

Back in Copenhagen the Bergstrøm family had a very different Sunday morning, marked by the small everyday routines that despite the occu-

Leo and Sarah Schüstin.

In the years 1882 to 1914 a great number of Jews—between ten and twelve thousand—immigrated to Denmark. Fleeing pogroms in Eastern Europe and Russia, they constituted a little surge in the huge wave of Jews who migrated from East to West during this period, many via Copenhagen. Most went on and settled elsewhere in western Europe, the United States, or South America, but around three thousand stayed in Denmark, where they constituted, by local conditions, a significant and strange immigrant group, known as "Russian Jews." The group contained a mixture of Orthodox families, Zionists, and socialist atheists. Yet they appeared to the surrounding communities as fairly similar, not least because of their common language, Yiddish, and their culture.

The melding of these "Russian Jews" into Danish society was not easy, and it took many years before the new citizens were reasonably assimilated. The newcomers looked exotic to the local Danes, and they settled predominantly in the same Copenhagen neighborhoods that during the first decades of the twentieth century were characterized by small Jewish traders in professions such as dressmaking and millinery. Not wealthy people, they had only limited contact with the surrounding community, including the well-integrated "old Jews" in Denmark.

The integration progressed, however, and by the time World War II broke out, most "Russian Jews" were well established in Danish society. Some were successful businessmen, and their children had learned Danish and Danish culture through school.

Leo and Sarah Schüstin are examples of this trend. They were both born in Copenhagen around 1910. Leo was the son of a young Jewish refugee from Lithuania, and he worked first as a hatter and later became a professional wrestler. His mother, Rebecca, joined her son and daughter-in-law in the escape. She was fifty-six years old when for the second time she had to flee her country.

Danish Jewish Museum

pation and the unfolding drama were still attainable—for some. Meticulously taking notes, Bergstrøm went on with his diary: "We slept until
9 o'clock and rested after the air-raid siren. I raised the blackout curtains. It was fine, sunny weather. Sat down to work on the war book [his
diary]. Then washed myself using the washbasin. At noon I called the
fish restaurant and reserved Tout Paris.

"Elsa [Bergstrøm's wife] and Tusse [their daughter] were seated
on the sofa. There were only a few people. The restaurant missed the
Swedes, the waiter said. We got a half bottle of Liebfraumilch for 14
kroner, before it was 2 or 3 kroner. Tusse is a connoisseur, she ate as
much as the rest of us. After the main course we had a pancake and Elsa
and I a glass of black currant rum each. The waiter talked about the old
customers, among them Mr. Hurwitz, professor of law. 'I wonder what
has become of him,' he said, worried. 'He has gone to Sweden with his
entire family,' I informed him. It seemed to please him. With the waiter
I met the same opinion as I have. Not fond of Jews, but they should not
be treated like animals."[4]

On the same day Bergstrøm decides—much against his custom—to
go to church. He gives the background: "At Vesterbro Torv we met Sergeant Godtfred Jensen. He said that even today some Jews had been
picked up . . . and that he intended to go to church for once, as it was
reported that a letter would be read from the bishop protesting against
the persecution of the Jews. With my book in mind, I decided to go to
church."

Bergstrøm was working on his monumental book about life under the
occupation, and wanted to include it all. Together with his wife and
daughter, he went to witness what would happen: "There were many
people in the church. Two white-clad girls with Danish flags were stationed at the foot of the stairs to the altar. It was a church festival. As a
result of the baby boom four children were baptized. Tusse went right
up close and followed the ceremony with the greatest attention. Then
she came back to us. She was aware that there was a uniformed cop sitting in the back. It was probably Godtfred Jensen. A church officer came
up to him and had him removed. Possibly to a less exposed position.
I was bored by a long homily on the mission in India. Then another
priest came to the pulpit. When he said he had a letter from the bishop
to read aloud, a little shock went through the congregation. The priest

read the protest against persecution of the Jews. One had to remember that Christ was from the Jews' land. And that Christianity had the Old Testament as its basis. You had to obey God rather than man. Persecution of Jews was also a violation of the Danish sense of justice. Therefore the church had to protest."

Bergstrøm "came to think about what had happened in Norway, when the priests protested. The Danes now walked in their Norwegian colleagues' footsteps. I wonder if it will have the same effect?"

It had long been a thorn in the side of Danish pastors that their Norwegian colleagues had protested already during Easter 1942. They protested against the growing nazification of Norwegian society, and their action had led to the bishop's arrest and several priests' resignations. Some in Denmark had begun to prefer "Norwegian conditions," where it was clear that the regime was imposed by the occupying power, to the more ambiguous picture in Denmark, where it still was the Danish authorities who managed things—but on terms partly dictated by the Germans. Normally the Danish state church keeps its distance from politics. The clergy may express opinions, but it is very unusual for the church to speak with an authoritative voice, and it has no institutional mechanism for establishing a common position on matters relating to politics—or even faith. The informal council of bishops can, however, under extraordinary circumstances, issue a declaration. Such a letter was now read in churches throughout the country, setting out a definite demarcation. The point was made quite plainly that under the circumstances the individual bore a responsibility to act, even if this entailed violating rules and regulations: "The leaders of the Danish Church have a clear understanding of our duty to be law-abiding citizens and not to revolt needlessly against those who exercise authority over us—but our conscience obliges us at the same time to maintain the law and to protest against any violation of rights. We will therefore unambiguously declare our allegiance to the doctrine that bids us obey God more than man."

As the historian Leni Yahil has pointed out, "this statement is in reality an expression of the spiritual and moral foundation of the Danish government," and she quotes a Jewish refugee's comment that the Danes did what they did, not as much for the Jews' sake, but because they wanted to protect their concept of justice. The pastoral letter is an unequivocal call for civil disobedience. A recognition that the individual, face-to-face with injustice, has a duty to act, whether or not that means a break with the legal authorities. There is more than one account of congregations, after hearing the pastoral letter read, spontaneously standing up and expressing their commitment with an "Amen!" King Christian in his diary that day limits himself to one short sentence that accompanies a copy of the letter: "The Jews are remembered in all churches."[5]

Without getting lost in these considerations, Bergstrøm followed events from his usual ironic distance: "After the reading of the bishop's protest the first verses of the solemn hymn 'A Mighty Fortress Is Our God' was sung. In his prayer the priest interwove prayers for the Norwegian, Swedish, Icelandic, and Finnish churches and for the Jews. Then we left. It had been a historic moment. The church took a risk. We went home, as it was past 6 o'clock in the afternoon."

The pastoral letter was drafted at the initiative of the bishop of Copenhagen, Hans Fuglsang-Damgaard, who had from the beginning of the occupation championed the idea of a visible church that took upon itself a spiritual responsibility for society and the state. He was known as an outspoken critic of anti-Semitism and as a moderate activist, who on the one hand restrained the more radical clergy, and on the other rejected attempts to make the church an instrument of politicians' attempts to keep the population quiet.

Among the bishops he was the one who was willing to go furthest in confrontation with the occupation, and the adoption of the bishop's pastoral letter to be read in churches on October 3 was possible only because Fuglsang-Damgaard hammered the idea through at a meeting among his colleagues convened for that purpose.[6]

Bergstrøm also noted that Sunday evening that a police officer told him "that the university was closed for 8 days. On Saturday a student stood up and said that they would not study alongside two Nazi students. They should either remove themselves, or the others would go. And then the students ended up leaving the premises. It looks like a whole lot of panic."

At the invitation of student organizations the same day, the senate of Copenhagen University adopted a brief statement: "Guided by the sufferings imposed over the last days on Danish citizens, the Dean and the Senate have decided to suspend classes at Copenhagen University for a week. Classes resume on Monday, October 11."

Bergstrøm busily sought further information on the situation: "I called and spoke with Næsh. Now the Jewish suicides had begun. Two old ladies had taken their own lives with gas yesterday. And today there was a harrowing drama in a seaside cabin near Helsingør Seabath. Solomon, a Jewish manufacturer, had cut the throats of his two children, his wife, and himself. His wife and children were dead, he was barely alive. 'Yes,' we both said quietly. 'There may be a good deal more to come.' I added that we live in ghastly times."

Unlike many other rumors Bergstrøm picked up, the horrifying story of the man who killed his wife and two children, and attempted suicide himself, referred to an actual tragic event. The man survived and received assistance from both doctors and the police. He was later helped to Sweden.[7]

Such tragedies had not previously been part of life in occupied Denmark. Now, people felt evil moving closer to themselves. It nourished the feeling that the German action was directed against the entire population, and that they all were now exposed to the occupation's arbitrary brutality. At the same time it deepened the gulf that separated them from the Danes who sided with the Germans, and who at one stroke became even more marginalized and outcast than before.

The Port of Ystad

On Sunday morning the boat loaded with refugees landed at long last in the Swedish port of Ystad. Poul Hannover recounts the arrival scene: "We were thrown past a buoy—now we saw the harbor entrance quite clearly—everything else was forgotten—and a moment later we saw a few workers on the outer breakwater come rushing out, waving their hats: 'Welcome here,' they said. I don't think there was a dry eye for any of us who saw it. Three men, who climbed down into a boat from a small warship—threw out a rope and led us toward the quay, where we put to. A few soldiers were present there—oh, surely they could not be green—the Swedish uniforms are not much different from the German—but no—here again, uniformed people who waved to us, friendly. And then we were at the dock. If it had not taken two minutes to get on board, it certainly took no longer to get on land—warm hands reached toward us: Välkomne—välkomne! Yes—we were saved—we were on dry land."

The relief is enormous. The uncertainty plaguing them to the last moment is replaced by the assurance that they have made it to safety: "We all hugged each other—and Inger, who before we departed had received a little hip flask from the maid with a little of our own good

Cognac, gave us a sip. Allan, who needed to get to the bathroom awfully badly, got a great big soldier who took him by the hand and very decently trudged off with him—yes, the guy was so exhausted that the soldier had to button his pants down and up for him. More and more officers and customs men came. They told us that the previous day 8 refugees had come—others had not reached Ystad—sure enough it was Ystad we had come to. The door to the customs house was opened—and we went in there and got our baggage. We went out again to get a little sun to dry ourselves. A little girl was up in the building with her parents—she opened the window, and lowered apples down to our children."

Kis's version is also full of relief: "When we got upstairs, we were received by Swedish sailors who greeted us, Welcome to Sweden. It was a wonderful feeling to be received this way and to know we were in a free country. There were not many dry eyes. Gunnar and I cried and hugged each other and Poul and Inger.

"We were now all led down to the Customs Station, where our bags were examined. We were medically examined, but only for typhoid, as they had heard that it existed in Denmark . . . and had to tell them how much money we had. It took some time, since we were many. We stood outside in the sun and waited, when a bag of apples was lowered down to the kids from a window above the Customs room. As a whole, all these people were so sweet and cordial that we really felt welcome. I talked to one of the functionaries about the German soldiers that we had left, and he said, 'They won't come here,' and it was really reassuring to see Swedish soldiers everywhere in the harbor."

The Swedish government's decision to build up the reception capacity for the refugees from Denmark now showed its strength. The Danes should feel not only that they had reached safety. They should also feel welcome among next of kin. Psychologically this gesture made a deep impression on the fugitives, who had just lived through the opposite experience, being turned from full citizens into lawless refugees. In Poul Hannover's words:

A doctor was called and examined us—it was typhus they were afraid of—one of Germany's many blessings. Casual and considerate. The same with customs examination—and with a short report of what kind of money we had. Then we had to leave for the police station—but Miss Ledermann was too exhausted—an ambulance took her. As it could take a while before we got our luggage, I took

Inger's bag—and we went up to the police station. They were so nice and as considerate as you could ask for. I was by the window and was about to fall asleep—but I had to try to get my clothes dry. Allan fell asleep. We were allowed to put him on a couch—he fell asleep immediately. Paperwork first the largest family—it was the Ledermanns—it took quite a long time—then it was our turn. We had visas, so it went pretty quickly. There was something we had to sign—we woke Allan up—but he was so out of sorts that we had to give up. They asked if we wanted to be in a first-class hotel and phoned the Hotel Continental and ordered rooms. To get Allan down there, we had to take a car. We got two rooms—one for the children and one for us—Kis and Gunnar got a room big enough for all four. Inger got Allan undressed—his clothes had not come—he was already asleep—she got Mette washed while I rushed to the phone and began to call.

Poul now reconnected to contacts and business links he could draw on. He needed to get family matters organized, and especially to obtain and share information on the fate of family members and friends—and, vice versa, to spread the message that the two small families were now safe in Ystad. Yet they knew nothing of the fate that had befallen their closest kin—just as little as anyone knew that they had come to a safe harbor.

The police report from the interrogation of Poul Hannover and the other refugees, immediately upon arrival, still exists. Each person gives a brief account of the last days' dramatic events. The short reports in general confirm the diaries but also show something else: The relief was great, but there was also caution. Hannover was asked to explain his escape route, and he tells the main features of the story—but without the critical details that would expose those who had helped along the way. Here it appears that the family had slept in the open, and that the contact with the fisherman in Stubbekøbing was purely coincidental. Poul Hannover also indicates he paid six thousand kroner for the contact—but not the payment for the actual transfer—maybe in order to protect the three Danish fishermen. The police in Ystad note that Poul Hannover on arrival was in possession of 2,345 Danish kroner and Gunnar Marcus something similar.[8]

For the Marcus family it was less easy, because they had no Swedish visas and no direct connections. But all benefited from the Swedish hospitality and the family ties that were now apparent on the Swedish side of the Sound. Kis tells of the Marcus family's arrival:

> When we were finished at the customs station, we went to the police. They were very gracious to us. Palle, Dorte, and Mette were allowed to write on their typewriters while we waited, and Allan was put on a sofa, where he promptly fell asleep. In return the officers got to eat the remnants of our sandwiches, which they were enthusiastic about. We were just to hand over our passports and then come back the next day, and our money was actually also kept by the police. It was easy for Poul and Inger, who had visas. They would soon be allowed to go wherever they wanted. The police called and ordered a room for us at the Hotel Continental, and we drove there by car, as Allan was so worn out that he couldn't stand on his own two feet.
>
> As soon as our suitcases came, I bathed the kids, washed their hair, and put them to bed.—We used the phone to call to see if any of the family had come; we were disappointed not to hear that Ada [Kis's older sister] was there, as we thought she had come over.
>
> We knew nothing about all the others. Poul called his cousin and found out a little about his family. . . . Later in the day we found out about more arrivals. We were happy about each one we heard about while we were extremely anxious for those who had not yet come.
>
> After having taken a bath myself I also went to bed. (Gunnar was sleeping with the newspaper lifted high in one hand.) At 9 p.m. we got up and had dinner in the restaurant.

Poul Hannover was fortunate because as a longtime director of the engineering and electronics company Titan, he had close contact with the great Swedish electronics company ASEA, which had interests in Titan. ASEA's CEO, Herman Wernekinck, was a close acquaintance: "I asked Wernekinck, who gave me a warm welcome and assured me that we had been in their thoughts in the last days, to telegraph ASEA in Copenhagen . . . and told him where we were. . . . Then our luggage came—and I now felt I couldn't do any more. In the meantime Inger had washed Mette and herself and put Mette to bed. We left a message that we would sleep until 7 p.m., and I fell asleep right away."

It was not a long sleep for the Hannover and Marcus families in Ystad. A few hours after they had gone to bed, they got up for their first evening in Sweden: "We managed to get a hot bath—it was wonderful. When we got up at 9, we all went to dinner. The police had said we should not worry about ration coupons—that would be arranged later. When we had eaten, I called Walter [a relative living permanently in Sweden] again—this time I reached him and got the first information about who had come—including Uncle Carl Johan and the whole family as well as Inger and Hans. It was great—but what about Mother? Yes—a man was sent over to try to get her and Aunt Ida over. Although the children, who had recently been put to bed, were dead tired, they were happy to hear the names—and not 10 minutes later Walter phoned: Poul—I am pleased to tell you that your mother and Aunt Ida came over here—and Father's going down to pick them up tomorrow.

"So we slept—as best we could—happy and grateful for those who had come—anxious and worried about those we knew nothing about. We had no idea if Else and Knud [Poul's brother and sister-in-law] had come over with Mom—and don't know yet."

Allan has his own account of the arrival in Ystad:

As we approached the harbor two workers jumped up on the dock and shouted "Välkommen," and the soldier who stood guard on the pier also greeted us. Then a rowboat came toward us with four sailors from a patrol boat, threw us a line, and came on board. When we came ashore and had taken leave of the fishermen, we were to go to the customs building. However, I had to use the toilet and asked a soldier to show me the way. When I finished, my hands were so frozen stiff that I could not even button my pants. Our suitcases were looked over in the customs building, and we were inspected for typhus by the doctor.

While suitcases were being examined, we found out that the fishermen, who had sailed further into the harbor, were now on their way out. Everyone in the customs building came out and waved good-bye to the fishermen and to the Dannebrog [the Danish flag]. While we stood outside the customs building and waited to see what would happen, a bag of apples was lowered down to us from the second floor.

We went on to the police station and presented our passports. As I was very tired, I was placed on a couch in the guardroom, where I fell asleep, and when it was Mother's and Father's turn to be questioned, they could not wake me up. They finished what was needed, and agreed that I could come and sign it the next day. I was eventually awakened, and we got a taxi to the Hotel Continental, where we—after being given a cup of tea—went to bed and slept until 7 p.m. At around 9:30 p.m. we went down and ate and then back up and slept again.

It is obvious that Allan's report, at least to a degree, reflects the versions of the crossing and the arrival that have already started to settle into the family's story. Because the processing of dramatic events is achieved partially through the telling and retelling of experiences, it can already be difficult after a short time, even for those who have lived them, to distinguish between what was seen and what is told. An additional entry in Allan's diary demonstrates that his report was written a little later than the other two: "By refugees who reached Sweden later from Falster, we were told that in Stubbekøbing, where the whole town was involved with our departure, an informer had made the Germans aware of our presence, and Frey's Hotel had been searched only a few hours after we had left it."

Allan's account is confirmed by the report from Vicar Niels Lund in Stubbekøbing about the families' departure: "The negotiations, which now appeared to be founded on more solid ground, continued in the afternoon and resulted in the whole group in the evening getting off happily to Sweden from Grønsund ferry landing. It was not a moment too soon. In the evening a small, private air-raid siren sounded in Stubbekøbing, while a company of Germans turned the police station and all the city's hotels and guesthouses upside down. Someone had kindly reported that there were Jews in Stubbekøbing. The expedition, however, yielded no result. The birds had flown, and naturally no one here knew that they had been here at all."[9]

If the families at the Hotel Continental in Ystad took a look at that day's edition of the leading Swedish newspaper, *Dagens Nyheter*, they would have seen that the action against the Danish Jews was front-page news, with the headline that sixteen hundred had already been deported. The newspaper also declared that all Danish Jews were welcome in Sweden. The editorial was titled "Sacrificing to Idols": "There exist some pseudo-religions with ritual murders as part of their cult. Sometimes it happens that a resourceful tribe first uses a threat as a means of pressure to achieve what it wants—and after that the prestige of the idol enters the picture. It can also happen that the highest leadership at a given moment is blind to anything but the holy mission—blood mission, extermination mission. In which direction such a leadership may guide itself and its people can be left unsaid. It provokes the horror one experiences in face of that which no longer belongs to the community of humanity."

These are strong words, significantly stronger than the Swedish press's past criticism of Hitler's regime and Nazism. The editorial concluded: "Pogroms in Copenhagen—this is the unfathomable, which has to arouse even the most complacent, open the eyes of those who have been willing to keep them closed harder and longer than the rest. Far stronger than before, popular sentiment, all the way down to the commonest people, will rise up against anything that can be construed as Swedish favors to the suppressors of our brothers and sisters. Between the Swedish people and the leaders of the German people, the vapors from the burned offerings now rise ever thicker, ever more suffocating and sickening. They infuriate people. Anything else would be shameful."

More subdued, but still not to be misunderstood, the competing *Svenska Dagbladet* headed its editorial "Against Divine and Human Order": "With deepest disgust and outraged feelings the Swedish people learn that racial hatred against the Jews, which last year led to such terrible scenes in Norway, now has been unleashed on Danish soil. . . . What it is about, and what is contrary to all divine and human order, is the sinister and ruthless disregard for humanity's advances through the long centuries of Western history, which these persecutions of Jews demonstrate."

The announcement that Sweden would accept all Danish Jews had already opened a perspective that no one had previously imagined. Now the Swedish authorities came up with orders for the Swedish navy to repel all German war vessels in Swedish waters, as well as orders to refuel the boats of Danish fishermen who came over with refugees.

Although all these practical measures were of great importance, perhaps Sweden's most important contribution was to publicize the German action directly and intensely, both in official statements and in the Swedish press. The press conveyed greatly exaggerated and dramatized figures about captives and deportees, and not least the Germans' persistent attempts to stem the flight and capture the fugitives. For the first time the Nazis had to pursue their persecution of the Jews under scrutiny by a free press, reporting daily on the situation in Denmark and the desperate situation of the refugees. This awareness was anything but welcome and may in itself have contributed to reducing the German authorities' desire to take effective action against the flood of refugees now gathering to flee Denmark.[10]

"The Psychopaths . . . Rule the World"

By Sunday, October 3, only a few Danish Jews had arrived in Sweden. But many had now set themselves in motion, and they sought very different roads to get across the Øresund. Hospitals in particular served as collection centers, and hospital doctors took action as coordinators of large refugee flows.

At Copenhagen's municipal hospital Ella Fischer followed the developments with growing concern. One report that gave cause for hope was the message that Jews would be welcome in a safe haven in Sweden, as shown by Ella's short diary entry from Sunday after a visit from her sister, who apparently continued to move about the city regardless of the prevailing conditions: "Edith came and visited me. She said that Sweden had offered Germany to create a haven for the Jews and was, in that case, quite optimistic. She said that if we were allowed to travel to Sweden legally, she would make sure that I could come along."[11]

In Ruds Vedby in the middle of Sjælland, the twin sisters' father, Dr. Meyer, sat in his friend's home with major concerns. There were still practical matters to be arranged and money to be deposited. In his brief record from that Sunday he notes that he has been told that the weather was good and would stay that way for a few days: "There was a good chance of crossing. . . . In the evening, when Hart came home, he told me about the raid and people's rage and helpfulness, and thought that my children were all safe."

That was the message Dr. Meyer had been waiting for. The time had come when the head of the family also had to take steps to reach safety.

The same day, not far from Ruds Vedby, where Adolph Meyer was hiding, twenty-five-year-old Herbert Levysohn, using an alias, sought out Dr. Stubbe Teilberg at the hospital in Dianalund. Levysohn was the grandson of the prominent textile merchant William Levysohn, and his father, Willie Levysohn, was among the leading members of the Jewish community who were taken hostage on August 29 and who were still in Horserød camp. Herbert had been hiding in the previous days with friends in the village of Stenlille, a few kilometers farther east, but like so many others he now realized that the situation was untenable and that he had to go to Sweden. The chief physician was helpful but would not, according to the report Levysohn wrote later in October, keep him in the hospital: "He continued, 'I cannot keep you in my department. It is the epilepsy department and it will hurt you more than benefit you. But you can go to a farmer outside the village of Kongsted. I often have patients there in need of rest. It's in a lonely place and won't attract attention, as there often are guests. I have spoken to the farmer, and you are welcome. There is also room for your mother and sister, who I understand may come in a few days.' I was happy with this arrangement and Wenzzel [a helper] and I went back again, after the doctor finally uttered the following truth: 'In 1930 we wrote major medical treatises on how to deal with psychopaths, and now it's the psychopaths who rule the world.' "[12]

That same evening another solo refugee, Bernhard Cohn, made his circuitous way to the tiny fishing hamlet of Gilleleje at the northern tip of Sjælland, where good friends had told him that refugees were being shipped to Sweden. All day long young Cohn had struggled with the leg he had strained when he let his temper get the better of him as he disembarked that same morning in Havnegade. About events in Gilleleje on Monday evening, "Bubi" Cohn writes:

So we traveled individually to Gilleleje. When we got up there, after some negotiation we were led to a house where others were waiting. . . . I could feel something had not worked out right. It turned out that the skipper with whom we should have sailed had run away. A connection with another skipper was then established, and we went down to the harbor. A strange sight. There were lots of fishermen with their hands in their pockets. Furthermore, Danish police officers strutted around as guards armed with rifles, etc. These officers showed us the way.

When we came out to the ship, the captain would not sail because he had heard that the Gestapo were on their way to the port. While we stood and anxiously discussed this with him, there was a cry: "Scatter, the Germans are coming!" I ran with the small suitcase I had stolen from Mogens up into the city. However, I was overtaken by someone who told me that I should just go back, they would sail anyway. When I came down to the cutter, an unbelievable 12 elegant suitcases were lined up at the deck. I loaded the suitcase into the hold, where all the others were sitting, and joined them.

And then came 45 minutes which I shall never forget. We heard people coming out on the pier in rhythmic steps. We heard them approaching and someone went up into the back of the ship. We heard a voice asking to see an ID, then a voice replied that he didn't damn well have such a thing. We were not supposed to utter a word. Ingrid Seligmann, who sat next to me, was very agitated. She had to hold my hand. Allan wasn't any better. They complained all the time: we won't get over, we won't get over. Old man Meyer and I were the calmest. I didn't do anything but tell the others in the group to shut up. Suddenly the bulkhead was lifted and a man with lit match looked over our faces. I thought that our time had run out. I had decided to jump into the water in the dark and maybe swim to the beach, or the like. But the man proved to be a fisherman.

Many years later the fisherman Poul Jorgensen tells of the events of that night, when two vessels had already slipped away from Gilleleje with refugees. Several fishermen would not sail because it was Confirmation Sunday, and many were either holding a confirmation party within their own family or were invited to attend one as a guest. Poul Jorgensen, however, had met the thirty-seven-year-old skipper Juhl Richard Svendsen, who agreed to sail, and together they got the group, which Cohn also belonged to, on board the cutter *Danebrog*, which lay in the inner harbor by an old wooden bridge. "At 7 to 8 p.m. the Germans came. They had been hanging around at the hotel. I cast off, and we drifted out from the pier—Juhl Svendsen lay hidden in the wheelhouse, and I lay flat on the deck. All boats in the harbor were searched but we got away, and we were the only ones who had Jews. The Germans were probably in the harbor for a few hours, but they did not set up spotlights and there were no shots fired.

"We drifted toward a pair of schooners that were next to each other by the north pier, and we laid up on the side of the outermost. A man on board told us that the Germans had already been there, and I moored. A little later I went ashore, but I ran straight into the arms of Gestapo-Juhl. I had my exit pass and gave him some cock-and-bull story and got away. I hid in a well-box, where I could see through the holes. When it was quiet in the harbor, I crept out of my hiding place, and ran into Sergeant Koblegaard, who was able to tell us that the Gestapo were about to leave the hotel. After this Juhl Svendsen wouldn't sail."[13]

Bubi Cohn continues his account, seen from the hold in the boat, which drifts quietly from one side of the harbor to the other, thereby avoiding the Gestapo raid. "After some time we were picked up and taken to another boat. [illegible] was pulled up around the harbor. It caused a huge racket. It was said that the Germans had left. After a quarter of an hour, we sailed out of the harbor, got some [illegible] and then our trip continued. I forgot a little intermezzo, which has some meaning [illegible] had only 2,000 kroner in assets and we had to pay 2,500 kroner. I immediately gave him 500 kr. It was all about a person's life."

The last detail is not uninteresting. Poul Jorgensen, one of the fishermen who sailed the group over, has a very different memory twenty-five years later of the five hundred kroner that changed hands because of a generous gesture that night: "I met Oluf Andersen and asked if he would take the Jews, and he said yes. One of the refugees was a Jewish farm worker who had no money. He wanted to row over, but I told him that he should come with us. He went to Oluf Andersen and said: 'I have no money.' Oluf said, 'Here's 500 kroner. You should not come to Sweden without money.' "

Both stories may be true, of course. But it is also possible that the story has changed over time. In that case it would be one of countless examples of the difficulties in unraveling a story that happened years ago, before the rationalizations of posterity. This is especially true for events where later knowledge completely changes our perceptions, as with the Holocaust. That is why this account tries to limit itself to the perspective of those who went through it.

Cohn tells of the route across the Øresund: "I will never forget that trip. There were some mighty seas. I stayed on deck where the air was clear. Unbelievable suddenly to be on the way to freedom, after having thought that you would be taken prisoner by the Germans, sent to concentration camps, etc.

"There were a few saboteurs along, young, [illegible] and nice people. Furthermore, some Poles who, as usual, could not behave."

The remark of Bernhard Cohn seems once again to reflect a general attitude among many within the "old" Jewish families in Denmark in regard to the "Russian Jews." But it is worth noting that these prejudices did not prevent a strong feeling of solidarity toward a group who were surely less privileged—but nonetheless still countrymen. Bernhard continues: "The lights approached. We were thrust north at the beginning and then east to get around a minefield. I did not think of mines at all. We continued toward the lights and after 1½ hours we reached the port of Höganäs. Soldiers were standing with bayonets turned toward us. When they saw our cargo, they helped us up and welcomed us. I've never seen anything like it."[14]

According to Swedish police Bernhard Cohn arrived in Höganäs at 2:30 a.m. Monday carrying eight thousand kroner in cash but without his wife and three-year-old son, who had stayed behind. As the reason for entry into Sweden the prickly lawyer notes "displaced by pogroms" and as for his status, "Danish refugee" or "political refugee." What had begun as the escape of individual families now began to develop into a mass movement. It is estimated that some five hundred refugees crossed over on Sunday, October 3. Yet fewer than one thousand of the seven to eight thousand people directly concerned had reached safety. The drama was only about to begin.[15]

Heinrich Himmler in 1943. Born at the turn of the century, Himmler played a key role in the Nazi leadership and in the planning and execution of the Holocaust. He became a party member in 1925 and soon advanced thanks to his organizational skills. In 1929 he was promoted to leader of the SS, and three years later he was instrumental in the bloody liquidation of the competing SA corps.

Himmler developed the SS into a powerful elite organization, based on vague ideals of race and strength, ultimately aiming to create a stronger human lineage. His brutality was notorious, and he was the brains behind the buildup of the concentration camps beginning in 1933. With the outbreak of the war, Himmler assumed additional responsibilities, and within the Nazi hierarchy he ranked third after Hitler and Hermann Göring.

After the assassination of Reinhard Heydrich in June 1942, Himmler took over leadership of the German security headquarters, overseeing the extermination of European Jewry. He was also the mentor of Werner Best, who had been working closely with Himmler to build up the inner security of the Third Reich.

Himmler was dangerous to his enemies, and his special elite army corps, the Waffen-SS, became a cancer on the Wehrmacht. In 1943 Hitler appointed him interior minister, in addition to his other posts.

At the end of the war, Himmler sought in vain to achieve a separate peace with the Western Allied powers. He was arrested in May 1945 but committed suicide before facing trial. Scanpix

CHAPTER 9

MONDAY, OCTOBER 4

THE VILLAGE OF RUDS VEDBY

Poznan

It is dangerous to underestimate our formidable ability to close our eyes to what we do not want to see. This ability also influenced contemporary knowledge in Denmark—and elsewhere—of the fate of the Jews in Nazi Germany and in the territories under German control. Despite the fact that from 1942 numerous eyewitness accounts existed and were reported, especially by the BBC, describing systematic mass murder including gas chambers, most people merely accepted the fact that the situation was very grim indeed. To go beyond this was quite simply too daunting, too unthinkable, and too threatening. If the Danish Jews believed or knew of what today is commonly known about the Holocaust, they would probably have sought to escape long before the action in Denmark was undertaken. And had the Danish authorities realized it, they would hardly have been able to cooperate with the occupying power. Most people vaguely knew that it was a grim fate to be a Jew in Nazi-controlled territory, but only a few realized the implication of the Nazi practices taken to their extreme and heinous conclusions.[1]

One of the reasons for this lack of insight was that the Nazi leadership had prepared for the genocide in glowing terms. Although hatred of the Jews exudes from virtually all Nazi writing and speech, it is often difficult to pinpoint the specific decisions that put the eradication into effect on an industrial scale. While a series of conferences and meetings have been identified as decisive in the organization of the genocide, there is no overall plan, though the Nazis followed roughly the same sequence in various countries. First, separation and labeling of the Jews. Then the deprivation of rights, confiscation of property, concentration in transit camps and ghettos, transportation under conditions that in themselves eliminated the most vulnerable, the selection of the "able" for brutalizing work details, and the murder of those who were judged "unable" or superfluous. It is not a simple matter to organize the killing of millions of people, and the physical arrangements required a lot of coordination, decision making, and logistics. But even so, all of this was shrouded in euphemisms and understandings, making it hard to nail down the concrete decisions. The only thing there was no doubt about was the intention.

In the spring of 1943 Berlin issued explicit orders about measures to hide the extensive genocide in the East. Although it is estimated that up to two million Jews had been killed by that time, these exterminations were a consequence more of a common, unspoken effort than of a concrete adoption of specific decrees or legislation. One of the horrors of the Holocaust is that such a comprehensive, systematic, and well-organized genocide could happen without it subsequently being possible to place responsibility at a single locus or on a centralized decision-making body. This is a contributing factor as to why the extermination of the European Jews still attracts so much interest and such intense research. Despite our extensive knowledge, broadly and in the details, the crucial question is still elusive: How did it work?

The Danish experience adds new features to the broader picture. Here, the perpetrators, the victims, and the bystanders acted in ways that are significantly different from the common patterns known from other occupied countries. Together these differences changed the logic of the genocide and caused it to fail in Denmark.

One of the few known examples where a leading member of the Nazi hierarchy spoke of the extermination of the Jews in no uncertain terms is a speech made by Heinrich Himmler on October 4, 1943. Himmler spoke to some one hundred prominent SS officers, who were gathered in Poznan, about halfway between Berlin and Warsaw in a section of Poland that was incorporated into Germany after the 1939 invasion. Had it not been for the action against the Danish Jews, Werner Best would probably have been among the participants listening to the words of their leader. He was one of those who were originally invited to the conference, and had actively sought authorization to participate. He belonged to the inner circle of trusted SS officers, who knew what was going on and who each carried their share of responsibility for it. But as it was, he had to stay in Denmark. He had important work to do.

Under Heinrich Himmler's ambitious leadership, the SS had gradually developed its influence and leverage in the Nazi power structure, which was characterized by unclear distribution of responsibilities and brutal rivalries between competing centers of power. Among other things, by virtue of its control over the concentration camps and forced labor, the SS was a significant center of gravity in the industrial and economic spheres. Despite significant military losses, the SS continued to grow. Like a cancer, the SS sucked strength from the Wehrmacht, both in Germany and through more or less free recruiting in the occupied countries, where everyone of Aryan origin was welcome. This also included Denmark. Within the Nazi organizations in Germany, the SS was a fast track to higher posts with more influence, and the undisputed leader of the SS, Heinrich Himmler, was in 1943 one of the Third Reich's most powerful men.

In June 1943 Himmler had initiated the first liquidation of all the Polish ghettos, followed by the ghettos in Belarus and the Ukraine. This led to a major expansion of the crematoria and gas chambers in extermination camps like Auschwitz. From July all Jews were formally treated as a matter for the police, and in August, Himmler was appointed interior minister in charge of all the police forces in Germany and in the occupied territories. On Monday, October 4, Himmler stood in Poznan before his most loyal supporters and those who were specifically responsible for putting his murderous plans into practice. For once Heinrich Himmler spoke directly about the extermination of the Jews. He spoke without a script, but his talk was recorded on wax disks and was carefully transcribed so that he could subsequently approve the precise formulations, which were sent to those of his people who had not heard him in person.

The speech, which lasted over three hours, dealt predominantly with other issues, but in one part, devoted to the *Judenevakuierung* (evacuation of the Jews), he reveals the mind-set making the extermination of Europe's Jews a common goal that for those directly concerned also entailed a strong sense of communality and shared destiny: "I also want to mention a very difficult subject before you here, completely openly. It should be discussed among us, and yet, nevertheless, we will never speak about it in public."

Himmler then refers to the so-called Night of the Long Knives on June 30, 1934, when an internal showdown laid the foundation of the SS's power through the liquidation of the Nazi Party storm troopers, the

Sturmabteilung, known as the SA, and the original security organization overseeing the SS: "Just as we did not hesitate on June 30 to carry out our duty as ordered, and stand comrades who had failed against the wall and shoot them. About which we have never spoken and never will."

Himmler's tone is understanding, friendly, and almost compassionate about the burden imposed on the chosen ones, and which they had undertaken. The aim is both to share responsibility and to spread it out, so no one can escape his part in it. It is also a warning against "weakness," which could cause the individual to hesitate in the face of atrocity:

> I am talking about the extermination [*Ausrottung*] of the Jewish people. It is one of those things that is easily said. "The Jewish people are being exterminated," every Party member will tell you, "perfectly clear, it's part of our plans, we're eliminating the Jews, exterminating them, ha!, a small matter." And then along they all come, all the 80 million upright Germans, and each one has his decent Jew. They say: all the others are swine, but here is a first-class Jew. And none of them has seen it, has endured it. Most of you will know what it means when 100 bodies lie together, when there are 500, or when there are 1000. And to have seen this through, and—with the exception of human weaknesses—to have remained decent, has made us hard and is a page of glory never mentioned and never to be mentioned. Because we know how difficult things would be, if today in every city during the bomb attacks, the burdens of war and the privations, we still had Jews as secret saboteurs, agitators, and instigators. We would probably be at the same stage as 1916–17, if the Jews still resided in the body of the German people.

Himmler's mission is to convince the assembled SS officers of the inevitability of the genocide. Even more than that, of its honor. Of the treacherous hazards of compassionate objections, he concedes that it may be difficult to be responsible for the death and destruction of so many people, but hastens to reassure his men that it is the victims who are guilty, and that those who have taken responsibility for the killings are the righteous. The credit for Germany's salvation goes to them.

Himmler then momentarily ventures into the importance of the SS officers not exploiting the situation to enrich themselves personally. The Jews' riches belong to the Third Reich, the state. He ends this section about the Jews with an assurance: "We have carried out this most difficult task for the love of our people. And we have taken on no defect within us, in our soul, or in our character."[2]

Himmler's repulsive words notwithstanding, we have to accommodate the paradox that the assembled SS officers, even though they shared a single and terrible goal, were also independent individuals with their own particular interests, ambitions, and strategies. Self-preservation was also a driving force that, at least in some cases, exceeded their hatred for the Jews. Werner Best is an example. He realized that he had nothing to gain by sending the Danish Jews to the gas chambers. On the contrary, he knew what he stood to lose. Therefore he tried to both soften the blow and shirk responsibility. This gave Danish activists the breathing space they needed to build a bridge to Sweden.

Werner Best's Pledge

That Monday, shortly after noon, Nils Svenningsen paid a visit to General Hanneken, whose headquarters was at the Nyboder School, and who wished to tell Svenningsen of the release of the Danish soldiers and the lifting of martial law, which was set for Wednesday, October 6. But before he got that far with this "happy news," Svenningsen interrupted, according to his own account of his conversation with the general. Danish officials were, the Foreign Ministry's director emphasized, "deeply shaken by what has happened. We feel our sense of justice has been profoundly violated. We have the greatest compassion for the poor people who are affected. For the purpose of relations between Denmark and Germany in the coming times, we deeply regret what has occurred. The combination of the Jewish action and the soldiers' release has attracted the most embarrassing attention."

About the general's response to this condemnation Svenningsen notes that he asserted that "he was not responsible for the Jewish action, and that, moreover, it had not been particularly extensive," a recital Svenningsen sharply rejected with the comment that it "was certainly not quantity it depended on. It was the principle."[3]

The minutes of the conversation are Svenningsen's own, and should probably be taken with a grain of salt. The permanent secretary knew that he had to distance himself quite explicitly. He was also aware that posterity would very carefully examine his actions in the aftermath of the roundup, and that what he had said and not said to the occupation's highest representatives would come under close scrutiny. No doubt he strengthened, rather than weakened, his lines in relation to how they were actually spoken face-to-face with the Wehrmacht's commander in Denmark. Even with this caveat, the image of the chastising Danish diplomat and the self-exculpatory German general is remarkable. Svenningsen's remarks were effective. Only a few hundred Jews had yet been captured, and the general's Wehrmacht soldiers constituted the largest German power in the country. The fewer that were assigned to the hunt, the fewer Jews would be arrested. Svenningsen had every reason to express the disapproval of the permanent secretaries.

Later that afternoon Svenningsen also went to see Werner Best at Dagmarhus. Since the action Friday night Best had done what he could to avoid having to see his closest Danish partner eye-to-eye. Best had lied to Svenningsen to his face, and he knew that the permanent secretaries' head man knew it. What Svenningsen could not know was the nature of the meeting in Poznan that Himmler had just hosted and that Best had been invited to participate in. Now, on Monday afternoon, Best could no longer decline a meeting with Svenningsen, which began with an urgent complaint about the action against the Jews in the same terms he had used with Hanneken. But Svenningsen went even further with Best in sketching out the damage the action would have on relations between the two countries: "The action against the Jews was very deplorable in terms of future relations between Denmark and Germany in the coming times, because with it so much had been destroyed in this country. In fact, for the immediate future it would not even be conceivable to start working to rebuild confidence between the two countries."

There was deep frustration among the heads of the administration, but it was Svenningsen's assessment that "provided that there were no new extreme actions against the Jews or in other areas, . . . there was no danger that officials, in general, would not continue to work at their posts. A prerequisite for this, however, was that we have quiet at the workplace, and that the Germans did not interfere in our affairs."

Svenningsen clearly is back in business, trying to use the situation to squeeze concessions out of the occupying power. If cooperation was to continue, the Germans had to refrain from more "extreme actions" and in general allow the permanent secretaries to work in peace. The warning was clear: If the arrest of a few hundred Jews had brought tempers to the boiling point and the permanent secretaries had been on the verge of resigning, what would the consequences be if they succeeded in arresting thousands, who were now deep in hiding?

Svenningsen did not let it go at that. He wanted firm guarantees for those who, according to the Germans' own announcements, were excluded from the roundup, mainly half Jews and Jews married to Aryans. Svenningsen pointed out that "for those concerned there was a strong anxiety and fear that the first action would be replaced by a new one in which they themselves could become victims." When Best willingly assured him that half Jews and Jews married to Aryans had nothing to fear, Svenningsen asked for a written guarantee. Best had to promise to further investigate this and to confirm his guarantees in a letter to his Danish counterpart. It was also important that Friday's action remain an isolated case, and that a further manhunt not be launched.

In addition Svenningsen asked whether visa rules could be relaxed so that more of those who were not covered by the action could leave legally. Best skirted around an answer, but he did make one observation, which may contain a key to his balancing act in the run-up to the raids and the lack of strength with which the action was carried out. Best explained that "he personally saw no reason to regret that a number of people had saved themselves by their flight to Sweden. From a German point of view it was important first and foremost to cleanse Denmark of the Jews, and whether this was achieved by the Jews traveling to Sweden or by deporting them to Germany didn't really matter. It was not about catching as many people as possible."[4]

Best's view was far from trivial. Regardless of whether he had anticipated, and perhaps even hoped, that a mass exodus would occur, or if he had sought to turn this to his advantage once under way, it was crucial that the occupation's top representative in Denmark now plainly stated that the flight was serving a German goal. Best had nothing to gain by capturing and deporting thousands of Danish Jews, but he still had much to lose by doing so, as was illustrated later the same day when he received a communication from the head of the Danish navy, Vice Admiral Vedel, who was among the Danish servicemen now being released. Vedel said in so many words that it "was a disgrace for the servicemen of the Navy to be released at the expense of other Danish nationals."[5]

To Best the stakes were clear. The question was whether Berlin saw—or could be made to see—things from the same perspective.

With the Politicians on the Tailgate

Svenningsen must have talked to the politicians' leading figure, former prime minister Vilhelm Buhl, immediately after the interview with Best, because that same day the politicians summoned the old inner circle plus a few ministers from the "dormant government." It was by no means obvious for the politicians to meet at a point in time where their strategy was to refuse to take any responsibility and where the Germans were exercising pressure for them to come together and resume the cooperation they had discontinued on August 29. Judging from the scattered handwritten notes by Oluf Pedersen, the chairman of the small Retsforbundet, a minor political party, Buhl briefed his colleagues on the commitments Best had given to Svenningsen:

> Svenningsen is told only 100% Jews, excepting those who are married to "Aryans," that is, mixed marriages. Also if there are mixed children from Jews whose spouses were Aryan. It was recognized that there had been mistakes—these would be redressed.
>
> From Best's side, they would seek to limit it to this action. . . . There is some suggestion that "from here" the Germans will announce that this raid is now done.
>
> There was an approach by industry on Thursday . . . they were unanimous in saying that the Jews were part of the Danish population. They went to the Foreign Ministry to obtain an audience with Best, who would not receive them. They . . . put something down in writing, and it was delivered. The king also approached—and the Supreme Court sent a request. The Attorneys' Council also . . .
>
> In addition, Sweden has sent a démarche which was very strong—it was said that it would provoke dramatic indignation. But all in all it has not helped anything. The bishops issued a pastoral letter. It was raised whether anything can be done?
>
> The permanent secretaries also made an approach through Svenningsen to Dr. Best. There have been discussions whether the permanent secretaries should stop work, from our side [that is, Buhl and thus the Social Democrats] we don't believe it should happen. You could say we should do something? I think that can only make matters worse. It can only be a protest.

Buhl obviously has a very clear picture of the situation, and he has discussed with Svenningsen both the possibility that the politicians approach Best, and the idea that the permanent secretaries stop working. Buhl dismissed both options to his colleagues. In that way the country's leading politician also made it clear that while the implementation of an action against the Danish Jews would have been a breaking point for the government, he did not consider it should be one for the permanent secretaries. The situation was different.

Knud Kristensen, leader of Venstre, the country's second-largest party, then took the floor: "Since the action has now happened—will it mean that those who were hunted are still at risk?" Buhl said, "Yes. Following their usual practice, the Germans took what they were after—but not individual searches. And nothing has happened on subsequent nights. Some Jews who were taken indicated who had helped them—and these helpers have been taken."

The Conservative Ole Bjørn Kraft believed that politicians had to do something, "if some form can be found." The politicians got lost for a while in the question of whether it was preferable to act on their own behalf or to let industry and other commercial interests run the protests. The prominent member of the Liberal Center Party Berthel Dahlgaard backed Buhl: "I do not think that any approach from the political side helps—however I am comfortable with the industries' approach."

Before the former prime minister tried to close the discussion, he also addressed the permanent secretaries' internment plans, which Svenningsen must have told him about: "There is talk of detention of those captured by the Germans, but we think it is dangerous. Svenningsen tried it. Could not, they had sailed away."

The Conservatives' chairman, the former pastor Vilhelm Fibiger, spoke with more clarity and apparently even had direct input with the permanent secretaries: "I have advised against interning the Jews here, which we cannot be a part of. It was dangerous for the permanent secretaries to direct such a request—it had a political character." Buhl interjected: "Svenningsen said it was for humanitarian reasons," but Fibiger continued with the more fundamental point of view: "I feel that we, in certain circumstances, can give advice [to the permanent secretaries]. On the other hand, I do not like a request from us to the Germans. We cannot feel called upon to do that."

Kraft provoked the big question as to whether Denmark should take the opportunity to opt out completely and declare the state of war that seemed to be moving closer and closer. It was the "Norwegian conditions" that haunted: "I think that we have to make our position clear. If we are belligerents we must say so in Berlin. I expect many other actions, such as the imposition of forced labor."

Buhl drily intervened: "We will not be allowed to make a declaration of war," a formulation that in itself reflects the deep contradictions in the whole situation. Usually a declaration of war is not something you ask your supposed adversary for permission to submit. Moreover, how does a government declare war if it refuses to work in the first place?

And how does a country declare war against another that has already occupied it? Oluf Pedersen, who took the notes, interjected: "No one can present such an idea in Berlin."

Dahlgaard of the Liberal Center Party, the former coalition partner to the Social Democratic Party, returned to the main track of the discussion. Was there anything the politicians could and should do? "I do not understand whether, from the Parliament's standpoint, we can do anything under the circumstances. One cannot refuse to take political responsibility—and still intervene. I imagine that the permanent secretary talks with various political circles, for example Buhl, privately."

Knud Kristensen was on the same page, and Buhl again tried to sum up: "Can I assume that if the permanent secretary asks us—that we do not believe that they should resign?" Oluf Pedersen records that it was "Yes, from all sides."

The question remained whether to approach Werner Best with the aim of limiting the action's further implementation. Buhl asks if "there may be situations where we can express the people's position?" But Dahlgaard insists: "I'm against it—at this point," while the somewhat unreliable Kraft still doesn't get it: "How about a request from the Conservative Party to Dr. Best?"

That was the last thing the politicians wanted. Such isolated contact, particularly from the Conservatives, would give the Germans renewed hope that some sort of a constitutional government with the participation of a few elected Danish politicians could still be formed and thus establish precisely the division the Danish politicians wanted to avoid at all costs. Buhl cuts in quickly: "I don't believe we can negotiate with Dr. Best."

Kraft explained: "Uncomfortable for me not to do anything," but Oluf Pedersen supported Buhl: "When the king, the government, and parliament will not work, it must be consistent." And Buhl follows: "I think Svenningsen has done what's possible. It would be too risky for Kraft to personally contact Best—he will ask about the government. We must keep ourselves away from him."[6]

In the end, four days later, on October 8, five leading politicians, each representing one of the five democratic parties in the parliament, delivered an official—but confidential—protest to the German plenipotentiary. The politicians expressed "the deep sorrow, which these actions have caused in the Danish people": "The Danish Jews are an integral part of the people, and therefore all the people are deeply affected by the measures taken, which are seen as a violation of the Danish sense of justice."[7]

The Last Resort

At Rådhuspladsen in Copenhagen it was still extremely difficult to obtain an overview of the situation. A flood of information and rumors crossed, and it was impossible to know what to trust. Over the weekend thousands of people had disappeared from their homes and from public life. But had they been deported? Or had they fled? Or had they perhaps seized some desperate last resort? At *Politiken* Bergstrøm followed the stream of rumors: "Holton said there had been 15 Jewish suicides or suicide attempts overnight. Went to the newspaper. The weather was gray and sad. Nielsen came home with a bagful from police headquarters. [The director of the Tuborg breweries] Einar Dessau had committed suicide in Horserød camp. Could there be a mistake here? I already knew that Einar Dessau's brother had killed himself. Barrister Leo Dannin is said to have shot himself, and Professor Kuhr had committed suicide one way or another. The most dismal story, however, occurred last night out in the Sound. A boat with Jews, including Supreme Court attorney Oppenheim, had been stopped by a German patrol boat. Mrs. Oppenheim and five Jews had jumped overboard and drowned."[8]

Almost all of Bergstrøm's information was wrong. But the wild rumors reflected not only great anxiety and uncertainty; they also applied to the reality that one of the major causes of death among Danish Jews was suicide—second only to accidents in flight—predominantly by drowning. The cases of suicide reflect how those directly affected saw their situation. They had heard enough about the fate of the Jews in Germany to prefer the only other option they could see. It is estimated in the latest research that at least sixteen committed suicide during the German action against the Danish Jews. The individuals' fates are very different and the circumstances, by their very nature, are often difficult to disentangle. The fact remains that individuals did seize this solution of last resort. Surely many more were considering the fatal option.[9]

Numerous statements from both refugees and civil servants reveal a profound anxiety over the fate awaiting Jews who were deported to Germany. Concentration camps were well known, and one of the reasons for the politicians' decision to discontinue cooperation with the Germans in August was the prospect that henceforth Danes would be deported to such camps in Germany. The very idea that Danes were now to be deported was shocking and provoked a strong reaction within the Danish and Swedish administrations. The Swedish government reinforced its efforts to get as many of the deportees as possible back to Scandinavia. On October 4 Richert, the Swedish minister to Berlin, followed up on his earlier démarche. The Swedes now proposed that all Jewish children from Denmark be sent to Sweden. The rationale was cunning. In the official reason for the exclusion from public life of the Danish Jews, the Germans had claimed that Jews "poisoned" the atmosphere in Denmark and were behind terrorism and sabotage. But this could certainly not apply to the children, the Swedes now pointed out. So they should be taken to Sweden, where they were welcome. The Germans' enthusiasm for this "offer" was not overwhelming, and they simply chose to ignore it.

The proposal also had an extra sting, since among the deportees were about forty young German Jews who in 1939 at the behest of the International Women's League for Peace and Freedom had been given German exit visas to Denmark, where they were in agricultural training. The German visas were granted with the express condition that the youth not be returned to Germany. In that light, as the Danish Ministry of Foreign Affairs was also quick to point out, the deportation to Germany was a contradiction. All to no avail. Nazi ideology could not be ensnared by logic, and the so-called League children had to stay in Theresienstadt.[10]

Calm After the Storm

After Friday's, Saturday's, and Sunday's violent events and dramatic decisions, it is as if Monday was the day when thousands of fleeing people licked their wounds and pondered their next move. Many had sought and found refuge in more or less safe hiding places. The question now arose of what would happen next? After the raid on Friday, few dared to have faith that they could ride out the storm hiding in Denmark, and interest focused on escape routes across the Sound to Sweden. The Swedish offer to accept all Danish Jews raised hopes and provided a goal and direction. But there was no organization, no precedent, and wild confusion around the crucial question: How to get there?

Herbert Levysohn, who had sought refuge on a farm in Kongsted, just north of Dianalund, was a case in point. He was received kindly, and the woman of the farm, Mrs. Marbo, was able to calm the young man, whose nerves were frayed by uncertainty. She treated him to good food and cordial words, both about his immediate family's destiny and what lay ahead. In his diary he muses over it all: "Uncertainty is the worst thing there is, and everything was uncertain. I wonder how Dad is? And poor mother and Kate? Will they come tomorrow? Or when? How many people knew I was in Kongsted? Would the Germans search for me here? And what would happen then? Who have the Germans taken? Were they in Denmark, the poor souls? No, they were probably on their way to Poland? This is how the cluttered thoughts bounced around in my head, while I felt miserable that I could not stand by my mother's side in this situation."

Haunted by all these thoughts, Levysohn also felt suspicious of the other guests at the farm: "And then that half-witted young lady. She might be a Nazi. Tomorrow her boyfriend will even come and visit her, and what would he say when he gets back to Copenhagen? I wonder how things are in Copenhagen? Was the house in Klampenborg okay? Or had the Germans taken it? And what about the business?"[11]

The assumption of both the fugitives and their helpers was that the German police would actively search for the refugees and seek to prevent their further flight, both on land and at sea. They had to assume that the Germans would quickly become aware of the Jews' seeking passage to Sweden, and that determined efforts would be made to block the flight and detain the refugees. But that was not the case, and in Stockholm the impression quickly began to settle in "that the Germans in Copenhagen are unwilling to act vigorously against the Jews and to some extent are turning a blind eye as they flee to Sweden," as the Swedish Foreign Ministry expressed it Monday.[12]

In London the Danish minister, Eduard Reventlow, received a visit from a representative of the Jewish World Congress, "who asked for information about how the Conference could help their fellow believers out of Denmark. Advised him to send ciphered telegram through the Foreign Office via the legation in Stockholm to the Conference representative in Stockholm inviting him to explore the possibility of authorizing local representatives in Helsingborg and other Swedish cities on the Sound to provide help . . . by paying the fishermen for transport."[13]

Vilhelm Bergstrøm's short diary note on Monday gives the impression of an observer who was in close contact with the Danish police: "Sergeant Godtfred Jensen arrived. He said there was a collection for the Jews. Some kind of federation had thus collected not less than 6,000 kroner. Jacob arrived and asked if it was hard to get across the Sound. I told him that the Germans were now on their guard, so the trip was not safe anymore."[14]

The helpers had only vague ideas about what might happen if they were caught in their work. Later attempts to reconstruct a realistic picture based on random, scattered material show only that nothing universal can be derived from it. Few had prior experience with underground work, let alone with active resistance. Most had probably been skeptical of armed resistance and sabotage, but now it seemed natural, even necessary, to help the fugitives. Many contributed passively by closing their eyes. But those who engaged actively by helping, who concealed the fugitives and sought to organize transport and cover, crossed the line to active, though generally unarmed, resistance. Given the state of emergency and the increased repression, no one had any idea how the Gestapo would react if they seized the helpers in the act.[15]

In Ruds Vedby Adolph Meyer was still considering his situation without knowing what had become of his children and the rest of the family: "I negotiated with Bülow on Monday the fourth of October, and Mary also gave him power of attorney. I asked him to cash in all my bonds and send me 100,000 kroner with a trustworthy man, Wednesday or Thursday. I called to allow Adam to move and store my furniture, Stavnsholm my wine, Munkegård my books, and let the girls remove the most valuable things. He did not seem inclined to do it, and I wonder if he has done it? He had no opportunity to send the 100,000 kroner. I asked him to give Honoré 1,000 kroner to stay at Nørager [a winter and summer vacation resort]. I allowed him to spend what he considered appropriate to help poor Jews to flee. . . . Despite my nervousness I did not sleep badly at night, with the help of 1 or 2 bromisoval pills. I did, however, feel eased prostate discomfort, and I was still thinking about the fate of the children."

A New Beginning

Meanwhile in Ystad, the refugees' perspective changed quickly. From the moment they set foot in Sweden, they were at once overwhelmed by

Architect Poul Henningsen was among those who felt the earth burn beneath him after the August uprising. The Nazis believed PH to be a subversive Communist, but the government had tried to protect the naughty-rhyme man by claiming that he was only a "salon Communist" and thus should not be detained. Danish Nazis, however, became more and more enraged at PH, who in cooperation with the like-minded CEO of Copenhagen's popular Tivoli Gardens, Kjeld Abell, was in the process of transforming the old garden into a hotbed of jazz and other liberal activity that—rightly—was seen as directed against Nazi bigotry. After several attempts Henningsen ended up fleeing across the Sound on September 30. A rowboat was transported from Bagsværd Lake to Høje Skodsborg, where he and his wife, Inge, joined fellow architect Arne Jacobsen and his girlfriend. Jacobsen was of Jewish descent, as was the fifth passenger, a young sports rower, Herbert Marcus, who manned the oars seated across from the two small, stout architects.

The five set out from Høje Skodsborg at nightfall. The trip was longer than expected, and only after five hours in rough seas, with the women bailing water continuously from the open boat, did they reach Landskrona. "We have fallen among human beings," PH wrote shortly afterward, moved by meeting friendly Swedes who bade the refugees a warm welcome.

In Stockholm, Henningsen quickly became part of the lively and highly combustible intellectual environment in which refugees from Norway and Denmark, together with Swedish peers, discussed the lessons of war for the impatiently awaited peace. The young German refugee Willy Brandt was part of this group, with distinct social democratic leanings and a pronounced rejection of Communism. When Willy Brandt later called himself a Nordic Social Democrat, he was referring not least to these years in Stockholm.

and grateful for the warm welcome, and simultaneously very focused on getting on with their lives as soon as possible under their new conditions in exile. Naturally they were very eager to hear news about family and friends who were also on the run, and there were large and small injuries to be healed. All the troubles of life in exile had to be met and overcome. This weighs heavily in the diary entries from those first days in Sweden. At the same time they reflect something that characterized the refugees from beginning to end: their insistence on maintaining self-respect in these unfamiliar new circumstances, now coupled with a great impatience to set about building a new life. The refugees refused to see themselves as victims. If part of the goal of the Nazi persecution of the Jews was to break their self-respect and determination, it didn't succeed with the Hannover and Marcus families.

Poul Hannover explains: "Yes—I could probably finish the story of the trip here. But anyway, let me briefly report further. The next day I was with the police several times—partly formalities dealing with the money—I was allowed to change 400 kroner—I was at the bank twice—I got my one pair of shoes fixed. . . . Inger took some of our clothes to the tailor to get them cleaned and pressed. The tailor was a story in himself. He had a sister in Denmark . . . and he was touching—it cannot be described. The different people who had been there could confirm that he was adamant in his refusal to take money. On the contrary, he filled the different parties' pockets with cigarettes and chocolate. When I came down and had to pick up our clothes—and it was not so little—there was no question of accepting my money. I burst into tears and asked to pay him for his work—but no, do not talk about it—and if I needed money—yes, he did not have very much—but a little might also be of some help. It turned out that he knew the fund manager Landin at ASEA, He went off and came back with a little box of Sedubrol—I should take a few pills with some broth to calm down—and barely had I come back to the hotel before a package arrived from him—and when I open it, there is both a box of sweets, some real chocolate with the sweetest little letter to me that here were some 'sweets to the children.' I shall never forget him."[16]

CHAPTER 10

TUESDAY, OCTOBER 5

GOING NORTH

Under Arrest

Many of the fleeing Jews had not gone far. They had sought refuge with neighbors, friends, and acquaintances, or they had gone to a vacation home in the country—their own or borrowed—to gain time and await further developments.

Some were also still admitted to hospitals under aliases. This included Ella Fischer, who was admitted to the municipal hospital with neuritis. In her diary she describes how things began to take off that Tuesday: "For a start, the head nurse and Miss Ring came and retrieved my bill, because Dr. Krabbe wanted the Jewish patients' names changed, and at the same time we were given notice that our clothes were to be brought up to the rooms, so that we [would be] ready for a quick discharge. When I asked if we were no longer safe in the hospital, the response was that they could not guarantee anything. They would certainly take their precautions."

In her diary there is a short report about a Danish helper, Mrs. Sorensen, who apparently quite inadvertently, from one moment to the next, had been thrown into a Jewish family's efforts to cope with the situation, stick together, and find ways to get to Sweden: "During visiting hours Mrs. Sorensen came—she lives in the same building as Johanne and Fritz—and told me that they had reached Sweden. She showed me a letter that Johanne had written from Swedish territorial waters, in which she had asked Mrs. Sorensen to visit me. She offered to help me leave, but then, of course, when I would not go alone, I gave her the address of Miss Raastøff, and she then went to talk to her."

After Mrs. Sorensen had gone to attend to this errand, the hospital chaplain arrived. He had spoken with Ella the previous Sunday without much success. This time it went better: "The hospital chaplain came soon after, and to my great astonishment, offered to help me leave. He did not want anything more, he said, than to help get us off, and I could just send for him if I wanted help. How this offer fits together with his preaching a few days before, I do not understand, but he may have changed his mind."

In a roundabout way Ella gets a message that "Mrs. Sorensen seems to think she can help me get away the next day. She will come to me during visiting hours." The problem now is money: Ella's employers are apparently not exactly generous or understanding: "Munksgaard had only wanted to give me 700 kroner—the stingy ass—although I had not yet received my salary for the month of September. He said that if it were necessary, I could ask for 300 kroner more. He also asked if there wasn't something I could sell. I have no idea how he imagined this business might be conducted when I was in the hospital and all my relatives and friends were scattered to the winds."

Her landlady was more helpful. She had packed what was needed from her tenant's room and showed up at the hospital with it: "Miss Abro came in with a suitcase with my clothes, so now I had everything ready to go. I gave Miss Abro the message to rent my room furnished because it was the easiest way out. I also said that if she vacated the apartment, could she make sure that my stuff was stored. I gave her Per Federspiel's address so the storage could be arranged with Leo's things. That night I barely slept although I had been given a strong sleeping pill."[1]

In Ruds Vedby, Adolph Meyer is aware that he and Mary, his sister-in-law, must move on. The hope that they could ride out the storm in this rural area and at some point return to town and resume their normal lives was shattered. They had to get away, and away meant to Sweden. Rumors from numerous directions indicated that escape routes were being established and that possibilities for shipping out were best from the north coast of Sjælland, where in part there had been the fewest German police, where there was a long and scarcely populated coastline, and finally, the coveted Swedish coast not so far away. It is also apparent from the doctor's entries that his hosts and colleagues are now starting to move to get the seventy-two-year-old and his sister-in-law out of the place before it is suddenly too late: "The next morning, Tuesday the fifth of October, to my surprise, Dr. Hart arrived at 8 or 9 in the morning (I had yet to see a doctor). He said he was with a friend. Erik Nyegaard had come to Ruds Vedby the night before at 11 p.m. When Hart opened the door to him, Nyegaard discovered that Hart was from his school and that they knew each other. . . . They sat together a long time. He stayed there that night, but did not close his eyes, and looked pale."

Although it is not clear from Adolph Meyer's diary, the connection must be that Erik Nyegaard, after the departure of the Hannover and Marcus families from Grønsund on Saturday night, went back to Copenhagen and was informed there that the twin sisters' father had taken refuge with his colleague in Ruds Vedby. Without knowing that he was an old schoolmate of Dr. Hart, Nyegaard must have gone to see if Hart's lodgers, the aging refugees, needed help. With his arrival in Ruds Vedby late Monday night, Nyegaard found that the host and he actually knew each other from their old days, and the two of them, Dr. Hart and Nyegaard, deliberated overnight over the old people's flight.

Dr. Meyer explains further: "Then Erik Nyegaard came in, and I did not immediately recognize him. He was fitted with a Danish police badge (this was stolen by a saboteur from a police officer. Nyegaard got it from him and went to police headquarters with it, and he was allowed to borrow it to help the refugees, and they informed him that according to the number, it had belonged to a cop named Nissen, whose name he should take. So police headquarters also helped)."

This must be the fake police badge Kis Marcus mentions in her diary, and which Svend Nielsen, a resistance man according to her information, had used to get through a checkpoint on his way to Falster. He had apparently passed it on to Erik Nyegaard, who had the audacity on the Monday to go to police headquarters in Copenhagen to clear up whom the stolen police badge belonged to. It is not clear whether Nyegaard had a confidential relationship with the police, or whether he might just have wanted to return the badge to the right person. However, he ended up keeping the badge, now helpfully provided with the false identity of a named Danish policeman.

To the refugees and their helpers, a major obstacle was the lack of cars. As gasoline was difficult if not impossible to obtain, private cars generally didn't run, and official cars were under tight control, with ambulances the most obvious exception. Thus many refugees were transported in ambulances as they transited through the hospitals en route to the coast. In other cases public transportation was the only option. Even if this was unrestricted, it was highly visible, all the more so as all railroads invariably led through Copenhagen. This was regarded as a significant risk, especially in the case of Adolph Meyer as he was a fairly public person who could easily be recognized. The idea, therefore, was that Meyer and his sister-in-law should be transported as Erik Nyegaard's detainees. Dr. Meyer explains:

> Then Mrs. Hart came with Mary. We had to pack in a hurry and only take the small bag. The red suitcase I had at Dianalund, Hart took along. There could be no nametags on any of our belongings, the name was ripped from my jacket, and I had to leave my passport, cane, doctor's ring, the pearls, extra gold cufflinks, all luggage. Fortunately I had a coat, galoshes, but in my attaché case only toiletries (minus tooth powder case), a set of silk pajamas, a wool sweater, my angora vest, extra glasses, mittens, and 5 handkerchiefs, no extra collar or shirt or undershirt, not Mathilde's picture in the silver frame and only the cigars I could fit in my case and a little tobacco in a tobacco pouch + a pipe. Some of this was probably excessive caution; if we were taken, the fake name would hardly have helped. I drank some milk and ate a little porridge and bread in a hurry; we went out to the waiting [doctors'] car after Hart had explained the situation to the doctors and I had said my farewells to the Harts.
>
> As arrestees we were led off, first to Sorø, where we waited in a separate room at the railway hotel after Nyegaard had presented his badge. The host asked if the prisoners were from the area. "No," said Nyegaard. Later he asked if it was Jews. "Do you think that the Danish police do the Germans' drudgery?" Nyegaard answered.
>
> After barely a half hour we were led to the railway station, where we were brought into the stationmaster's office, which led to a back door that Nyegaard locked and gave the key to stationmaster. The previous evening in Korsør he had ordered a compartment for our transport. He called express to police headquarters in Copenhagen, as it was said that trains were being checked in Copenhagen, but fortunately it turned out not to be the case.

Rush Hour

Adolph Meyer continues the story of his journey:

> The train came and we were brought to the rear compartment, where passengers were taken off first. They had forgotten to give

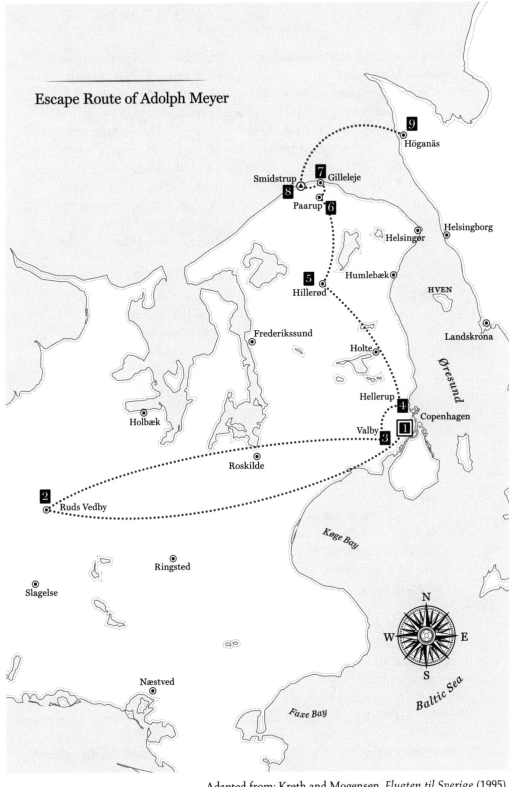

Escape Route of Adolph Meyer

Höganäs

Smidstrup Gilleleje

Paarup

Helsingør Helsingborg

Hillerød

Humlebæk

HVEN

Frederikssund

Holte

Landskrona

Hellerup

Øresund

Copenhagen

Valby

Holbæk

Roskilde

Ruds Vedby

Køge Bay

Ringsted

Slagelse

N

W — E

S

Baltic Sea

Næstved

Faxe Bay

Adapted from: Kreth and Mogensen, *Flugten til Sverige* (1995).

the train conductor notification of the transport in Korsør, and he was a little fussy, but a pack of cigarettes from Nyegaard, which were actually some of my packs from Dianalund, did wonders. "Be a little nice," Nyegaard said to him, and soon after signs were put up on the windows with the word "Occupied." The curtains were drawn. We did not dare travel to the central train station, where there were Gestapo. We went as far as Valby, where we arrived about 2 o'clock. We were on the platform, our backs to the train, until people had gone and the train had departed, went out from the station to the left, got a taxicab, and drove around town to Hellerup; where we got another car that drove us to a villa in nearby Charlottenlund.

In the car I hid myself as best as possible. In the villa that I think belonged to Nyegaard's sister, only the maid was home. We stayed there for 5 minutes, then we went for a few minutes to a villa belonging to the merchant Johan Hansen, inhabited by his daughter, a local teacher, Miss Hansen. Her mother and a couple of older ladies were present, they soon left, and Mrs. Hansen gave us lunch, during which Miss Hansen, who was very charming, came home. The father came later, he had not, apparently, understood the seriousness of the situation. Nyegaard, to whom we had said good-bye, had immediately informed me in the morning that Inger and Poul, Kis and Gunnar and their children were safe in Sweden. He had also informed me of the wording of the telegram we should send after arrival in Sweden. The idea was that we were leaving in the evening with Axel and Ingrid Salomonsen and their children [another Jewish family], and when we all came over the telegram should read: "Asea, Bredgade 45, Copenhagen, 6 engines were unfortunately delayed"; if we came over alone, it should read: "2 engines unfortunately delayed."

So far so good. But Dr. Meyer actually was nearly back at his own home, and there were still many stops to come. The escape had not yet been efficiently organized, and each of the helpers was drawing on his personal contacts. Even if everyone was supportive and hospitable, it brought Meyer and Mary no closer to the coveted transport over to safety: "At 4:30 p.m. or a little later there was a call, and I heard a voice say: 'Is Uncle Adolph here?' It was Director Henry Nielsen, and he took us immediately with his car, said that Ada, Jørgen, and family were safe—in Copenhagen. We drove to a villa Højbo in Gentofte, I went straight in and heard some voices. When I walked into the room, they said they were sorry but that the car with some others who were about to leave had driven off about a half an hour ago, it could not wait for us; luckily Henry Nielsen had not yet paid for the car. We should have gone via Hornbæk to Gilleleje on the north coast, but we only managed to reach the North Rail train in nearby Holte and go over Hillerød on the Gribskov train. It was pouring rain, and we had to stand a large part of the way. Henry Nielsen came with us. It rained heavily in Hillerød, we were in a carriage that was completely full of refugees, several carriages were used, and we were at least half an hour late, there were about 200 refugees on the train."

One has to imagine here an old provincial train with two wooden carriages and normally only a handful or two of passengers. That afternoon it was all different, and among the many refugees who passed through the station in Hillerød was Herbert Levysohn, who after many vicissitudes during the previous days had followed a route not unlike Adolph Meyer's, and who now ended up on the same train as the pediatrician and his sister-in-law. We thus have two independent contemporary accounts of the events that ensued.

Levysohn recounts in his journal how he was greeted by two assistants at Holte station, one probably a trusted employee at his father's business, the other an uncle:

I sat in Holte station in the waiting room and immersed myself in a newspaper. Soon after clerk Stridsland and Mr. Wenzzel came. There is a forest behind the station where we walked around for the next hour, where I got an explanation about it all. That evening one of the vessels from the coastal police was to leave from Gilleleje. We would be 5 people in it, all in all it was very safe. I only needed to approach a man in Gilleleje with a Band-Aid on his right cheek. If I saw him on the train I had to pretend to know nothing. Then I got some of Mom's jewelry that Mrs. Stridsland had made a small bag for, for me to hang around my neck. I got some money, including 1,500 kroner that the trip would cost. Eventually Stridsland gave me the royal emblem in gold as a parting gift, for which I was very touched. Finally I signed a document that gave them the right to sell my papers as they thought best. Stridsland then went into town and bought some food for me, but I never ate it, it was lost in the confusion. Both went with me down to the train to Hillerød, and I departed. In Hillerød I was to switch over to the local train to Gilleleje. It was rainy and very dark, I still had not seen the fellow with the Band-Aid.[2]

The scene at the train station in Hillerød reflects the situation in many parts of North Sjælland that week: Fleeing families and large groups of refugees approaching the coast with only faint ideas of how to proceed from there. That particular afternoon the pressure was so heavy that the railways had to add extra cars and dispatch densely packed carriages. It would have been an easy matter for any authority, Danish or German, to intervene and arrest the refugees. But German Wehrmacht soldiers who randomly observed the fugitives had no desire to see anything, military police were not deployed to transportation hubs, and the few eager Gestapo officials and their Danish collaborators could not be everywhere. In most cases the only authorities operating were Danish police and railway personnel, who at worst closed their eyes but more commonly helped the fugitives on their way. The problem, however, was the reception on the sparsely populated north coast, where the locals were completely unprepared for the influx coming on the afternoon trains.

Herbert Levysohn, who like several other young refugees was able to see the funnier aspects of this impossible situation, gives a lively description of the situation on the evening train from Hillerød to Gilleleje: "The train was overcrowded, most particularly the two carriages going all the way to Gilleleje. There were so many black-haired people that it was absolutely fantastic. I had been told that we were only 5 going over that night, but there were at least 70 here. Parents with small children, old people, young people, and very few could hide their nervousness. 'How long is the train delayed?' 'When will we get to Gilleleje?' 'Give the boy something to sleep so he calms down,' etc. Idiots, I thought, they can't shut up. This is all going to fail when they actually advertise that they are about to flee. The congestion in the two small carriages was incredible, the heat unbearable. I pushed myself out onto the platform and got fresh air, amply mixed with rain and coal dust."[3]

Dr. Meyer describes the train's stop at the small unmanned station just before Gilleleje: "When we got to Paarup, there were shouts: 'Director Nielsen, passenger to Gilleleje, must get off here!' As the young girl who brought the message did not know otherwise, Henry Nielsen did not think it had anything to do with him and us; he would follow his instructions, which had been typed up in the Gentofte villa. So we stayed on the train. In Gilleleje we had to wait a very long time in the waiting room, and met several acquaintances."

There was general confusion, not aided by the great secrecy that contributed to important messages being whispered into the wrong ears—and when they found the right ones, they often gave rise to mis-understandings. Levysohn has this version of Paarup station and then the arrival at Gilleleje: "At the station before Gilleleje there was a longer stay. Some people entertained themselves quietly with one another as if there was nothing wrong. One didn't feel comfortable with the sit-uation. Finally we got to Gilleleje, around 9 p.m. to be precise. I still had not seen the fellow with the Band-Aid, and now it was pure chaos. In pitch darkness people rushed around among themselves and called out to one another. Suddenly someone says, 'Hello Mr. Levysohn.' It was headwaiter Bendixen from Marienlyst Hotel, and he was there to help. Shortly afterward I met Jørgen Jacoby, who was also there to help. Finally the guy with the Band-Aid popped up, and gave orders to go into the waiting room inside, where we all gathered. It was not pleasant; everyone was nervous and talking at one another. A man reassured us that the police were there to protect us and there was no danger. The Danish police swarmed in and out and gave orders, but they didn't seem calm, and I found it all chaotic, as if it wasn't going to succeed. But one was in the middle of it now, and so one had to hold on."[4]

Gilleleje Harbor

There are multiple contemporary reports of the dramatic events in Gil-leleje that evening. A Norwegian engineering student from Copenha-gen, Vilhelm Lind, was actively involved in the efforts to help out on the north coast during the first days of October. In an account written at the latest just after the war, he noted how things developed after he and a few others had helped to organize the first major shipment of refugees out of Gilleleje, including those arriving at the fishing ham-let on the afternoon train from Hillerød—the train before the one that Meyer and Levysohn came on: "At around 7 p.m. a special train arrived from Copenhagen bringing approximately 175 Jews. Because of the large number and their arrival so late in the afternoon and without any prior organizational work, it was impossible to spread them throughout the town. Therefore they were pushed onto a side track so they could stay put in the carriage until the ship, a schooner they had bought, could sail."

There were several other, smaller transports planned that evening, and the coastal police undertook to give a signal when the time was best for the individuals to depart: "At 8 o'clock, after it was pitch dark, the train from Copenhagen was driven down to the harbor and up to the side of the schooner, where the contents were loaded on board, after which the schooner sailed immediately. The coastal police were busy investigating something suspicious at the other end of the harbor at the time, and the Germans had not yet appeared in the harbor.

"When the schooner was well away, the other students began to board their ship, and everything seemingly went well and the ship departed."[5]

It was around this time that the new, crowded evening train, with Meyer and Levysohn among hundreds of new refugees, arrived Levysohn explains further about the chaotic events at the small station:

> We were then divided into teams, I was not in the first team, but I didn't care if those who were most nervous pressed ahead and ended up in front. After a bit the first team of 19 people marched off from the station and into the dark and the rain. After a while it was us who marched away. Gilleleje was quite dark, only the lighthouse illuminated the town with flashes as we walked along the muddy road. . . .
>
> We went on for a while, where to was not easy to see, but it appeared to be the main street in Gilleleje. Then we came through some small winding alleyways, through a house, back out into an alley, and then we stopped at a house. We, i.e., 13 people, 12 refugees and 1 police officer. The house we stopped in front of was a mission hotel where the policeman had his little room on the ground floor. We entered. In the room there was a bed, a table, and a chair, and we were to stay until we got further instructions. We stood and sat around and we were ordered to keep quiet, which was difficult for most people. The policeman came back a few times and said we should just wait, how long it would last, he did not know, but as a precaution he gave orders to turn off the lights. Being in the dark without air did not bother me, but the ladies were not happy about it.

The many people in the small, stuffy, dark room were apt to get nervous, but there was still the prospect of making the crossing that evening. It did not last long: "Then he came and told us that the first boat was now departing. We waited. Suddenly there was a shot. The policeman came rushing: 'The Gestapo is in the harbor, and is shooting at the first boat that was just about to go out.' A short while later he came again. 'The Gestapo took the first boat and everyone's been captured. You must keep yourselves calm, the situation is not good.' "[6]

It seems that Dr. Meyer and his sister-in-law were taken to the same room at the Mission Hotel, where they waited together with Levysohn, and we also have Meyer's account of the journey from the station:

> So we were picked up in teams. It was probably between 9 and 10 p.m., when we were led, sprayed and blown, by a Danish coastal policeman who had borrowed my little flashlight, down to the harbor. We heard from him that a large boat had departed, but the next one with 19 passengers had been shot at, so they dared not send more boats away; moreover, there were German guards coming to the port.
>
> We were tired, hungry, nervous. Together with 8 others we came into a small room with 2 beds on the ground floor in the so-called Mission Hotel. Henry Nielsen also had to spend the night in the "hotel" but we did not see him later. We were not allowed to have lights or open windows, which were inadequately blacked out. After some time, 4 or 5 of the 12 were placed upstairs. We tried to sleep. I lay dressed in one bed, Mary and Mrs. Jespersen on the other, two lay on the floor, one sat in a chair (fortunately there was a WC outside in a corner of the hallway). We could only open the door if there was a specific knock. The cop came by now and then, a bit nervous. He feared that they would not dare to sail the first days.

It was Gestapo-Juhl at work again, and the Norwegian Vilhelm Lind, who was present at the port while the dramatic events unfolded, has given his report of the failed departure of the cutter *Danebrog*. It was the same boat that had drifted across Gilleleje harbor Sunday night with "Bubi" Cohn and others on board, an experience that already had frightened skipper Juhl Svendsen. On Sunday evening he had managed to talk his way past Gestapo-Juhl and to save his cargo of refugees. This time Gestapo-Juhl set eyes on him just as the *Danebrog* was about to depart, loaded with nineteen refugees: "When the ship had just left, a car drove down the harbor and out jumped three Schalburg men and began firing at the boat. . . . I could not figure out whether the skipper was hit or not, but the boat began to drift out of control."[7]

The Danish coastal police sergeant Mortving was also present at the harbor, and the same evening he reported on the ensuing incident: The cutter *Danebrog*, led by Juhl Svendsen, had just put to sea with nineteen refugees on board when Gestapo-Juhl surprised it with three or four other Gestapo men. Juhl shouted at the cutter and demanded "that it stop, otherwise more shots would be fired, but the captain did not respond and continued sailing, causing Juhl to fire an additional 20 to 25 shots at the cutter, whose engine now immediately stopped."

At the sight of the Gestapo, Svendsen had immediately started the *Danebrog*'s engines and left the quay. At Gestapo-Juhl's cry the skipper gunned the engine, but he panicked when the bullets began to smash into the wheelhouse where he stood. Svendsen put the engine into reverse, whereupon the boat's stern ran into the tip of the pier. Svendsen and his assistant, fisherman Peter Johannes, jumped ashore and disappeared into the darkness.

On the other side of the dock Gestapo-Juhl stood with the Danish coastal police officer Mortving, who was not nearly as busy as his German counterpart. While some of the refugees were desperately trying to gain control over the abandoned cutter and go full speed ahead, the wind pitched the boat out into the middle of the harbor, where it ran aground on the sandy bottom at the east pier. Mortving reports: "Criminal Inspector Juhl now turned to me and asked me to provide a dinghy, so that he could get on board the cutter, which was now driven toward the east pier. Sergeant Koblegaard then rowed out with the harbormaster, Christian Svendsen, and Juhl to the cutter, now driven completely into the stone wall on the east pier.

"Koblegaard came back immediately afterward and announced that on the cutter he found a gentleman and a lady as well as a minor child. Furthermore, several people were lying on the stone wall on the east pier, including several women and children of Jewish descent.

"Juhl then took up position on the east pier to cut off those people's way back along the pier toward land. Immediately after, more German military personnel arrived at the port by truck and immediately arrested the fleeing Jewish people."

Sergeant Mortving adds for good measure the blatant lie that "none of the police officers had noticed any of the persons referred to arrive at the port tonight."[8]

The nineteen captives were transported to Helsingør and then on to Horserød, which was the collection point before further deportation to Theresienstadt.

Some groups of the latest arrivals were on their way through the dark streets when they heard the shooting. They had to turn back and seek refuge. The helpers found many who had stayed in primitive hiding places for hours, and brought them into shelter. At the Mission Hotel the situation was untenable. Levysohn gives a report of the mood in the room (where according to his notes there was one bed, but according to Dr. Meyer, two): "These were strange hours passing by. My thoughts turned to Mom and Kate, happy as I was to know that they were over, but for Mother's sake, I had to figure out how to get over, but what now? Well, we had to keep ourselves calm and wait out the events. After an hour or more, the cop came again. 'The Gestapo is still in the harbor, so the prospect of sailing tonight is extremely low, if not hopeless.' "[9]

While the twelve refugees were still crammed into the coastal police's temporary office at the Mission Hotel, and many others in other places in the small town, Gestapo-Juhl and his small team of collaborators raided both the hotel and the inn. They had no luck at either of the sites because they had been evacuated shortly before. But Gilleleje was full of refugees, and had the Germans entered the coastal police's office right next door, they would have had a great catch. Gestapo-Juhl retreated with his men but left no doubt that he would come back. Nevertheless all the accommodations were put back into use, although it was obvious to everyone that things were completely untenable with so many refugees in the town.

Levysohn is among those being evacuated from the Mission Hotel that same evening:

One lady had a place with some friends where 4 people could stay, and they were allowed to go. Another lady had a place to which she had the key, it was an empty house, with room for 6, and I went with them. We carefully snuck out, with our friend the policeman in the lead. As we approached the main road we had to press ourselves against a wall when 2 cars with Gestapo drove right past. We went on. The lady with the key to the house went in front. The policeman and I were last. In the darkness the policeman and I got separated from the others, and as the officer, who was employed by the coastal police, had only arrived in Gilleleje the day before, he didn't know his way or where I was supposed to go.

We passed 3 fishermen who stood and talked. The officer approached them and asked if there was one who would take me for the night. It was midnight by now. One of them offered right away. I had to take it as it was. I was happy if I could just lie down for a few hours. He had a small two-room apartment. In one room he slept with his wife and two small children, the second was the living room, where there was a couch. The wife got up and gave me a cup of coffee, and then made up the couch for me. Half-dressed and ready to rapidly respond, I lay on the sofa. There was no thought of sleep of course, since you listened to every step, but just to lie down did me good.[10]

It is no wonder that both the refugees and the helpers in Gilleleje felt that their number was up. Today we know that to a great extent Gestapo-Juhl constituted an exception to the rule that the German authorities did little to capture the fugitives, and the testimony of the fugitives also reflects a general feeling that the Germans as a rule were not particularly zealous in their manhunt. This is noted on October 5 in the diary of the town doctor in the tiny Swedish coastal town of Höganäs, who was responsible for examining the incoming refugees, and who spoke with some of the first to come in: "They reported that the Danish people did everything to help, and that the German soldiers wanted to see them slip through."

Unfortunately Gestapo-Juhl was not a German soldier but an active Nazi and Gestapo officer. And he did not want anybody to slip through.

The Mobilization

While the refugees and the helpers tried to cope with the evolving situation in Gilleleje and other coastal cities, the country was still struggling to understand what was happening and to digest the consequences. The legal press and radio were silent on the unfolding human drama, so rumors and hearsay traveled fast, creating confusion. In general the reaction was as expected—and feared—by the Germans, except with no tendency to demonstrations or civil unrest. But the raid against the Jews provoked a new sense of defiance that for many became the crucial nudge in the direction of active resistance. Armed struggle and sabotage were still the acts of a very few, and the majority of the population probably still viewed sabotage with great skepticism, because many feared it would just provoke the Germans and increase the repression. But there is no doubt that the center of gravity in public opinion was shifting, and more and more people felt that the time had come to push back harder.

While hatred of the Germans only grew, many also retained strong reservations about the Communists taking a leading role in the armed resistance. For the same reason the elected politicians still harbored strong reservations in regard to the militant freedom fighters. What were their intentions if the Soviet Union won the war? Even if the Communists had begun to use national slogans hailing the defeat of fascism and the liberation of Denmark, few trusted their patriotic sentiment, and many feared that they were using the fight against the Germans as a springboard for their continued desire for social upheaval and revolution on the Soviet model. The battle lines were sharply drawn, and when the Communist-inspired underground newspaper *Free Denmark* was released in October with its commentary on the action against the Jews, it was permeated by the underlying struggle for what was now at stake.

Free Denmark first notes that the action against the Jews, "which today has resonated through all walks of life," has led to a flood of indignation: "The persecution of the Jews has hit Danes at the tenderest point of their consciousness, even the overly tolerant, the passive, the lukewarm, feel this baseness and they shrink at the thought. . . .

"The Germans must not think that either the repatriation of soldiers or the pro forma lifting of the state of emergency will dampen the wave of indignation spawned by this outrage. There are those who bitterly claim that 'if we had just behaved and refrained from sabotage' or 'had caved in to the German demands and formed a new government then we would have avoided this blow against the Jews.' We do not agree with these embittered people: Denmark is a country at war. And we cannot give up this fight, which is about our freedom and our future—we cannot give it up *for anything*, not even to save a group of countrymen from the terrible fate that 1,600 Danish Jews now have to share."

Free Denmark takes issue here with the core rationale of the policy of cooperation and with the legitimacy of the claim that it saves many from a worse fate. Not only was the resistance on the offensive against the policy pursued by the elected politicians, it was also out to defend itself against popular accusations that it was the resistance itself that had unleashed the German reprisals against the civilian population: "You might answer that we can easily say that, as we are not Jews ourselves, and not having Jewish lineage—it's not for us to pay! But saying so ignores the fact that many Danish freedom fighters have already had to suffer harsh penalties, some even death for Denmark's sake, and that all of us who continue today to lead the fight for freedom from the occupation put our lives on the line every day, thus showing that for us there is no higher calling than the good of the fatherland. It is this that allows us to put Denmark's struggle for freedom above all else—even more than the individual's fate, however cruel and unfair it be."

This is the fundamental argument of the active resistance against the complacency and convenience of accommodation, and *Free Denmark* concludes its pamphlet with the following declaration: "The battle is raging and the battle exacts its victims.—*143 Danish Communists were deported to the concentration camp Stutthof near Danzig, side by side with the Jews.*—And no one knows who will be next."[11]

In its first edition after the roundup, another illegal newspaper, *Free Danes*, with an independent leaning, expounded on the action and what it meant. If anyone is in doubt about who were the "us" and who the "them," they could find help in this commentary and its vivid description of the offense: "For us Danes it was particularly shameful that there were 'Danish' Nazis of all kinds involved in the removal of the Jews; SS men, Schalburg people, and civilians. People who helped the German executioners. They showed them the way around in the dark capital, and they performed with even greater brutality and rawness than the Germans."

Although *Free Danes* also mentions the figure of sixteen hundred internees, which proliferated in the Swedish and illegal press in the first days after the operation, the underground press is aware that the flight is very large in scope, and that the result of the raids is ambiguous: "As far as is known in the capital, it is mainly the poorest Jews around Nørrebro, Vesterbro, and the inner city's side streets who have been taken at present. Its shoemakers, dressmakers, secondhand dealers and other small-business owners—the honest and industrious people who have never done anyone any harm. Seen in even the most favorable light, it's impossible to accept what war-justified purpose their abduction could serve for the German Reich."

For *Free Danes* it is of vital importance to emphasize "that the Danish police have not in any place or any way had anything to do with this crime. It is solely on the Germans and their cronies' bill!"

It is reported that in some places the Germans had requested police assistance in breaking down front doors, but also that this was "rejected with indignation." On the other hand, *Free Danes* notes "that in a few cases the German military police have shown an ounce of consideration for their hapless victims," and it speculates: "Some of them have been ashamed of what they had to do. They apologized to non-Jewish family members of the victims saying that they only followed orders, otherwise they would be shot."

Free Danes expresses gratitude to the Swedish government for its offer to provide all Danish Jews sanctuary in Sweden and also tells the story of the Swedish démarche in Berlin. Then the paper ventures into the delicate question of the role of the Jews in armed resistance. Here the paper needs to work its logic carefully between firm support for armed resistance, and Germany's claims that the Jews are responsible for sabotage: *"The Danish Jews are innocent. It cannot be stated strongly enough!* The claim that the Danish Jews took part in sabotage and other illegal activities . . . is a deliberate and baseless lie. . . . It must be said here that the Jewish community in this country has repeatedly been blamed for not supporting various illegal undertakings. Jews have always rejected this. They have taken the view right from the beginning of the war, since they knew that the spotlight was on them, that they would not engage in any kind of illegal acts. And the Germans know well enough that not one of the arrested saboteurs has been a Jew."

Although the reference to the Jews' blanket rejection of the illegal is of course a generalization, the passage reflects at once the position the leadership of the Jewish community had taken—and the resistance movement's tacit acceptance of this view—and the paper's closing clarion call also shows that the resistance, even at this early stage, understood very well that the crime committed against the Jews was also a turning point for their cause: "THE FREE DANES repeat: 'This is the vilest crime that has yet been committed in Danish society.'"[12]

These are strong words, coming only one month after the resignation of the legitimate government and the imposition of martial law with draconian penalties, which hit the resistance fighters hardest. This statement is amplified and explained in a short note in the underground newspaper *Danish Monthly Post*, which wrote in its October issue: "The Germans are mistaken if they believe that Danes forget or forgive the Jewish action out of sheer joy at the release of the detained soldiers. . . .

This simplistic idea has only cast their action in an even worse light. We Danes don't barter with our Constitution and least of all in the matter of citizens' equality. No distinctions are made in Danish society between one or the other race. But from now on the distinction between Danes and Germans will be sharper than ever before."[13]

Cooking the History: Round Two

While the many Jewish refugees still crowded along the coastline of Sjælland, Werner Best at Dagmarhus concentrated on mitigating the unfortunate impression the failure of the action had made in Berlin, and the harmful effects it had caused in relation to his Danish counterparts, the permanent secretaries. In the relationship to Berlin, especially the headquarters of the Reich Security Head Office, which was administratively responsible for the extermination of the Jews, this constituted a problem, and in a telegram on October 5, Best tried to erase the impression that the roundup in Denmark had not led to the desired result, while he also shifted as much of the blame as possible to everyone but himself.

Thus Best reminds Berlin that it was Mildner who "gave all the orders." When apartments were not broken into, it was because the Jews had been warned beforehand and were therefore not home, and also so as not to make a bad impression by breaking in. It was Hanneken who had not issued the follow-up orders regarding those who fled and those who helped the refugees, but this was of less importance as Mildner believed that German police would gradually be able to locate the Jews who were still in hiding. Denmark's coastline made effective surveillance physically impossible, which Best had also previously emphasized several times. And incidentally, the problem had actually been solved, as Best pointed out in his reporting to Berlin: "Since the factual purpose of the action against the Jews in Denmark was to cleanse the country of the Jews and not to conduct a manhunt, with as much success as possible, it has to be stated that the action has achieved its goal. Denmark is now *entjudet* [de-Jewed] since not a single Jew, who comes under the relevant decrees, can henceforth legally reside and act here."[14]

In relationship to Berlin, it was good for Best to be able to issue the information that on the night of October 4 an additional sixty refugees were arrested. And if he could deflect further German actions, Best would also have something to deliver in his efforts to rectify the battered relationship with Svenningsen. The cards were back in Best's hands with the repeal of martial law the following day, and he maneuvered with great skill to ensure that the recent course of events, which had threatened to tear asunder the whole laboriously built-up cooperative structure, was replaced by a situation in which Best again became the key figure in the German occupation of Denmark. Best had made a huge bet. As things were on October 4, he stood to win.

In order to ensure Best's victory, Svenningsen had to return to the line of cooperation. To obtain this result, on October 5 Best took a most unusual step: He issued to Svenningsen the written guarantee the latter had demanded the previous day: "Half Jews and those with a lower percentage of Jewish blood remain untouched by the measures taken in regard to pure Jews. This also applies to full Jews married to non-Jews."

At the secretaries' meeting on the same day, Svenningsen could provide information about Best's oral and written commitments, with the addition that Kanstein had also spoken to the same effect. For the time being these assurances were circulated only by word of mouth, but before a week had passed, one of the best-informed underground papers, the independent *Information*, published the exact wording of Best's guarantee to Svenningsen. The paper could not possibly have known how much trouble this would cost Best. But if it had, it would surely have found all the more satisfaction in the publication.[15]

Although no one dared rely on Best's promises, they were still better than nothing, and it is remarkable how much confidence leading Danes still had in the official German assurances. As mentioned before, the wealthy C. L. David, who was of half-Jewish descent, was unsure if he should flee. Through the Supreme Court lawyer H. H. Bruun, on October 1, he had already received reassuring messages from the German authorities, and even though he had taken measures to escape, he had not yet left by that Tuesday. Bruun now thought that if David could get to Sweden legitimately, it would be advisable because of "the fact that he is generally perceived as being of Jewish descent, and the fact that in the domestic Nazi press he was loathed and cast as a typical representative of big capitalism." But Bruun would "in his place be reluctant to flee illegally," and moreover felt that David "could present himself at the office as usual." Neither the man directly concerned nor his adviser could bring himself to cross the boundary into the illegal. That evening Bruun's advice for David to stay was confirmed, as he received reliable notification of Best's commitment to Svenningsen.[16]

Based on the latest move by Best, the permanent secretaries reinforced their engagement. This was a delicate move. With each passing day, more were managing to escape, and even a limited postponement of further action against those now on the run could save many lives. At the same time Svenningsen and his colleagues in the Foreign Ministry put every effort into rescuing as many detainees as possible from the clutches of the Germans before their deportation. Despite all German assurances, it was quickly apparent that for those already deported, arguments helped little. Therefore it was all the more crucial to avoid the deportation of anyone who fell outside the Germans' own criteria. Before long the efforts to limit the scope of the assault and to soften its consequences for the victims became one of the most important activities of the permanent secretaries.

These were all strong arguments for the permanent secretaries to engage—as they did. But by doing so they also moved one step further down a road no part of the Danish administration had previously been willing to travel. Hence Danish authorities were working with categories such as half Jews and *Mischlinge*, the Nazi term for "less than half Jews." When individuals asked Svenningsen and his colleagues in the Foreign Ministry whether they were in danger or safe, Svenningsen referred them to the assurances received from Best. In order not to be personally committed to the promises, Svenningsen chose to authorize copies of the October 5 letter from Best to be forwarded in confidence to those concerned. Even so, it was inevitable that the engagement in the ongoing effort to soften the blow against the Danish Jews forced Danish authorities to base their moves on at least a recognition of the racial criteria established by the German action. There is no evidence that this meant that the permanent secretaries at any point or to any extent began to internalize the Nazi concepts—but continued cooperation at the practical level did presuppose a degree of confidence and mutual respect between the permanent secretaries and their German counterparts. This was a price the Danish authorities chose to pay.

An Old Man with White Hair

In Ystad the two families struggled at their own pace to get a firm footing. Much was done by the Swedish refugee aid organization—but there were many formalities and great uncertainty about what to do next. Poul Hannover had set course for ASEA, Titan's Swedish partner and co-owner, which was headquartered in Västerås, some one hundred kilometers west of Stockholm. Hannover had friends and business associates there who committed themselves to help him. It was a matter of urgency to get there and begin a new life. His son, Allan, describes in his diary how on Tuesday morning, only two days after the exhausted family reached salvation in the port of Ystad, he was roused by the porter at four in the morning to begin the train journey to Stockholm and Västerås, which they reached late in the afternoon. There they were received by colleagues from ASEA: "We went to the City Hotel, where we were assigned rooms and then the aforementioned gentlemen invited us to a meal in the hotel restaurant. On the table was a Swedish and a Danish flag, and while we ate, the orchestra played some Danish songs. Right after dinner Mette and I went to bed."

Allan's aunt, Kis Marcus, and her family also leave Ystad the same day. But they are not on the same social level, and they do not have the equivalent business relationship. Therefore the family has to take the stipulated path through the Swedish reception system:

Palle woke up pretty early. He got himself ready and ran down to the porter, who he had a good time with. He had been with him to the confectioner's, where he gave Palle some candy and a box with a fine piece of cake for Dorte. I packed our clothes and went to the police. After lunch, which was pretty confused as half of the group went over to the bank to change money, we were supposed to travel by bus to Snogeholm Castle, which was converted into the refugee camp.

At the hotel we met a Mr. Salomonsen, whom Gunnar knew from Iceland. He had come to Ystad on the night between Monday and Tuesday in the same boat as we sailed in. The weather had been far worse than the night before, and the fisherman said that he would not have sailed over in that weather with all of us.

We then said good-bye to Ystad and traveled by bus and car to Snogeholm together with the Ledermanns, the Goldsteins, and Margolinsky. The first thing we saw when we arrived was the Dannebrog waving from a high flagpole. We were received by Danish men, most military personnel, police, and saboteurs, as well as some sailors, many of them fine people. We also entered to greet the director, who was Swedish.

We got careful instructions about how we had to behave both

at Snogeholm and in Sweden in general. We had to sleep in large rooms, Gunnar with a lot of gentlemen. I was luckier and was together just with Mrs. Goldstein and the kids alone. We were to help make beds and put things in order, clear the table, and wash the dishes.

Dorte was very unhappy that evening, both because we still knew nothing about Grandfather, and because she was disappointed with the place as she had thought it was a castle in the true meaning of it. Now she found everything so menial, as she said. She was obviously too tired and confused by all the impressions she had received over the last week. She said to me: "If tomorrow we hear that an old man with white hair has arrived ('Yes, and goatee,' interjected Palle), I would be so happy."

To make the crossing was crucial. But as soon you were over, new questions arose. It was not ideal for the Marcuses, who were used to living in their own house, now to be suddenly accommodated in a refugee camp. The refugees were welcomed. They were treated well and more than correctly by the Swedish authorities and warmly by the local population. This was highly appreciated and there was no murmur to be heard from the refugees, quite the contrary. But reading between the lines of the contemporary accounts, it appears that even with all their courage and determination it was hard on the families, now in safety, to accustom themselves to life as refugees. A few days before, they had felt safe in their homes and within their daily lives. Now they longed to get out of the refugee reception organization and to become part of their new country. Kis cautiously puts it into words: "We so wanted a little more peace and quiet than there was in the camp, but we were told that first we had to take care of a lot about passports, ration cards, etc., before we could move forward. They also needed to know that we had someone in Sweden who would take us in [before we were] to be allowed to travel, and Gunnar therefore called Henry, who immediately called the director who said that he could give us shelter."

In his diary entries from Copenhagen that Tuesday, Bergstrøm gives a vivid impression of how the dramatic events during the escape filtered back to those who were following things from a distance: "Up at the paper everything was in a commotion. They had been told that Valde-

KUNGL. UTRIKES
DEPARTEMENTET Söderblom/AA

ang. danska flyktingar

Sthlm den 5.10.43.
Överl.f. kännedom till
Env.Prytz,London/536
   "   Richert,Berlin
xp 6/10.åå.(v)Söderblom/537
   Årade Broder,   U. n.

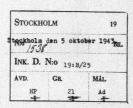

STOCKHOLM   19

Stockholm den 5 oktober 1943
        1538   BIL.

INK. D. N:o   19:B/25

AVD.   GR.   MÅL.

HP   21   Ad

            Redan i förrgår (söndag eftermiddag) gavs or-
der till marindistriktschefen i Malmö att med alla tillgängliga
honom underställda sjöstridskrafter övervaka vårt territorialvatten. Dessutom utlämnades ur flottans förråd olja till alla fis-
kare, som frivilligt ville deltaga i patrulleringen, allt i syfte
att på ett så tidigt stadium som möjligt taga hand om ankommande
danska flyktingar. Det föreligger ingen rapport om någon kränk-
ning av vårt territorialvatten från tysk sida i samband med den
nu pågående flyktingströmmen.

                                        Söderblom

Envoyén von Dardel,
    Köpenhamn.

On October 5 the Swedish Ministry of Foreign Affairs informed its envoys
in London, Berlin, and Copenhagen of orders to the Swedish coast guard to
protect its territorial waters with all means at its disposal. Also, fuel from
military stocks was distributed to some thirty local Swedish fishing boats,
so they could voluntarily participate in the search for Danish refugees and
pick them up as quickly as possible. Local authorities were later ordered to
shield landing sites and ensure the illegals freedom of passage. The telegram
notes that "no reports have been received on German violations of our territorial waters in connection with the ongoing stream of refugees." Swedish
marines' patrol boats were posted outside all Swedish ports from Höganäs
in the north to Trelleborg in the south. In order to lead the Danish refugee
transports to safe harbor, the patrol boats were given the exceptional order
to display full lighting at sea.   Kreth og Mogensen

mar Koppel [former editor in chief of *Politiken,* a member of the board of the newspaper since 1937] had been arrested that night in the coastal village of Humlebæk with wife, son, and daughter-in-law. They were on their way to Sweden. The family had probably been released, but Koppel had been driven to Horserød camp. Everyone found it very sad about the old man."[17]

CHAPTER 11

WEDNESDAY, OCTOBER 6

GILLELEJE

"Before the End of the Year"

On the third day of Heinrich Himmler's meetings in Poznan, the Third Reich's third most powerful man addressed a closed group of senior Nazi officials. Again he raised the issue of the extermination of the Jews, explaining how difficult a decision it was also to order the killings of women and children, but that it was necessary if the problem was to be solved once and for all and not leave someone who could or would avenge the killings. "The difficult decision had to be taken to ensure that this people disappear from the face of the earth." Almost like an ominous comment on the situation in Gilleleje during these very same days, Himmler added: "The Jewish question in the countries we occupy will be resolved before the end of the year. Only traces of random Jews who were able to find hiding places will be left."

The genocide of the Jews was not a plan that ran amok but a decisive effort by the Nazi leadership. It was a project that was considered vital for Germany's survival and essential for the Third Reich's victory. Therefore it was central both politically and administratively. It was a goal that Hitler and his closest aides did not think they could afford to lose sight of—a goal they pursued with ever greater zeal in step with the growing problems at the fronts, and with ever greater vigor as the more or less voluntary allies of the Third Reich became less and less enthusiastic about their role in this barbarous endeavor.

In one crucial point, however, the action in Denmark distinguishes itself clearly from all previous raids and actions against Jews initiated by the Nazis; in Denmark it took place under the eyes of an immensely indignant and protective society, while the Swedish press delivered live coverage, so to speak. This is exactly why the Nazi apparatus failed in this case.

As events unfolded in Denmark, of course no one knew the exact wording of Himmler's speeches in Poznan. But the men who represented the occupying power were schooled in the mind-set the speaker expressed, and they knew that the extermination of the Jews was to be implemented at all costs. As a very senior SS officer, Werner Best knew this better than anyone else. At the same time Berlin wanted the peaceful occupation of Denmark to continue. The two goals were difficult to reconcile, and the risk was extremely high if it failed. It was not only the Danish Jews' lives that were at stake. The development could also be fatal for Werner Best and his people. If Berlin got the impression that he opposed the deportation of Denmark's Jews, he risked reprisals and ultimately even his own life. Conversely, if cooperation with the Danes were at risk, the ground would crumble under him. For Best, there was no alternative to going all out. That is why he told Svenningsen, on the same day that the state of emergency was lifted, that he, Best, would henceforth again be fully responsible for all German interests in Denmark.

So Werner Best was hanging on to the reins as best he could. The first riddle he had to crack was how to accomplish the cleansing of Denmark while stemming the wave of indignation and protest from all parts of Danish society. Perhaps it is true, as Duckwitz later testified, that Best exclaimed that what he needed most was a bridge to Sweden.[1]

Morning in Gilleleje

Adolph Meyer and the other refugees in Gilleleje also needed a bridge. After a long, strenuous journey on Tuesday, with only a few hours' sleep in the coastal police officer's stuffy room, Wednesday began no better. Meyer noted:

> I do not remember if I slept a little, it was not nice, and I was not brave. On Wednesday, October 6, at 4 a.m the officer came in and said we had to get up to a nearby farm that was 2.4 kilometers away. We trotted off, did not really know, but felt that the worst

was still to come. The farm we came to was called Blaksheide; Mary was placed in the cowshed, I got the son-in-law's, the Chinese man Wang's, bed, I lay there, dressed, from around 5 or 6 o'clock for a few hours, we got coffee and bread, and were told to walk 5 to 10 minutes to a neighboring farm, Lysgård.

We were 12, I think, that trudged over, including Ragna and Jespersen. The farmer was not home, and the wife and the people did not dare put us up, after a 10-minute stay in the barn we went back, we did not complain as there was no phone in Lysgård. On the way Mrs. Jespersen suggested that we and she and her son should go to Majorgården in Hellebæk [on the coast farther to the east, closer to Helsingør], where she believed that a crossing could easily take place. We telephoned around 11 o'clock for a car, it did not come.

The experience was consistent. Nothing functioned normally, and the fugitives had difficulty knowing what they could—and could not—count on. At the municipal hospital in Copenhagen, Ella Fischer still had not left either. Several had offered their help, but she chose to rely on Mrs. Sorensen, who lived in the same building as some of her relatives: "During visiting hours Mrs. Sorensen came to me and told me that the previous night police patrol boats from Gilleleje had sailed with 150 people on board. She was certain that my family would be among them, and I felt very relieved."

This is undoubtedly the echo of the first successful trip from Gilleleje the previous evening, the news having reached Mrs. Sorensen in Copenhagen. The impression was that the coastal police had assisted, which gave the story the twist that it actually was their patrol boat that sailed refugees over. But the rumor was not true. And Ella's confidence that her family had been carried to Sweden from Gilleleje would prove to be wishful thinking. In fact her father, the Jewish community's librarian, Josef Fischer, was arrested the same day on the main road between Helsingør and Gilleleje. He was with his wife and two of their daughters, Edith and Harriet. The entire family was deported to Theresienstadt.

However, neither Ella Fischer nor Mrs. Sorensen knew this, so they took an optimistic view: "Mrs. Sorensen thought I could get away the same day and wanted to take me to her home immediately. Then I called Miss Ring and the head nurse and got dressed in a hurry. I did not say good-bye to anyone in the room, except for Mrs. Vitha Jensen, who came in while I was getting dressed. She had been fully aware of the situation and helped me in many small ways. Most of the others in the room did not understand a word of it all and were not aware that I was thinking of escape. I drove in a car with Mrs. Sorensen out to Hellerup. She said that I should squeeze myself completely into the corner of the car and close the curtains completely, so I felt like the worst criminal. Sometime after we got home, Mr. Sorensen came. He was to have met a gentleman concerning my departure on that same day, but that man never came, and although he had received a written message, he didn't believe that it was advisable to send me off. It was then that I decided I should stay with them that night."

Two days later, on October 8, Ella Fischer succeeded in getting to Sweden—the only member of her immediate family to do so.[2]

The general confusion that characterized the escape at the beginning of the week was also fueled by the growing doubts about German intentions. As mentioned above, the prominent lawyer H. H. Bruun was advising members of the Jewish community and also C. L. David, who was half Jewish. As late as Tuesday, Bruun passed along the reassuring messages from Best, which had been given to Svenningsen, in regard to the safety of half Jews. Bruun now sought out Svenningsen personally, and the lawyer's notes from the conversation leave the impression of a permanent secretary who no longer knew what he dared to believe. But even if Svenningsen was visibly shaken, he still did not seem to have realized fully how unscrupulously the Nazis could behave. Bruun, on the other hand, saw this continued confidence in the German authorities as a major liability—even if he himself to some extent shared it. Svenningsen gave Bruun a clear confirmation of his conversation with Best and of his assurances in regard to half Jews. But at the same time Svenningsen, according to Bruun, "severely weakened the impact of his own assurances," as the barrister apparently began to press harder for details: "Best had not made promises for the future, but only mentioned the fact that the raid had been aimed at pure Jews.

"Svenningsen said that they would try to obtain approval for the half and quarter Jews, and Jews in Aryan marriages, to be allowed to go legitimately to Sweden. Svenningsen thought those groups to be without risk, but if they felt insecure, they had to have an option. However, those in question first had to submit a petition to the Ministry of Foreign Affairs. They wanted to see how many were involved and then refer the matter to the German authorities. I argued that the half and quarter Jews with Danish names . . . would be reluctant to reveal their Jewish lineage and fear that the documentation would be misused. Svenningsen acknowledged this, but said that people had to weigh those odds themselves. Whether an arrangement could be worked out, he did not know, but it would at any rate only be possible when the petitions were submitted, and it was possible to examine what it was about."

Bruun was far from convinced, and thought that there was a real danger if half Jews were to register. He headed straight to the Swedish minister, Gustav Dardel, who explained that obtaining legal exit papers for Sweden was difficult. All in all Bruun concluded that it remained safest for David to stay. Although there could well be unpleasantness, the dangers of illegal escape still seemed to outweigh the prospect of safety. But the same day David wrote a letter to Bruun, in which he asks that he make some arrangements if David should choose to flee to Sweden. The letter reflects that David is still undecided, but also that he is moving toward the decision to leave. Thus the letter ends with a PS: "If I choose to go to Sweden and succeed, I think my law firm should be maintained until it is clear whether I can come back again, just as I have hopes in other respects that times will be such that I can resume my activities."[3]

The Schooner *Flyvbjerg*

While Adolph Meyer and his fellow refugees had to move quickly from one hiding place to another near Gilleleje, the situation around Gilleleje's harbor was coming to a head. It started with an embarrassing episode, which is reflected in a report from Sergeant Mortving of the coastal police. He had already been an involuntary participant the previous day in Gestapo-Juhl's raid against the cutter *Danebrog*, just as it was heading out of the harbor with seventeen fleeing Jews. After the gunfire and the arrest of the Jews, the cutter was seized by Gestapo-Juhl and berthed "in the immediate vicinity of the control house," where the Danish coastal police was housed. But when another boat, the *Ingeborg*, came into the harbor shortly after 9:00 a.m., the duty officer left his post to check it. Mortving reports with tongue in cheek on further events: "When [the duty officer] came back after approximately 10 minutes, the cutter [the *Danebrog*] had sailed and was well outside the harbor. The duty officer immediately reported the development to the undersigned [and states] that he did not notice people on board the cutter, and did not hear the cutter's motor start, but he declared that the cutter sailed under its own power.

"The owner of the boat, fisherman Juhl Richard Svendsen, born 4/7/1906 in Gilleleje . . . who after Ocotber 5 was wanted by the German police, disappeared from his home on the 6th so it must be assumed that it is he who has sailed with the cutter (probably to Sweden)."

The bone-dry report concludes with a laconic remark in which one can discern a faint undertone of Sergeant Mortving's quiet triumph: "Criminal Inspector Juhl, who later in the day arrived here on patrol, was notified."

In other words Gestapo-Juhl was told to his face that the cutter he had arrested the previous day and placed under the control of the Danish coastal police at the harbor had been taken by its owner, who was a wanted man, and sailed off in full daylight right in front of the Danish guards who claimed to have seen and heard nothing—just as they had not the previous days and nights. What Mortving did not feel he had to tell Gestapo-Juhl, and what is not revealed in his report, is that the *Danebrog* had run aground in the harbor and could not get out on its own. Fisherman Axel Sorensen had to tow him out with his boat, *Maagen*, and only then could *Danebrog* leave the port. The fishermen in Gilleleje had every reason to trust that the Danish police were on their—and the refugee helpers'—side, just as Gestapo-Juhl had every reason not to trust his Danish colleagues.[4]

The influx into the small town was hard to keep a secret. At the butcher's on Vesterbrogade there were about thirty Jews, and the fishmonger also had a house full of refugees. It was clear that they had to be dealt with as soon as possible—preferably shipped out. Some refugees jumped to conclusions and left Gilleleje with their mission unaccomplished. Among them was Levysohn, who had spent a restless night in the fisherman's small home: "The hours crept on. At 5 a.m. Wednesday morning the fisherman went down to the harbor to see how things were. He came back to tell me that the Gestapo were still in the harbor, so escape was out of the question. I had to get back to Copenhagen as, in his opinion, it was too risky to be in Gilleleje. The train went at 6:30 a.m. I got a cup of morning coffee, and he followed me down to the little station outside Gilleleje where I got onto the train. . . . Of those who wanted to escape, there were not many along; most stayed in Gilleleje to wait and see.

Whether they subsequently crossed over I have no idea. The mood on
the train was somewhat dull and nervous, but the ride was smooth. At
one place a lot of German soldiers got on, but those clodhoppers obviously were not dangerous."[5]

Back in Gilleleje a visiting helper, assistant professor Mogens Schmidt
from Helsingør, cycled down to the harbor early in the morning, where
he had spotted a dozen "wind drivers," many of them large schooners,
which were moored one next to the other along the piers. If their sails
could be raised it would do the trick. Schmidt made several unsuccessful
attempts to get in touch with skippers, and finally made contact with a
captain from Fyn, Gunnar Flyvbjerg. He hesitated. He was not the sole
owner of the schooner, and would also be putting his brother's share at
risk if he ventured to transport a boatload of Jews. Eventually Schmidt
persuaded skipper Flyvbjerg and the two young men who constituted
the crew. At the control post on the center pier they got the coastal police
officer's approval of the plan. The sailing was scheduled for 1 p.m., and
preparations for the quick departure were made on board the schooner.

The *Flyvbjerg* could take several hundred refugees, and the message
that there was now the possibility of a ship spread by word of mouth
among the helpers, who each had knowledge of small groups of refugees
hiding in various locations in and around the town. Thus the news also
reached Adolph Meyer's small traveling party, which had just given up
trying to obtain a car: "Now, another car came an hour later in a hurry
to get us to a crossing, we flew off, and the car would have to return to
pick up the young folks who were following us on foot."

The local helpers wrote multiple contemporary accounts of the ensuing events at the harbor that morning. Although great efforts were made
to manage the influx of Jews to the harbor, the situation with so many
refugees in the tense atmosphere could not be kept under control. Only
a few hours after Gestapo-Juhl had left the port area, men and women,
young and old, children and luggage, all flocked down to the center pier
where the *Flyvbjerg* was moored. The helpers were not organized or
coordinated, and they all wanted their own groups to reach the boat.
The rush was at once a moving and deeply disturbing sight, as Vilhelm
Lind, participating in the futile attempts to control the situation, amply
described:

> The departure was originally intended for 12:30 p.m. but already
> by 10 o'clock the coastal police gave the ready signal, and because it
> was important to use the time while the Germans were not around,

it was determined that it should sail immediately. At the same time the message was given throughout the town, and scenes there could not be depicted more dramatically in any film. The once so peaceful seaside resort, now sitting there quietly in autumn, with almost empty streets, was suddenly full of life. In a moment all the house doors sprang open and Jews flowed out of almost every house. In an instant the whole main street was full of people, women and men, from the youngest toddlers to gray-haired old men, poor and rich—all on the run from the barbarians. The entire town's population helped, and all kinds of vehicles were used. Old gouty women were carried by weatherbeaten fishing hands, while others were rolled off by wheelbarrows and other odd transport devices. I found a little girl who seemed to have become separated from her family. I got her up on my bicycle bar and rode at full speed toward the harbor. She cried when I picked her up, but gradually as I was yelling and screaming in Norwegian, pushing myself forward through the crowd on the pier, her fear turned into enthusiasm, and it was a very excited little youngster I delivered on board the ship. It was a strange sight to see all these people on the run along the main street, down toward the harbor, people who had done nothing wrong but whose only sin was to be Jews. They were now being chased away with empty, expressionless, or resigned faces, without understanding a bit of it all. As for myself, having handed over the little one, I swallowed and swallowed and found it hard to hold back the tears, whether it was the joy that everything seemed to go so well, or . . . the bitterness of having to witness that kind of thing in a Nordic country in the year 1943—or maybe because of both.

The tension was constantly at the breaking point, for the Germans could get there at just any moment. But everything went well until suddenly there was a cry: "The Germans are coming!" and in an instant the moorings were cast off and the schooner sailed toward Sweden and freedom with 210 Jews on board.[6]

It is impossible to say where the rumor originated, but the cry of the Gestapo's arrival spread like wildfire and created panic on the center pier. Although it turned out to be a false alarm, the embarkation of several hundred Jews from the port in full daylight put the local Danish authorities in an impossible situation. While they did the best they could to facilitate the operation, they had to assume the worst if it became too obvious to the Gestapo that they were actively assisting in the escape they were supposed to prevent. This dilemma also shines through a short telegraphic report Mortving submitted that same day on the situation at the port up to the *Flyvbjerg*'s departure. The sergeant is clearly aware that the report will be read not only by his own superiors but also by their German counterparts: "Today at 10:30 a.m. I became aware that there was a large influx of Jews to *Flyvbjerg* . . . which lay at the eastern quay in Gilleleje. I set off immediately to prevent the departure, but I was asked by many unknown persons not to prevent departure, as they would otherwise make use of machine guns. The persons referred to were wearing coats, so it could not be ascertained whether or not they were in possession of firearms. As I was alone at the harbor along with one reserve officer and there was no possibility of calling for reinforcements for as large an assembly as around 300–400 people, I let *Flyvbjerg* depart unimpeded with the Jews at 10:45 a.m. According to the information obtained there were about 230 Jews on board."

For Meyer and other refugees streaming into the harbor, the early departure was fatal, which Meyer already realizes: "When we came, the ship had sailed (because information had come indicating that the Gestapo had set off from Helsingør). The ship could easily have waited until we had come; the Gestapo had not yet come, and for all of us it was cause for many troubling hours and for more a cause of fatal accidents."

On board the schooner the many Jewish refugees were able to breathe a sigh of relief, although they undoubtedly feared for a while that the Gestapo would sound the alarm and take up the pursuit. The skipper and his crew had sailed with the certainty that they had been seen, and that the police would have to report on their departure. The police report confirms this, as it inevitably concludes with the information that could be fatal for those concerned: "The said schooner *Flyvbjerg*, which is 81 tons, is owned and led by Captain Gunnar Flyvbjerg, born 5/20/1915 in Uggerby, and also had a crew of two men."

The harbor report from the Swedish authorities contains a telling footnote concerning the *Flyvbjerg*'s arrival at Höganäs later the same day with, according to the exact head count by the Swedish authorities, 186 refugees on board: "When *Flyvbjerg* arrived in Höganäs port . . . a German cargo ship was also here . . . which took cargo to Bremen, where it would sail on October 7."

It was no wonder that skipper Flyvbjerg and his crew decided to stay as refugees in Höganäs until the war was over.[7]

Above right, the motorized schooner M.A. Flyvbjerg, *painted in 1943. The Flyvbjerg was built in 1911 and in 1943 had recently been renovated after a shipwreck in 1941. The schooner, which was co-owned by two brothers from Fyn, was one of the first big boats that went to Sweden from Gilleleje with Jewish refugees.*

On October 1, the coastal police had ordered all smaller private vessels to be removed from the harbors and nearby surroundings. Therefore, the transfer by small private vessels, such as rowboats or kayaks, occurred infrequently.

Most transfers, by far, departed from harbors on Sjælland and the southern islands, both because of their proximity to Sweden and because some 80 percent of the Jews lived in the Copenhagen area. For the same reason, the Copenhagen harbors were the most frequently used for the escape. But from Hundested in the north to Gedser in the south, there are seventy harbors along the coastline of the eastern Danish islands, and in 1943 a total of 1,300 fishing vessels were registered in those harbors. Mostly, smaller cutters were used for the nightly transports, and it is estimated that a total of 600 cutter passings were conducted, on average holding 10 refugees each, and probably engaging 200 to 300 smaller boats. But larger vessels like Flyvbjerg were also used, especially at the peak of the escape during the first two weeks of October when there were seven major transports totaling 1,400 refugees, three of which departed from Gilleleje.

Most of the vessels involved no longer exist, but a few do, and the schooner Flyvbjerg still sails Danish waters, now under the name of Brita Leth.

Below right, the center of the fishing hamlet Gilleleje. The church is in the middle. The harbor is located a bit beyond the top of the postcard. Behind the church to the left is Østergade with Marie Olsen and her husband's stables.

Photo of painting by Fr. Ernlund, 1943 (above)

The Church of Gilleleje (below)

Parti fra Gilleleje.

. . .

While the confusion was approaching a climax in Gilleleje, Herbert Levysohn had, via Helsingør, returned to Copenhagen's northern suburbs, where he had friends and acquaintances. But it turned out that several contacts with whom he sought refuge were at least as vulnerable as he. In his distress he sought out the parents of a classmate he had recently come to know: "I felt that the best place was with my good friend Jacob Grauer's parents on Bøgevej, it was nearby. . . . I took a taxicab there and rang the bell. Mrs. Grauer opened the door. 'Good God, child, you haven't left yet?' she exclaimed when she saw me. 'Hurry and come in and stay.' . . .

"When in distress you have to know your friends, the old proverb says, and this was again brilliant proof of the unique friends one has. Despite the fact that my friendship with Jacob is of a relatively recent date, and the family does not know me as well as so many others do, I felt that day that they had known me since I was born, and even more than that, like I was a son of their own, so well did they treat me. First I got a tremendous meal that I needed without any forethought, for it had been about a day since I last had anything, but one was not hungry in those days, there was no time. Then I got at least five buckets of hot water so I could wash myself thoroughly, which I also really needed, and in the end I came up to Jacob's bed wearing his pajamas to get some sleep."[8]

Between the Church Loft and the Stable

In Gilleleje there was no time to rest. In the panic on the pier at the *Flyvbjerg*'s sudden departure, families were separated; some were on board, other family members not. Many refugees were left on the pier desperate to find new hiding places. One such place nearby was in the private home of the local parish council chairman, A. Christian Petersen, who lived on Havnevej. Many from the harbor sought refuge there, while others who were headed for the harbor, hoping to catch the schooner, were redirected to the local church. This latter group included Dr. Meyer: "We were now brought up to the church loft, probably 50 people, after some time a whole host of other refugees arrived. . . . We got sandwiches, beer, and milk there. After a good hour when it was around

1:00 p.m., someone came to subscribe us for the crossing, the ship would cost 50,000 kroner, Mary and I each paid 5,000 kroner, and the required sum was quickly subscribed, but the great majority didn't subscribe, nor could they. Then the priest came and held a short religious speech. We went down and were led along the harbor, where there were a lot of residents who stood and watched us, as we went to the parish council chairman or a fisherman's house. He [A. Christian Petersen] was touching, very unhappy for our sake, cried, and promised that they would do everything to help us get over. Some others came to this house; we took up all the rooms and kitchen and had a total of 60."

The close packing of the many refugees at the parish council chairman's home was a big risk, and the helpers were nervous. The groups were constantly moved and interchanged, which contributed to the fugitives' stress while inevitably whipping up emotions. Meyer speaks drily, in a businesslike way, and he sticks to the facts. But it is precisely in these passages that it emerges how deeply affected the confident doctor was when someone—it is not known who and for what reason—decided to evacuate the group: "At 2 or 3 o'clock we were rapidly led along some back roads up to a loft by a stable. At the back of the loft there was some hay. We were 50 up there, including several young children, where I met several acquaintances. We were not allowed to smoke or light candles, it had windows on one side ajar; we had been warned not to talk."

The group was accommodated in the stables of the carrier Kaj Olsen, who was out working with his horses. Therefore the practical details were arranged by his wife, Marie, who was one of the active local helpers whose houses, farms, and stables were filling up with desperate refugees. The helpers estimated on Wednesday afternoon that the small fishing hamlet contained up to five hunded Jewish refugees, and after the incident at the port earlier in the day, there was no embarkation. The Danish police were at a loss. There was imminent danger that the Gestapo would come back. The situation grew increasingly tense. The church loft was filled again, and still more came from all sides. The local residents acted haphazardly without any overall plan, while the city's leading citizens began to gather to discuss how the relief effort could be organized. They worked to arrange a major new transport with another schooner whose skipper was willing to depart when police felt the time was favorable.

The Mutiny

While far too many refugees jammed together in too little space in Gilleleje, Herbert Levysohn was pleased to find the shelter and solace of his friend's parents, who immediately activated a large network to find a safe way to Sweden for their new lodger. In the meantime they let him use their son's clothes and room, assuring him that he could safely stay with them until a way out was found. But late that afternoon a message arrived for Levysohn to stay clear and expect to spend the night at the national hospital. At around 5 p.m. he was picked up by car, still assuming that he was going to the hospital, which in those days served as a transit point for many refugees. But new plans were constantly developing:

> It turned out that I should not be at the hospital, but on the contrary I had to leave immediately. At the corner of Stockholmsgade and Upsalagade we stopped again, and a couple jumped in; to my great astonishment one was Preben Holten [an acquaintance], who also had to flee because he had helped 46 over, and the Gestapo were looking for him. And so we went on down Østbanegade and Århusgade past the Danish Industry Syndicate and down to Skudehavn. Here our helper said goodbye to us 5, after we had arranged payment of 1,500 kroner. We were hidden in a shed, and a little later we were taken in 2 teams in a roundabout way that led down to a fishing boat. Yes, no matter how reluctantly, one had to leave one's fatherland, let's hope only for a short while. . . .
>
> It was about 6 p.m. and it was light. There were already some passengers; we were a total of 12, also the skipper and a helper. Some were crammed into a small hold, some into the cabin, and 3 men, among them myself, were hidden behind the nets inside the railing on the deck. Was I nervous? No, I can't say that. Now you were out, and hopefully it would work, but you could not possibly turn around, so there was no reason to be nervous. My thoughts were as before with my mother and Kate, thinking of the joy that we would have when we met; thoughts went to Father, but there they entered in a vacuum, at this moment it did not help, the thoughts only made it all worse.

Among the larger group of prominent Danes the Germans had taken as hostages on August 29, at least seven were known to be Jews. Two were later released, one because of illness, the other because he had been arrested by mistake. The five remaining hostages were prominent members of the Jewish community, including the businessman Willie Levysohn, Herbert's father. They were all deported, four to Theresienstadt and one to Poland. The last died there.

Levysohn's account generally stays on the lighter side, seeking to apply a more humorous tone to his personal hardships. This excludes mention of his father's fate—and for good reason, as it turned out. The son's tribulations were not over either. The fisherman who was to sail the refugees over was obviously not used to sailing across the Øresund—let alone on a dangerous journey, pursued by unknown enemies. Levysohn's description of the voyage gives an excellent firsthand impression of the anxiety that prevailed among some of the helpers, and of how much the actual experience of being hunted differed from the cooler assessment in hindsight of the real risk of being seized by German patrol boats:

> At the same time the skipper did everything to make us nervous. It was the first time he was out, he did not know the waters, and he was overly nervous himself. In the beginning it went fairly well, but by the Middelgrundsfort [at the exit from Copenhagen harbor] he began to cover us even more, and then he began to see Germans everywhere. At intervals he said, "I hope it works out—what kind of ship is that approaching?—right there—I guess it'll be the Germans—it's all going to hell." Later it turned out to be a Danish ship, but he wasn't quieted for long: "So now it's fucking all wrong, here comes a German patrol boat." The boat's nationality was never cleared up since it only appeared on the horizon, which Preben Holten could see, but we who lay under the fishing nets while the water splashed over us had no idea how bad it was. It was not exactly cozy. Eventually the skipper got so nervous that he took down the lantern and turned it off. The hours slipped away. The idea was first that we were meant to dock at Malmö, but he abandoned that in favor of Landskrona, he thought, anyway. I think the time was about 8:30 p.m. when we were allowed to come out of the fishing nets, for now the skipper felt there was no more danger, which in Preben Holten's opinion there had never been anyway.

It is telling that the experienced helper, Holten, who had apparently already been involved in several transports, was aware that the risk was limited once the boats were out on the water. But the fisherman seems not to have known, and the attempt to escape from real or imagined enemies leads him both off course and away from elementary seamanship:

> Now the words began to flow, spirits rose as the lights in hospitable Sweden appeared, and even the skipper livened up, went from his rudder, and sat down to chat with one of the young ladies. He should never have done that; suddenly the keel scraped the bottom, and so we sat there stuck. Using poles we got off the bottom, but with the result that we got stuck on a different place and so forth. The situation was quite hopeless, and I was seasick. The light was turned on again after much discussion, and we tried alternately to swing it and to call for help, but to no avail. We had heard that the Swedish boats were out to help the Danes in, but that night we did not see any. Finally we had been sitting so long on the bottom that the propeller broke, and at this point the engine also stopped completely. "Now only God can help us," said the skipper, and gave up. His assistant and another who was sea savvy had to deal with it. One of us who knew about engines finally got the engine going again, the propeller remained quite inactive, no sails were to be found, so we had to make do with the poles until the seas also carried us. It is probably exaggerated to say that the atmosphere was good, however our spirits weren't completely gone. There was no question of swimming ashore, we were too far out, and it was neither Malmö nor Landskrona we saw in the distance; if anything it was Barsebäck, but that wasn't sure either.

There is in fact talk of a small mutiny on board, where the crew of a single assistant and the fleeing passengers remove the confused skipper and take matters into their own hands. So close to freedom and safety, the refugees are determined to make a last effort to get the boat afloat and find safe harbor. They work with poles and the engine and have the sound judgment not to try to swim ashore in cold water on an October night in the Sound:

> After sitting aground for 2 to 2½ hours we finally got completely free, and so the trip went on. At this time we definitely did not know where we were, only the lights told us that it was not darkened Denmark, the chance did not exist that it was anything other than Sweden, but beyond that we didn't know anything. Finally

we reached something that looked like cliffs in the distance, and as we approached we saw some lights between high slopes. After much discussion with the completely exhausted skipper, we sailed between the cliffs and approached the lights, and we finally sailed into a port, but where? It was neither Malmø, Landskrona, nor Barsebäck, that much we knew. Had someone said it was Australia, we would have gladly accepted it as no one knew anything. We ran into the harbor and in the strong harbor lighting we saw some gray-green uniforms. If only they were not Germans!? "Welcome to Sweden!" cried the gray-green soldiers in Swedish. "Where are we?" we shouted back. "On Hven," was the reply, and a moment later we set foot on Sweden's small outpost to the west, the former Danish island of Hven. Never in my life have I been happier that it is Swedish than at this hour. We were all rescued and under the Kingdom of Sweden's protection. The skipper disappeared soon after we all had come ashore.[9]

The island of Hven has a population of a couple of hundred souls and is situated approximately in the middle of the Øresund, to the north of both Malmø and Landskrona and quite a distance from Copenhagen. It was Danish until the mid-seventeenth century, when the ancient Danish provinces in the southern part of the Scandinavian peninsula were captured by Sweden.

The Raid

In Gilleleje late that evening, no solution had been found for the many refugees who huddled together in almost every house, in every loft, and behind every shelter. The Gribskov line's evening train, with about fifty refugees following the same route as Meyer the day before, was halted in a daring action. A couple of helpers organized a regular holdup at the tiny station in Paarup, before Gilleleje, where they boarded the train and shouted that everyone who was going to a destination beyond Gilleleje should get off there. The train emptied of passengers, who sought refuge in the farms outside Gilleleje, leaving only three perplexed local people in the ongoing train.

Meanwhile Danish coastal police seized the harbor. A force of thirty men occupied the entire port area in accordance with a police notice issued the same morning by the central authorities in Copenhagen following events on Tuesday. The order put into immediate effect a ban on any unauthorized person moving in the harbor areas in all the ports in North Sjælland. The intention was to forestall a German intervention, which in Gilleleje in particular seemed imminent. That same evening the Danish Press Service in Stockholm reported the new order, which was also read on Danish radio. The press service stated that violations would be punished with fines and imprisonment up to two years and did not hide the fact that the new measures were intended to curb the flood of refugees from the Danish ports. The press service's addition worried the Danish helpers: "It is alleged that several fishermen have been arrested in the ports of Northern Sjælland, suspected of helping refugees across the Sound."[10]

By 7 p.m. Wednesday night, as soon as the big police force was in place at the port of Gilleleje, its boss, Sven A. Holten, was contacted by the helpers' leading men, including the parish council chairman, who had housed Meyer and numerous other refugees earlier in the day. Holten, who was head of the Danish coastal police, indicated that they would check the port and that shipping out from there would not be possible. In turn he assured the helpers that the police would not investigate what happened outside the port area, any more than they would initiate or participate in any raid to find refugees who might be hiding in or around the town.

Holten warned the refugees' helpers that the Germans would most likely return in the evening, and he urged that the town be vacated of refugees hiding there. He probably knew that earlier in the afternoon Gestapo-Juhl in Helsingør had received the telegraphic police report on the *Flyvbjerg*'s departure the same morning. Therefore it was crucial to get the refugees out of the vicinity, but the helpers did not consider it feasible at this late hour to start an evacuation of the many hundred refugees hiding all over town. If the refugees were to be shipped from the beach, it would take time to organize transport from land to the schooner in small dinghies. The helpers discussed many plans, all of which had to be abandoned. A group of young people who seem to have arrived from Copenhagen to help out were apparently preparing to try to open the harbor by force, and a group of armed resistance fighters had gathered in the garage under the barn loft, where Meyer, along with a large group of refugees, spent the night. It was the local helpers who thwarted this idea, because they feared an armed confrontation could lead to a massacre of the huddled refugees and the local people, all of whom were to a greater or lesser extent involved in the relief effort. Marie Olsen, hosting Dr. Meyer's group in the loft above the stables, described that fateful night in a letter a few weeks later: "At 8 in the evening a big German car stopped outside our garden, while 8 men were here—with friends—and loaded firearms. . . . The idea was to take over the harbor at night, so all the Jews could come over, but it had to be abandoned; two large trucks came with Copenhagen cops, and so ours dared not start something as they did not know if the police from Copenhagen were trustworthy. So it was decided that we should deal with it calmly the next day. The Gestapo was also in the city—and then it turned out to be such a horrible night."[11]

Both at the church loft, where about eighty refugees were huddled, and in the loft above Kaj Olsen's stables, the hours crawled by in the intense atmosphere of heightened anxiety. Adolph Meyer writes: "We lay on the bare floor, but at least got a little straw beneath us. They diligently brought us sandwiches, eggs, and drinking water. We were able to relieve ourselves inside the stall, as the hatch could be lifted up and we climbed down the ladder. It was a horrible night. I first was under the sloping window, later to the side with my bag under my head, on my coat, with galoshes and clothes on. Suddenly in the darkness someone stepped on my genitals and I yelled out loud."

Between the hours of 9 and 10 p.m. Gestapo-Juhl showed up in Gilleleje with a small contingent of plainclothes Gestapo men. They found the harbor lit by spotlights and completely deserted, except for the Danish police force. Gestapo-Juhl demanded that they assist in searching homes, but Holten flatly refused. Then the Gestapo went to the parish hall and from there to the church. The Danish helpers fled after trying unsuccessfully to evacuate refugees from the church, and at midnight the little church was surrounded by Gestapo-Juhl and his armed men. Wehrmacht soldiers were called in and arrived. Some still remained hopeful that the Germans would not violate the traditional sanctuary of the church, but the Gestapo thundered on the door and demanded it be opened. The key was inside. At 3 a.m. Gestapo-Juhl woke up the gravedigger Jørgensen and demanded that he hand over the spare key to the church. According to a later report, Jørgensen, who for several days had been working with refugee traffic both in and out of the church, exclaimed to Juhl (who held a flashlight to his face): "The poor Jews!" to which Juhl is said to have replied, "It is written in the Bible that this shall be their fate." Jørgensen answered: "But it is not written that it has to happen in Gilleleje!"[12]

Marie Olsen's property was on Østergade between Lille and Store Strandstræde. It consisted of three wings in a U-shape around a courtyard. The farmhouse faced toward Østergade; the livestock barn with the hayloft was farthest back. It was here that Meyer was hiding out together with other refugees who intended to sail on the *Flyvbjerg* that morning. In a letter smuggled to Dr. Meyer a few weeks later, Marie Olsen tells further how she experienced the events that night: "At 11 in the evening the Germans came . . . , and how terribly it now unfolded . . . those gruesome people took over the parish hall and the Jews who were hidden there—said to be around 40—and they went on searches of almost all the houses. The house beside ours—not ten steps from where you all were hiding here with us—was also examined, oh, thank God they went past our door. When it was 3:30 in the morning they went to the gravedigger at the church and forced him, with a gun to his chest, to hand over the key to the church—his wife fainted, and in the morning the priest had a nervous breakdown when this was told to him—it was all so awful."

Gestapo-Juhl could have saved himself the trip to the gravedigger. The wretched and frightened refugees in the church loft asked their helpers to open the door. The impact of the storming of the little church was unimaginable, even for people confronted with the realization of their worst nightmare: capture by the Gestapo and deportation to Nazi concentration camps.

Marie Olsen goes on: "Then the Germans went to the church and opened it and broke into the high loft and dragged all these poor people down and put the car lights on them. Then they were all separated into different groups and were collected in the parish hall; all this was going on while you and your friends were with us. We were so unhappy when around 5 a.m. that morning we came out and learned all this. We stayed up all that night watching and praying for you who suffered and endured such hardship, and this saved you all. Yes, such is our faith."[13]

(If there is a hint of Christian mission in Marie Olsen's last remark to Dr. Meyer, it is a point in itself, because it illustrates again that the dividing line for her did not run between the Christian and Jewish faiths but between those who persecuted innocent citizens on the one hand, and the persecuted and their helpers on the other.)

Only one escaped from the church loft: A young man had climbed up the ladder from the loft to a dormer in the bell tower, where he hid in the open air, until he was found by helpers next morning and brought down, more dead than alive. This young man, Bruno, died tragically just a few days later, when he and nine other people tried to cross over to Sweden in a rowboat that capsized not far from the Danish coast. Of the ten passengers three drowned, including Bruno, while five of the others were rescued by a dredger. The last two managed to swim ashore. In the country as a whole, at least twenty-two people of Jewish lineage are documented to have drowned in their attempt to get to safety in Sweden. The figure is probably higher, because the fates of all of them are not known, and many took the chance alone or in small groups in miserable vessels and without knowing enough about conditions on the water in those cold and windy October days.[14]

In Copenhagen on Wednesday, Bergstrøm writes a brief but telling passage in his diary, returning to the protest the bishop had ordered to be read out in all the country's churches on Sunday. With priests as sources the journalist could report: "On Sunday the priests had been prepared to be arrested for reading the bishop's protest. The letter was distributed to several who were prepared to read it out loud if something had happened. It had been said that the Germans did not like this protest, which also reached the farmers."[15]

The cynical Bergstrøm identified an important point. Protests by townspeople were one thing for the occupying power. It would be even worse if the popular response to the Jewish action provoked a situation that had an effect on production and deliveries to Germany. Here agriculture and the farmers stood front and center—not the cities. It was also an important shift in the entire strategic picture that many refugees were now hiding in the countryside, where for many farmers and fishermen the refugees were their first direct encounter with the human consequences of the Nazi exercise of power. This was another good reason to proceed cautiously—unless, like Gestapo-Juhl in Helsingør, one was consumed by an unholy fire.

In Safety

While these fatal events unfolded in Denmark, Poul Hannover was already in Västerås deeply involved in the process of arranging things for himself and his family:

> On Wednesday morning I was at ASEA, where Dector Lilliekreutz took me up to the managing director, Thorstein Ericsson. I could not have wished for a more beautiful and dignified reception—the sincere and cordial way in which he assured me of his joy at seeing me, and knowing we were here, went straight to my heart. How different things would be arranged we could always talk about—for the time being I was not to worry about anything—but sleep, rest, and eat. One could hardly ask for more.
>
> Later in the day I met Wernekinck—an equally warm reception. As I sat there the telephone rang from Göteborg. It was one of our technicians—I knew he had taken the trip and had asked our friends to make sure that he took some of my clothes along—they were already there. He was told to send them on—he sent greetings from everyone at Titan, regretting my absence—our house was still standing when he left—probably untouched Monday or Tuesday—and he thought everything had been removed as agreed. A large stone fell from our hearts.

There was ongoing concern for family members, and every phone call brought further clarification: "At lunchtime Knud called and said that Hjalmar had come over with the family. Again a wonderful message. A small soldier who had come to the hotel in Ystad, and who knew that Esther's brother, Julius, had come over, had initially said that he believed that Hjalmar had been taken—so it helped considerably to learn this."

Hannover is also aware that he must help his sister- and brother-in-law come north as soon as possible: "God knows how many times that day I sent a card off to Gunnar, who was on the way—but I had spoken with him by phone to see if he needed money because I immediately had what I needed from ASEA. For dinner we ate with the Wernekincks here at the hotel—they have a nice boy who is a few years older than Allan—he was very sweet to play with the kids, and they were delighted."

Criminal Adjutant Hans Juhl, better known as Gestapo-Juhl, was solely responsible for around half of all arrests of Jews after the German action on the evening of October 1, including the raid on a church loft in Gilleleje the night of October 6–7, in which eighty-five Jews were arrested.

The thirty-nine-year-old Juhl was born and raised in Schleswig-Holstein in the old border region between Germany and Denmark and was originally a farmer not far from Flensburg. He spoke reasonably good Danish. Shortly before the Nazi takeover in 1933, he became a member of both the Nazi Party and the SS, which earned him a ticket to the Gestapo, where he pursued a mediocre career. Juhl came to Denmark shortly after the German invasion and as the head of the Gestapo border police in Helsingør (Elsinore) had the responsibility of combating all illegal traffic across the Øresund. We do not know Juhl's precise orders for the Jewish action, but it is reasonable to assume that his activities were part of the general fight against illegal routes.

Juhl was far down the hierarchy and had only a few helpers to carry out his duties. It is characteristic that he had to summon soldiers and vehicles from the Wehrmacht to the raid in Gilleleje. There was no help available from Mildner, the Gestapo chief.

Juhl testified during the trials following the liberation of Denmark, but walked away without being punished. Frihedsmuseet

Allan also describes the evening: "Once again both nations' flags were on the table. During dinner the orchestra played the overture to the Danish national music play *Elverhøj*, and we heard the national anthem, 'King Christian' standing up, played by the Swedish orchestra."

In her diary Kis Marcus relates the family's new lives as refugees in the reception center: "In the morning I immediately went to the doctor with Palle. The rest of us had already been checked the night before. We were photographed for our passports, were questioned about various things, etc. I played with the kids for part of the day. They were slightly bored. In the evening more refugees came, and we got an old blind lady, a young girl, and a wife with 2 kids in our room. I slept really very well despite everything, but we could not wash ourselves properly and everything was in general so primitive that I was happy at the thought that we would move on the next day."

On the same day Kis Marcus and her husband completed their visa applications for the Swedish social authorities. The completed forms still exist. In the section concerning the purpose of the visit both Gunnar and Kis wrote with a new tone of defiance: "political refugee." It was a different world from the one they left less than two weeks before when they had first started to take the idea of escape seriously.[16]

CHAPTER 12

THURSDAY, OCTOBER 7

THE HOPE

Night Harvest

In the small hours of the night the search in Gilleleje was also extended to several farms in the surrounding area, including Søborggaard, where the Germans found about fifteen of the refugees who had arrived on the Wednesday evening train to Paarup. All the captives were taken to the parish hall, where they were searched and interrogated, after which they were driven to Horserød camp for new interrogations. Here half Jews and Jews married to non-Jews were separated and released. These were almost half of the 107 who were taken prisoner in Gilleleje during the night. The others were deported on October 12 to Theresienstadt, where three later died.

Although a German action was expected and in some ways almost inevitable with the massive and overt refugee pressure on Gilleleje at the beginning of the week, Gestapo-Juhl's targeted action raised the question of who had told the Germans that a large group of Jews were hidden in the church loft and on Søborggaard. Local suspicions focused on three named individuals, all of whom had been seen in questionable circumstances, or were known for their contact with Gestapo-Juhl. In particular a waitress from the Gilleleje Beach Hotel, a known hangout for Gestapo and Danish collaborators, was locally proclaimed an informer. After the liberation two of them were brought to justice. The waitress was sentenced by the district court after testimony from, among others, Gestapo-Juhl, but she was acquitted in the Supreme Court. Another who was active in Gilleleje was later convicted of informing, but not for the action in Gilleleje. And the third, who according to several of the refugees in the loft was present both at the church and in connection with interrogations in Horserød, was not charged in the case. Thus it has never been resolved whether Gestapo-Juhl had active informers in Gilleleje, or whether he raided the church at random.

That same morning, while hearings of those arrested were being held in Horserød, Supreme Court lawyer Bruun talked again with C. L. David, who was becoming more and more nervous about staying in Denmark. As he had in previous days, Bruun advised his friend to wait and see, but only until later that day when he spoke to a senior police contact, who told him that Danish Nazis had participated in Friday's raid. That was news to Bruun, who again went to David, this time with a different set of considerations. It was probably still possible to trust German officialdom, but Bruun had "become more afraid of excesses against David from the Danish Nazis' side." Clearly Bruun remains confident that the Germans themselves will stick to their line—but he is losing confidence that they can—or will—control their local cronies. According to Bruun's notes David is now "more shaken than in the morning. He said he was aware that he had to take responsibility, but that he had only asked for my help to get as much information as possible."

H. H. Bruun ends his notes on his advice to David with two short paragraphs that reflect the excruciating question of whether to attempt escape or to stay. The lawyer was aware that both decisions were risking David's life, and he felt the weight of having counseled his friend in a matter that could have fatal consequences. It is probably also the reason why the Supreme Court lawyer asked his friend to countersign a short summary Bruun drew up describing the sequence of their conversations on the matter: "I was aware when I left him that his decision was probably departure and that our conversation had helped push in this direction.

"I was very upset by the whole situation and deeply moved at having to say good-bye, so tragically, to a close friend. As always, David preserved his outward calm, sober and clear, balancing the pros and cons without expressed fear or bitterness. It was a deeply sad good-bye and my joint responsibility in his decision rests like a weight on my mind.

"Whether the decision was right or wrong, maybe the answer can never be given. Ultimately, it depends on David's strength of nerve, and that would be tested only by living through what David evaded by leaving."[1]

Hven and Horserød

Herbert Levysohn spent his first night in safety at the improvised refugee reception center on the small island of Hven. Here he shared his fate with strangers who had not necessarily felt any sense of community before they arrived at Hven. Seen though the eyes of the wealthy heir to a large family enterprise, it was a motley crowd, including some who were not nearly as privileged as Levysohn himself:

> Solid ground under the feet, friendly soldiers who continued to bid us welcome. Now everything was good, the most exciting hours in one's life were over, and now it could not last too long before I connected with mother, yes everything was, under the circumstances, as well as it could be. We were now led into a kind of passport office where we had to present a passport or other papers. I, like several others, had nothing on me that could prove that I was Herbert Levysohn, as everything was burned as I had taken the cover name of Larsen. Well, Preben Holten knew me very well and could vouch for me. From there we were led in the middle of the island to the small "town" Sankt Ibb. It was a 20-minute walk, but we young people were not tired at all, and the atmosphere was good. Here in Sankt Ibb there is a combined hotel-restaurant-theater, which is currently used as a collection point. We went first to the commander, who like everyone else received us very graciously. Papers were prepared and questions and answers exchanged back and forth. The few hotel rooms there were already taken when we arrived, only the boat's oldest passenger, a lady of about 70 who had fallen and hurt herself, got a bed, we others came to the cinema where we would be the rest of the night, the time was already almost 2 a.m. A real refugee life unfolded here. Some sat and played cards, some slept on paper mattresses on the floor, others tried to sleep on the chair seats but since these, like any other cinema seats, swung up as soon as you lifted them a little, this sleep was quite hopeless. We could buy some sandwiches and beer with Danish money, and it felt very good to get something to eat again. Many had no money, but

fortunately Holten and I had so much that we could help the others, so everyone was well fed. The fact that most who came to the island that night were less fortunate exemplars of expelled Poles and Germans was of course sad for the race as a whole, but one could avoid those. Still more and more came to the island, and the cinema became more and more full, the air worse and worse. Luckily we could help them a little, and gradually it all calmed down.

Levysohn's description of his fellow refugees reflects the deep divide between the well-integrated families who had been in Denmark for many generations, and the so-called Russian Jews who had come much later, not to speak of the most recent arrivals from Poland and Nazi Germany, many of whom still lived at the bottom of society without social or cultural integration. Not without reason were half the Danish Jews at this time estimated to belong to the working class. Typically, those who had arrived more recently were more religious and attached to the culture they came from. Many spoke Yiddish at home and had a less than perfect command of Danish. Most of this group had either weak or no social contacts with non-Jewish Danes (or for that matter with the well-assimilated Danish Jews), and most of them were among those who escaped rather late, compared with families like the well-connected Hannovers or the Marcuses. Often their first contact with the helpers came from the family doctor, who forged links with hospitals or further to the help groups that sprang up in the week after the action. For the affluent young Levysohn, these people were a class he had not previously encountered:

> I want to always remember two old, indeed ancient, farmwomen who had been driven from Lithuania at the time, in their worn clothes where they sat huddled together, they could not speak Danish, only a little German, they did not have a dime, and they shook with terror and horror. At one place sat a woman who was expecting a child not later than 10 October. She could not sit down on the hard benches, so I let her sit on my coat. For the rest of the night I was in constant fear that she would give birth on my only decent piece of clothing. Neither Holten nor I could sleep as it was pretty unbearable in the hall, but the weather showed its amiable side, so sometimes we went for a walk in the area where it was allowed.
>
> Holten was not really in a good mood. He had to leave his wife and children home and flee without having said good-bye to any-

one. He had helped 46 over, and now had to leave himself because the Gestapo was after him. He belongs to the kind we all have to remember with gratitude. Well, the night passed at last, and the day appeared.[2]

The Conspiracy

In the days leading to that fatal raid Wednesday night, the rescue work in Gilleleje was characterized by randomness. The small fishing hamlet of less than 600 households and 1,700 residents was a closely knit community where everyone knew everyone else. The primary business of Gilleleje was fishing, but it was also a popular beach resort, and in the hinterland, city people had summerhouses that stood empty at this time of year. In the remote settlement no one had predicted the stream of Jewish refugees now seeking shelter there, and the inhabitants had to improvise as the numbers kept growing. At one point that morning the number of refugees in Gilleleje is estimated to have amounted to one-third of the town's population. Everyone was involved, and the vast majority of the citizens participated in the efforts to cope with the emergency. But with the Gestapo raid on the church in the evening the whole enterprise had gone awry. The night of horror with its arrests and deportations had brutally exposed the fugitives and their protectors alike.

Now, in the early hours of the morning, some ten citizens of Gilleleje got together at mechanic Peter Petersen's place. Here they set up what amounted to a conspiracy, later to be known as "the Jewish Committee." At first the men suggested that the local police officer act as their chairman, but he declined, citing the fact that it was too dangerous for him to undertake this duty. He would, however, remain a member and do whatever he could to sustain the efforts to avoid further arrests. The group then turned to the local elementary school consultant, L. C. Jensen, who accepted the "nomination" and immediately emerged as the committee's dynamic leader. Other members were the local parish council chairman who had housed Meyer and his group the preceding day, the cabinetmaker, the teacher, the two grocers of the village, as well as a local manufacturer and the town physician. With the exception of one person, grocer Lassen of the nearby settlement of Smidstrup, none of the ten men had any prior experience with illegal work or active resistance. Half of them had been engaged in the relief effort for less than a day, prior to their gathering at Petersen's house this early Thursday morning. The ten men had little in common. But they shared a strong determination spurred by the tragic events of the past night: Something had to be done to organize help for the many remaining refugees. And if nobody else would undertake this task, they would.

We have several later accounts of the discussions within this self-appointed action group, and the driving motivation of the men is worth noting. It was Gilleleje's reputation that was at stake. The honor of the local community—and thus that of its inhabitants. "History will be written these days in this town," the school consultant is quoted as having said that morning. And the group agreed, sharing a sense that somehow they had been called upon to stand up and do their part in a big struggle that so far had seemed very remote from their village. Also there was no disagreement about the task at hand: The Jews who had not been found by the Gestapo the night before had to be saved at any price. The first step was to get them out of town. Food also had to be provided for everybody. Longer term, the committee had to set up a system for transfer to Sweden. Contacts had to be established with the fishermen on the boats, money was to be collected among the refugees, transfer prices negotiated, and arrangements made for those who had no means to pay for their escape. All this had to be accomplished within hours and under great uncertainty as to the further plans and intentions of the Gestapo. Strangely, the members of the conspiracy do not seem to have been concerned with their own fate, should their activity be disclosed. They seem to have trusted that no member of the community would betray the activities of the helpers—or the hundreds of refugees still hiding in almost every house and stable.[3]

The initiative for the Jewish Committee in Gilleleje follows the same pattern as the simultaneous formation of similar groups in Stubbekøbing and elsewhere, where local communities organized themselves spontaneously to help stranded refugees. In Stubbekøbing the men who a few days earlier, hesitant and bewildered, had tried to help the first refugees at Frey's Hotel, formed a strong and effective organization based on "Næsgaarden," the major estate in the area, from where several hundred refugees during the following weeks were shipped off via the Grønsund ferry berth. The previously mentioned Lyngby Group, formed far from any harbor, developed into a management entity, playing a central role in coordinating the work in the area north of Copenhagen during the following weeks.[4]

Like other similar groups, the citizens' group in Gilleleje had few features in common with traditional freedom fighters. They were not young and not particularly politically engaged—and did not at all belong to the political extremes. They had no particular issue with the policy of cooperation and were not otherwise in opposition to the existing society; nor for that matter did they take a particularly strong line against the occupation. Rather, they were local patriots, each in his own way a prominent member of the small community on the north coast that suddenly saw its fateful hour arrive. None of the ten had previously stepped onto history's stage, and none of them appeared there again. They were driven by a belief that the situation required immediate action, and that no one was better positioned than themselves to take responsibility for what was going to happen. They regarded with considerable skepticism the young refugee helpers who began to stream in from Copenhagen—young men, as the locals feared, who would not show the well-considered restraint that in their view was now required. None of the more-resistance-oriented young people who had stood ready with their weapons in Marie Olsen's stables joined the committee, which worked almost entirely without weapons, and sought to avoid any confrontation with the occupation forces.

For the ten men now forming the Jewish Committee as well as for all the inhabitants of Gilleleje, the events of the preceding day and night had completely changed their perception of the occupation. It had dawned on them that Denmark was not only occupied by neighboring Germany but ruled by a criminal regime that arbitrarily perpetrated violence against the defenseless. It was the first time since the occupation of April 9, 1940, that ordinary citizens were directly confronted with Nazism's ugly face. Yes, one had heard and seen things, and the occupation forces were not popular even if they behaved correctly. But by and large one's life could continue relatively undisturbed, and the Danish social order prevailed. Now, from one day to the next, the Nazis had shown what it meant when the rule of law and humanism were cast aside and a group of criminals persecuted and terrorized Danish citizens who had done nothing to provoke the occupying power's anger. To the villagers of Gilleleje this was a dramatic turning point, and it seemed to most of them that standing by passively would somehow damage their reputation and indeed that of their village. Suddenly it became imperative to take action and to demonstrate that Gilleleje did not take part in the crime but—very much to the contrary—took action to stop it. Seen this way, there was no going back: The fate of the refugees now crowding the town had been inseparably linked to the town itself.

Also, something else was at stake. The refugees hiding in Gilleleje were anything but an abstraction, a story, or an anonymous group. These were real, ordinary men, women, and children, families with the old and the fragile, the magnanimous and the petty, everyday people who were hurting—frightened and desperate to get away to safety. They had descended upon Gilleleje in great numbers, forcing every citizen of the village to look into the eyes of misery and to realize that these wretched refugees might as well be themselves. It was impossible to look the other way and pretend not to see. One could not be deaf to the knocks on the doors, the pleas for help.

If everything Gilleleje citizens believed in and what the minister— literally—preached in the church were to have the slightest credibility, this was the moment when the town had to step up. If they did not do so, it was not only their reputation that was at stake: It was the very social order the ten citizens represented, in their different ways. It was the democracy they swore to, and the respect for the individual on which it was based.

The pressure was overwhelming, the task unmanageable, and the consequences unpredictable. But the arrests in the church showed that it now had to be met with full force. The small church had been on the main street for four hundred years, and it featured in the high points in its parishioners' lives: baptisms, confirmations, weddings, and funerals. There is a long tradition of the church's sanctity, which lived strongly in the collective sense of justice. Only the most ruthless assailant does not respect church peace—and even secular society usually steps back from violating it. Conflicts and disputes are settled elsewhere. With the arrests in the church Gestapo-Juhl had demonstrated the ruthlessness that permeated the Nazi mind-set. It was a slap in the face of the local community, and it was perceived as a demonstration of contempt for the values they treasured most.

The reaction was not a sort of popular uprising; there were no riots, no resolutions, no demonstrations. It was the profound realization that Denmark wasn't occupied by Germany, but by a violent regime of criminals that could in no way be trusted. The action was a watershed because it made perfectly clear that there was no possible compromise between what Nazism stood for and the societal norms of ordinary Danish citizens. Before the action against the Jews, the Danish public in general resented the occupation forces. After those days, they opposed them. The difference may seem subtle. But the leaders of the occupation authorities knew and feared that difference.

The reaction was not long in coming. It took root in mechanic Peter Petersen's living room where the ten men swore to one another that such a thing would not happen again. Not in their community. Fate had momentarily handed history's pen to Gilleleje. And the town had no doubts about what story it would write.

"A Gripping and Unsettling Thought"

That very morning the first results of the committee's efforts began to affect the refugees hiding throughout the village. Fresh milk was brought from the dairy, eggs and sandwich packs for the hidden, and plans were made for their immediate evacuation to safer shelter.

The situation was bleak, noted Adolph Meyer in his diary, and spirits low at the hayloft Thursday morning after a long uneasy night. Though in an impossible situation, the doctor tries a bit of black humor about the night's inconvenient bed:

> Naturally, the night was uneasy with interrupted sleep, but we did sleep some, and on the morning of October 7 I found a beer bottle and an iron file underneath me. Hands and especially nails were dirty. The parish council's chairman came and told us that we would be split up for a few days among the town's residents, but shortly after, we heard that house searches were taking place both yesterday and today all over Gilleleje (I learned that many unhappy refugees were found in the apartment in the parish house and in the church attic).
>
> Later we heard that the Gestapo had been in the horse barn, where six horses stood stamping away, fortunately the ladder behind the troughs was not discovered by the criminals. Later in the afternoon the chairman came again, and we noticed that he was very nervous. "You will all be helped, let's just not get nervous," he said. We heard that there had been an informer, who helped the Gestapo get wind of the refugees in the church.

For the coastal police the night's actions were difficult to handle, caught as they were between their efforts to protect the refugees and the risk of being caught in the act by the Gestapo. The two sides had no mutual trust, and the local police had to act with utmost care, knowing that the reports to Copenhagen were also scrutinized by German police there. That morning police chief Mortving sent in a report on the German raids with a note that the Germans now seemed to be loosening their grip on the harbor and leaving more to the Danish police: "Chief Criminal Assistant Juhl from Elsinore arrived today at 10:30 a.m. at the police office at the harbor, declaring that the German Wehrmacht would discontinue the occupation of the harbor at 11:00 a.m. He requested, however, that the harbor henceforth be controlled by Danish police. Five posts were established, spread throughout the entire harbor.

"Chief Criminal Assistant Juhl also announced that last night, here in Gilleleje and environs, 107 people were arrested, including women and children as well as two Swedish citizens. The Swedish nationals are soon to be released. In addition, today in nearby Paarup at 5:00 a.m., a seriously injured person was arrested. The prohibition on sailing from the port is lifted."[5]

Part of the Jewish Committee's activity was to set up a system for payment for the crossing. Those who had declared themselves able and willing to pay were now asked to actually make the payments, and Dr. Meyer was among those who paid willingly. He seemed satisfied to be in a position where he and his sister-in-law jointly provided for one-fifth of the entire amount collected within their group. He notes that others—among them probably the agricultural students—could pay nothing and didn't have to: "We now paid for the crossing. We might have achieved it cheaper, but paid for many who had no money, so I don't regret it."

The affluent doctor was also aware that many who helped in the little fishing community were far worse off socially and economically than most of the refugees. The entire situation entailed a distinct social paradox: A good part of the refugees in Gilleleje were well-off city dwellers, while their local helpers were mostly from the opposite end of the social spectrum. Dr. Meyer was among those who recognized this dilemma and together with the more prosperous of the other refugees he acted to address the issue: "In the attic we pitched in for the poor in Gilleleje, because the residents of Gilleleje had been magnificent to us. We collected 1,270 kroner, which we gave to the local priest to hand out. (Mary gave 200, I gave 500 kr.)"

This gesture bears witness not only to the mental strength of the refugees who, in the midst of their own compromised position, collected for those who were most disadvantaged in the community. It also testifies to the very state of mind that made the escape possible. (And in a curious way it links up with Poul Hannover's reluctance to break into the abandoned summer colony in the forest, and his preoccupation with taking responsibility and making good the damage done.) The Jewish refugees in the attic over the stable in Gilleleje were certainly exhausted and terrified, but they insisted on maintaining their dignity. They refused to be reduced to fugitives on the run, desperate, hungry, and without a will of their own, and this refusal constituted a resistance to the very purpose of the Nazi assault against them. It was a dramatic revolt against the deliberate strategy to characterize Jews as outcasts, antisocial creatures who were unworthy of the surrounding community's respect. It was precisely this view of the Jews as barely human that elsewhere had robbed them of their fellow citizens' natural sympathy and protection. In Denmark, however, this attempt was met not only with massive rejections by their fellow Danes, but also with an active defiance by the Jews themselves.

No one could know what was in store for the refugees in the attic, but the 1,270 kroner they entrusted to the priest, in a church that was not theirs, for distribution to the poor without regard to whether an individual had helped with the escape or not, constituted the refugees' confirmation of the underlying social contract and of mutual solidarity within society—the solidarity on which their lives now so acutely depended. Their gesture was one of trust, not only the trust uniting the refugees and their helpers, but trust in society. However, by no means should the moment be construed as one in which all social divisions and internal strife, conflicting interests or contradictions, were abandoned. Among both the fugitives and those who aided them, all opinions and differences were represented as well as individual antipathies and sympathies. The situation changed none of that, and neither the refugees nor their local helpers were homogeneous groups. But overriding all these differences and tensions, the imperative was now to act in unity against the very purpose of the German roundup.

Meanwhile, in the attic, there wasn't much the confined could do. Time seemed to stand still as the hours crawled by. It was quiet, so quiet that Dr. Meyer and his sister-in-law had ample time to think through the eventuality of a new Gestapo raid revealing their hiding place and leading to their arrest. The two seniors faced their situation without sentimentality, and they were in no doubt what line to take in such circumstances. The doctor reflected upon their decision in his journal: "The day passed slowly, I was tired and everyone was nervous but admirably calm. I had a 10cm^3 syringe ready and 2x10 cm^3 morphine for injection, and I promised Mary that if the Gestapo came, I would inject her first and then myself. (I had the syringe from home, the morphine I got the morning of October 5 from Dr. Hart, who had promised to give it to me the day before.) It was a gripping and unsettling thought, but I wouldn't have hesitated."

There is no reason to doubt Dr. Meyer's determination. As a doctor he was accustomed to facing death, and several days earlier he had made the necessary preparations. Now the agreement with his sister-in-law was set, and the doctor knew what had to be done if it came to that. It would have comforted him to know that by this time his children and grandchildren were all safely in Sweden, and it would have saddened him to know how much they now worried about his fate. Mary and he had endured their hardships with calm and with their dignity intact. Now they had decided to take their own last, definitive step in accordance with their own willpower.

The Hope

Meyer continues his report: "I could not bear the thought of another day in the barn, but luckily we got a message at 6 p.m. to go downstairs for transfer. The stay down there was almost the worst thing. We were told that we would be picked up in cars, but it dragged on and dragged on, and we felt our friends' nervousness, which infected all of us."

Marie Olsen, the mistress of the house, helped organize the delicate relocations of the many refugees from the hayloft. There was reason for anxiety. A German car was posted at the corner of Østergade and Hovedgade, just twenty-five meters from the Olsens' property, and after the night's experiences everyone feared that the Gestapo would show up any minute. A journalist had turned to Marie Olsen to hear how things were, which only caused more anxiety. County Officer K. V. Kirkeskou, who was on the Jewish Committee, stood near the German car in civilian clothes and thereby kept in touch with other guards, while the mechanic

Petersen and his sons led Meyer and his companions past the church, through the courtyard of the local cooperative shop, past the railroad to the gas company.[6] Meyer writes: "Finally at 7 p.m. a car came, and now in the space of half an hour more cars, we were up to 7 in each car, we drove deep into the country, a significant detour to an orchard in Smidstrup, where we were 60 accommodated in 4 houses, summer cottages, which belonged to one Miss Fanny Cohn (ownership was now transferred to another name). It was called 'Hope 1' (the others Hope 2, 3, and 4), which was the password, followed by three knocks. The grocer of Smidstrup, whom we called the Scarlet Pimpernel, arranged for our meals; there was hot and cold water, toilets, electric cooking in the big house, where we were 12 people. . . . We were not allowed to go out of the house and not recommended to open windows, it was poorly blacked out, there was a fireplace, which gave good heat. I got a private bedroom, the Gelvans one together, and all the others were in the large living room on couches and mattresses and a cot. It was a relief to go to bed, and I slept until 5 in the morning."

It's quite clear that the helpers have better control of the organization, locally represented by the thirty-seven-year-old grocer Gilbert Lassen, the only member of the Jewish Committee who had a little experience with resistance work, and who was responsible for shipping from the coastal settlement of Smidstrup, some five kilometers west of Gilleleje. It was Lassen who for Adolph Meyer was the Scarlet Pimpernel, as August Jensen had been for his twin daughters' families departing from Falster the preceding week. Shortly after the liberation Lassen himself described his role in Smidstrup:

When the summer of '43 was over, I got a chance to get into the unified security company that patrols along the beach here from Gilleleje to Vejbystrand, overseeing approximately 60 cottages. I had to ride by bicycle 3–4 times a week between 10 at night and the next morning.

It was a dirty job, but it gave me more liberty—I could move everywhere, regardless of the curfew which was in effect at that time—I could bear arms and I could take underground papers along at night, and those I placed along small streets in all garden gates, particularly in the Gilleleje region.

Sabotage also developed more and more as a form of struggle, and we were several who had more or less good plans for such, including about the Gilleleje Beach Hotel and Cinema, owned by a German-friendly man, and which was used a lot by the Germans and the German Gestapo men, among whom were several Danes who now often came for raids along the coast and later settled in Gilleleje and Raageleje.

Around August–September rumors began to leak that the Danish Jews would be interned, where previously only Communists and a small number of other saboteurs were incarcerated in Horserød camp.

In mid-September a young Copenhagener suddenly showed up at his mother's summer cottage and was living there alone. I understood that something was wrong and had a confidential conversation with him. He said he had to flee to Sweden.... I knew that wealthy Jews had begun family by family to pack up and either by motor or fishing boat travel to Sweden from the coast here or elsewhere. Therefore we drove to Gilleleje and felt our way with the most sympathetic fishermen, and one evening luck was with us, and we got him over with a rich Jewish group that had paid many thousands to the fisherman for the trip—he only got a few packs of good tobacco from us to give—that was what we had.

In those days when it began, the wealthy Jewish families came out to the summer cottages, and a few days later they were gone. One evening, just as I was sitting at home alone with my young maid, a frightened young married couple came, two young Jews I had dealt with several years ago in Copenhagen. Could I help them? I biked to Gilleleje, leaving them behind to eat the roast pork, which it turned out was the first time they tasted it. In Gilleleje I felt my way with various acquaintances, and during the evening I found an old outbuilding in the backyard, where there were already some Jews gathered, ready for departure. My two Jews had 1,000 kroner for the trip, and managed to agree to what was necessary, so they came up with that amount, I hurried home and retrieved them with a car, and they were happy in all their nervousness.

After such lending a hand from time to time it all went fast, the Jews now came in large numbers, and I had to let business take care of itself in the first days of October, as I was now known to help, and a rumor travels quickly, I knew many Jews, and they gave their friends and family a hint that there were many of my "white" customers with the belief that I, living on the coast, could help. The other permanent residents here on the coast also knew a little about my national attitude and turned to me when they had Jews living with them.

The grocer Gilbert Lassen is an example of a man for whom assistance to the Jewish refugees gives the final push into organized, illegal work—and on to active, armed resistance. His report also reflects the ethos he shared with most other helpers, that in addition to general human considerations, they also saw helping from a national perspective. As a result of this, Lassen even calls it his "national attitude." This was the key to the helpers' success. Having a national attitude implied helping other nationals—including as a matter of course Jewish citizens. That was the whole point.

Lassen writes further about the events on Wednesday and Thursday and about Meyer's move to Smidstrup: "On the evening of October 4 we got a large boat away, and in the morning the *Frydendal* went with approximately 200 on board. For this boat 40,000 kroner were gathered in butcher Olsen's outbuilding. One of the organizers was Assistant Professor Schmidt from Helsingør. The boat was departing prematurely as Jews rushed like mad along the harbor quays with children, suitcases, and bundles, and all of a sudden there were false warnings that the Gestapo were coming. The boat left amid great confusion and did not even get money, which was buried in the butcher's garden, and later a man came out to me with the package. In the meantime we started a committee in Gilleleje, to whose treasurer, Dr. Vilstrup, I handed the money.

"There now began to spread some panic caused by the steady influx of Jews by train and by car, and one or more families lived with the majority of the city's residents, or they huddled in attics, in sheds, in stalls, in the shipyard, and all other places."

Lassen describes the confusion among Gilleleje's residents on Wednesday, as there seems to be no end to the arrivals. He participates in the previously described improvised stopping in Paarup of the evening train to Gilleleje, takes part in the placing on farms of refugees from the train, but when he returns to Gilleleje late in the evening, he finds the situation much changed: "Our meeting place at teacher Frederiksen's was closed and dark, and after a long time knocking the only reply was that the Gestapo was in town. All the town's good citizens had completely lost their heads and were hiding under the covers, and there was no one to find. I hurried to the harbor, and luckily I had my raincoat and watchman's hat on, so I could continue unimpeded."

Lassen passes the church as the Germans are chasing the refugees out, and he continues his reconnaissance: "The port was occupied by Danish police and it was illuminated by floodlights. At some corners in town there were German soldiers and several Danish and German cars stood by. . . . I went around during the night and found that there were still many refugees in the lofts, the brewery, the hayloft above a horse stable, and with many individuals, who dared not move in the night."

Lassen recounts the formation of the Jewish Committee the next morning, the first contacts with skippers concerning embarkation from the coast, and organizing transport of the Jews to the holiday cottages at Smidstrup to which he had access as a watchman:

> In the meantime I found 3 or 4 men from Smidstrup who would undertake the ferry from the coast to the boats and have two boats ready. Similarly, we called the skipper of the *Jan*, a ship from Aarhus, which was in Gilleleje, up to the meeting. We offered him 50,000 for the human cargo and 5,000 to the men who ferried them out to the ship. We took the car out to look at the departure point in Smidstrup and to agree on a signal.
>
> I stayed behind to bring the Jews out there, now that there were still Germans in the town and on the roads. We used all means, mostly large trucks with straw and hay, vehicles with herring boxes along the sides, medical cars, and the like, and all the transports went around the town a little and towards the country first, then along secondary roads to Smidstrup. Eight of the largest houses were ready for use, we did not ask the owners, but simply borrowed everything we needed. Food and drink we brought from the grocery store and from the guesthouse Havregården. Many Jews found themselves at peace with their fate, others were totally nervous and hysterical. We let the blinds and blackout curtains cover the windows, and in many cases we even locked them inside. . . . My sons and a few others that I could trust were used as sentinels in the corners that led into the orchard and farther on to the houses. We also had an agreement with officer Kirkeskou concerning a telephone warning if something bad was on its way from Gilleleje.

The concentration of Jews inside Gilleleje itself was now limited after the raid the day before, and the Jewish Committee took a firm grip of the organization. The refugees who continued to flow into Gilleleje were transferred to holding residences, typically in the summer cottages at Smidstrup, where they awaited their embarkation for Sweden. Accommodation in the deserted cottage areas was safer and more convenient, guards were placed to warn if something unexpected should occur, and the vital connection between collection and shipment became far more effective than before.

The organization is also clear to the fugitives, and Meyer's report reflects the immense relief that someone—personified by Gilbert Lassen—now seems to have a grip on things.

Like Salt in a Hollow Tooth

Rumors about the dramatic events in Gilleleje reached Copenhagen the day after the big raid. As usual, Bergstrøm was quick to gather the information at *Politiken,* and that evening he noted in his diary: "Up at the paper, I heard that last night there had been a great panic in Gilleleje. Many hundreds of Jews had been up there. Whole travel groups were arranged. A ship had gotten away. But then the Germans came in large cars. The Jews had sought refuge in the church and parish hall. There were 103 persons, men, women, and children, taken. It was miserable. It was said that saboteurs had arranged several things up there, but had to yield to superior force. In the parish hall all the Jewish property was deposited, and lists were written there, which were held by the Germans. All of Gilleleje, with the priest in charge, was implicated in the emigration. The fishermen had earned floods of money. Now the coast to the north and down to the other side of Copenhagen has been closed by the Germans. But is it not partly the Swedes' fault because they have talked so much about the crossings on the radio? Of course, it has been to reassure those remaining in Copenhagen, but it has also alerted the south [the Germans]."

Although Bergstrøm could see only part of the game, he, like other contemporary observers, perceived that the German representatives in Denmark had an understanding of the Danish attitude that differed substantially from the one prevailing in Berlin: "As for the Germans here in the north, you have a feeling that they really had the greatest desire to make themselves human. Here you understood better that it was a sore thing to touch the Jewish question. It directly touched the Danish legal consciousness. It is like salt in a hollow tooth. But they have not understood this in the south. One cannot escape this thought, when one considers that so many have come over."[7]

Bergstrøm's diary from those days also bears the mark of intense rumors that journalists would be the next to be interned by the Germans. Arrest lists were to have been drawn up, and in the unrest all sorts of rumors flourished about an imminent action. Bergstrøm kept his cool distance, but was obviously pondering whether it really could be true. He also felt more and more personally exposed because of his meticulous documentation of life under the occupation, including a large collection of clippings and documents from underground newspapers. Still, he can't help being sarcastic in his depiction of the release from prison of the onetime editor of *Politiken*, Valdemar Koppel, who had been arrested with his family during an escape attempt a few days earlier:

> Priemé [a colleague at *Politiken*] had just talked on the phone about Koppel, when he came out of the editorial office and saw—Koppel, as if he had seen a ghost. He nearly had an accident. It was Koppel. Freed. He immediately began to make calls. Where was his family? Well, it was said that they got over. The employees gathered at a distance and looked at Koppel as if he had been a ghost. When he had finished telephoning, we gathered around him, and he willingly gave his story. He had no collar on, but a vest that ended with a zippered neck. It had been pretty hard on him. He was standing with his hands clasped in front of his chest. He wrung his hands. With eyes on the floor he recounted his story. But he had not lost his sense of humor. . . . He grunted a laugh when he said that Jews had taken refuge in the Christian church in Gilleleje. He talked whimsically about his arrest. The skipper in Humlebæk had asked Koppel and his group to go a little further up the coast before they were taken on board. A German car came. He had not had time to hide. When he was interrogated, he could not figure out any lie, but said straight out that he had intended to flee. So he had been driven to Helsingør. From there to the Vestre Prison. The Jews had to stand facing the wall. But he had finally been driven to the Horserød camp, where things went very well. He was released because he was married to an Aryan woman.[8]

Shortly after the liberation, the editor Koppel wrote a description of his experiences, among them a brief exchange of words with one of the Gestapo men who had captured him. When he protested at the arrest, pointing out that he was married to an Aryan, one of the German guards was strongly provoked: "I decided to make another attempt and turned around and explained that there was a misunderstanding. But at that moment a furious Gestapo man came toward me, a little fat guy, and turned me around, and when I still protested, he gave me a kick in the back and at almost the same moment a resounding smack that sang and crashed in my head: I could even feel it the next day. But I had become mighty angry. 'You hit a 76-year-old man,' I shouted. 'I have not ever experienced that.' 'You're going to experience what is much worse,' roared the beast, grabbed me from behind with a strong grip on my neck, and firmly banged my head against the wall again and again; happily my hat took the brunt of it, otherwise I probably would have had a concussion. The other Jews stood during this scene rigid as pillars of salt, without moving."

Koppel's description of his experiences in the Vestre Prison and later in Horserød is also remarkable in that the German police, who have found him in possession of a large amount of cash, tease him with it but neither confiscate nor steal it. In Horserød, Koppel witnesses the arrival of the exhausted prisoners from Gilleleje: "From the much-talked-about church loft in Gilleleje a whole long troupe came, some 60 heavily damaged people, betrayed in their hiding place, and having endured an entire siege by the Gestapo. The German officers laughed and enjoyed themselves greatly when they came by, exhausted, with their bags and bundles, shielding as best they could and comforting the children. Most of them, as well as the others, had endured terrible hunger and especially the cold in their hiding places, and their nerves were at the breaking point."

Koppel was released from Horserød, and after his stopover at the newspaper, he sailed to Sweden a few days later.[9]

On October 7 the prison inspector in Horserød announced, at the request of the Foreign Ministry, that "the number of Jews collected at the Horserød camp by midday today had risen to 177. In addition, 12 fishermen." The following day it had climbed even further to 215, although releases of half Jews and those married to non-Jews pulled the number in the opposite direction. Svenningsen argued that they should be handed over to Danish justice, "as attempting an illegal exit from the country was an act that fell under Danish jurisdiction." He was obviously aware that this could not save those whom the Germans considered pure Jews. But for everyone else, including the twelve fishermen and other helpers, coming under Danish laws would mean a world of difference.[10]

While the flood of refugees went on day after day, the permanent secretaries intensified their efforts to accomplish the return of those deportees who did not fulfill the Germans' own criteria, or for whom there could be any doubt. On Thursday, Svenningsen called Mohr, the Danish minister in Berlin, and asked him to pursue these cases "with all his energy." The same day Mohr again presented the Danish arguments at the Foreign Office for the immediate repatriation of those "wrongly" deported. He also built further on the Swedish proposal to repatriate children and the old, who could in no way be suspected of involvement in acts of sabotage. The Danish authorities were also prepared, Mohr declared, to detain those concerned in Denmark. Mohr's German counterpart promised tepidly to "convey the message," which indeed happened the same day in a short note to Adolf Eichmann, who on October 12 had his second-in-command, Rolf Günther, reply that the matter was under investigation and that there were no mistakes. Although during an earlier interview at the Foreign Ministry in Copenhagen, Mildner had made himself more sympathetic, the permanent secretaries ran up against a German wall of sluggish hostility, often personified by the same Rolf Günther, who already during his short stay in Copenhagen had come to believe that the Danish Jews had gotten off too lightly. The Danes got nowhere with their arguments. The Nazis' motives did not follow a rational logic, and they did not let themselves be caught in the inconsistency of their own arguments.[11]

Moral Support

While dramatic events played out in Gilleleje, Smidstrup, and Humle-bæk, the two young families who had fled south via Falster were already beginning to establish themselves in their exile in Sweden. Smaller problems and hardships replaced the great existential challenges that had confronted them only a few days earlier, as Poul Hannover's notes reflect: "Thursday morning I got an engineer—Borg from ASEA—to go around with me to get coupons. We also found out that we could stay a lot cheaper—and also actually more practically, at the hotel AROS from Tuesday on. Mrs. Linden rang—and Inger and the kids went out there. Wernekinck, who is tremendously helpful, brought a typewriter to the hotel—it's been great to have. In the evening Gudrun called, saying that Ada and the kids had come with Jørgen—Allan, who was about to sleep, was overjoyed. The Lindens wanted to take us out, but we needed to stay at home—although there was so much to do that we still did not get to bed early."

His sister-in-law, Kis Marcus, relates her experiences that day:

We had to rush from the table in the middle of luncheon to reach the train station in time. Dorte was a little unwell, had nausea and got an aspirin at the station. It was probably just fatigue. I discovered that I had forgotten my bag at the castle. I called over there, and luckily the driver came with it before the train left.

In Malmö we parted from our travel mates and went with the children to a few hotels to check, searching for relatives and acquaintances—Gunnar tried to get in touch with a business contact, who turned out no longer to live in the city. We went down the main street and bought a toy for each child, as we had promised them. Dorte got a dress-up doll and Palle some small soldiers. We came to Hässleholm around 5:30 p.m. and got a lovely room at Bern's Hotel. After tidying ourselves up a bit, we went into the restaurant and had a lovely dinner. Dorte really enjoyed it. Palle had been happy and satisfied for the entire trip, and thankfully did not understand much of the horrors. Before we went to bed, each of us took a hot and luxurious bath.

The same day the Swedish minister to Copenhagen, Dardel, sent a report back to Stockholm, describing the sentiments of goodwill and gratitude flowing toward Sweden from the troubled Danes. The minister also commented on the impact the action had had on the mood of the occupied country: "Since no trace of anti-Semitism seems to exist in any part of the population, the Danes have hardly ever before been so united and so filled with indignation as is now the case. Although the démarche we carried out in Berlin, as one might expect, did not lead to a result, it does constitute a strong and gratefully received moral support toward the Danish people."[12]

Herbert Levysohn after the war. His father, Willie Levysohn, had become co-owner of a big textile wholesaler in 1918. As a successful businessman, Levysohn was among the Danish Jews who, like a number of other prominent Danes, in the days after August 29, 1943, was taken hostage by the occupation forces and interned in Horserød prison camp. In Sweden in late October, Herbert Levysohn described his father's attitude this way: "As soon as they knew that I had arrived here safely, Stridsland [a friend] went to Father, and with 3 Swedish flags on the back of his coat made him understand that we were in Sweden. Mogens Fisker [another friend] thought that we could get Dad out of the camp, partly by their own people and by bribery, but on inquiring of Father about escape, he refused to be involved in something [illegal] like this. Of course we do not know whether such a flight would have been successful, but there was great potential for it. What can be the reason that Father would not? It's currently hard to say. One can assume that Father still did not realize the seriousness. . . . In addition, we who know Father so well imagine that he still insisted on the fact that he is Danish and therefore would not leave the country, a doctrine that after October 2 unfortunately can only be damaging, and not to anyone's benefit. But all these assumptions have to be pushed aside to face the sad reality that Father did not come from Horserød camp to Sweden. So far as is known, Horserød camp's Jewish department, to which Father had been transferred, was emptied Tuesday, October 12."

Willie Levysohn had a heart problem. Despite several attempts, efforts to secure his release from Theresienstadt failed, and he died there on March 16, 1944.

CHAPTER 13

FRIDAY, OCTOBER 8

THE BEACH AT SMIDSTRUP

The Report

It was imperative for many of the fugitives to resume as soon as possible, if not normal lives, then the responsibility for their own destiny in Sweden. One of Poul Hannover's first steps was to enable all former Titan employees who had fled to be employed by ASEA, so that they could support themselves. Meanwhile he started transcribing his notes from the escape into the coherent report that has been quoted here: "I had a lot to write—also started this long report—the children were with the Lindens for dinner, while we ate with the parents here at the hotel—they were very sweet and helpful—it's great to have such good friends. I have already met a great number of ASEA's engineers here at the hotel where they have bid me welcome."

Kis and Gunnar Marcus also made contact on Friday with residents they already knew: "We woke up early, had breakfast in the room, and traveled by train to Linköping and switched to Gullberg. When we got there Eva and Henry met us by car, and we arrived at their lovely small house in Ljungsbro at around one. Our reunion was great, and we had plenty to talk about."

Eva and Henry Frænkel were Danish; he was of Jewish descent. They had resolutely traveled to Sweden on April 9, 1940, with the last free ferry from Helsingør, immediately after they had seen the first German aircraft and understood that the country was under occupation.

. . .

While the two displaced families were finding permanent places in Sweden, the story of their dramatic escape the week before was reaching Bergstrøm's ears on Rådhuspladsen in Copenhagen. He writes in his diary for October 8: "I heard a story about Jews from Stubbekøbing. A Jewish family of 10 members had to spend a night in the woods because it was not possible to come up with the boat they should have had. They were helped by another boat and escaped through the northern straits, while another fisherman was doing tricks to the south of them and attracted police attention, whereby the right boat got out unnoticed. The man who pulled the antics just said that he was doing sea trials. The Jewish family got to Sweden safe and sound."[1]

The idea that the search for the Jewish refugees continued unabated was trumpeted by the Swedish press, although the Swedish authorities were very well aware that it was otherwise. In a telegram to the Swedish legation in Berlin on October 8, the Foreign Ministry in Stockholm wrote directly that "it seems obvious that the Germans are letting things slip through with the escape."

At the same time the situation in Copenhagen was tense. As Helmuth von Moltke stopped over in Copenhagen on his way back from Norway, he noted after a few hours' stroll in the streets: "The atmosphere in town is considerably hardened. Never before have I in any occupied country seen such hatred in the eyes of people as they see the German uniforms. People are simply out of their minds. The removal of the Jews has left the impression that they are all exposed."[2]

Alarming bulletins were still fueled by the Danish Press Service in Stockholm, which in its morning broadcast of October 8 reported that the Germans were continuing action against the Jews by all available means: "The special SS units that were sent to Denmark to carry out the pogroms are constantly active and drive hundreds of Jewish families to despair and suicide.

"One of the leaders of the persecution in Helsingør has been the notorious SS officer Juhl, formerly Foreign Minister Ribbentrop's driver, who has stayed in Denmark since the German onslaught on the country. There are rumors that he has been shot by the Danes because of his zeal in pursuit of the Jews."

Svenska Dagbladet supported the image of active German efforts to stop the wave of refugees in its Saturday edition. Here, Danish refugees tell of dramatic events on the Danish coast, where a boat is sunk, and German surveillance is stepped up day by day.[3]

Neither the information about the SS units nor the rumor about the liquidation of Gestapo-Juhl was true.

In Berlin by contrast, the diplomatic wrangling about the deported Danes continued. Minister Mohr insisted that a clear German commitment had been made that half Jews would not be deported, and that accordingly those who had been should be returned. And the German Foreign Office was not completely reluctant to support this view. Best had promised that "only pure Jews" would be deported, so if a mistake could be demonstrated, it was a breach of that commitment. Mohr also continued his efforts to convince the German Foreign Office that the elderly and the young should be returned. But again, the Nazi regime's logic was quite different, as shown by the official German record of a conversation in which Mohr made yet another attempt but was rebuffed by his German interlocutor: "Simultaneously I pointed out to the minister that because of our experience we think of all Jews as being at war with Germany and treat them accordingly. Age plays no decisive role here."

Judging from the German minutes from the conversation, the Danish minister did not pick up this argument. But he did persist with his own, which simply appealed to humanity: "Mohr expressed understanding for this view, however, opined that one generally does act differently in dealing with the very old and the children, even when enemy aliens."[4]

In Copenhagen the leading politicians gathered to assess where the country stood after the action against the Jews and the lifting of martial law. Would the Germans continue to press for the establishment of a new Danish government? And would the hunt for the fleeing Jews really keep going? According to former foreign minister P. Munch's record of the meeting, Buhl reported "that he had spoken with Svenningsen . . . to see if there was any message from Berlin. Svenningsen announced that no answer had come from Berlin, but he understood that the capital had accustomed itself to the facts on the ground; it was not desirable to seek more clarity, you had better come to terms with the relationship as it was. Best came again instead of General Hanneken. . . . Buhl asked if Best had again made remarks about the formation of a government. Svenningsen had said no, that he regarded that as useless after the measures against the Jews."[5]

Svenningsen's statements can be seen as the beginning of a "new normal." There was not only a "before" and an "after" August 29. Now there was also a "before" and an "after" the action against the Jews, and although the state of emergency had been lifted, a Danish government was no longer a viable option. The fragile construct of the permanent secretaries and Werner Best remained with the politicians in the wings. It held until the liberation of Denmark on May 5, 1945.

Via Skudehavn

Among those who still took the commotion with reasonable serenity was a twenty-six-year-old Copenhagen resident, Henrik Martin Schall Meyer, who was relieved that his parents had gotten away earlier in the week but who had long hesitated to follow himself. He had, like his older sister, Wanda, stayed with various friends and acquaintances, and it was Wednesday before they decided to try to get over the Sound. All Wednesday and Thursday, Henrik Meyer investigated different options, judging from his contemporaneous notes, without being much troubled by the situation. On the contrary, he used the many visits for festive gatherings, apparently without worrying much about being listed, let alone arrested. On the other hand, the various counsels and rumors he took down reflect that he thought it could be dangerous to be apprehended during the flight.

After a shipping opportunity failed Thursday night, Henrik and Wanda spent the evening with a friend who offered "lovely sherry, and a lot of good advice about how we should go to Nykøbing F, if everything else failed." But the next morning, Friday, things began to develop, and Henrik Meyer tells in detail about the day's events: "We were up in time. Wanda was wearing all her woolen layers, but as yet not looking noticeably fat. Asmussen picked us up at 7:30 a.m and then a small car with a Mr. Heymann arrived. In that we all huddled up. We then drove out quietly to Aarhusgade, where Asmussen got out, and we got another driver. From there we went out into the civilian harbor to a boatbuilder, where we got out. There were already several people gathered. . . . Now old Janson headed in. He could not walk, and his wife was also very decrepit. After some delay, during which we were treated to apples and cigarettes, one boat passed, and then another one. Old Janson was carried out by two men and groaned terribly. Wanda and I, as the two youngest, had to wait, as there was no room for us in the boat."

With two boats departed for freedom, and uncertainty about what would follow, the spirited young man bears further witness to the gravity of the situation:

> Then a terrible waiting came, in which we were still promised that we would soon get going, but there was still no one to fill the boat. At a certain point we had to hide in one of the boats, as there were some suspicious people along the road. Finally at approximately 2 p.m. some people came. "Rentier" Selbiger and wife and their niece. . . . Selbiger was terribly nervous, he had not said a word in 8 days. He fled first from Germany and then from Poland. On the other hand, his wife talked. She had dyed her hair red, like a madwoman. After some waiting we were moved to a fish shack. . . . At last we were crammed into the cabin in the bow of a fishing ship, and we sailed at 3:20 p.m. (Luckily we got lunch and a few beers in the boathouse.) The weather was fine, and the trip went smoothly. There was a strong smell of kerosene in the cabin, but only Mrs. Selbiger got sick. The fishermen were very nice. They accepted our cigarettes and promised to call home with messages. We had already handed over our ration cards . . . , but the fishermen were quick to ensure that we did not take them out of the country.

Henrik Meyer tells of the reception in Sweden, where he has clearly regained his good humor:

> After going through 2½ hours' sailing we arrived at Barsebäck. As we crossed the territorial boundary the jubilation was great! In Barsebäck's well-fortified port we were greeted by the Swedish military and a large crowd of curious residents. We were led to a house where a Mrs. Larson regaled us with coffee and bread that local inhabitants had provided. A military person came and registered us. Wanda and I could have wrung Mrs. Selbiger's neck.—After coffee we were driven to Kävlinge on a big truck about 20 km away. It was great to see the lights shining out of houses and on the streets.
>
> In Kävlinge we gathered at the firehouse with a dozen other refugees and together we marched up to the school. About 100 people were gathered there, and we put our clothes in the dormitory and went over for dinner: lovely peas with sausage. The Swedes were very friendly toward us, and the Danes talked like hell.
>
> After dinner . . . we went for a little walk in the town and then back to the dormitory. We were preparing to go to bed, but they

couldn't find mattresses for all of us. There was a worker next to me lying directly on the floor all night, despite the fact that I offered him half of my mattress. The Jews talked, and then they snored. Later that night a migration of older people began, and they generally stumbled over my legs. The air was stifling.[6]

That afternoon Niels Bohr visited the Danish minister in London. He had been flown the day before from Stockholm to Scotland and was immediately taken to London, where he stayed for some time before he went on to the United States to play a key role in the Manhattan Project. Reventlow notes in his diary: "Bohr talked about conditions in Denmark and about the outstanding assistance that was granted to the Jews by the entire nation. All in all he was full of praise for Denmark's position. He was greatly concerned about the Jewish question, and assumed as a matter of course that those now arrested faced death."[7]

By Hidden Paths

In Fanny Cohn's summer cottage, the Hope, in Smidstrup, life looked brighter than when Adolph Meyer and his sister had prepared themselves only a day earlier to put an end to it all if the Gestapo discovered their hiding place at Marie Olsen's. But it was still quite uncertain what the future would bring to those trapped in the summerhouses, and the whole situation and the previous night's drama took their toll:

> We did not know how long we would stay here. Mrs. Abrahamsen...was very worried about her mother and sister, the children—especially the 11-year-old son—very nervous. It was Yom Kippur evening, and old Mrs. Gelvan and the Sokols were emotional.
>
> On the afternoon of October 8, a Miss Damm came in quickly and said that we should get ourselves prepared by 6 p.m., as we had to leave in the evening, but only the minimum of luggage—we could easily comply. We were very excited. During the day runners with white armbands had brought us food and messages. At 6:45 p.m. old Mrs. Gelvan was picked up, and approximately a ½ hour later we others, we were excited—would we eventually

manage?—"Everything is going smoothly," Miss Damm encouraged. For 3 days she had been absent from her office without a medical certificate and had not slept for 2 nights, I asked her to say hello to the clinic if she knew we had crossed over. The weather was beautiful, clear moonlight, mild. We walked the 500 meters through the forest, our way was guarded by young people with white armbands (we heard later that the Danish police had cordoned off the plantation in a 10 kilometer circumference), and relays (watchful young men and women) started by bike right from Hornbæk to check on the situation.

Shipping out from the beach was to take place just two days after the Gestapo raided the church and other hiding places in Gilleleje, a few kilometers away. For the rapidly established refugee organization it was a risky affair both to concentrate so many refugees in holiday cottages in Smidstrup and also so soon after the disaster on Wednesday night to begin embarking from the beach on a grand scale. Tensions ran high, also for the helpers, and particularly at the critical time when Dr. Meyer and his flock were reaching the embarkation point. It was, according to grocer Lassen, just about to go wrong: "The first sign of nervousness was on the beach, since one of the guards came running and told me that there were two Gestapo men behind a garage. Together with a later-known saboteur, Hansted, we went there with revolvers ready, very troubled, it was the first time, but it turned out to be 2 friends whom I later came to work with a lot."

Dr. Meyer did not notice anything in this episode, but portrays the shipping out from the beach a little differently than Lassen remembered a few years later: "We soon reached the beach and saw a large schooner to which fishing boats rowed back and forth from a jetty. Floodlights behind the orchard searched for airplanes, the moon grinned at them, because they were looking in the air instead of searching the sea. It was quite calm on the water. We rowed easily over to the schooner and climbed aboard, the fisherman shook our hands and wished us well over, we were then placed in the hold, where we were 124 in number and had ample space. There could easily have been 3 to 4 times as many."

In his report from 1945, Gilbert Lassen relates his version of how the shipment was organized that evening:

At 11 p.m. that evening the first boat left from Smidstrup Strand with 180 people. Earlier in the evening everything was made ready.

The diary of Thomas Brandes.

Among the Jews in Denmark were about a thousand young agricultural students, who came between 1933 and 1938 with a view to further immigration to Palestine in cooperation with the Zionist organization Hechalutz. However, 377 of these students were stranded in Denmark by the German occupation in April 1940. Among them was Thomas Brandes, who came to the village of Voldbro on the island of Fyn, where he met the local Gerda Petersen on the first evening. The young couple married and settled there a few years later, and Brandes converted to Christianity.

In 1942 Thomas Brandes received a letter from his father, who had escaped to Paris. Now, he was on transport to Auschwitz, and, realizing what this portended, he wrote a farewell letter to his son in Denmark, who later the same year learned that his father had indeed vanished in the camp together with several other members of the family.

As a private language teacher, Brandes had a German officer among his students. Late in September he advised Brandes to escape and as the warning was confirmed also from others, Brandes decided to leave. Gerda was

Flugt til Sverige Okt.1943

Fredag 1.Okt. Kl.9 Advarsel af Lydia
Kl.20.30 sidste Gang i Lejligheden
natten fra Fredag til Lørdag sovet
hos Nine *illegible* Gerda og Kirsten.
Lørdag 2.Okt. Kl.8 Radio Extra-Udsendelse
Kl.10 hos Fru Gryhold
Kl.11 per Cykel til
Glamsbjerg.Med Toget,hvor Gerda og Kir-
sten var i,til Ebberup, saa med Cykel
til Engmosegaard.
Lørdag,9.Okt.Svigerfar og Gerda til
Odense,tilbæge om Aften.Beslutning til
Flugten til Sverige Kl.10 Aften
Søndag,10.Okt.Afsked af alle Kære
kl.19.30.Natten fra Søndag til Mandag
sovet hos Nine med Svigerfar. iOdense
Mandag,11.Okt. Kl.12,20 med Toget fra
Odense.Afsked med Svigerfar.
Kl.18 Ankomst i Valby,medTaxa til Læge-
boligerne paa Lyngbyvejen;
Kl.20 tilbæge med Taxi til Valby Station
Kl.20.15 til Nykøbing Falster med Toget
Ankomst Kl.1 om Natten,Ophold 1/2
Time paa Hotel Fønix saa med Falk
Ambulance til   /12.Okt
Grønsund Kl. 2.10 Tirsdag Morgen med
xFiskerbaad til
Trelleborg,Ankomst Tirsdag Middag Kl.14
Man 13.Okt. Kl.7.30 fra Trelleborg,
Ankomst kl.13.30 i Floda,Ankomst
i Bockaberg Kl.14.

pregnant and they judged it too risky for her to follow, all the more so as
she as a Gentile was not at risk.

During his escape, which lasted from Friday, October 1, to Tuesday, October 12, Brandes kept a brief diary in a small notebook. Once safely arrived in Trelleborg, Sweden, he transcribed his own pages with a typewriter and pasted his notes onto the first page of a scrapbook he compiled on his time as a refugee in Sweden.

It appears that he stayed in his home until less than an hour before the action started, and that the final decision to flee to Sweden was only made a week later. The escape route went via Copenhagen, a stop at Bispebjerg Hospital, and by train to Falster, where a well-oiled local organization was responsible for the further transport by ambulance out to the Grønsund ferry dock, where the Marcus and Hannover families had left the week before.

After the war Thomas Brandes resumed his life on Fyn. The scrapbook is kindly made available by his son, the artist Peter Brandes, who was born in the town of Assens during his father's Swedish exile.   Private collection

The refugees had food; we had a doctor for some, and a few received calming pills and medicine. An accompanying person was taken to every house, and they led them by hidden paths to the shipping spot, a small grove of trees that went down to the sea and where some stone jetties went further out into the water. I got down to the signal house in good time, a high-lying two-story cottage, clearly visible from the sea. From the middle window in the top floor, at the stroke of 11, I had to flash the ship in with a very sharp floodlight I had borrowed from a factory.

The very large schooner came exactly on time with dimmed lights, as it got the signal to go as close to the coast as it could get, likewise the two small motorboats came, which were also signaled into the breakwater with a small flashlight. Embarkation could only begin when I gave the message to my helper farthest out on this breakwater, who was the young lieutenant Erik Bennicke, who later helped me many times, but approximately one year after, he was shot by the Gestapo when they came up to his office to arrest him, and he and his clerks defended themselves.

The successful outcome gave Lassen and his people renewed courage, and according to his account the very next evening, an additional 110 people sailed this way, distributed in two boats, from Smidstrup: "In 14 days to 3 weeks we sent people out every or every other night, as we soon came into contact with many groups, committees, and individuals. . . . During those weeks the Germans figured that shipping could only happen from ports, and at that time did not have as many people available, Danish and German, as they later got. The transports continued steadily in October. The number of people was, however, less and less, from 15 to 25 each time. These stragglers were often sick, the poor, the elderly, and invalids, many were found in hospitals and poor neighborhoods, each had been hiding in small rooms for weeks. For these last transports of Jews, I had many occasions to go to Copenhagen to arrange it, often gathering these poor souls at the Biophysics Institute with Professor Ege. These stragglers rarely had the means for crossing, and fishermen got about 5,000 for such a crossing shared between boat and crew, but this rarely caused anguish as several committees still had money from the so-called big days. Thus, at the end of the year, when Jewish transports had long since ceased, the Gilleleje Committee still had approximately 30,000 kroner in holdings."[8]

Safely aboard the schooner *Jan*, out of Aarhus, Dr. Meyer and the rest of the refugees in the cargo organize themselves as best they can. The tension is far from released: "I sat on my little bag and supported myself against the ship's wall, and then at 8 p.m. we sailed, the engine worked well. From a Mr. Katz, I got through Valdemar 6 cigars to smoke in Sweden. I did not feel calm until we were confirmed to be in Swedish territorial waters. We sailed 3½ hours, as the schooner made a detour into the Kattegat. At 11:30 p.m. we were in Höganäs port. We sang the Danish national anthem followed by the Swedish. We were saved."

CHAPTER 14

SATURDAY, OCTOBER 9

REALITIES

The Town Doctor

The town doctor in Höganäs, H. G. Widding, took pride in the fact that the small town itself was able to mobilize the forces needed to handle the increasing flow of Danish refugees. In his own words he had already been worn out like a slave for a week with the reception and medical examination of the arrivals, but he liked the job and went to work with heart and soul. At the same time he kept a diary of things large and small, also following the events early Saturday morning on October 9: "I will never forget the night between October 8 and 9. I had fallen asleep around half past midnight when the police called and said that they had 124 refugees at the port. I quickly got dressed, found [a few aides] and soon the work flowed wonderfully. By 4:30 in the morning we had examined all so they could get to their accommodations. A family—Grundkin—(the father is the newspaper editor) composed of wife, husband, and three children, had to stay with us because one child had something of a cold and I had neither the opportunity for isolation nor the heart to separate them."

Adolph Meyer talks about his arrival and the friendly reception, which is in huge contrast to everything the fugitives had just been through. But Meyer also notes that the sincere solidarity is the same on both sides of the Sound: "The reception in the harbor was as gracious and sincere as our compatriots' actions. Customs officers, sailors and the tall Swedish soldiers welcomed us. The weather was beautiful, moonlit and warm. After waiting awhile we walked the very long way to People's Park, where we had milk and coffee and cookies, then we had to fill out questionnaires and were registered and examined by a doctor. I introduced myself as a doctor, and Dr. Hakon Widding offered 'a 2 bedder.' Mary and I were picked up by car and driven there, it was now 3:30 a.m. October 9, so it was nice to go to bed, we shared the room and slept soon."

The town doctor not only has a family of five in his home but also accommodates Meyer and his sister-in-law, who both the next day tell their host about their entire journey. Widding in turn tells them that several of the children have difficulty understanding why they have been forced to flee. They're Danish, as they explain to the doctor, and had never thought that they were also Jews. Widding also recounts an episode: After he checks a newly arrived refugee the man thanks the doctor and observes: "Yes, you may send the bill to Hitler!" Widding pleasingly notes that Danish humor is still in evidence even under these tragic circumstances.[1]

It's also in evidence at the reception camp in Kävlinge, some twenty kilometers from Barsebäck, where the young refugees Henrik and Wanda Meyer have not had a pleasant first night but are in good spirits. That same day Henrik describes life in the troubled camp: "We struck out early. It was not possible to wash, and we were gradually getting filthy. In the women's dormitory there had been even more turmoil, and some infants had howled the whole time. It was nice to get some fresh air. Some young people had been up all night, others had arrived during the night. The toilets are indescribable. Wanda and I help in the kitchen. . . . I'll collect and empty trash and later help with the morning coffee. . . . Registration begins, and we line up in good time. After completing a form we are called one by one. . . . We're queried there whether we want to obtain [ration] cards for tobacco, and it is confirmed. After some waiting, we come to the doctor. He looks like an uncomfortable mountain troll, and the examination is quite a parody. He listens to my heart, we're screened, and the throat is looked at (the doctor uses a spatula rinsed only in lukewarm water!). Then we go to the bank and convert 100 Danish kroner on my passport. The exchange is 80."[2]

Henrik and Wanda Meyer are already looking forward to going to Göteborg, where his parents are lodging with acquaintances. The hunt for a new life has begun, and for the young ones for whom the change feels less dramatic, the worries are less intrusive. Letters are written home to caregivers and family, delivered through a Swedish soldier who promises to pass them on to a Danish fisherman who can mail them in Denmark.

In Västerås, Poul Hannover's last entries are characterized by daily life that is already beginning to appear. "Yesterday—Saturday—I was at the bank. It was Mette's birthday—we had some small presents for her. . . . But perhaps the best gift was that we were told that grandfather had come. Wernekinck called, if we would come out there last night—after which grandfather called, so we talked with him—and were told to wire home. At 6 p.m. we went to dinner with Mr. and Mrs. Wernekinck singing—on the table there were two packages for Mette."

In Ljungsbro, Kis and Gunnar Marcus were now also settling down with their friends, the Frænkels: "We went for a walk along the Göta Canal with Eva and the kids. It was very beautiful with all the autumn colors on the trees. Drank hot chocolate when we got home on the occasion of Mette's birthday.

"Eva and Henry gave us their bedroom right away when we came, and they had borrowed a few beds for Palle and Dorte. They slept in one of their living rooms. We also borrowed nightclothes, underwear, and the like from them."

Now it's Adolph Meyer's turn to deal with the many practical issues after arrival. The overriding consideration is to inform the immediate family that they are safe and to get information about who else has come over. About the accommodation at his colleague's in Höganäs, Meyer says:

It was a very luxurious villa with nice furnishings and a large garden. We had breakfast there, but ate all subsequent meals in the Hotel Switzerland together with the refugees; Mary moved during the day to a family who had given Valdemar, Ulla, and Ragna shelter. By telephoning Göteborg . . . I got permission to go there Sunday, got Mary and me photographed (which was done with the help of the Kaminkowitz ladies), and I obtained the police emergency travel document for Mary and me. In the morning I was immediately told that Hjalmar and Esther were going the same day to Göteborg, I took a car to the 11:30 train, but they had gone with the morning train. I met Mogens and was told about everyone. I had talked to Carl Mannheimer [a wealthy Swedish relative who offered to house the family] who promised to telegraph that I could go to Göteborg and asked Dr. Widding to lend me money. I borrowed 200 kroner which was returned on Monday the 11th of October.... I was happy to learn that all my family was saved, later it turned out that nephews and nieces were also in Sweden. The weather was still summery. Widding and all other Swedes helpful and hospitable.

Meyer had reason to heave a sigh of relief. After almost two weeks of flight, he could now start to build a new life in Sweden. On Saturday the ninth alone, when the inflow peaked, it is believed that more than fourteen hundred Danish Jews came over. In the following days the flow of refugees began to slow. Most had reached safety.

Upon his arrival Adolph Meyer, like all other Danish refugees, had to fill out an application to get an alien passport. The form can still be found in the Swedish police files. The pediatrician inserts his personal information on the preprinted form with neat handwriting. About the reason for his visit to Sweden, he cites "Jewish persecution in Denmark," and to justify why he did not have a valid Danish passport upon arrival, "Had to flee." But Dr. Meyer left no doubt that he considered his stay in Sweden as temporary. Asked how long he wants permission to stay, he doesn't enter a date but writes, from his own perspective: "Until the day when it is possible to return to Denmark."[3]

The most recent figures show that a total of 7,742 Jews fled from Denmark to Sweden because of the German action. In addition, 686 non-Jews

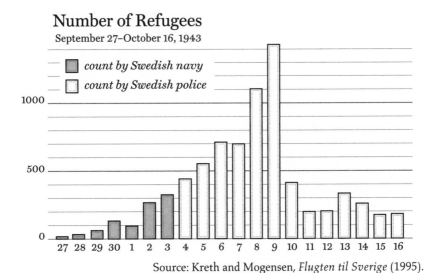

Number of Refugees
September 27–October 16, 1943

count by Swedish navy
count by Swedish police

1000

500

0

27 28 29 30 1 2 3 4 5 6 7 8 9 10 11 12 13 14 15 16

Source: Kreth and Mogensen, *Flugten til Sverige* (1995).

went into exile with their Jewish familes. Some 1,376 of those who fled were German refugees, including stateless Jews. After the war 348 of the stateless chose to remain in Sweden. The young Danish historian Sofie Lene Bak, who has researched the refugees' fate extensively, concludes: "The Danish government care included all who were deported from Danish soil, and the Danish legation in Sweden decided that anyone who had fled from Denmark to Sweden, regardless of nationality, was covered by the official refugee assistance."[4]

Support for all, whether they were Danish or not, gave the non-Danish Jewish refugees who had come to Sweden via Denmark hope and a belief in a future in Denmark. After the war it turned out that for many of those concerned, these aspirations were not fully realized. In 1945 Denmark resumed its restrictive refugee policy in regard to the stateless who had escaped to the country in the lead-up to the war. This policy was maintained until March 1946, when it was slightly relaxed by providing them with one-year residence and work permits. Gradually the stateless were able to apply for Danish citizenship when they had resided in Denmark for fifteen years, and the last of those who had escaped via Denmark to Sweden in October 1943 and had returned after Denmark's liberation got their citizenship in 1974.[5]

The culmination of the mass flight from Denmark on the weekend of October 7–9 gave rise to questions in regard to the Germans' strategy. While the Swedish press during the previous days had overflowed with dramatic stories of the Germans' attempt to stem the flight, the Sunday edition of *Dagens Nyheter* featured a much more sober assessment based on Saturday's impressions along the Øresund coastline. The headline establishes the puzzling fact that the dramatic increase in the number of refugees had to be happening with "the Good Will of the Germans." The newspaper estimated fairly accurately that about five thousand Danish refugees had arrived in the past week, which was possible only if the Danish police were assisting in the escape and the occupation forces turning a blind eye to it. But how *was* this possible? The question was raised, but it has taken seventy years of debate and research to provide the answers.

Reality on the Water

As early as 1942 the German minister to Copenhagen, Werner Best's predecessor, the career diplomat Renthe-Fink, gave Berlin a sobering lesson in the coastal geography of Denmark, a nightmare for anyone aiming to control maritime traffic: "Because of Denmark's very long coastline, which in some places is only four kilometers from the Swedish coast, illegal border traffic can be kept under control only with the greatest difficulty. Effective blockage is technically not possible. At best the goal can be to reduce the element of risk as much as possible by the application of every conceivable measure. This work is done by Danish police and the German navy in close and good cooperation."[6]

That was an optimistic interpretation. And since 1942 the conditions had deteriorated to the point of complete collapse only after August 29, 1943, when the cooperation between the German and Danish navies was discontinued, and the efforts of the Danish coastal police significantly hampered. The German navy's main tasks in this sector were the securing of Danish waters and the German lines of transport to Norway, with the vital provisions of iron ore to Germany; they also had to see to it that Allied units did not penetrate into the Baltic. Those tasks of high strategic importance were supplemented by coast guard minesweeping, which until August 29 was carried out by the Danish navy in cooperation with the Danish coastal police. With martial law and internment of Danish military personnel, this cooperation broke down altogether, and even though in September the Germans made several attempts to restore it, this was not possible as long as the state of emergency lasted.

On September 6 the Germans had a mere six Danish coast guard cutters stationed in the port of Helsingør. These were provisionally manned by German sailors transferred from a minesweeper. On September 30 the punctilious German admiral stated that this patrolling would be suspended in the near future because the crew was going back to the minesweeper. The following day, October 1, it was announced from Helsingør that patrols by the Danish cutters had ceased. The primary military coast guard, in other words, ended its patrols the same day that the German action was put into effect. They were not resumed until early November. The result was that *not one* of the some seven hundred illegal transports across the Sound following the action against the Danish Jews was intercepted by German patrols.[7]

G. F. Duckwitz, in a postwar report, declared that the German port commander in Copenhagen, at his request, made sure that the German navy ships were in dry dock during the crucial days in October—adding yet another myth to the history of the rescue. No contemporary sources support his assertion. But even if it was so, guarding the coast was not the German navy's task. It was a task for the six Danish coast guard cutters, which were fully operational and subject to the authority of the German port commander in Helsingør. The problem was that in October there were no personnel to man the six cutters.[8]

This did not mean, however, that there were no German patrol boats on the Sound. On the contrary we have reports from the Swedish coastal monitoring service's observations of the German navy's movements in the Sound during the critical days of October. For example, on October 4, two days after Poul Hannover stared blindly into the Baltic dark, a large number of German patrol vessels were observed, although it was difficult to establish whether it was about five, ten, or fifteen. A number of other sources also support the assertion that the Germans patrolled very intensely. But none of these patrols was tasked with overseeing civilian traffic, let alone with an attempt to stem the flood of refugees. Their tasks were military in relation to hostile operations in Danish waters and entry to the Baltic, and the German squads were probably barely aware of and certainly not interested in the drama that was playing out on the Sound right through their lines. In a laconic reference found in the war diary of the German Naval War Command for the second of October 1943, it is noted that the Jewish action in Denmark the previous night had failed, because the Jews had been warned and the majority of the six thousand Jews had gone into hiding. A mass exodus to Sweden was now in progress, it says, without a hint that the navy had received—let alone was eager to receive—orders to stop it.

The impression that the German patrols were passive bystanders during the escape is also confirmed by later reports from the skippers on the boats that crossed. Thus skipper Aksel Sørensen reports that during a voyage with a cargo full of refugees they met a German patrol boat in the open water. There was nothing to do but to stay the course. The two vessels sailed right past each other, with only customary greetings exchanged.[9]

The night when the action took place, the police leadership, as mentioned, ordered that Danish policemen should not participate in the arrests of Jews. This order also applied to what was left of the coastal police force. Through informal channels another instruction followed not to arrest Jews during attempts at illegal exit—although the coastal police's main task was precisely to prevent illegal exit. A recent thorough study of the many reports from countless refugees finds that the Danish coastal police did not cooperate in the deportation of Jewish refugees. In October

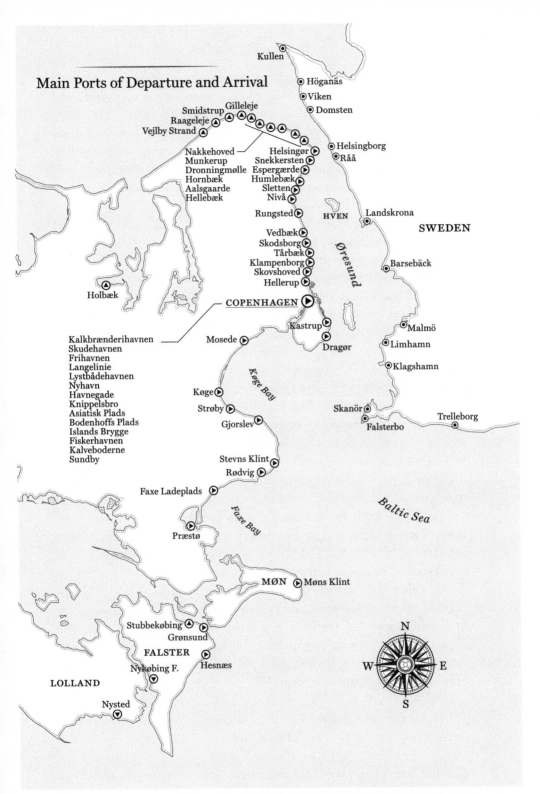

Main Ports of Departure and Arrival

Kullen

Höganäs

Viken

Domsten

Smidstrup Gilleleje
Raageleje
Vejlby Strand

Nakkehoved
Munkerup
Dronningmølle
Hornbæk
Aalsgaarde
Hellebæk

Helsingør   Helsingborg
Snekkersten   Råå
Espergærde
Humlebæk
Sletten
Nivå

Rungsted   HVEN   Landskrona

SWEDEN

Vedbæk
Skodsborg
Tårbæk
Klampenborg
Skovshoved
Hellerup

Øresund

Barsebäck

Holbæk

COPENHAGEN

Kastrup   Malmö

Dragør   Limhamn

Klagshamn

Kalkbrænderihavnen
Skudehavnen   Mosede
Frihavnen
Langelinie
Lystbådehavnen
Nyhavn
Havnegade
Knippelsbro   Køge
Asiatisk Plads
Bodenhoffs Plads   Strøby
Islands Brygge
Fiskerhavnen   Gjorslev
Kalveboderne
Sundby

Køge Bay

Skanör

Falsterbo   Trelleborg

Stevns Klint
Rødvig

Faxe Ladeplads

Baltic Sea

Faxe Bay

Præstø

MØN   Møns Klint

Stubbekøbing
Grønsund

FALSTER   Hesnæs
Nykøbing F.

LOLLAND

Nysted

N
W   E
S

Adapted from: Kreth and Mogensen, *Flugten til Sverige* (1995).

the Jews were freely allowed to travel to Sweden, apart from a few tragic cases where coastal police, because of an accident or the many refugees in the ports, could not avoid assisting with German arrests. The situations could be hard to cope with out in the more than seventy fishing ports, as virtually all were guarded by officers from the coastal police, one of whom in November noted: "From the Jews' side there was a complete lack of understanding of the situation, as they showed up at ports in large numbers carrying large amounts of luggage."

Nevertheless the study found that the coastal police not only closed their eyes but in many cases directly helped and assisted the fugitives, as is also documented in Gilleleje. From the Copenhagen area, where more than one hundred men and three boats from the coastal police controlled traffic between Tuborg Harbor and South Harbor, between two and three thousand refugees shipped out during the first two weeks of October. Not one was arrested by the police. The Germans could, of course, smell a rat, and there are instances when coastal police officers were subjected to searching questions and threats. But what could be done? The problem went, as a Gestapo man remarked to a Danish helper, right up to the top police officials in Copenhagen.[10]

The attitude of the police authorities is also reflected in the handling of a case from Gilleleje, where a coastal officer serving during the days when Dr. Meyer and his sister-in-law were in town, was caught pocketing some of the refugees' money. The officer was dismissed and brought to justice. The indictment, dated December 1, 1943, charges the officer "while working for the coastal police in Gilleleje to have helped the Jews' illegal departure from the country and for this involvement having received a total of 2,800 kroner, which he kept, and an amount of 4,500 kroner, which he distributed to 9 reserve officers."

The officer was sentenced to three months in prison—not for helping Jews to escape but for having taken money for it. What's more, the prosecution appealed the case, requesting increased punishment. The Supreme Court, however, upheld the judgment—and thus also the clear decision by the legal system that the offense lay not in helping the refugees but in taking payment for it.[11]

The Money

Did the Danish Jews pay exorbitant prices for transport to Sweden? The question has haunted the debate about the rescue since the dramatic

October days, and already at the time many sarcastic remarks were heard about fishermen's earnings, as the quoted diaries also reflect.

As a predominant rule helpers on land were not paid. On the other hand, the fishermen and others who sailed larger and smaller groups over *were* paid. As is already apparent from the cited reports, prices varied greatly and there were far from transparent fixed rates. But gradually, as the helpers' network organized the routes, there was also increasing control over payments, so the worst fluctuations were avoided. Yet there is no doubt that among the fishermen there were some who exploited the situation, just as it is equally clear that there were more who acted without regard to personal gain. Some refugees had to pay unreasonably high prices, but no one was left behind because they could not—or would not—pay.

Over the years numerous attempts have been made to calculate payments in relation to today's prices and wages. Such comparisons are difficult. It gives an impression of scale that a fisherman on a single successful transport could earn enough for a new boat, or more—and many fishermen sailed many of these tours. Conversely, as a previously cited story shows, there are examples of a skipper who, after just a single crossing, did not dare sail back and thus had to spend the rest of the war in Sweden.

It is estimated that the average price for a ticket was around one thousand kroner per person. That was around one-third or one-fourth of the annual salary of a skilled worker, and almost half the refugees belonged socially to the working class. Studies of the payments from Gilleleje suggest that there was some correlation between supply and demand. In September, when only a few refugees sought passage, and at the end of October, when the number of refugees had dropped significantly, prices were lower than when the large influx characterized the town in the first weeks of October. While the price in September appears to have been below one thousand kroner, it rose during the first two weeks in October to between one thousand and two thousand, whereafter it dropped to about five hundred kroner. It was especially at this late stage that the poorest Jews fled, and in many cases groups of helpers had saved money so they could ensure that all came over.[12]

The contemporaneous reports quoted here are very direct about the payments. But they do not reflect that the fugitives felt blackmailed or cheated when they dealt with those who actually sailed or organized the crossings. They had another fear, namely of falling into the hands of charlatans who would trick the refugees out of their money without delivering the crossing. It is equally striking that none of the fugitives who wrote close to the action was in doubt that both they and their helpers were being hunted. Today we know that the risk was minimal—especially when the refugees were on board and on the way to Sweden. But that was neither the fishermen's nor the refugees' perception at the time. And it is characteristic that, despite the large amounts of money involved, throughout the period it was difficult to find skippers who were willing to sail at all.[13]

Fishermen put not just their boats but their lives at risk and most asked a solid payment, especially from the most wealthy refugees. Most of the fugitives do not seem to have felt exploited or extorted. For the majority two things seem to have been crucial: that they and their relatives come over, and that no one be left behind because they could not afford the crossing. Several factors contributed to achieving the last goal. Had the fishermen sailed only for money, we would find reports of people without means who didn't come over. But we do not find any. Ultimately the helpers simply insisted that no one be left behind. It was a matter of individual conscience and national honor. It was strongly felt that ultimately anyone who had to flee to Sweden be granted the opportunity.

It has been argued that the issue of the money, and the fact that Danish fishermen gained large sums on the transits in October 1943, has been a taboo subject in the myths surrounding the rescue of the Danish Jews. Much to the contrary, this aspect is an integral part of the history and is seldom left out in the numerous accounts of the events. At the same time, few of those returning to Denmark after the war raised the issue. It was obviously not an issue for the rich nor for those less fortunate who had been supported by the authorities during their exile. Also, a special compensation arrangement was adopted in Denmark after the war for damage caused by the Nazis. This arrangement also provided compensation to Jews who escaped to Sweden.[14]

The need for money was huge in the help groups, which sprouted everywhere, and many were extremely creative when it came to obtaining large amounts of cash. It was far from the case that only the fugitives themselves donated. One group carried out a successful collection tour at Sjælland estates. Others sought to raise large amounts through regular credit. After the war Supreme Court lawyer H. H. Bruun, who just before the action was hurriedly given the responsibility for the Jewish community's property and assets, provided a vivid description of how he administered the 11 million kroner involved. For Bruun it was crucial that no involvement in any illegal activity could give the Germans a pretext to confiscate Jewish assets. On the other hand, he felt it appropriate to use some of the funds to "help the many needy Jews with the expensive trip to Sweden." The way out was to take out a loan of 250,000 kroner from a known shipowner against the security of the community's assets. The loan could then be used to fund the illegal exits.

Bruun also mentions an episode that reflects the ambiguous conditions in Denmark in the weeks following the action. A few days after the operation the concierge of the community building in New Kongensgade phoned and said that two Germans and two Danes had arrived and stolen a number of books, including a very rare and valuable Talmud. After having slept on the matter, Bruun chose to report the theft in writing to the police commissioner, who a few hours later phoned and asked if the barrister "was mad and did not know that the Germans had the power in the country?" Bruun replied, according to his own report, that he "thought the police director still had the task of maintaining law and order within his official area," and "insisted that the notification was forwarded to the Germans": "It happened, and 8 days later the concierge phoned again: All the books, including the edition of the Talmud, were handed to him by two unknown men—not the police—and the same night everything was moved over to the Royal Library, with whose leadership I had previously made an agreement."

Bruun added that he was delighted when the war was over, "to surrender all possessions to the community in undamaged condition, plus assets increased by a not inconsiderable amount thanks to current interest rates."[15]

The Blind Eye

While in practice it was difficult for the Germans, without Danish assistance, to stem the flight by sea, there were much larger German forces in the country. The interesting question is whether their inaction, already noted by contemporary commentators, was due to politically imposed restraint by the German authorities, more or less explicitly encouraged by Werner Best?

Surely the problem was not lack of manpower. In addition to Danish police the occupying power possessed its own security police, uniformed police, and Wehrmacht soldiers. It was the security police who had primary responsibility for the action against the Jews. As noted, there was no cordial relationship between the German forces and their respective commands, and neither the Wehrmacht nor the uniformed police, who had thirteen to fourteen hundred officers under them, showed any eagerness to help the security police search for the Danish Jews. A certain practical assistance was granted in connection with the action as such and subsequently in a number of specific cases, but in general both the Wehrmacht and the policemen dragged their feet. If a blind eye could be turned toward the fugitives, this as a rule was done, and we have numerous reports of trains and ports filled with fleeing families who were ignored by passing German soldiers and police. Herbert Levysohn's quoted note about the German "clodhoppers" also bears witness to this.

Of course no guarantees were given, and there were exceptions with the direst consequences. Refugees were caught, and some were shot. But overwhelmingly the German police and the Wehrmacht turned their backs—first and foremost because each was dependent on further cooperation with the Danish authorities. Their lack of enthusiasm was due neither to a lack of manpower nor to a matter of capacity. It was due to a lack of will.

This left the German security police pretty much alone with the responsibility of carrying out both the action itself and the subsequent attempt to stop the escapes. Here the picture is more fragmented, but it is marked by Werner Best's fundamental belief that the action was completed during the first night. There was no organized or systematic pursuit of the fugitives or any issuing of orders to make a special effort to intercept them. On the contrary, Best makes it explicit in his reports to Berlin that there will be no "manhunt." Much was therefore left to the initiative of individual commanders. Most took it easy, and, with the exception of Gestapo-Juhl, do not seem to have been eager to catch as many as possible. Conversely, there are also examples of Jews who were tracked down during their flight, captured, and later deported. But the overall impression is one of a halfhearted effort to arrest the refugees who accidentally bumped into the arms of the security police.

Rudolf Mildner and other high-ranking German police and security personnel gave several—and conflicting—explanations, after the war, of why they chose to carry out the raid one night and then almost ostentatiously turn a blind eye to the thousands of refugees flocking to railroad stations and the ports. The explanations are characterized by the prominent Nazis' need to shed a positive light on their own deeds—and thus carry little credibility. More trustworthy are explanations based on the realities in Denmark as they presented themselves to the occupying authorities in September and October 1943.

The general unrest in August 1943 was still fresh in the collective memory, and from all parts of Danish society the strongest possible warnings were sent that an attack on the Danish Jews would be perceived as a brutal strike against society at large and thus poison the relationship of trust that was being laboriously rebuilt between Werner Best and the permanent secretaries and between Mildner and the Danish police force. All German authorities who had even the slightest feel for the situation in Denmark were well aware that the action crossed a critical line. This resulted in a significant nervousness about new unrest, while those directly responsible, most crucially Best and Mildner, had a strong desire that their Danish partners perceive them as moderate, if possible even as direct opponents of an action that was imposed on them from Berlin.

While Best would soften the blow to maintain peace, order, and good relations with the permanent secretaries, Mildner was interested in the same thing, because his main task was to rebuild a working relationship with the Danish police after the imposition of martial law on August 29. Mildner was aware that this task was possible only if a renewed cooperation with German security authorities was seen to spare Denmark what was worse. If the worst had already occurred, the Danish police would not reenlist in any cooperation.

While the mass flight increased in terms of numbers, Mildner and representatives of the Danish police met to discuss the resumption of police cooperation. Both Nils Svenningsen and the permanent secretary of the Ministry of Justice, Eivind Larsen, participated in these negotiations. According to the Danish historian Henrik Lundtofte, who has studied the Gestapo operations in Denmark during the occupation, the occupying power was deeply dependent on the more than ten thousand Danish police officers cooperating with far fewer German uniformed police forces. The focus of Danish police was ordinary law enforcement, but for the Germans it was especially crucial in relation to the sabotage and political turmoil they feared would be reignited after the Jewish action. In order

to create a real stimulus for the reluctant Danish side in the negotiations, Mildner offered a mechanism whereby Danish courts under
Danish law could judge the saboteurs whom the Danish police arrested
themselves. The alternative was SS conditions based on the Polish and
Czech model—a specialty Mildner had personally practiced at his previous post. Thus the Danish negotiators were again caught in the dilemma
of rejecting responsibility for the terrible—in this case the Danish police
participating in the hunt for Danish resistance fighters—in return for
the prospect of being able to avert the even worse: German summary
courts, torture, executions, and deportations.[16]

There is little doubt that this perspective weighed heavily in the Germans' considerations and that continued cooperation with the Danish
authorities was more important to the Nazi leadership than the physical extermination of the Danish Jews. This applied to both Mildner and
Best, but both also exercised their authority in a delicate and dangerous balancing act between the intersecting expectations of different
branches of the Nazi leadership in Berlin. It may also have occurred to
the two men that the judgment they would be facing after the war was
lost depended greatly on their behavior in relation to the action against
the Danish Jews.

In Stockholm later in 1943 the Danish journalist and opposition figure Erik Seidenfaden analyzed the German authorities' apparent pas-
sivity in their search for the Danish Jews. Even at that stage the astute
observer grasped the essential elements:

> The times had changed. The easy victories and the war machine's
> invincible efficiency belonged to the past.... Hitler's regents and
> henchmen began to understand how things were going. Some
> understood that they would come to reap what they had sowed,
> and that there was no rescue for them—they might as well play
> the game to the end. It was they who set the Jewish persecution
> in motion in Denmark at the eleventh hour. But there were oth-
> ers who believed in at least a personal rescue through the upcom-
> ing defeat and collapse, and who sought the safe harbors. It was
> those men who in Denmark turned a blind eye to the Jewish Danes'
> escape. A few years earlier, the same men would have done every-
> thing possible to prevent it.

In this way, at this stage of the big war, Denmark came to experience the noticeable symptoms of Nazi Germany's first metamor-

phosis. You could say that the civil war began here. On the one hand, the passive surveillance vessels on the coast and the reluctant Wehrmacht. On the other, continued eager Gestapo raiding teams with their Danish aides and homegrown Nazis, who at the last minute would try to implement some of the atrocities from which under the occupation's peaceful years they had been barred.[17]

Gestapo-Juhl in Helsingør belonged to the latter category; he conducted himself exactly as those fleeing feared that all German officials would: zealously and without mercy. He did not close his eyes or change his ways. As a result he and his small team had the dubious honor of capturing more than half of the total of 190 Jews who were deported from Denmark to Theresienstadt in the days and weeks following the first deportations on October 2, 1943.[18]

The Promise of Adolf Eichmann

Although much appeared chaotic and random, not least for those directly affected as they hovered in fear and uncertainty, and although it can be difficult to accept the logic behind the action, there was a kind of method to the madness. What's more, the occupying power was careful to respect it. Apart from a few "mistakes," particularly in regard to the raid and the shipment of the first captives, "only" the "pure Jews" were deported from Denmark. However, few of those concerned dared trust the German guarantees. The vast majority, like C. L. David and Valdemar Koppel, chose to flee to Sweden at the earliest opportunity.

In London, after another conversation with Niels Bohr, the Danish minister noted that he was "optimistic about the future of Denmark." The nuclear physicist said about the action against the Jews that "the Germans raged over the Swedish intervention." Bohr was aware that at least one ship seemed to have left Copenhagen with Jews on board, and he assumed that it was destined for Poland.[19]

When Svenningsen, in an conversation with Best on October 9, asked if he could make public his written understanding that only "pure Jews" would be arrested, Best refused. It would be "too embarrassing." But Svenningsen had already let the word out and now brought up another problem: Arrests were still occurring in the streets. Could that not be changed? First, it harassed everyone "who even appeared to be Jewish," and then it was a source of unrest. Best was accommodating. It was reprehensible that there were arrests in public places. He would put a stop to it.[20]

On the same day Werner Best also received a letter from his former Danish partner and closest confidant, Erik Scavenius, who had not been heard from since he submitted his resignation to the king on August 29. Now Scavenius broke his self-imposed silence in a letter in which he sought to support efforts to at least get the mistakenly deported sent home immediately. He would "not fail to take this opportunity to tell you how strongly I feel that where people of Jewish descent have been arrested by mistake and deported, it be redressed as soon as possible by them being sent back to Denmark."[21]

The letter is a unique example of Scavenius emerging from the shadows after August 29. Although his inquiry did not lead to the desired result, it helped build up considerable pressure on the occupying power. Denmark had not written off the deportees. On the contrary, it began to be clear that the Danish deportees could not just disappear without causing sharp reactions with significant implications for future Danish-German interaction. A long period of conflict began. It ended only in the spring of 1945, when the war in Europe entered its final stages.

From the very outset, writing the history of the action against the Danish Jews became part of an ongoing fight that began on the eve of the raid and could have vital—if not fatal—consequences for those directly concerned, including the 472 individuals deported to Theresienstadt. Ever since, this history has been the subject of dispute and wrangling. On October 12, after the preliminary rounds, a long telegram from the German consul in Malmö, the Swedish city on the Sound, just across from Copenhagen, arrived at the Foreign Office in Berlin with a first fairly accurate and blunt description of how over the past ten days some five to six thousand Danish Jews had fled to Sweden. What Berlin had so far heard only in roundabout ways and learned through deduction was now in a telegram framed in no uncertain terms. The German Foreign Ministry kept the explosive report at arm's length and sent it quietly on to the Reich security police, who were ultimately responsible for the extermination of the Jews.

At the same time the ministry conducted its own investigation of what had caused the failure of the action against the Danish Jews. Over the following days the Berlin authorities slowly began to unravel the prelude to and implementation of the action in Denmark. Telegrams went back and forth between the various authorities concerned, and Best did his best both to maintain the view of a conditional success, which he had begun in the days right after the operation, and to disclaim any responsibility for what had gone wrong, while simultaneously arguing that half Jews and the very old among the deportees be sent home. Best's reports also reached Goebbels and other hard-liners, who could read that the action in Denmark had led to shock and turmoil in the occupied country and in the rest of Scandinavia.

In a provisional reply to the requests for getting those deported by mistake returned, the office of Ribbentrop declares on October 15 that he agrees with Best because he is "basically in favor of a flexible treatment of the Jewish issue in Denmark." If Best had the lukewarm support of the foreign minister, Himmler was anything but happy, and a few days later he vetoed an expected promotion of Best.

In the Foreign Office in Berlin the matter became a source of irritation, because the Danish authorities kept on raising the issue of those who were deported by mistake as well as the suggestion to let the young and the old "harmless" detainees return. As time went by it was dawning on the authorities in Berlin that Best had issued not only an oral but also a written promise to the Danes guaranteeing that half Jews and Jews married to non-Jews would not be affected. But upon whose authority had the German plenipotentiary in Denmark issued such a document—and why had Berlin not seen a copy of the October 5 letter now being discreetly circulated by Danish authorities to those who asked?

On October 28 a senior diplomat from the ministry called Best and demanded that he account for what he had actually promised the Danes, who continued to claim that they had concrete commitments to rely on. Best had to confess to having furnished the Danes with the said promises—and in writing.

The reaction from Berlin was not long in coming. Best was called home for immediate consultations. He had to try to explain to the Reich security authorities and to Adolf Eichmann personally how he could have given such promises without a mandate and without informing the competent authority—that is, Eichmann. In a few days it looked as if Best had overplayed his hand and could not get out of the predicament he had brought on by his double games with Danish and German authorities. For reasons that are not clear, it ended up being Adolf Eichmann who traveled to Copenhagen, where on November 2 at Dagmar-

Above, the rescue of Scandinavian concentration camp prisoners from the collapsing Reich in the spring of 1945 was a nerve-racking and dramatic humanitarian action, conducted in close collaboration by the Swedish Red Cross and Danish authorities. The key vehicles were the white buses and, of course, the volunteers driving them.

Below, Dr. Adolph Meyer and his close family shortly after their arrival in Sweden. Beside him, from left to right, are Kis Marcus, his daughter; an unidentified Swedish woman; Mayer's sister-in-law Mary Goldschmidt; and Else Hannover, his daughter and the wife of Knud Hannover, the younger brother of Poul Hannover.

By September 1 the Danish legation in Stockholm had already declared that it would undertake all costs in connection with the Danish refugees in Sweden, making it explicit that this social guarantee included also stateless refugees coming through Denmark. With the mass exodus in October these costs exploded, and the Swedish government intervened with credits. By the end of the war, these credits amounted to some 30 million kroner. Another credit was opened to finance and equip the Danish Brigade, set up with Danish volunteers, the accumulated costs amounting to 25 million kroner by the end of the war. Though Denmark offered to cover these costs after her liberation, the Swedish government in 1945 decided not to reclaim the 50 million kroner spent on refugees from Denmark.   Royal Library (above)
Private family collection (below)

hus he had long conversations with, among others, Best and Mildner. On the same day Günther Pancke arrived in Copenhagen at Himmler's initiative to take up the position as the senior SS and police leader in Denmark, side by side with Werner Best and General Hanneken.

What we know about the conversation at Dagmarhus that afternoon comes partly from a short telegram from Best of November 3 with a brief summary of the conclusions sent to the German Foreign Office, and partly from a more detailed report the ministry sent Best on November 5 after Eichmann returned and after follow-up discussions in Berlin with the German Red Cross.

Best's summary if astonishing. In almost all respects he had apparently succeeded in convincing Eichmann of his views:

1) Jews older than 60 shall henceforth not be detained and deported.

2) Half-Jews and Jews living in mixed marriage who have been detained and deported shall be released and returned to Denmark.

3) All Jews deported from Denmark shall remain in Theresienstadt and be visited by representatives of the Danish Central administration and Danish Red Cross as soon as possible.

What's more, Eichmann confirmed his decisions in a classified document to the Foreign Office, which was then forwarded to Best:

RSHA SS-Obersturmbannführer Eichmann has approved implementation of proposals. . . . However, proposal 1 is to be understood as follows: Jews older than 60 shall <u>henceforth</u> not be detained and deported. Those already deported remain where they are. Regarding Half-Jews and Jews living in mixed marriage, mentioned in proposal 2, individual examination will be actuated, and a release and recirculation to Denmark is only to take place if irreproachably determined that in fact Half-Jews or Jews in mixed marriage. With respect to proposal 3: RSH principally willing to let Jews living in Theresienstadt and having been deported from Denmark be visited by representatives of Danish Central Administration and Red Cross. Visits before spring 1944 however undesirable. Furthermore, Jews in Theresienstadt will be allowed to communicate with Denmark, whereas consignments of food parcels to Jews from Denmark are <u>initially</u> undesired.[22]

These commitments provided a platform for the continuation of the very exceptional treatment of the Danish Jews. The struggle over the following eighteen months to keep Adolf Eichmann firmly to his November assurances was no less dramatic than the process surrounding the escape of the Jews. Danish authorities fought an uphill battle for the Danish detainees in Theresienstadt and other German concentration camps, and from the last weeks of 1944 convoys were sent to some of the camps to rescue Danish detainees. When Germany's protracted collapse reached a critical phase in the first months of 1945, these efforts were combined with those of others who were working to bring the Danish and Norwegian prisoners home from the German concentration camps before it was too late. These efforts succeeded to a great extent when a dramatic operation led by the head of the Swedish Red Cross, Count Folke Bernadotte, who had managed in the first months of 1945 to negotiate with Heinrich Himmler and other senior Nazi officials the release of thousands of Scandinavian prisoners out of German camps—including 423 of the 472 Danish Jews who were originally interned in Theresienstadt.[23]

The Nazi Hesitation

What ultimately stopped the extermination of Jews on Danish soil was the expressed and entrenched Danish opposition to the project. This, together with our insight into the cynical trade-off between the different policy objectives that were guiding the leading Nazis in respect to the occupation of Denmark and action against the Danish Jews, opens a troubling perspective: Those responsible shrank back when they faced a clear choice between pursuing their overarching interest in Denmark or persecuting the Danish Jews. The many protests from high and low, from church and business, from politicians and state secretaries, confirmed what Best and his people had long known and told Berlin: There was a deeply rooted aversion in the Danish population to the idea of introducing special laws or measures against the Jews. Since 1933 the Danish government had forcefully rejected any attempt to create a divide between the Danes based on descent. Rather, those who attacked democracy had been excluded from the national "us," while the leading politicians succeeded in equating the nation with the values its social order rested on. This adherence to humanism had become a bulwark supported by a very solid majority of Danes.

In Sweden shortly afterward, Erik Seidenfaden considered the reasons for the strong Danish reaction and provided a first, well-considered explanation that still largely holds true. It was, he wrote before the end of the year, "the first time you saw a whole people rise up as one against the disgrace of racial persecution. The special Danish triad showed its strength in this crucial situation. The underground organizations had their apparatus in order, the Danish administration's well-preserved machinery functioned optimally and with the right attitude, and the population's widespread passive resistance demonstrated that the ambiguity of the policy of cooperation had not undermined its attitude toward the concrete requirements of humanity and love thy neighbor. The unarmed people rebelled against power with all kinds of tricks, with adventurous artifice and disguise, with ingenuity and courage—but first and foremost with solidarity fueled by deep indignation."[24]

By completely rejecting the ideas that excluded the Jews from the national "us," Denmark deprived the Nazis of the fig leaf they needed to justify discrimination and legitimize the deed.

This rejection explains not only the people's spontaneous support of their Jewish countrymen, but also the Nazi hesitation that made the rescue possible. And this is where the troubling perspective arises: Would something similar have been possible elsewhere? Could the rejection of the logic of the Jewish extermination have stopped the project in other occupied countries—even in Germany itself? The answer is yes—of course. But the point is not to moralize that people in other occupied countries could "just" have rejected persecution of the Jews, or that the responsibility rests on each individual who didn't do so. The history of the Holocaust tells a different story, and the terms of occupation, local conditions, and much else differed radically from place to place and over time, making the situation unique in each case. The special Danish example cannot be used to reproach others who experienced the German occupation under far worse conditions than Denmark.

However, there is another—and in the current perspective, important—lesson to be learned: Politics makes a difference. It was not the Danes' reaction that made the Nazi leadership bend. It was the expectation of that reaction and the certainty that it—or something worse—would surely be forthcoming.

Statistics and Fatalities

The question of what the Danish helpers knew or thought about the real risk has been thoroughly discussed over the past seventy years. Opinions are divided, and there is no reason to believe that the helpers had any kind of a common view. The most thorough historical study finds that "there is evidence to suggest that there were many who were aware that they were not performing an extremely dangerous form of resistance work, and that this forms part of a nuanced understanding of why thousands of people dared to launch themselves into illegal aid work in those October days."[25]

Historians base this assessment mainly on the case law, already beginning to accumulate in October 1943, which showed that even fishermen who were caught in the act escaped relatively unscathed. Some who helped organize the transports also subsequently concluded that "for the Jewish transports the boat was confiscated, but no more." It was totally different if there were saboteurs or other resistance fighters among the refugees, and there is evidence that they may have impersonated Jews in order to get across. The experienced helpers distinguished between the transports of resistance fighters, for which there were severe penalties, and aiding the Jews, an activity that was punished much more lightly.

But there are also examples proving these generalities wrong. When a police officer fled on the night of October 9, his wife subsequently explained to a colleague that the reason was that he had helped Jewish refugees across and feared being shot by the Germans. His nervousness turned into panic after he heard that the German police had arrested twelve fishermen from Snekkersten, including the parish constable, for helping Jews to Sweden. The police officer who wrote up the report on his colleague's fear of being shot coolly noted, "whether or not these fears were unfounded." Still, the point actually lies in the very fear and uncertainty. In the rumors and half-truths. In the terror and the sleepless nights. In the effects of imagination and bad nerves. In the concern for family and future. Many had probably been clear-eyed enough eventually to arrive at a fairly realistic picture of the risk, and cold-blooded enough to wager that things would probably not go so wrong. But others did not have that overview or that fearlessness: They acted in spite of their uncertainty, and they overcame their own fears.

However, even if the risk was small, it did exist. The very same night that Adolph Meyer was finally able to rest safely in a real bed in his colleague's house in Höganäs, shots were heard from the coastal police office in Tårbæk Harbor, north of Copenhagen. Two sergeants went down to see what had happened. They found a German security police officer there who explained that he and a colleague had gone to Tårbæk after receiving a message that there was a boat in the port with Jews ready to depart. The German police soon realized that Jews had been led aboard the fishing boat *Matador*. They fired some shots in the air and shouted: "It is the German police!" A firefight ensued with the Danish helpers, during which a young student, Claus Christian Heilesen, was fatally struck by a bullet.[26]

It is true that statistics were with the fugitives and their helpers. Only a few were caught and even fewer were killed. Even the Jews who were caught and deported from Denmark got exceptional treatment, and the vast majority survived. But statistics were of no help to Claus Heilesen at that moment in the port of Tårbæk. And no matter how rare the instances of death being the price of their activities, both the fugitives and their helpers had every reason to believe that they were risking their lives.

The Danish Exception

In 1996, Daniel Goldhagen published an extensive study of the general public's knowledge of and involvement in the implementation of the Holocaust. *Hitler's Willing Excecutioners* is a disturbing account because Goldhagen shows how many Germans were implicated in the nefarious project. But it is especially disturbing because it reveals chauvinism's roots in Germany, and how appallingly widespread the thinking was that led to the mass extermination of fellow citizens. It shows how deeply the problem was rooted in the general population, who allowed themselves to put so much credence in the systematic description of the Jews as a threatening foreign body that they lost their basic compassion and empathy—the starting points for all peaceful coexistence. Goldhagen makes little mention of the few exceptions where the Holocaust failed—such as Bulgaria and Denmark. His focus is on the general picture and the underlying driving forces, and he concludes: "The destruction of the Jews, once it had become achievable, took priority even over safeguarding Nazism's very existence." Goldhagen points out that this priority was so high that the extermination continued to the bitter end—long after it was clear that the Third Reich would be defeated.[27]

The German historian Peter Longerich has a somewhat different interpretation. He agrees with many of Goldhagen's observations, but gives different answers when it comes to what the German population knew—or avoided knowing. *Davon haben wir Nichts gewusst!* ("Of this we had no knowledge!") is the apt title of Longerich's 2006 study of the Nazi propaganda against the Jews and the public knowledge in Germany of the mass murder. In Longerich's interpretation the Jewish extermination was an open secret. All the elements were commonly known, and anyone had the opportunity to recognize mass murder as the objective, and to know about the scope of the genocide. But that still does not mean that most Germans knew what was going on. Longerich believes that most closed their eyes and ears and shied away from seeing the scale of the criminality, and many protected themselves against the sense that insight entailed responsibility. The closer the Nazis came to defeat, the more their propaganda sought to promote a sense of collective guilt and responsibility. "Of this we had no knowledge" is an assertion that reveals more than it denies: It was clear that something was going on, and that everyone suspected the worst. But Longerich's point is that the majority wanted anything but the transformation of their fears into certain knowledge: "Between knowledge and ignorance, there was a broad gray area marked by rumors and half-truths, fantasy, forced and self-imposed limitations in communication. It lies between not wanting to know and not being able to understand."[28]

The history of the Danish Jews in many ways differs from that of the Jews in Germany, and the account of their escape can shed only limited light on developments within the Third Reich. Still, one persistent question remains: Did special historical circumstances make it possible for Hitler and other leading Nazis to mislead an entire people so that eventually, with regard to the Jews and other minorities, they went astray and allowed the heinous oppression of their universal humanity? Or did these special historical circumstances rather in their own right create a brief rupture in civilization's control of the individual, lifting the lid and allowing people to live out their inherent brutality, xenophobia, and selfishness? In other words, are human beings fundamentally good but weak? Or are we brutal by nature, checked and controlled only by civilization?

On two important points the story of the Danish Jews supports the first interpretation.

First there is the uplifting experience that the Danish population, whose political leaders soon realized the terrible consequences of the totalitarian mind-set, and who consistently refused to let it gain a foothold in national politics, spontaneously turned against the injustice exercised against their countrymen. The vast majority were completely alienated by the idea of separating Jews from the rest of society, seeing them as an explicit part of the "us," as part of the nation. Leni Yahil put it that although the Danish people, its leaders and authorities, had placed solidarity with the Jews up front from the beginning of the occupation, "the rescue operation nevertheless came as a surprise—no one could have foreseen that in the hour of need the mass of the nation would give this identification the full force of action. No other example had ever been known"[29]

It is certainly true that among the Danes, more or less innocent prejudices against the Jews flourished, as some of Bergstrøm's comments also reveal. But anti-Semitism had not been allowed to take root, and most of the countless Danes who in the crucial days in September and October 1943 helped fellow citizens, did not see these fugitives as Jews. They saw them as distressed countrymen, as families harmed by injustice and misery, as elderly people, women, and children who were experiencing what no one ought to experience; as neighbors, colleagues, and relatives, as countrymen who through no fault of their own were suddenly hit by a crime instigated by the occupying power. Therefore they perceived it as both a human and a national duty to take personal responsibility, to assist in the exodus—without regard to personal consequences. And when the number who helped was so massive, and those who pulled the other way were so few, it was a reification of this strong connection between compassionate instincts and national duty. Among the rescue's greatest heroes were the political leaders who through a decade in which it would have been easy and popular to talk about "them" and "us" had the courage to stick with the fundamentals of democracy: that all citizens are subject to the same laws and entitled to claim the same justice.

The story also sheds light on the question of whether the executioners were seduced or freed from the shackles of civilization. On the occupying power's side a number of prominent Nazis contributed to making the flight possible. Each of them had their own opportunistic reasons, and it is not difficult to show how any of them could see the advantage of appearing as one who had tried to mitigate the blow. Yet it is remarkable that both the leading German Nazis in Copenhagen and their superiors in Berlin shied away from a consistent implementation of the persecution of the Danish Jews.

We are not talking about a group of especially "soft" Nazis but of men who all bore their personal share of responsibility for monstrosities elsewhere in occupied Europe. The logic that softened the blow against the Danish Jews found its way up to the very top of the Nazi leadership, which even on issuing the order mentioned reservations to avoid a perceived public reaction. Why? What made the Danish Jews something special, and how was it possible for Best to persuade even Adolf Eichmann to spare them? What made Denmark an exception?

The answer is undeniable: The Danish Jews were protected by their compatriots' consistent engagement. Hannah Arendt, in her 1964 book on the trial of Adolf Eichmann, wrote: "Politically and psychologically, the most interesting aspect of this incident is perhaps the role played by the German authorities in Denmark, their obvious sabotage of orders from Berlin. It is the only case we know of in which the Nazis met with open native resistance, and the result seems to have been that those exposed to it changed their minds. They themselves apparently no longer looked upon the extermination of a whole people as a matter of course. They had met resistance based on principle, and their 'toughness' had melted like butter in the sun, they had even been able to show a few timid beginnings of genuine courage."[30]

Today, Hannah Arendt's observations can be taken even further, as it is clear that the orders from Berlin were also softened in relation to the Jews in Denmark. It turns out that even leading Nazis in Berlin and Copenhagen needed the local understanding and support that would give the crime an aura of necessity and justice. Without this even the most hardened Nazis shrank back. Public participation was therefore not only a practical condition for implementation of the project; its support was also a prerequisite for the leading Nazis' daring to set the atrocities in motion. Even these experienced Nazis with blood on their hands could not or would not go all the way alone. Even they depended on the understanding and support of the project, which was absolutely missing in Denmark.

Without it they faltered, and extermination of the Jews came to appear as a goal that had to be weighed against other, more practical considerations, particularly the further cooperation with Denmark and the maintenance of essential supplies from the country.

The leading Nazis' complicity in making the flight possible suggests that they were led by practical and opportunistic considerations. In the Danish context, continued interest in cooperation with the "model protectorate" weighed more heavily than the desire to annihilate the Jews.

Paul Hennig was the most centrally placed Dane in the preparation and implementation of the action against the Danish Jews. As a manager from 1941 in the Danish Nazi Party's "Central Office for Race Policy," he was an avid anti-Semite and was given the responsibility of separating Aryans from Jews—which he acknowledged was a difficult task in Denmark. In September 1943 Hennig was permanently employed by the Gestapo at Dagmarhus. In this position he took part in the raid on the Jewish community office to obtain its membership lists.

On the night of the action Hennig was responsible for the cross-examination of the detainees in order to single out half Jews who were not supposed to be deported. During the following days he was engaged in the efforts to track down and arrest those fleeing, both with the help of informers and through direct actions. Thus he and his colleague Fritz Renner were responsible for the October 9 shooting of the student Claus Christian Heilesen while he was in the process of helping a group of refugees board a boat in the port of Tårbæk.

After the liberation Paul Hennig succeeded in staying hidden until December 1945, when he was arrested in South Jutland. In 1947 he was sentenced to death for his part in the action against the Jews. After an appeal to the Supreme Court, Hennig was sentenced to life imprisonment. He served until October 1956, when he was released. Private collection

The senior Nazis' involvement was not driven by personal necessity. Hatred of the *different* was not some primordial force that was unleashed. Rather, it was a political convenience that could be used as needed, and in most occupied territories the Nazis followed their interest in pursuing this with disastrous consequences. But without a sounding board the strategy did not work. It could be countered by simple means—even by a country that was defenseless and occupied—by the persistent national rejection of the assumption that there was a "Jewish problem."

The idea is both edifying and terrifying. When it is so easy to arouse national chauvinism, it is not because we all ultimately fear and despise those who are different. It is because from time to time we allow political leaders to use suspicion of "the other" as their political tool.

Allan Hannover ends his diary with a few notes on the everyday life of the family in Västerås. He tells how they move to the more practical hotel, and then in January 1944 on to their own apartment. On October 15, less than two weeks after the crossing, his little sister, Mette, entered the local public school, and Allan started school four days later. The family liked to go to the movies and watch the American films that had been banned in occupied Copenhagen.

Allan's grandfather, Adolph Meyer, traveled with his sister-in-law, Mary, to Jonsered, just outside Göteborg, where they were accommodated in Skogshem, a large summer home that belonged to his wealthy cousin. In the following months several of Meyer's children and their families gathered there and stayed for the rest of the war. Adolph Meyer was licensed and worked as a physician for the many refugees in Göteborg.

Poul Hannover continued his involvement in the businesses of ASEA and went all around Sweden. He was also active as a volunteer in the Danish Brigade, a military corps with volunteers from the Danish refugee community, established in Sweden to provide the Danish politicians with a nascent army. Hannover spent the last period up to the liberation with the brigade in Tingsrud. Poul returned to Denmark with the Danish Brigade; Inger and Mette soon followed, while Allan stayed until June 1945 and finished his middle-school exams in Sweden. On their return to Søholm Park the family found their house unharmed. Friends and neighbors had emptied it of valuables but maintained what was necessary, and according to Allan's report, "the only visible sign that the

Germans had been after us were marks on father's old desk, where a bayonet had tried to open a drawer that did not exist."

The Marcus family stayed with their friends for three months in Ljungsbro, where the children went to a Swedish school. In January 1944 they moved to Jonsered, where they could live with Adolph Meyer and other family members. Dorte and Palle entered the Danish school in Göteborg, while Gunnar Marcus found employment with the Oceanographic Institute. Like his brother-in-law he joined the Danish Brigade, and on May 5, 1945, he returned with the brigade to Denmark as a truck driver.

Kis and the children followed a month later, and the family moved back into their house, which had been rented out. Gunnar also reclaimed his rented business premises. The landlord had sold the stock and sent the proceeds to Sweden, but had kept the office space, from which Gunnar was able to resume his business.

Many years later both Palle and Dorte Marcus told me that for the rest of their lives their parents didn't want to talk about the escape or about their time in Sweden. It was like a parenthesis, a sequence of events both they and their children lived with but rarely touched on. The diaries, completed during the first days in exile, were stored away and kept in a safe place—but the entire experience was not a subject of conversation within the family. The family's close friendship with Erik and Else Nyegaard dwindled away in the years after the war, and the Marcus family never returned to the places and people they encountered in Sweden. Palle Marcus and his older sister remember little from the flight, but they—like Allan Hannover—have kept the records, which run like a red thread through this book.

The librarian of the Jewish community, Josef Fischer, was arrested on October 6 on the road between Helsingør and Gilleleje with his wife and daughters Edith and Harriet. The whole family was deported to Theresienstadt but returned home at war's end. The third daughter, Ella Fischer, saved herself, reaching Sweden on October 8. She had no connections in Sweden but found a job in January 1944 when Bonnier's publishing house employed her in their book club.[1]

The cashier of the Jewish community, Axel Hertz, who had asked the Gestapo by what right they requisitioned the membership list, arrived in Limhamn on a fishing boat from Copenhagen early in the morning of October 10.

After his arrival on the Swedish mainland Herbert Willie Levysohn was reunited with his mother and other close relatives, who all went on to Stockholm. He wrote his account there in the last days of October 1943. According to the Swedish immigration authorities Levysohn carried eight thousand Danish kroner in cash, which he supplemented in Stockholm with his monthly salary of two hundred kroner from employment at a warehouse. After the war he took over the family business, succeeding his father, who died in March 1944 in Theresienstadt.

Permanent Secretary Einar Cohn arrived in Sweden on October 13 and immediately proceeded to Stockholm, following his wife. He gave two Swedish references on his entry form: Permanent Secretary Dag Hammarskjöld and the governor of the National Bank of Sweden, Ivar Rooth. Hammarskjöld was later to become the second secretary-general of the United Nations.[2]

C. L. David reached Sweden safely and returned to Copenhagen after the war, where he resumed his business. In 1945 he donated his unique art collection—which among other things included one of the world's finest assemblages of Islamic art—to the C. L. David Foundation and Collection. At his death in 1960 David bequeathed his summerhouse, Marienborg, to the Danish government. Marienborg has since served successive Danish prime ministers as their official residence.

Henrik Kauffmann remained in Washington until the end of the war as an independent envoy for "free Denmark." His contact with James Wise of the World Jewish Congress in Washington later led to an agreement with Jewish organizations in the United States on a shared fund-raising drive that before the end of 1943 had reached fifty thousand dollars. At the same time the campaign helped to put Denmark, the Danish Jews—and Kauffmann himself—powerfully on the map with the American public. Thus the activities of the envoy for "free Denmark" succeeded in achieving his most important goal: making the American public aware that Denmark stood firmly on the side of the free world. By their successful escape the Danish Jews helped their country immensely in this regard. Nothing contributed more to the general impression in the United States that Denmark rejected Nazism than the fact that it rejected the persecution of its Jewish citizens. And nothing cemented this reputation more strongly than the fact that the escape was made possible not by the Danish government but by the Danish people.

Kauffmann was appointed a minister without portfolio in the liberation government, and he represented his country at the San Francisco conference in 1945 where the United Nations was created. Subsequently he returned to Washington, where he remained Denmark's ambassador until his retirement in 1958.

Paul Kanstein left Denmark as he desired at the end of October 1943 to take up a position in northern Italy. He felt that what he had stood for—and taught his boss, Werner Best—had been undone by the state of emergency on August 29 and the action against the Jews. Rudolf Mildner had to leave the post of chief of the security police in Denmark in January 1944 after just three months of service. But it was not, as often interpreted, to punish him because of the failure of the action against the Jews. The reason was rather Mildner's dislike of Himmler and Hitler's requirement at the time to launch "counterterror" in Denmark. Mildner was not sensitive, but he was a good policeman, who thought that such counterterror would strengthen rather than weaken the Danish resistance. At the end of the war he was the deputy chief of the security police in Vienna. During the Nuremberg trials Mildner was a witness for the prosecution in the case against one of the organizers of the extermination of the Jews, Ernst Kaltenbrunner. Mildner was released from custody in 1949 and disappeared soon after escaping prosecution—probably to Argentina.[3]

Werner Best was sentenced to death in 1948 by the district court in Copenhagen. It did not help that Scavenius testified in his favor; in fact, it probably had the opposite effect. Police psychiatrists found Best highly intelligent and a psychopath to a minor or moderate degree. In prison Best wrote almost maniacally in his own defense. He felt very unfairly treated and portrayed himself as the rescuer of Denmark and the Danish Jews. Best claimed to have waged a war on two fronts: against armed resistance in Denmark and against other German authorities to fend off much tougher repression. Indeed, this self-image, which was the one Best fought hard to uphold, is widely reflected in the common perception of his role, not least in regard to the persecution of the Danish Jews. It seems as if this allowed Best to displace the real purpose of his presence in Denmark as part of the criminal Nazi executive. An almost whimpering appeal runs through his self-defense to take his moderate policy in Denmark for real and credit it to his personal effort—though at no time in the postwar period did he distance himself from the Nazism he was part of. Werner Best aspired to be respected as a "good Nazi"—and never seems to have realized the fundamental contradiction inherent in his claim.

In 1949 the Supreme Court acquitted him, on appeal, of having launched the action against the Jews, but sentenced him to twelve years' imprisonment for his part in the murders of prominent Danes. In 1951 Best was pardoned and expelled from Denmark. In 1952 he settled in Essen as a legal counsel and began to advise the old SS-Kameraden and the Hugo Stinnes Industrie und Handel GmbH. In 1969 he was charged as the principal and co-perpetrator of the murder of ten thousand men in Poland; however, he was then conditionally discharged on grounds of fragile health. Neither the main proceedings nor a later retrial was initiated, while his capacity to act in court was only established in April 1989. But Best died in June 1989, before his criminal past managed to catch up with him.[4]

G. F. Duckwitz remained after the war for a while as a trade counselor in Denmark, where he was hailed as the savior of the Danish Jews and as a much-needed "good German." He got credit for warning of the impending action and for a marked lack of zeal in the ensuing manhunt—an image he actively sought to consolidate in his own accounts. But as a conservative German patriot and member of the Nazi Party, Duckwitz never distanced himself from Werner Best, and he kept defending his former boss. He was also known to share the contemporary Nazi stereotypes about Jews, at least up until the beginning of the war. Nevertheless, historical research generally accepts that Duckwitz did indeed play a key role, claiming he was driven by a personal conviction that the action was a crime and that he had the civil courage to stand against it.

Duckwitz had established contact with the organized German opposition, but this was never disclosed. In the 1950s he entered the Foreign Office of the Federal Republic and from 1955 to 1958 he was the first German ambassador to Denmark. From 1967 to 1970 he was state secretary under Foreign Minister Willy Brandt and in this capacity was deeply involved in the development of his Ostpolitik, which culminated with the signing of the Polish-German treaty in 1970. When Duckwitz died in 1973, Chancellor Brandt said to Annemarie Duckwitz that her late husband "had secured for himself a lasting place in our memory by his humanity, his integrity and his friendly determination."[5]

General Hanneken was discharged in January 1945 from his command of the Wehrmacht in Denmark, accused of corruption. It is unclear, though possible, that the accusations were planted by the SS as part of a power struggle. After the war he went to trial for war crimes in Denmark and in 1948 was sentenced to eight years in prison in district court. The following year, however, he was acquitted by the Supreme

Court and deported to the Federal Republic, where he remained until his retirement, serving as an economic adviser to German industrial companies. He died in 1981 at the age of ninety-one.

Immanuel Talleruphuus, who was the Marcus and Hannover families' first contact in Falster, was an underwriter from Copenhagen. He survived the war and died in 1968, at the age of sixty-five.

Sven Otto Nielsen, the young resistance fighter who helped the Hannover and Marcus families in Grønsund, but who would not go to Sweden because he thought there was still work to be done, involved himself a few weeks later in the resistance group Holger Danske, where he became a leading member, known as "John." It is conceivable that it was meeting with Erik Nyegaard in Grønsund that drew him into the organized resistance. In civilian life he was a teacher at the Skovshoved elementary school north of Copenhagen. He participated in a series of daring sabotage actions. On December 9, 1943, he and a friend were stabbed by a female traitor. During the escape from the Gestapo he was badly wounded, captured, and subjected to brutal interrogation at Dagmarhus, but he revealed nothing. He was later transferred to the Vestre Prison, where he was incarcerated for several months without medical treatment for his injuries. In April 1944 he was sentenced to death by a German court-martial, and on April 27 he was executed in Ryvangen.

Erik Nyegaard was in Denmark throughout the rest of the occupation and maintained his relationship with Holger Danske, though it is unclear what role he played. His villa on the Strandvej, where the Marcus family spent their first nights as refugees, was blown up in October 1944 by the Germans after the renowned freedom fighter Bent Faurschou-Hviid, known as "the Flame," was surrounded there and committed suicide with a vial of cyanide.

Erik Scavenius exercised no influence on Danish politics after August 29, 1943. His last action in government service was on May 5, 1945, immediately after the German capitulation, and while there still was shooting in the streets, when he set off on foot toward Amalienborg Palace to receive his formal dismissal from King Christian. He knew that responsibility for the cooperation that the politicians had wanted, which was now deeply resented, would be placed on his shoulders, and that many of the armed resistance fighters who were in the process of consolidating their positions in Copenhagen considered him a traitor. That is not how he perceived his role, and shortly after the war he published a book in which without equivocation he accounted for "the policy of negotiating during the occupation." It was, in Scavenius's own words, a policy that was "determined by the difficulties of the moment. The goal was to avoid disaster, and the policy would be the same regardless of who you thought would win. . . . My policy was justified until the day Germany was finished."

Throughout his long retirement Scavenius maintained personal contact with Werner Best, who never tried to hide his personal admiration for the Danish statesman, whom he regarded almost as a father.

Scavenius pursued realpolitik to its extremes, and in his vision Denmark's perpetual closeness to Germany dominated. Here, no room was left for more lofty considerations—not even those most urgently warranted. At the same time, he drew a clear line in regard to concessions that could and should not be made, and it is impossible not to give him part of the credit for the survival of the Danish Jews. Scavenius died in 1962 at the age of eighty-five without having been forgiven by his people and without overcoming his bitterness at not being recognized for having saved his country twice at critical junctures during the two world wars.[6]

Nils Svenningsen retained his position as head of the permanent secretaries right through to the liberation of Denmark, and he remained in office under the liberation government in 1945, although he was a red flag to the resistance movement. Later that year he was sent on a kind of retreat as minister to Stockholm, where he had been born. Few expected to see more of him in the forefront of Danish diplomacy. However, they underestimated the assertive official, who in 1951 made a spectacular comeback as director of the Danish Foreign Service, a post he retained for an additional ten years.

Svenningsen enjoyed a long retirement, during which he vigorously defended the policy of negotiating—in tandem with his master and colleague, Erik Scavenius. He remained an inveterate critic of the armed resistance and those who had chosen what he until his death in 1985 considered "the easy solutions."

Both Erik Scavenius and Nils Svenningsen were caught in what the American diplomat George Kennan during his posting in 1940 to occupied Prague described as "one of the oldest and most sticky humanistic dilemmas" consisting of the choice between "a limited cooperation with evil in order to alleviate ultimately its consequences" as opposed to "an uncompromising, heroic, but suicidal fight against it." Kennan saw that everyone who "participated one way or another would end up being impaled on the horns of this dilemma." Kennan, of course, was referring to Czechoslovakia after Munich—but his observation is equally true for Denmark during the German occupation.[7]

King Christian X lived to regain full constitutional powers at the liberation on May 5, 1945, and to install a liberation government supported by both the armed resistance and the old politicians. The king was physically weak but more popular than ever. He died two years later in April 1947, at the age of seventy-six.

The king had managed at one and the same time to fully back the policy of cooperation with the Germans while standing as a popular symbol of Denmark's dream of freedom and the will to resist. The king did not distance himself from Scavenius or his policies even though the two men vehemently disagreed at many places along the way. King Christian did not leave notes from their last conversation when Scavenius, as acting prime minister, arrived at Amalienborg on liberation day to be dismissed. According to Scavenius the king remarked: "Our achievement after all was that Copenhagen was not bombed, and that the country was not destroyed." That short phrase says it all. The "after all" refers to the lack of struggle and therefore to lost honor. But it also serves to highlight the crucial point that democracy had passed its toughest test.

The escape of the Danish Jews happened because they acted on their own initiative when warned of the impending threat against them. But how did they even get the opportunity? The hesitation of the Nazi leadership in Berlin and of their officials in Denmark was caused primarily by the expectation of the Danish reaction and its negative ramifications for both the "model protectorate" and the continued shipment of Danish provisions to Germany. What made the escape possible, therefore, before anything else, was the fact that Danish society as a whole had so quickly, so consistently, and with such determination turned against the very idea underpinning the persecution of their fellow countrymen. This attitude was anchored in the preceding ten years of antitotalitarian Danish politics. The miraculous escape of the Danish Jews cannot be understood outside that political context.

The way in which the civilian population assisted both the Danish and stateless Jews in October 1943 remains without precedent or parallel. Indeed, two years before, in the summer of 1941, only a few had risen up to defend the many arrested Communists. Societal inclusiveness did

Volunteers in the Danish Brigade. It was not an obvious choice for middle-aged family men like Poul Hannover and Gunnar Marcus to sign up as volunteers for the Danish Brigade in Sweden. But there was a war, and they both volunteered and served as drivers. The upper photograph shows Gunnar Marcus, second from the right, at a shooting exercise. Below, both men are together with the other drivers of the brigade immediately before they were deployed to Denmark on May 5, 1945. Poul Hannover is standing beside his brother Knud in the back row, fourth and third from the left; Gunnar Marcus is seated in the middle row, third from the left.

By April 1945 the Danish Brigade had three thousand men under arms, corresponding to almost one-fifth of the registered Danish refugees in Sweden. It played an important political role and could, as the largest standing force under the Danish politicians' command, have come to play a crucial military role if Denmark's liberation had developed less peacefully than it did.

Formed after August 1943 by agreement between leading Danish and Swedish Social Democratic politicians, the brigade was modeled on the exiled Norwegian police force, which was being developed to assure the Norwegian government in exile of a loyal force as a counterweight against the Nazi-infected Norwegian police. In all three Scandinavian countries leading Social Democrats were deeply concerned that if there should be a chaotic final battle on Danish or Norwegian soil, the elected politicians would be left without legitimate means of power. At the same time they feared that the Communist-controlled factions of the armed resistance would be able to obtain permanent political concessions following the German capitulation, particularly if the liberation of Denmark or Norway were carried out by the Red Army. In this situation a well-trained and well-equipped brigade under the command of professional and loyal officers would constitute a decisive power center for the restoration of democracy.

It was an immense relief to all that no such situations developed—but the possibility had in no way been excluded when the brothers-in-law Hannover and Marcus put on their uniforms.　　　　　Private family collection

not extend to those who were perceived to be hostile to democracy. Conversely, the escape of the Danish Jews was due to the penetration deep into the population of the idea that everyone who declared themselves part of democracy belonged to the national community. Because of this a great majority of Danes knew that the intimidation of one individual is a threat to the entire society. In October 1943 they acted upon that insight.

NOTES

Author's Note

1. Jespersen, *Rytterkongen*, p. 441f.

Prologue

1. Kis Marcus's journal is privately owned; a copy has been provided for this book. The handwritten journal, which begins on September 26 in Charlottenlund and ends in Sweden on October 14, is apparently based on contemporary entries that were transcribed by October 14. Her journal resembles that of her brother-in-law, Poul Hannover, and the two of them seem to have glanced at each other's entries before they parted ways in Ystad on October 3. In translating this and other contemporary diary notes from their original Danish, minor editorial adjustments have been made to ease the reading and provide necessary context.

2. Poul Hannover's journal is privately owned. A copy has been provided for this book. The journal begins sporadically in Charlottenlund on September 26 and ends in Sweden on October 14. His journal resembles that of his sister-in-law, Kis Marcus, and the two of them seem to have glanced at each other's entries before they parted ways in Ystad on October 3.

Chapter One: Sunday, September 26: The Last Day of the Past

1. *Rigsdagstidende*, Landstinget, January 26, 1939, column 443f.
2. Rünitz, *Danmark og de jødiske flygtninge*, pp. 114ff.
3. Lidegaard, *Kampen om Danmark*, pp. 110ff.; Åmark: *Att bo granna med ondskan*, pp. 467ff.
4. Jespersen, *Rytterkongen*, p. 393f.
5. Ibid, pp. 440f.
6. Ibid.
7. *Gads leksikon om dansk besættelsestid*, pp. 500ff.
8. Jespersen, *Rytterkongen*, pp. 448ff.
9. *Gads leksikon om dansk besættelsestid*, pp. 140ff.; Vilhjálmsson, *Medaljens bagside*.

10. Jespersen, *Rytterkongen*, pp. 449ff.

11. Longerich, *Holocaust*, p. 400.

12. Lidegaard, *Kampen om Danmark*, pp. 300ff.; Jespersen, *Rytterkongen*, pp. 452ff.

13. Arendt, *Eichmann in Jerusalem*, pp. 154ff.; Yahil, *The Rescue of Danish Jewry*, pp. 82ff.

14. Wannsee Protocol, January 20, 1942, quoted in Longerich, *Holocaust*, pp. 305ff; Kirchhoff, "Endlösung over Danmark"; Arendt, *Eichmann in Jerusalem*, pp. 153ff.

15. Herbert, *Best*, pp. 251ff.; Danielsen, *Werner Best*, pp. 92ff.; Lauridsen, *Werner Best og den tyske sabotagebekæmpelse i Danmark*; see also Lauridsen, *Die Korrespondenz von Werner Best*, vol. 1, pp. 58ff.

16. Of Best's views on anti-Semitism, see Herbert, *Best*, pp. 203ff. and 298ff.

17. An exhaustive discussion of Best's self-defense, including a view of its influence on historical research, is found in Lauridsen, *Die Korrespondenz von Werner Best*, pp. 135ff.; Bak, *Jødeaktionen oktober 1943*, p. 50; see also Herbert, *Best*, pp. 323–400.

18. Longerich, *Holocaust*, p. 372. A comprehensive and balanced review of historical research into the action against the Danish Jews was published in 2012 as part of the introduction to the publication of Best's correspondence with the German Foreign Office. See Lauridsen, *Die Korrespondenz von Werner Best*, vol. 1, pp. 106ff.

19. Kirchhoff, *Den gode tysker*, pp. 124ff.; Kirchhoff, "Oktober 1943 set 'från hinsidan,' " pp. 94f.; *Gads leksikon om dansk besættelsestid 1940–1945*, pp. 254ff.

20. Bruland, *Jødeforfølgelserne i Norge*, pp. 225ff.; Åmark, *Att bo granne med ondskaben*, pp. 535ff.; Levin, *Flukten*; see also Longerich, *Holocaust*, p. 372.

21. Kirchhoff, "Endlösung over Danmark," p. 143.

22. Jespersen, *Rytterkongen*, pp. 484ff.

23. Ibid., p. 489.

24. Joseph Goebbels's diaries, September 8, 1943, quoted in Lauridsen, *Die Korrespondenz von Werner Best*, vol. 4, pp. 47f.

25. RA, Ministry of Foreign Affairs, Gruppeordnede sager: 1909–1945, 120–20, Svenningsen's memorandum, September 25, 1943.

26. The motives behind Best's initiative have been the subject of intense debate, summarized by Lauridsen, quoted above; see also Longerich, *Holocaust*, p. 398, who has a slightly different interpretation. The telegram is quoted in German in Lauridsen, *Die Korrespondenz von Werner Best*, vol. 4, pp. 42ff.

27. Conze et al., "Das Amt und die Vergangenheit," pp. 243ff.; Kirchhoff, *Den gode tysker*, pp. 160ff.

28. Kirchhoff, *Den gode tysket*, pp. 164ff. A reservation concerning Duckwitz's journal is appropriate: Even though much points to the journal's authenticity, some historians have argued that it may have been written later in order to make Duckwitz's role appear more heroic. A few conditions support this assumption, but indisputable documentation of his role in relation to the crucial warning of the Danish Jews is also found in other contemporary sources. On the basis of an exhaustive study of the underlying source materials, the leading historian in this field, Hans Kirchhoff, reasons that there is no basis for questioning the authenticity of Duckwitz's journals.

29. Kirchhoff, *Den gode tysker*, p. 164f.

30. Yahil, *The Rescue of Danish Jewry*, pp. 172ff.; Mogensen et al., *Aktionen mod de danske jøder oktober 1943*, pp. 35ff.; Lundtofte, "Den store undtagelse," pp. 182ff.; Lauridsen, *Die Korrespondenz von Werner Best*, vol. 4, pp. 42ff. and 102ff.

31. Kirchhoff, *Den gode tysker*, pp. 165ff.

32. Yahil, *The Rescue of Danish Jewry*, pp. 161ff.; Lauridsen, *Die Korrespondenz von Werner Best*, vol. 4, pp. 155f. and 192f.

33. Arnheim, "Jødernes historie i Danmark 1619–1969," (manuscript), chap. 16.

34. Allan Hannover's journal is privately owned. A copy has been provided for this book. The journal begins in Hellerup on September 26 and continues until the end of the war, though only sporadically after October 16, 1943. It appears to have been written shortly after the arrival in Sweden in the beginning of October, undoubtedly with backup from entries by his father, Poul Hannover.

35. Bak, *Nothing to Speak Of*, pp. 23ff.

36. Bak, *Da krigen var forbi*, pp. 33ff.

37. *De frie Danske*, September 1943.

38. Kreth and Mogensen, *Flugten til Sverige*, pp. 73ff.

39. An annotated excerpt from Bergstrøm's journal is in Lauridsen, *En borger i Danmark under krigen*. Entries from October 1943 are in vol. 2, pp. 761–840. September 28–30 are included in this chapter, but not the preceding days of September. For that reason quotations from September 24 to 27 are from vol. 154 of the original journals, which are in the Royal Library in Copenhagen.

40. KB, Vilhelm Bergstrøm's journal, vol. 154, September 24, 1943.

41. The financial situations were stated on arrival in Sweden, October 3, 1943. Swedish National Archives (Poul Hannover), Ystad police report, October 7, 1943.

42. Adolph Meyer's journal is privately owned. A copy has been provided for this book. The handwritten journal begins on September 27 and ends in Sweden on November 4. It appears to be based on contemporary entries that were transcribed in early November.

43. Yahil, *The Rescue of Danish Jewry*, pp. 219ff.

44. Arendt, *Eichmann in Jerusalem*, p. 161.

45. Yahil, *The Rescue of Danish Jewry*, pp. 219ff.; Ring, *Hitler beskyddar Danmark*, pp. 141ff.

Chapter Two: Monday, September 27: At Home

1. KB, Vilhelm Bergstrøm's journal, vol. 154, September 25, 1943

2. KB, Vilhelm Bergstrøm's journal, vol. 154, September 27, 1943.

3. Åmark, *Att bo granne med ondskan*, pp. 643ff.

4. Kirchhoff, *Den gode tysker*, p. 170f.; Kirchhoff, "Georg Ferdinand Duckwitz" (1999), p. 18.

5. Åmark, *Att bo granne med ondskan*, pp. 536ff.; Kirchhoff, "Oktober 1943 set 'från hinsidan' "; Kirchhoff, "Broen over Øresund."

Chapter Three: Tuesday, September 28: The Message

1. See Hans Hedtoft's introduction to Bertelsen, *October '43*, pp. 16–19; see also Hansen and Bomholt, *Hans Hedtoft liv og virke*, pp. 72ff.; Hæstrup, . . . *Til landets bedste*, vol. 1, pp. 148f.

2. Frisch et al., *Danmark besat og befriet*, vol. 2, p. 247.

3. Kirchhoff, *Den gode tysker*, p. 172f.

Chapter Four: Wednesday, September 29: Departure

1. Kirchhoff, *Den gode tysker*, p. 173f.

2. Kirchhoff, "Endlösung over Danmark," p. 174; see also Yahil, *The Rescue of Danish Jewry*, pp. 180ff., and Lauridsen, *Die Korrespondenz von Werner Best*, vol. 4, pp. 214ff.

3. *Gads leksikon om dansk besættelsestid*, pp. 341ff.; Leni Yahil describes how the employees at *Politiken* actively took part in the spreading of the warning, September 28, 1943, *The Rescue of Danish Jewry*, p. 238.

4. DJM, Personal Archives, Lise Epstein, JDK207A24/1/125, typewritten account of her escape to Sweden in 1943, typed in 1944.

5. Foss, *Fra passiv til aktiv modstand*, p. 214.

6. KB, Gunnar Larsen's journal, September 29, 1943.

7. DJM, Personal Archives, Ella Fischer, JDK207A103/1, account of her escape in September–October 1943. The account is used as a case in Bak, *Da krigen var forbi*, pp. 24ff.

8. RA, Archive of King Christian 10, 1943: Attachment no. 57.

9. The discussions of the permanent secretaries during the decisive days are referenced extensively by the head clerk of the Foreign Department, Jens Rudolph Dahl, who attended the meetings. A transcript of Jens Rudolph Dahl's reports has kindly been provided to the author by the chief consultant at the Danish National Archives (RA), Poul Olsen. See also Sjøquist, *Nils Svenningsen*, pp. 74ff.

10. The discussions are cited extensively by Jørgen Hæstrup, . . . *Til landets bedste*, vol. 1, pp. 150ff. Nils Svenningsen's contemporary memorandums are filed in RA, Ministry of Foreign Affairs, Gruppeordnede sager, 1909–1945, 120–20. See also Hans Kirchhoff's representation in "Endlösung over Danmark," pp. 166ff. Permanent Secretary Jespersen's detailed contemporary memorandums are filed in RA, Ministry of Business and Growth 1943–45, Permanent Secretary H. Jespersen's notes on meetings of the Council of Permanent Secretaries.

11. Lauridsen, *Die Korrespondenz von Werner Best*, vol. 4, p. 197, Best's telegram, September 29, 1943, 14:40.

12. Nils Svenningsen's contemporary memorandums in RA, Ministry of Foreign Affairs, Gruppeordnede sager: 1909–1945, 120–20.

13. Oluf Pedersen's notes from the politicians' meeting in RA, archive of Oluf Pedersen, archive no. 6104, optegnelser fra Nimandsudvalge, September 29, 1943.

14. Kirchhoff, "Oktober 1943 set 'från hinsidan,' " pp. 80ff.

15. Lidegaard, *I kongens navn*, pp. 286ff.; Kirchhoff, "Oktober 1943 set 'från hinsidan,' " pp. 80ff.

16. DJM, Objects, Bernhard "Bubi" Cohn, JDK207X40, journal from September 29 until November 21, 1943.

Chapter Five: Thursday, September 30: The Escape

1. Yahil, *The Rescue of Danish Jewry*, pp. 240ff.

2. Hæstrup, ... *Til landets bedste*, vol. 1, 1966, pp. 158ff.; Sjøquist, *Nils Svenningsen*, pp. 74ff.; Kirchhoff, "Den glemte interneringsplan"; RA, Ministry of Foreign Affairs, Gruppeordnede sager: 1909–1945, 120–20; RA, Ministry of Business and Growth 1943–45, Permanent Secretary H. Jespersen's notes on meetings of the Council of Permanent Secretaries; Jens Rudolph Dahl's reports.

3. KB, Gunnar Larsen's journal, September 29, 1943.

4. Lauridsen, *En borger i Danmark under krigen*, vol. 2, p. 768.

5. Foss, *Fra passiv til aktiv modstand*, p. 215.

6. Kirchhoff, "Oktober 1943 set 'från hinsidan,' " pp. 80ff.; Hæstrup, ... *Til landets bedste*, vol. 1, pp. 158ff; Lauridsen, *Die Korrespondenz von Werner Best*, vol. 4, pp. 207ff.

7. Foss, *Fra passiv til aktiv modstand*, p. 216.

8. RA, Archive of Eduard Vilhelm Sophus Christian Reventlow, Diary (1941–53), Binders 2–3, September 30, 1943.

Chapter Six: Friday, October 1: The Action

1. DJM, Personal Archives, Ella Fischer, JDK207A103/1, account of her escape in September–October 1943.

2. Kirchhoff, "Endlösung over Danmark," pp. 174ff.; Lauridsen, *Die Korrespondenz von Werner Best*, vol. 4, p. 237, Best's telegram, October 1, 10:15.

3. Kirchhoff, "Oktober 1943 set 'från hinsidan,' " pp. 80ff.

4. RA, Ministry of Foreign Affairs, Gruppeordnede sager: 1909–45, 120–20, handwritten letter from Hans Rasmussen to Nils Svenningsen dated October 1, 1943.

5. RA, Archive of King Christian 10, 1943: "Bemærkninger med bilag," Attachment no. 57.

6. RA, Ministry of Business and Growth 1943–45, Permanent Secretary H. Jespersen's notes on meetings of the Council of Permanent Secretaries.

7. Jens Rudolph Dahl's reports.

8. Lidegaard, *Kampen om Danmark*, pp. 399ff.

9. RA, Archive of Eduard Vilhelm Sophus Christian Reventlow, Diary (1941–53), Binders 2–3, October 1, 1943.

10. Kirchhoff, "Endlösung over Danmark," p. 166.

11. Handwritten note by the Supreme Court lawyer H. H. Bruun, dated October 10, 1943, and countersigned by C. L. David, kindly made available for this account by his grandson, H. H. Bruun.

12. The telegram, including a transcript of the king's letter, is reprinted in Mogensen et al., *Aktionen mod de danske jøder oktober 1943*, pp. 26f.; Lauridsen, *Die Korrespondenz von Werner Best*, vol. 4, pp. 240ff.

13. RA, Ministry of Foreign Affairs, Gruppeordnede sager: 120–20, Svenningsen's memorandum, October 2, 1943.

14. RA, Archive of King Christian 10, 1943: "Bemærkninger med bilag," Attachment no. 57.

15. Kirchhoff, *Den gode tysker*, p. 173.

16. RA, Ministry of Foreign Affairs, Gruppeordnede sager: 1909–1945, 120–20, Svenningsen's memorandum, October 2, 1943.

17. Yahil, *The Rescue of Danish Jewry*, pp. 175ff.; Mogensen et al., *Aktionen mod de danske jøder oktober 1943*, pp. 27f.; Lauridsen, *Die Korrespondenz von Werner Best*, vol. 4, p. 237, Best's telegram, October 1, 10:15.

18. Himmler's letter is reprinted in Lauridsen, *Die Korrespondenz von Werner Best*, vol. 4, pp. 246f., which also includes a summary of the international discussion of the letter's dating, plus persuasive reasoning for the above-presented interpretation; see also vol. 1, p. 113.

19. RA, Manuscript Collections, IV, Danmark-Norges almindelige historie 125; IV T1, Politirapporter 29/8 1943–4/7 1944.

20. Lauridsen, *En borger i Danmark under krigen*, vol. 2, pp. 771f.

21. Foss, *Fra passiv til aktiv modstand*, p. 217.

22. *Gads leksikon om dansk besættelsestid 1940–45*, p. 258; Lundtofte, *Gestapo!*, pp. 103ff.

23. Longerich, *Holocaust*, pp. 386f.

Chapter Seven: Saturday, October 2: The Transfer

1. Quoted in Kirchhoff, "Endlösung over Danmark," pp. 176ff.

2. Lauridsen, *En borger i Danmark under krigen*, vol. 2, p. 772.

3. Yahil, *The Rescue of Danish Jewry*, pp. 186f.; Mogensen et al., *Aktionen mod de danske jøder oktober 1943*, pp. 32ff.; Lauridsen, *Die Korrespondenz von Werner Best*, vol. 4, p. 248f., Best's telegram October 2, 1943, 07:00.

4. Mogensen et al., *Aktionen mod de danske jøder oktober 1943*, pp. 28ff.; Lauridsen, *Die Korrespondenz von Werner Best*, vol. 4, pp. 253ff.

5. Lauridsen, *En borger i Danmark under krigen*, vol. 2, p. 773.

6. Mogensen et al., *Aktionen mod de danske jøder oktober 1943*, pp. 30ff.; *Gads leksikon om dansk besættelsestid 1940–1945*, p. 277f.; RA, Ministry of Foreign Affairs, Gruppeordnede sager: 120–20, Svenningsen's memorandum, October 2, 1942.

7. The financial situations were stated on arrival in Sweden, October 3, 1943. Swedish National Archives, Archives of the National Board of Aliens, Dossier (Poul Hannover), Ystad police report, October 7, 1943.

8. Dardel's telegrams are available at bogwebs.systime.dk/bogwebs/FlugtenTil Sverige . . ./aktionen_txt.htm.

9. Lauridsen, *En borger i Danmark under krigen*, vol. 2, p. 775; Ring, *Hitler beskyddar Danmark*, pp. 141ff.

10. Handwritten note, Supreme Court lawyer H. H. Bruun, dated October 10, 1943, and countersigned by C. L. David, chapter 6, note 11.

11. Kirchhoff, "Oktober 1943 set 'från hinsidan,' " pp. 111ff.

12. Åmark, *Att bo granne med ondskan*, pp. 536ff.; Kirchhoff, "Oktober 1943 set 'från hinsidan,' " pp. 113ff.; see also Munck, *Døren til den frie verden*, pp. 138ff.

13. DJM, Objects, Bernhard Cohn, JDK 207X40, account of his escape written in October 1943.

14. Jens Rudolph Dahl's report, October 2, 1943.

15. RA, Archive of Eduard Vilhelm Sophus Christian Reventlow, Diary (1941–53), Binders 2–3, October 2, 1943.

16. Bak, *Da krigen var forbi*, pp. 35ff.

17. Gross, *Golden Harvest*, pp. 120ff.

18. Longerich, *Holocaust*, pp. 397ff. and 422ff.; Friedländer, *The Years of Extermination*, pp. 483ff.

19. www.yadvashem.org.

20. SL, Drawer 48, jødetransporter 28–97, undated typewritten account by Niels Lund.

21. Bak, *Da krigen var forbi*, p. 32; Bak, *Nothing to Speak Of*, pp. 45ff. See also Sofie Lene Bak's foreword, "Den lange tavshed," in Nilsson, *De gemte børn*.

22. Tortzen, *Gilleleje oktober 1943*, p. 94.

23. DJM, Objects, Bernhard "Bubi" Cohn, JDK207X40, journal from September 29 until November 21, 1943.

24. Bertelsen, *Oktober 43*, p. 17.

25. Dethlefsen, *De illegale Sverigesruter 1943–45*, pp. 36ff.

26. Kreth and Mogensen, *Flugten til Sverige*, pp. 117ff.

27. Tortzen, *Gilleleje oktober 1943*, pp. 104ff.

28. *Information*, October 2, 1943; see also Lund and Nielsen, *Outze i krig*, pp. 64ff.

29. Pundik, *Det kan ikke ske i Danmark*, pp. 68ff.

30. Lauridsen, *Die Korrespondenz von Werner Best*, vol. 4, pp. 253ff., Erik von Himburg's telegram, October 2; see also Lundtofte, *Den store undtagelse*, pp. 182ff.

31. Lauridsen, *Die Korrespondenz von Werner Best*, vol. 4, pp. 249ff., Best's telegram, October 2, 1943, 13:45; see also Yahil, *The Rescue of Danish Jewry*, pp. 178ff.

32. Lund, *Hitlers spisekammer*, pp. 283ff.; Lauridsen, *Die Korrespondenz von Werner Best*, vol. 1, pp. 86ff., in which Lauridsen refers in detail to the underlying research; see also *Gads leksikon om dansk besættelsestid 1940–1945*, 2002, pp. 309ff.

33. Lauridsen, *Die Korrespondenz von Werner Best*, vol. 4, pp. 267ff., Scherpenberg's report, October 4, 1943; see also Hæstrup, . . . *Til landets bedste*, vol. 1, pp. 168ff.

34. *Life*, November 28, 1960, p. 101; Yahil, *The Rescue of Danish Jewry*, p. 187f. See also Lauridsen, ed., *Die Korrespondenz von Werner Best*, vol. 4, pp. 240ff., Best's telegram, October 1, which includes a transcript of the king's protest. The telegram was sent at 19:30, one and a half hours before the operation was initiated; RA, Archive

of King Christian 10, 1943: "Bemærkninger med bilag," Attachment no. 57. The quotation from the Sassen tapes is from Stangneth, *Eichmann vor Jerusalem*, p. 346.

35. Kirchhoff, *Den gode tysker*, pp. 124ff.

Chapter Eight: Sunday, 3 October: Ystad

1. DJM, Objects, Bernhard "Bubi" Cohn, JDK207X40, journal from September 29 until November 21, 1943.

2. DJM, Personal Archives, Leo Schüstin, JDK250A1/4/275, records from October 1943. His depiction is slightly edited; Swedish National Archives, Archives of the National Board of Aliens, Dossier (Leo Schüstin). Leo Schüstin's escape is also described in Bak, *Da krigen var forbi*, pp. 30ff.

3. DJM, Personal Archives, Leo Schüstin, JDK250A1/4/275, records from October 1943.

4. Lauridsen, *En borger i Danmark under krigen*, vol. 2, pp. 776ff.

5. The protest is quoted from Yahil, *The Rescue of Danish Jewry*, pp. 235f.; RA, Archive of King Christian 10, 1943: "Bemærkninger med bilag," Attachment no. 57.

6. *Gads Hvem var hvem 1940–45*, p. 112f.

7. Lauridsen, *En borger i Danmark under krigen*, vol. 2, pp. 776ff.; Bak, *Nothing to Speak Of*, p. 80f.

8. Swedish National Archives, Archives of the National Board of Aliens, Dossier (Poul Hannover), Ystad police report, October 7, 1943.

9. SL, Stubbekøbing Regional Archive, Drawer 48, jødetransporter 28–97, undated typewritten account by Niels Lund.

10. Kirchhoff, "Oktober 1943 set 'från hinsidan,' " pp. 313ff.

11. DJM, Personal Archives, Ella Fischer, JDK207A103/1, account of her escape in September–October 1943.

12. DJM, Personal Archives, Herbert Willie Levysohn, JDK80/A2/1, account of his escape written in October 1943. A slightly abridged version of his account is published in Thomsen, *En Skildring om et enkelt Tilfälde under Jödeforfölgelsen i Danmark*. Here quoted from the original source filed at DJM.

13. Tortzen, *Gilleleje oktober 1943*, pp. 232ff.

14. DJM, Objects, Bernhard "Bubi" Cohn, JDK207X40, journal from September 29 until November 21, 1943.

15. Swedish National Archive, Archives of the National Board of Aliens, Dossier (Bernhard Cohn).

Chapter Nine: Monday, October 4: The Village of Ruds Vedby

1. Longerich: *Davon haben wir Nichts gewusst!*, 2006.

2. Several authoritative versions are accessible on the Internet in English as well as in the original German. Here quoted from www.holocaust-history.org.

3. RA, Foreign Ministry, Gruppeordnede sager: 1909–1945, 120–20, Svenningsen's memorandum, October 4, 1943.

4. Ibid., Svenningsen's memorandum, October 5, 1943; see also Hæstrup, . . . *Til landets bedste*, vol. 1, pp. 166ff.; Yahil, *The Rescue of Danish Jewry*, pp. 187ff.

5. Quoted from *Information*, October 11, 1943.

6. RA, Archive of Oluf Pedersen, archive no. 6104, optegnelser fra Nimandsudvalget, September 29, 1943, October 4. A few of the words are questionable, and illegible passages have been omitted; see also Hæstrup, . . . *Til landets bedste*, vol. 1, p. 179, and Munch, *Erindringer*, vol. 8, pp. 224ff.

7. *Den parlamentariske kommission*, vol. 8, book 3, p. 1552.

8. Lauridsen, *En borger i Danmark under krigen*, p. 779.

9. Bak, *Nothing to Speak Of*, pp. 67ff.

10. Hæstrup, . . . *Til landets bedste*, vol. 1, pp. 190ff.; Kirchhoff, "Endlösung over Danmark," p. 174.

11. DJM, Personal Archives, Herbert Willie Levysohn, JDK80/A2/1, account of his escape written in October 1943.

12. Kreth and Mogensen, *Flugten til Sverige*, p. 106.

13. RA, Archive of Eduard Vilhelm Sophus Christian Reventlow, Diary (1941–53), Binders 2–3, October 4, 1943.

14. Lauridsen, *En borger i Danmark under krigen*, vol. 2, p. 781.

15. Kreth and Mogensen, *Flugten til Sverige*, pp. 94ff.

16. Bak, *Nothing to Speak Of*, pp. 137ff.

Chapter Ten: Tuesday, October 5: Going North

1. DJM, Personal Archives, Ella Fischer, JDK207A103/1, account of her escape in September–October 1943.

2. DJM, Personal Archives, Herbert Willie Levysohn, JDK80/A2/1, account of his escape written in October 1943.

3. Ibid.

4. Ibid.

5. Vilhelm Lind's notes are quoted in Tortzen, *Gilleleje oktober 1943*, pp. 107ff.

6. DJM, Personal Archives, Herbert Willie Levysohn, JDK80/A2/1, account of his escape written in October 1943.

7. Vilhelm Lind's notes are quoted in Tortzen, *Gilleleje oktober 1943*, pp. 107ff.

8. RA, Public Prosecutor for Special Affairs, AS-sager for provinsen 1940–1944, 7, Hillerød Købstad 87–149, Sergeant Mortving's report October 5, 1943; see also Kreth and Mogensen, *Flugten til Sverige*, pp. 118f.; Tortzen, *Gilleleje oktober 1943*, p. 45.

9. DJM, Personal Archives, Herbert Willie Levysohn JDK80/A2/1, account of his escape written in October 1943.

10. Ibid.

11. *Frit Danmark*, October 1943.

12. *De frie Danske*, October 1943.

13. *Dansk Maanedspost*, October 1943.

14. Lauridsen, *Die Korrespondenz von Werner Best*, vol. 4, p. 248f.; see also Hæstrup, . . . *Til landets bedste*, vol. 1, pp. 171ff.; Yahil, *The Rescue of Danish Jewry*, pp. 187ff.

15. Hæstrup, . . . *Til landets bedste*, vol. 1, p. 182; *Information*, October 11, 1943.

16. Handwritten note by the Supreme Court lawyer H. H. Bruun, dated October 10, 1943, and countersigned by C. L. David, chapter 6, note 11.

17. Lauridsen, *En borger i Danmark under krigen*, vol. 2, p. 782.

Chapter Eleven: Wednesday, October 6: Gilleleje

1. Lauridsen, *Die Korrespondenz von Werner Best*, vol. 4, p. 281, Best's telegram to the German Foreign Office, October 6, 1943, 12:30; Duckwitz's memoirs, here quoted from Yahil, *The Rescue of Danish Jewry*, p. 161f.

2. DJM, Personal Archives, Ella Fischer, JDK207A103/1, account of her escape in September–October 1943; her family's fate is reflected by the Ministry of Foreign Affairs list of deported Jews filed at RA, Foreign Ministry, Gruppeordnede sager: 1909–1945, 120–20; see also Bak, *Da krigen var forbi*, pp. 24ff.

3. Handwritten note by the Supreme Court lawyer H. H. Bruun, dated October 10, 1943, and countersigned by C. L. David, chapter 6, note 11.

4. RA, Public Prosecutor for Special Affairs, AS-sager for provinsen,1940–1944, 7, Hillerød Købstad 87–149, Sergeant Mortving's report, October 13, 1943; Kreth and Mogensen, *Flugten til Sverige*, p. 78f.

5. DJM, Personal Archives, Herbert Willie Levysohn, JDK80/A2/1, account of his escape written in October 1943.

6. Vilhelm Lind's notes are quoted in Tortzen, *Gilleleje oktober 1943*, pp. 107ff.

7. RA, Public Prosecutor for Special Affais, AS-sager for provinsen, 1940–1944, 7, Hillerød Købstad 87–149; Tortzen, *Gilleleje oktober 1943*, pp. 46ff.

8. DJM, Personal Archives, Herbert Willie Levysohn, JDK80/A2/1, account of his escape written in October 1943.

9. Ibid.

10. Tortzen, *Gilleleje oktober 1943*, pp. 104ff.

11. The October 28, 1943, letter is reprinted in ibid., pp. 99ff.

12. Ibid., pp. 54ff.

13. Ibid., pp. 99ff.

14. Bak, *Nothing to Speak Of*, pp. 67ff.

15. Lauridsen, *En borger i Danmark under krigen*, vol. 2, pp. 784f.

16. Swedish National Archives, Archives of National Board of Aliens, Dossiers (Kis and Gunnar Marcus), visa applications, October 6, 1943.

Chapter Twelve: Thursday, October 7: The Hope

1. Handwritten note by the Supreme Court lawyer H. H. Bruun, dated October 10, 1943, and countersigned by C. L. David, chapter 6, note 11.

2. DJM, Personal Archives, Herbert Willie Levysohn, JDK80/A2/1, account of his escape written in October 1943.

3. Tortzen, *Gilleleje oktober 1943*, pp. 64ff.

4. SL, Stubbekøbing Regional Archive, Drawer 48, jødetransporter 28–97.

5. RA, Public Prosecutor for Special Affairs, AS-sager for provinsen,1940–1944, 7, Hillerød Købstad 87–149.

6. Tortzen, *Gilleleje oktober 1943*, p. 62.

7. Lauridsen, *En borger i Danmark under krigen*, vol. 2, p. 788f.

8. Ibid., p. 789f.

9. *Politiken*'s supplement, "Magasinet," January 13, 1946.

10. Hæstrup, . . . *Til landets bedste*, vol. 1, pp. 186ff.

11. Lauridsen, *Die Korrespondenz von Werner Best*, vol. 4, pp. 288ff. and 308ff.; see also Hæstrup, . . . *Til landets bedste*, vol. 1, pp. 188ff.; Yahil, *The Rescue of Danish Jewry*, pp. 296ff.

12. Kirchhoff, "Oktober 1943 set 'från hinsidan,' " pp. 324ff.

Chapter Thirteen: Friday, October 8: The Beach at Smidstrup

1. Lauridsen, *En borger i Danmark under krigen*, vol. 2, p. 793.

2. Kirchhoff, *Den gode tysker*, pp. 174ff.; Kreth and Mogensen, *Flugten til Sverige*, p. 106.

3. Tortzen, *Gilleleje oktober 1943*, pp. 104ff.; *Svenska Dagbladet*, October 9, 1943.

4. Lauridsen, *Die Korrespondenz von Werner Best*, vol. 4, pp. 291ff.

5. Munch, *Erindringer*, vol. 8, p. 226.

6. DJM, Personal Archives, Henrik Martin Schall Meyer, JDK275A18/2/278, journal, "Flugten til Sverige," October 1943.

7. RA, Archive of Eduard Vilhelm Sophus Christian Reventlow, Diary (1941–53), Binders 2–3, October 8, 1943.

8. Gilbert Lassen's description from 1945 is reprinted in Tortzen, *Gilleleje oktober 1943*, pp. 135ff.

Chapter Fourteen: Saturday, October 9: Realities

1. Doctor Widding's account is reprinted in Tortzen, *Gilleleje oktober 1943*, pp. 92ff.

2. DJM, Personal Archives, Henrik Martin Schall Meyer, JDK275A18/2/278, journal, "Flugten til Sverige," October 1943.

3. Swedish National Archives, Archives of the National Board of Aliens, Dossier (Adolph Meyer), Göteborg police report, October 21, 1943; *Dagens Nyheter*, October 10, 1943.

4. Bak, *Da krigen var forbi*, pp. 30 and 16; see also *Gads leksikon om dansk besættelsestid 1940–45*, pp. 254ff.

5. Bak, *Nothing to Speak Of*, p. 175f.

6. Dethlefsen, *Ud af mørket*, pp. 202ff.

7. Kreth and Mogensen, *Flugten til Sverige*, pp. 106ff.

8. Ibid., p. 115f.

9. Ibid,, pp. 46 and 110ff.; Tortzen, *Gilleleje oktober 1943*, p. 42f.; Lauridsen, *Die Korrespondenz von Werner Best*, vol. 4, p. 261.

10. Dethlefsen, *Ud af mørket*, pp. 202ff.; Kreth and Mogensen, *Flugten til Sverige*, pp. 69ff.

11. RA, Public Prosecutor for Special Affairs, AS-sager for provinsen 1940–1944, 7, Hillerød Købstad, 7–148.

12. Bak, *Nothing to Speak Of*, pp. 36ff.; Kreth and Mogensen, *Flugten til Sverige*, pp. 86ff.; Dethlefsen, *De illegale Sverigesruter 1943–45*, pp. 44ff.

13. Hjortsø, *Den dyre flugt*.

14. Bak, *Da krigen var forbi*, p. 103; Hjortsø: *Den dyre flugt*.

15. Dethlefsen, *De illegale Sverigesruter 1943–45*, p. 40f.; Tamm, *Bag kapperne*, p. 118f.

16. Lundtofte, *Gestapo!*, pp. 114ff.

17. Ring, *Hitler beskyddar Danmark*, pp. 141ff.

18. Kreth and Mogensen, *Flugten til Sverige*, pp. 106ff.

19. RA, Archive of Eduard Vilhelm Sophus Christian Reventlow, Diary (1941–53), Binders 2–3, October 9, 1943.

20. Hæstrup, . . . *Til landets bedste*, vol. 1, p. 182f.

21. Ibid., p. 185.

22. The chain of events leading to Adolf Eichmann's promise is discussed in Lauridsen, *Die Korrespondenz von Werner Best*, vol. 1, p. 114. The underlying documentation is in vol. 4, pp. 288–454.

23. Persson, *Vi åker till Sverige*.

24. Ring, *Hitler beskyddar Danmark*, pp. 141ff.

25. Kreth and Mogensen, *Flugten til Sverige*, p. 101.

26. Ibid., p. 94.

27. Goldhagen, *Hitler's Willing Executioners*, pp. 158ff.

28. Longerich, *"Davon haben wir Nichts gewusst!,"* pp. 313ff.

29. Yahil, *The Rescue of Danish Jewry*, p. 278f.

30. Arendt, *Eichmann in Jerusalem*, p. 157.

Epilogue

1. Swedish National Archive, Archives of the National Board of Aliens, Dossier (Ella Fischer).

2. Ibid., Dossier (Einar Cohn).

3. Lundtofte, *Gestapo!*; *Gads Hvem var hvem 1940–45*, p. 253f.

4. Kirchhoff, "Erik Scavenius og Werner Best," pp. 21ff.

5. Kirchhoff, *Den gode tysker*, pp. 358ff.

6. Kirchhoff, "Erik Scavenius og Werner Best," pp. 21ff.

7. Quoted in Madeleine Albright, *Prague Winter: A Personal Story of Remembrance and War, 1937–1948* (New York: HarperCollins, 2012), pp. 146ff.

BIBLIOGRAPHY

Books and Articles

Åmark, Klas. *Att bo granna med ondskan: Sveriges förhållande till nazismen, Nazityskland och förintelsen.* Stockholm: Bonnier, 2011.

Arendt, Hannah. *Eichmann in Jerusalem: A Report on the Banality of Evil.* New York: Viking Press, 1963.

Bak, Sofie Lene. *Jødeaktionen oktober 1943.* Copenhagen: Museum Tusculanum, 2001.

―――. *Nothing to Speak Of.* Copenhagen: Danish Jewish Museum, 2010.

―――. *Da krigen var forbi: De danske jøders hjemkomst efter besættelsen.* Copenhagen: Gyldendal, 2012.

Bertelsen, Aage. *Oktober 43.* Aarhus: Jydsk Centraltrykkeri, 1952.

―――. *October '43.* New York: Putnam's Sons, 1952.

Betænkning til Folketinget. Vol. 8, bk. 3. København: J. H. Schultz, 1947.

Bruland, Bjarne. "Jødeforfølgelserne i Norge." In *Danske tilstande—Norske tilstande: Forskellige og ligheder under tysk besættelse 1940–45.* Edited by Hans Frederik Dahl, Hans Kirchhoff, Joachim Lund, and Lars-Erik Vaale, pp. 225–41. Copenhagen: Gyldendal, 2010.

Conze, Eckart, Nobert Frei, Peter Hayes, and Moshe Zimmermann. *Das Amt und die Vergangenheit. Deutsche Diplomaten im Dritten Reich and in der Bundesrepublik.* Munich: Karl Blessing Verlag, 2010.

Danielsen, Nils-Birger. *Werner Best. Tysk rigsbefuldmægtiget i Danmark, 1942–45.* Copenhagen: Politikens Forlag, 2013.

Dethlefsen, Henrik. *De illegale Sverigeruter 1943–45, studier i den maritime modstands historie.* Odense: Odense Universitetsforlag, 1993.

―――. "Ud af mørket: Redningen af jøderne." In *I Hitler-Tysklands skygg: Dramaet om de danske jøder 1933–1945.* Edited by Hans Sode-Madsen, pp. 202–25. Copenhagen: Aschehoug, 2010.

Foss, Erling. *Fra passiv til aktiv Modstand: Breve, Microfilmsrapporter til London og Skildring af Frihedsrådets Fremkomst dækkende Perioden April 1940 til Februar 1944.* Copenhagen: Gyldendal, 1946.

Friedländer, Saul. *The Years of Extermination: Nazi Germany and the Jews, 1939–1945.* London: Weidenfeld & Nicolson, 2007.

Frisch, Hartvig. *Danmark besat og befriet.* Vol. 2. Copenhagen: Fremad, 1947.

Gads Hvem var hvem 1940–45. Copenhagen: Gads Forlag, 2005.

Gads leksikon om dansk besættelsestid 1940–45. Copenhagen: Gads Forlag, 2002.

Goldhagen, Daniel Jonah. *Hitler's Willing Executioners: Ordinary Germans and the Holocaust.* New York: Alfred A. Knopf, 1996.

Gross, Jan. *Golden Harvest: Events at the Periphery of the Holocaust.* Oxford and New York: Oxford University Press, 2012.

Hansen, H. C., and Julius Bomholt. *Hans Hedtoft, liv og virke.* Copenhagen: Fremad, 1955.

Hjortsø, Thomas. *Den dyre flugt: Pengenes strøm under redningen af de danske jøder i 1943.* Copenhagen: People's Press, 2010.

Hæstrup, Jørgen. *. . . til landets bedste, hovedtræk af departementschefsstyrets virke 1943–54.* Vol. 1. Copenhagen: Gyldendal, 1966.

————. *Kontakt med England 1940–45.* Copenhagen: Trajan, 1967.

Jespersen, Knud J. V. *Rytterkongen, et portræt af Christian 10.* Copenhagen: Gyldendal, 2007.

Kirchhoff, Hans."Endlösung over Danmark" In *Føreren har befalet!* Edited by Hans Sode-Madsen, pp. 57–107. Copenhagen: Samleren, 1993.

————. "Oktober 1943 set 'från hinsidan.' " *Historisk Tidsskrift* 97, no. 1 (1997): 80–115.

————."Oktober 1943 set 'från hinsidan.' " *Historisk Tidsskrift* 97, no. 2 (1997): 313–55.

————. "Georg Ferdinand Duckwitz." In *Tyskere imod Hitler.* Edited by Johan Dreher, pp. 7–24. Copenhagen: Forbundsrepublikken Tysklands Ambassade, 1999.

————. "Den glemte interneringsplan." In *Nyt lys over oktober 1943,* Edited by Hans Kirchhoff, pp. 37–48. Odense: Syddansk Universitetsforlag, 2002.

————. "Endlösung over Danmark." In *I Hitler-Tysklands skygge.* Edited by Hans Sode-Madsen, pp. 136–81. Copenhagen: Aschehoug, 2003.

————. "Broen over Øresund: Redningen af de danske jøder i oktober 1943." In *Grænse som skiller ej! Kontakter over Öresund under 1900-talet.* Edited by Kjell Å Modéer, pp. 93–108. Copenhagen: Museum Tusculanum, 2007.

————. "Erik Scavenius og Werner Best." In *Sådan valgte de—syv dobbeltportrætter fra besættelsens tid.* Edited by Hans Kirchhoff, pp. 21–44. Copenhagen: Gyldendal, 2008.

————. *Den gode tysker. G. F. Duckwitz, de danske jøders redningsmand.* Copenhagen: Gyldendal, 2013.

Kreth, Rasmus, and Michael Mogensen. *Flugten til Sverige, aktionen med de danske jøder i oktober 1943.* Copenhagen: Gyldendal, 1995.

Lauridsen, John T., ed. *En borger i Danmark under krigen.* Copenhagen: Gads Forlag, 2005.

————. "Werner Best og den tyske sabotagebekæmpelse i Danmark 1942–45." In *Samarbejde og sabotage—seks mænd 1940–45.* Edited by Henrik Lundtofte, pp. 144–209. Esbjerg: Historisk Samling fra Besættelsestiden 1940–45, 2006.

————. *Die Korrespondenz von Werner Best mit dem Auswärtigen Amt und andere Akten zur Besetzung von Dänemark 1942–1945.* Vols. 1 and 4. Copenhagen: Museum Tusculanum, 2012.

Levin, Irene. *Flukten.* Oslo: Senter for studier av Holocaust og livssynsminoriteter, 2007.

Lidegaard, Bo. *I kongens navn: Henrik Kauffmann i dansk diplomati 1919–1958*. Copenhagen: Samleren, 1996.

——. *Defiant Diplomacy: Henrik Kaufmann, Denmark, and the United States in World War II and the Cold War, 1939–1958*. New York, Peter Lang, 2003.

——. *Kampen om Danmark 1933–45*. Copenhagen: Gyldendal, 2005.

——. *A Short History of Denmark in the 20th Century*. Copenhagen: Gyldendal, 2009.

Longerich, Peter. *Der ungeschriebene Befehl: Hitler und der Weg zur Endlösung*: Munich: Piper Verlag, 2001

——.*"Davon haben wir Nichts gewusst!": Die Deutschen und die Judenverfolgung 1933–1945*. Munich: Siedler, 2006.

——. *Holocaust: The Nazi Persecution and the Murder of the Jews*. Oxford: Oxford University Press, 2010.

Lund, Erik, and Jakob Nielsen. *Outze i krig, med skrivemaskinen som våben*. Copenhagen: Informations Forlag, 2008.

Lund, Joachim. *Hitlers spisekammer: Danmark og den europæiske nyordning 1940–43*. Copenhagen: Gyldendal, 2005.

Lundtofte, Henrik. "Den store undtagelse—Gestapo og jødeaktionen." In *I Hitler-Tysklands skygge: Dramaet om de danske jøder 1933–1945*. Edited by Hans Sode-Madsen, pp. 182–201. Copenhagen: Aschehoug, 2003.

——. *Gestapo!: Tysk politi og terror i Danmark 1940–45*. Copenhagen: Gads Forlag, 2003.

Mogensen, Michael, Otto Rühl, and Peder Wiben, eds. *Aktionen mod de danske jøder oktober 1943: flugten til Sverige*. Aarhus: Systime, 2003.

Munch, Peter. *Erindringer*, vol. 8. Copenhagen: Nyt Nordisk Forlag, 1967.

Munck, Ebbe. *Døren til den frie verden: Erindringer 1939–45*. Copenhagen: Schønberg, 1967.

Nilsson, Kirsten. *De gemte børn, beretninger fra anden verdenskrig*. Copenhagen: Gyldendal, 2012.

Persson, Sune. *Vi åker til Sverige, de vita bussarna 1945*. Rimbo: Fischer, 2002.

Pundik, Herbert. *Det kan ikke ske i Danmark*. Copenhagen: Munksgaard, 1994.

Rigsdagstidende, Landstinget, January 26, 1939, column 443.

Ring, Erik. *Hitler beskyddar Danmark: Fakta och refexioner kring den senaste utvecklingen*. Stockholm: Albert Bonniers Förlag, 1944.

Rünitz, Lone. *Danmark og de jødiske flygtninge 1933–40, en bog om flygtninge og menneskerettigheder*. Copenhagen: Museum Tusculanum, 2000.

Sjøquist, Viggo. *Nils Svenningsen, embedsmanden og politikeren, en biografi*. Copenhagen: Christian Ejlers Forlag, 1995.

Stangneth, Bettina. *Eichmann vor Jerusalem: Das unbehelligte Leben eines Massenmörders*. Hamburg: Arche Verlag, 2011.

Tamm, Ditlev. *Bag kapperne, danske advokater i det 20. århundrede*. Copenhagen: Forlaget Thomson, 2007.

Thomsen, Lis Hygom."En Skildring om et enkelt Tilfälde under Jödeforfölgelsen i Danmark." *RAMBAM, tidsskrift for jødisk kultur og forskning* 10 (2001): 29–44.

Tortzen, Christian. *Gilleleje oktober 1943, under jødernes flugt fra nazismen.* Copenhagen: Fremad, 1970.

Ulrich, Herbert. *Best: Biograpische studien über radikalismus, weltanschauung und vernunft 1903–1989.* Bonn: Dietz, 1996. Reprint, 2011.

Vilhjálmsson, Vilhjálmur Örn. *Medaljens bagside. Jødiske flygtningeskæbner i Danmark, 1933–1945.* Copenhagen: Vandkunsten, 2004.

Yahil, Leni. *The Rescue of Danish Jewry: Test of a Democracy.* Philadelphia: Jewish Publication Society of America, 1967.

Newspapers and Magazines

Dagens Nyheter, October 1943.
Dansk Maanedspost, October 1943.
De frie Danske, September 1943.
De frie Danske, October 1943.
Frit Danmark, October 1943.
Information, October 1943.
Life, November 28, 1960, pp. 19–25.
Politiken, January 13, 1946.
Svenska Dagbladet, October 1943.

Internet Sources

www.yadvashem.org
www.holocaust-history.org

Unpublished Sources

Arnheim, Arthur. "Jødernes historie i Danmark 1619–1969." Unpublished manuscript, 2012, chap. 16.

Archives and Collections

Dansk Jødisk Museum (Danish Jewish Museum), DJM
Genstande og personarkiver (Objects and Personal Archives):
Ella Fischer (JDK207A103/1), Lise Epstein (JDK207A24/1/125), Henrik Martin Schall Meyer (JDK275A18/2/278), Herbert Willie Levysohn (JDK80A2/1), Axel Hertz (JDK207A28/2/256), Leo Schüstin (JSK250A1/4/275), Bernhard Cohn (JDK207X40), Inge Løve (JDK207B86).

Kongelige Bibliotek (Royal Library), KB
Vilhelm Bergstrøm's journal, vol. 154; Gunnar Larsen's journals.

Rigsarkivet (Danish National Archives), RA
Kong Christian 10's arkiv 1943 (Archive of King Christian 10, 1943): "Bemærkninger med bilag,"Attachment no. 57.

Eduard Vilhelm Sophus Christian Reventlows privatarkiv (Archive of Eduard Vilhelm Sophus Christian Reventlow)
Diary (1941–53), binders 2–3.

Oluf Pedersens privatarkiv (Archive of Oluf Pedersen)
Archive no. 6104, nos. 1–2.

Erhvervs- og vækstministeriet (Ministry of Business and Growth)
Archive no. 15, Permanent Secretary H. Jespersen's notes on meetings of Council of Permanent Secretaries.

Erstatningsrådet (Compensation Board)
Personsager 1945–1993, binder 171, case no. 5822 (Erik Elliott Nyegaard).

Håndskriftsamlingen (Manuscript Collections)
IV: Danmark-Norges almindelige historie: IV.T: Besættelsen: Pakke nr. 125, Gruppe IV.T nr. 1, Politirapporter 29.08.1943–04.07.1944.

Statsadvokaten for særlige anliggender (Public Prosecutor for Special Affairs)
AS-sager for provinsen 1940–1944, Pakke nr. 30, Politikreds 7 Hillerød: AS 7–116, AS 7–132, AS 7–148.

Udenrigsministeriet (Ministry of Foreign Affairs)
Gruppeordnede sager 1909–1945: 84–17, 84–23, 84–24, 120–18, 120–20, 120–21, 120–22, 120–23, 120–24, 120–25, 140–164, 140–165, 140–166.
Efteraflevering 1908–1985, no. 30.

Riksarkivet (Swedish National Archives)
Statens utlänningskommissions arkiv (Archives of the National Board of Aliens): Dossierer og Registerkort (D2AB).

Stubbekøbing Lokalarkiv (Stubbekøbing Regional Archive), SL
Drawer 48: Jødetransporter 28–97.

Private Collections

Handwritten note by the Supreme Court lawyer H. H. Bruun, dated October 10, 1943, countersigned by C. L. David.
Allan Hannover's journal.
Poul Hannover's journal.
Kis Marcus's journal.
Adolph Meyer's journal.

Bo Lidegaard is the editor in chief of the leading Danish newspaper *Politiken* and the author of several books on modern history. He served as a diplomat in the Danish Foreign Service before joining the Office of the Danish Prime Minister as Ambassador and Permanent Undersecretary of State tasked with responsibilities corresponding to those of National Security Advisor. He later led the team preparing the 2009 United Nations conference on climate change in Copenhagen. He is one of the most respected and widely read Danish historians, and his work has focused on U.S.-Danish relations in the twentieth century, as well as on the modern Danish welfare state. He lives in Copenhagen.

A NOTE ON THE TYPE

The text of this book was set in a typeface called Aldus, designed in 1952–1953 by the German typographer Hermann Zapf (born 1918 in Nuremberg). Based on the classical proportion of the popular Palatino type family, Aldus was originally adapted for Linotype composition as a slightly lighter version that would read better in smaller sizes.

Composed by North Market Street Graphics,
Lancaster, Pennsylvania
Printed and bound by Berryville Graphics,
Berryville, Virginia
Designed by Peter A. Andersen